THE FUTURE LASTS FOREVER

THE FUTURE LASTS FOREVER

FOREVER

A MEMOIR

LOUIS ALTHUSSER

Edited by

Olivier Corpet and Yann Moulier Boutang

Translated by

Richard Veasey

The New Press
NEW YORK

Published in the United States by The New Press, New York
Distributed by W. W. Norton & Company, Inc.,
500 Fifth Avenue, New York, NY 10110

Published in the United Kingdom in 1993 by
Chatto & Windus Limited, Random House, London.
Originally published in France in 1992 as *L'avenir dure longtemps*,
suivi de *Les faits* by Editions STOCK/IMEC.

ISBN 1-56584-087-9
LC 93-83621

Established in 1990 as a major alternative to the large,
commercial publishing houses, The New Press is the first full-
scale nonprofit American book publisher outside of the
university presses. The Press is operated editorially in the public
interest, rather than for private gain; it is committed to publishing
in innovative ways works of educational, cultural, and
community value that, despite their intellectual merits, might not
normally be "commercially" viable. The New Press's editorial
offices are located at the City University of New York.

Printed in the United States of America

HC   93 94 95 96   9 8 7 6 5 4 3 2 1
PB   95 96 97 98   9 8 7 6 5 4 3 2 1

CONTENTS

INTRODUCTION: LOUIS ALTHUSSER 1918–1990

Louis Althusser was one of the most original and controversial of French intellectuals: with Antonio Gramsci he was the most influential of western thinkers on Marxism. His career as a philosopher had been spent entirely at the prestigious institution of the École normale supérieure and his fame was associated with the seminars that he held in that part of the University of Paris. But after Sunday, November 16th 1980, his name became known to a wider public in France. At eight or nine that morning he ran from his rooms into the courtyard of the École, wearing a dressing-gown over his pyjamas. He was shouting dementedly: 'My wife is dead, my wife is dead', he cried again and again and again. The resident doctor at the École normale, Doctor Étienne, was called and came immediately. He found that she was indeed dead. But by then Althusser was shouting, 'I killed my wife, I strangled her, I've killed her'. He was in a terrible state of confusion and excitement, and as he wandered about his screams attracted considerable attention, especially from students who stood around, bewildered, not knowing what they could, or should, do.

Doctor Étienne had known Althusser for many years and he, better than anyone, knew that he had a long history of mental instability. He went to the Director of the École normale and told him that the police would have to be called. It appears that the Director not only did this, but that he also consulted various authorities as to what should be done. As a result of these consultations it was decided that Althusser should be taken immediately to the mental hospital of Sainte-Anne where he had been a patient on several occasions. Thus when the police from the local commissariat arrived, Althusser had already disappeared, the ambulance taking him to the hospital having left some ten minutes earlier.

At first the police could find no trace of strangulation on the dead woman's throat. Nor were there any signs of violence. It seemed possible that Althusser, overwhelmed by this death, had, in his despair, imagined that he was responsible. It was only the next day, after the post-mortem, that it was discovered that Hélène Althusser had, in fact, been strangled and that her windpipe had been broken by force.

An examining magistrate was appointed. He went promptly on the evening of November 17th to the hospital, Sainte-Anne, in order to inform Althusser that he was accused of 'voluntary homicide'. But there he was told that Althusser was in a state of total mental collapse and that he was incapable of understanding the legal procedure. He could not be served with any warrant. The magistrate had no alternative but to appoint a panel of three psychiatrists, who were to examine Althusser. After receiving their reports, more than two months after the murder, the magistrate declared that there would be no further proceedings. In French terms, he declared a non-lieu (in English law the term non-suit, or 'no grounds' is usually used), a refusal to order prosecution.

Althusser stayed in hospital until 1983. He then went to live, by himself, in the north of Paris, well away from the Latin Quarter where the École normale is situated. He was regularly visited by a few loyal friends, who helped him in many ways. They included his former pupil, Régis Debray, who had fought with Che Guevara but who, by then, was adviser to President Mitterrand. He gave a few interviews, usually about philosophy and psychology. He wrote the occasional letter to the press, sometimes protesting that his work had been misunderstood or that parts of it had been published without his consent. He read books that were written about him (his copy of Gregory Elliot's study of his work, *The Detour of Theory*, was copiously underlined and commented upon). Since he often said that others were always ready to talk about him whilst he never had the opportunity to talk about himself, he wrote these two versions of his autobiography, *Les Faits* and *L'Avenir dure Longtemps*, and told his life story to his biographer Yann Moulier Boutang, in whom he had complete confidence. From time to time, in his despair, he would walk in the streets of northern Paris, a shabby, ageing figure, and would startle passers-by as he shouted 'Je suis le grand Althusser'. He was always in and out of hospitals. It was in one of them, in the department of the Yvelines, that he died of a heart attack on October 22nd 1990. He was 72.

Althusser usually aroused strong feelings. The circumstances of his wife's death added scandal to polemics. There were those who claimed that he should have been arrested on November 16th. It was suggested that an old-boy network was functioning in favour of a criminal. For a long time it was expected that there would be a trial, and some newspapers had looked forward with relish to a court scene where the most controversial of philosophers would call, as a witness for the defence, the most controversial of French psychiatrists, Jacques Lacan. When this did not happen and the non-lieu was announced, disappointment gave rise to further complaints. It was pointed out that Althusser was a communist and that his major contribution to intellectual life had been his re-statement of Marxism. The government in power was in no way left-wing (it was some months later that the socialists were elected), but it was alleged that all French governments were soft on intellectuals, particularly left-wing intellectuals. After all General de Gaulle himself had given the order that Jean-Paul Sartre should not be troubled by the police when he was acting provocatively in public demonstrations ('one does not arrest Voltaire', the General is supposed to have said). Similarly it was murmured that smart Parisians liked to talk about Althusser and his theories, as if they understood them. It was because he was an intellectual, a fashionable Marxist and a *normalien* with powerful connections, that he had been able to kill his wife and get away with it. There were reports that even when he was in hospital and undergoing treatment, he had been allowed to go out and to walk the streets of Paris. There were those who were more sympathetic to the unfortunate victim than to the man who had killed her and who was, after all, alive and living in Paris, even if admittedly, he was far from well. This resentment surfaced again, both in England and France, when he died.

The École normale supérieure has produced some of the greatest figures of French intellectual, scientific and political life. Entrance is by competitive examination and once the students are there they prepare for another, particularly arduous competitive examination, the *agrégation*. The title of *agrégé* gives many privileges to those who hold it, especially to school and university teachers, and it can serve as a passport to many desirable positions. In July 1939 Althusser, then aged twenty, succeeded in passing the entrance examination. He was placed sixth in the order of admission, having particularly distinguished himself in Latin. But he had to do his military service, and he got caught up in the war, and then in the defeat of France. As he describes in his autobiography, in June 1940 he was captured by the Germans, in Brittany, and transferred to a prisoner-of-war camp in Schleswig-Holstein. He was there for more than four and a half years. Only after the liberation, in 1945, was he able to begin his university career and to start working for the *agrégation* in philosophy.

It was in the autumn of 1947 that I met Althusser. On my first evening as a student at the École normale I sat next to him, by chance, at dinner. He was particularly pleasant to me, a British student of history who knew no one in Paris, and the next day he suggested that I should continue to have lunch and dinner at the table for eight which he shared with other philosophers. I therefore saw him regularly. I learned that his room was in the sanatorium (or Infirmerie) and I was told that this was because he was *fatigué*, still suffering from his experience as a prisoner-of-war. Our relationship became closer when I too moved to the Infirmerie. I stayed as long as I could (since there I had a room to myself and was not obliged to share), and for some time Althusser and I were the only students present. It was then that I met Hélène Légotien, or Rytman, who became his companion and later his wife.

In 1948 Althusser passed the *agrégation* in philosophy. He was immediately made tutor at the École and given certain administrative functions. From then onwards I saw less of him, especially when I returned to England, but we continued to meet in Paris. From him directly, particularly when I gave a course of lectures at the École, and from friends, I learned about three important elements in his life. The first was that he had joined the Communist Party and had embarked upon a major re-interpretation of Marx. This surprised me, because in 1947 and 1948 he had, in conversations, shown little interest in either politics or Marxism.

It so happened that I had been planning to go to Prague about the time that the Communist coup took place in 1948. Jacques Le Goff, now a distinguished French historian, had been in Prague and he came to see me in the Infirmerie. He gave a fascinating account of what was happening there, but Althusser, who was in my room at the time, was in no way concerned. He grew impatient and said that he would be late for lunch. He had often told me that he intended to write his thesis on the Scottish philosopher David Hume, and had embarrassed me by asking my advice on this project. There was no mention of Marx.

He subsequently embarked on a study of French classical philosophy (which produced a short but perceptive book on Montesquieu). However, I learned that his articles, at first unnoticed, and then misunderstood, were becoming important and were seen to be challenging some of the orthodoxies then reigning in the French Communist Party. As is well known, this work culminated in the famous seminars and in the publication of such works as *Pour Marx* and *Lire 'Le Capital'*. Written in collaboration with two or three colleagues, and appearing in 1965, these were regarded as a fundamental renewal of Marx's thought.

The second thing I learned concerned his health. I had not known that before I met him, in 1947, he had received electric-shock treatment at Sainte-Anne and that he had come near to postponing his third year. From the 1950s onwards he was under constant medical attention and undergoing analysis. It is true that his illness sometimes involved the element of the practical joke. When he stopped students in the corridor and asked them who he was, and told them that he had forgotten his name, it seemed to many that he was playing a game with them. He wanted to see how they would react. But these games were probably a means of dealing with the reality of his alarming lapses of memory: after having edited and translated a number of Feuerbach's writings (published in 1960) he claimed that he had totally forgotten having done this. His dependence on psychiatry was enhanced by his interest in Freud, and as he embarked on his textual examination of Marx he was struck by its similarity to the work that Jacques Lacan was carrying out on Freud. The renowned seminars that the two men held emphasised this parallelism.

The third fact that I learned about Althusser over this period was the overwhelming importance to him of Hélène Légotien, whose real name was Hélène Rytman. She was his companion from 1946, although he only married her thirty years later. Hélène, who was eight years older and who was of Lithuanian origin although she was born in France, was the dominating influence. Apart from his mother and sister, she was the most important woman in his life. He was totally dependent on her, whether in terms of his health, his teaching, his publications, his friends. I once asked one of the philosophers who had shared our table at meals whether we should call on Althusser. 'Oh no,' he replied, 'that woman who holds him would not allow it'. (*'cette femme qui le tient'* was the phrase he used). She revised his writings, sometimes adding to them and sometimes, at the last moment, removing whole sections, although Althusser denied this. Critics (and enemies, needless to say) claimed that there was an element of affectation in this relationship. Although there were times when Althusser despised and detested Sartre, it was said that he was jealous of him. So he too would have his Simone de Beauvoir, an intellectual companion who vetted as well as promoted. But I thought that there was little pretence in his dependence on her, especially after he stayed with me in London in the late 1970s. Hélène was then in the south of France. He would telephone her at least twice a day. Before speaking to my seminar he asked for a recording machine, so that he could send her the tape of his talks. He constantly evoked the necessity of consulting her. Why then did he kill her?

What was the nature of their long relationship? Readers of the autobiography must judge for themselves. Was it that she brought to him a past of revolutionary action (however controversial), and that he was for her the potential revolutionary hero that she had always dreamed of (however unstable)? It was a relationship of mutual possessiveness, of shared fragilities, of implacable suspicions. But why then did he kill her?

For some there is no mystery. Althusser had suffered from mental instability all his life. He was a manic depressive who was getting progressively worse, and some sort of dramatic climax was inevitable. His autobiography shows how he suffered as a child and as a young man. He portrays himself constantly as the victim and this work is his escape from his 'tombstone of the non-lieu, of silence and public death'.

Sometimes he himself was responsible for the silence. When we were students I remember telling him that there was a good deal of interest surrounding Michel Foucault, then in his second year, who had begun his study of how madness was treated by visiting the Sainte-Anne hospital and questioning doctors and patients. He was then contemptuous of Foucault. 'They should keep him there', he said. There was no mention of his having been there himself, only a few months earlier, when he had been seriously ill.

Electric shock treatment, different methods of analysis, constant medication, none of these could prevent the depressions from progressing and getting worse. There were times when he would turn up to a meeting and dominate it. On a celebrated occasion in 1961 he orchestrated a debate with Sartre, and to the delight of his students, he devastated him. But these moments of hyperactivity were inevitably followed by periods of depression, inactivity and isolation. Each article was written, each seminar was conducted, with the thought that everything had to be done before the next onslaught of darkness. He set out to write a book with a colleague, but had to withdraw, and the colleague, and pupil, Étienne Balibar, had to complete the work on his own. It's significant that many of his contributions take the form of short articles or interviews. As he grew older his pessimism increased. People who visited him at the École normale found that his room was always in disorder, but then they saw that it was a disorder that did not change. The papers lying on the floor, and gradually turning yellow, had been there for a long time. He was not renewing himself and he was aware of this. He passed the summer of 1980 in hospital. On November 3rd, overcome by depression, he arranged to have a month's leave. There followed the tragic events of November 16th. In an amateurish way, which can claim the rights of common sense, one can say that something had to snap. And it did.

But can we consider the fate of the Althussers without reflecting on the type of philosophy that made Louis Althusser famous? Did its impersonal nature have its effect on his behaviour?

Introduction

Althusser broke with the ideological aspects of Marxism. He did not see history as a story of human effort or emancipation; he was not interested in humanism, whether it was socialistic or bourgeois; he was not preoccupied by messianic idealism, by ethical obligations or by calculated incantations. He set out to show that Marxism was a scientific theory and he sought to complete it. Only through a well-founded science would there be a scientific consciousness in society. It so happened that there was an intellectual climate in France into which Althusser's work could fit. Although usually isolated as an individual, the moment was right for him to appear in the company of other French thinkers. The success of Althusser was not a unique phenomenon. Just as the anthropologist Lévi-Strauss claimed to perceive a universal mental structure existing behind a diversity of empirical facts, or as Lacan believed that he could understand the human psyche in general, so Althusser believed that society was a unity and a totality even if it were the unity and the totality of complexity itself. Lévi-Strauss argued that he could relate the customs of particular primitive peoples to a greater structure, Lacan sought to link the therapy of individual patients to a greater human subject, and Althusser believed that a dominant structure existed in every social formation. Thus he wrote little about men, but rather about modes of production and about the ideological apparatus of the state.

Althusser's ambition was to give back to Marxist theory something of its status as a revolutionary theory and thereby to make it effective in producing results in the real world. He saw himself as making a fresh start in revolutionary politics, and rescuing the movement of the French workers from their ghetto, a ghetto that existed because the movement had no theoretical culture. If Althusser's critics have attacked this ambition, referring to it (as did the late E.P. Thompson) as 'the poverty of theory', Althusser was attacking the poverty of opportunism, of political manoeuvring, of 'spontaneism'. He was, as he put it, absolutely committed to a theoretical destiny, and to establishing Marxism as the science of society. If one could have a science of management, one could also have a science of revolution, of liberation. What excited the students of the 1960s was the revelation that Marx was the creator of such a science. They readily accepted Althusser's dismissal of 'the humanist ravings' that characterised those left-wing intellectuals who were blind to this science, and they felt that they were encountering truth and certainty.

Althusser himself was a kindly and gentle person. Literally hundreds of students can testify to his patience and to his readiness to help them. A professor of Colonial History at the Sorbonne had heard of him through a young relative who had sat the *agrégation* in philosophy. He told me how Althusser accompanied his students to the examination hall and then met them when they had finished. Such courtesy was rare in the somewhat impersonal University of Paris, where professors were usually distant figures, unconcerned by the problems of those to whom they delivered magisterial lectures. But when, in 1968, the students of Paris launched a movement which many considered to be revolutionary and when they needed the guidance of their master, Althusser retired to a sanatorium.

The problem of the events of 1968 is difficult. There is no question that students, influenced by the Maoist interpretation of revolution that had been put forward by Althusser, saw themselves as taking part in a movement in which everything was possible. The absence of Althusser appeared to be catastrophic: 'À quoi sert Althusser? Althusser – à rien.' was written on the walls of the Latin Quarter. Later, in 1969, he made disparaging remarks about the student movement. It was part of his philosophy that the order in which events happened should not determine their importance. That was the mistake of history. He believed that the fact that the student movement touched off the general strike should not cause one to imagine that the student movement was more important than the workers' movement. It is said that the question of how one should interpret these happenings was a subject of much disagreement between himself and Hélène. But for a time he supported the official Communist Party line that the situation was not revolutionary. In conversation with me he assured me that Paris was not France, and he thought that a communist intellectual who had refused to rush to Paris in May 1968, but who had preferred to stay in Poitiers, was right. However, perhaps because his name was so associated with 1968, and perhaps because he became so disappointed with the party, he changed his mind and he denounced the inaction of the party. It is as if he saw 1968 as the last chance of revolution. It is natural that when one looks back at events nearly ten years old, that one should have a reappraisal. But, remembering how he reproved me for my admiration for Pierre Mendès-France in 1954, I am surprised to find him regretting that the Gaullist party and the communist trade unions did not make contact with Mendès in 1968.

There were always difficulties in the theory. The self-confident Althusser of the 1960s believed that philosophers should admit their mistakes, just as scientists confessed to error and re-ran their experiments. But by the 1970s he was less certain. His revisions and self-criticisms were complicating, even undermining, the nature of Althusserianism. 'It is difficult to be a Marxist philosopher', he said, in 1975. And there were difficulties in the practice. The civilised and kindly person was aware of the disappointments and the discouragement of party workers. In 1978 he launched a scathing attack on the Communist Party. Four articles, published in *Le Monde*, were written with a magnificent vigour. 'We didn't know he could write like that' was the reaction of many who had struggled over the intricate and demanding prose of the theoretical philosopher. But these sentiments could have been expressed by many party activists. Was Althusser, someone who had been immersed in the École normale for most of his life, the person to demand more democracy within the party? When he spoke at my seminar at University College, London, his superb intellectual analysis was in contrast to his naïveté. He only just seemed to have discovered, for example, that a shift system existed in French factories.

Thus it could be that, approaching 1980, one was approaching the end of Althusserianism. At times he disregarded this by indulging in dreams about world revolution. In 1978 he envisaged the possibility of establishing himself in London. Had not de Gaulle done this in 1940? And Marx himself? From such a base he could be in touch with Marxists throughout the world. But such exaltation was probably only passing. He found himself faced with nothing. In such circumstances he killed the one person who was the key to it all. His wife. Perhaps it was a suicide, like that of his pupil Poulantzas, who found himself at the end of his understanding of revolution and who threw himself out of the window. This was the opinion of those who gave the news of October 22nd 1990 as 'the second death of Louis Althusser'.

Perhaps the rigorous and impersonal philosophy should be viewed in a wider context. There were certain keys to Althusser's existence. One was the Communist Party. But he despised the leadership, in particular the man who was in charge of the party's cultural activities, Jacques Chambaz. He saw himself as being in constant conflict with the Secretary General, Georges Marchais, who attacked him on television, with a reference to 'the intellectual, seated at his desk, who thinks he can tell us what to do'. The only leader whom he appreciated was Roland Leroy, who had been displaced in the party hierarchy by Marchais, and even he, when director of *L'Humanité*, the official communist newspaper, had refused to publish Althusser's articles, and Althusser changed his mind about him. Then there was always the problem of Hélène, rejected by the party, and a subject of intense controversy in the communist controlled peace movement. (Did Hélène tell all her past to Althusser?)

Another element is the Catholic Church. He was brought up in a strict Catholic tradition and before the war he was one of the leaders of the Catholic youth movement. After the war he probably renounced his faith but he remained (with his sister) a supporter of the Social Catholic movement and a champion of the worker priest experiment. The revelations of one of his former teachers at Lyons, Jean Guitton, suggest that he never broke off relations with Catholics. It is said that in the neighbourhood of the École normale there was a community of nuns that he visited regularly, though secretly. Another of his teachers at Lyons, also a Catholic, wrote an enthusiastic account in *Le Monde* of the occasion when Althusser defended, and revised, his work, when he received his doctorate at the University of Lille. In 1979 he sought an audience with the Pope, John Paul II. Perhaps this was a sign of megalomaniac madness (akin to his idea that he should, like de Gaulle, establish himself in London). But he did believe in the necessity of reconciling Communism and Catholicism. If his wife accepted this, it is difficult to believe that she did so with enthusiasm.

Once again one finds that a vital element in Althusser's being is fraught with frustration. Although he insisted that he wished to maintain his friendships with individual Catholics, and although he assured Jean Guitton that he would turn to him when he needed him, he had no relationship with the Catholic Church. His quarrel with Emmanuel Mounier, the director of the socially conscious Catholic review *Esprit*, and his contempt for the Catholic interpreter of Marx, Jean-Yves Calvez, probably did not help matters.

There was also frustration with the École normale, which had been his home since 1945. French academic procedure is invariably slow, but the authorities of the École were apparently oblivious of the fact that at Lille, in 1975, he had been received as a docteur d'état. The normal procedure is for someone having this title to be placed on an official list as being available for an appointment. Althusser could then have been approached by any university, and by this time there were thirteen in Paris, and appointed. This could have given him a stimulus. Whilst one understands why the authorities at the École normale did not wish to do this, one must also understand that this was another reason for his increasing depression. Also the atmosphere at the École had changed. Just as the role of the intellectuals was declining in France as a whole, students were less interested in the theory of Marxism. Classical philosophy had regained its prestige. Marxism seemed dated in a world where modernism reigned supreme.

There was a further and even more acute frustration. Althusser seems to have become increasingly troubled by psychiatry. Having praised Lacan for revealing the true Freud, he then accused him of having distorted his teachings. In the spring of 1980, on what was to be his last public appearance, he denounced Lacan with great brutality. But perhaps it was via his own psychiatrist that the real crisis developed. When he was staying with me in London, in 1978, I noticed that after telephoning his wife, he telephoned his psychiatrist. What I did not know was that his wife was also a patient of the same psychiatrist. It was, according to Althusser, he who suggested that she should undergo analysis, but there are those who think that it was she who arranged this, so that she could, all the more completely, supervise him. Rumour has it that he discovered that after sessions, there was a discussion about him between the wife and the psychiatrist. There could be nothing sinister about this. Both were devoted to his health and well-being. But to the sick mind it could have appeared as a betrayal. Hence he killed her.

But that is only surmise. We shall never know for certain. A simpler explanation occurs to me. When Althusser was staying in my house I discovered, for the first time, that he was a sleep-walker. He would wander around, come into the room where my wife and I were sleeping, play gramophone records, and the next morning he did not appear to have any recollection of any of these things. There are stories of men who dream that they are strangling their worst enemy and who wake to find that they have killed their wife. There has been at least one case recently, in England, of a man committing murder whilst sleep-walking. This would also be compatible with Althusser's having played a record during the night and then, the next morning, having no remembrance of doing so.

Other suggestions have been made. One is that Hélène had decided to leave him. Therefore it has been argued that the act of destroying her was a more traditional manifestation of anger, mixed with jealousy and fear. Another story suggests that, unexpectedly, the drugs he was taking were having the wrong effect. When this was discovered it was decided to hospitalise Althusser, but arrangements were made too late. Important messages were not delivered. Friends of Hélène have found it strange that, if she had felt in danger, or if she had indeed decided to leave her husband, she did not get in touch with them. All these possibilities emerge in the autobiography.

When reading it one should not forget that Althusser was a *normalien*. Part of the culture of the *normalien* is the practical joke, or *canular*. In the earlier, shorter version of the autobiography, the story of Althusser being approached by General de Gaulle in the street and being asked for a light, is a typical *canular*. Equally one should not take his suggestion that, as a philosopher, he was a fraud, too seriously. The *normalien* despises the man who works all the time (in *normalien* slang he is called a *chiadeur*) and it is common to claim to have passed one's examinations brilliantly without doing any work. To state that one became a renowned expert on Marx without having read the whole *oeuvre* is in this tradition. There are other examples.

Why should we read this work by Althusser? In the summer of 1993 a 35-year-old man coldly shot and killed a young girl whom he did not know, in Brittany. Five days later he committed suicide in a Brest hotel, not far from the scene of his crime. He left a note saying that his life had been a failure, and that life was foul. He admitted that he had killed the girl, but he could not explain why he had done it. This is the autobiography of a murderer, and nothing else. Althusser has not written the autobiography of a murderer, and to refer to him as 'the Paris strangler' (as a London literary review has) is wrong. *The Future Lasts a Long Time* is filled with details which one can read, irrespective of the destiny of the Althussers. We may not believe the stories of his adventures with women. We can note a certain simple romanticism when he hopes that some day society will become just, and that someone like Madame Poré, who for many years organised the École normale supérieure, would be able to have a decent retirement. We can note that he is unfair to his fellow Marxist philosopher, Desanti, to whom he undoubtedly owed a great deal. We can follow an intellectual adventure as well as *une histoire à sensation*.

It has frequently been said that the tragedy of the Althussers was also the tragedy of Althusserianism. No one, it has been claimed, would read Althusser any more. He, even more than traditional Marxists, had become unfashionable. But there are reasons for believing that this is not so. Althusser moved Marxism away from a mechanical evocation of economic principles. His description of the ideological state apparatus which manipulates people into positions of oppressor and oppressed, through education, the family, the media, has never been more relevant. There are those who learn to rule, and there are those who learn to be ruled.

Althusser's theoretical work was always surrounded by the idea of violence. There is a danger when a gentle person writes a literature that is inherently violent. But I find it difficult to envisage the Althusser whom I knew (or thought I knew) deliberately murdering his wife. At all events, without neglecting the tragedy of the dead woman, one must also have great sympathy for Althusser. His last years were years of unbearable sadness. His autobiography is magnificent in its depiction of a victim.

Introduction

Douglas Johnson

The fullest account of Althusser's work in English is by Gregory Elliott: *Althusser: The Detour of Theory*, Verso, 1987.

EDITORS' FOREWORD

Louis Althusser died on October 22nd, 1990. The two autobiographical texts published in this volume had been carefully preserved in his archives and were found when these were handed over in July 1991 to L'Institut Mémoires de l'édition contemporaine (IMEC), whose task it was to verify everything in the archive from a scholarly and editorial point of view.

The two texts were written at an interval of ten years, but in the middle of that period, on November 16th, 1980, Louis Althusser's life took a tragic and unimaginable turn with the murder of his wife, Hélène, in their flat at the École normale supérieure in the rue d'Ulm, Paris.

When he read these two autobiographies –the second of which, *The Future Lasts Forever*, had an almost mythical status – François Boddaert, Althusser's nephew and sole heir, decided they should be published as the first volume of the posthumous edition of unpublished work found in the Althusser archive. As well as these two texts, the edition will include his *Prisoner's Diary*, written during his imprisonment in a German camp from 1940 to 1945, a volume of strictly philosophical works, and finally a collection of various pieces (political, literary . . .) and of letters.

In preparing this edition we have obtained a number of sometimes divergent points of view from those of Althusser's friends who at one time or another knew something about these manuscripts or had come across them. A few had read them either partially or completely when they were written. We have also gathered together documents of all kinds (diaries, notes, press cuttings, letters . . .) which were often scattered throughout the archive, but which provided us with evidence, proof even, or references as to the 'sources' used by Louis Althusser. The dossier used in the preparation of this edition, including of course the manuscripts themselves and the different versions and additions, may be consulted in its entirety. This will enable those with specialist research interests to study the genesis of these autobiographies. We shall simply confine ourselves here to an outline of the basic facts concerning the texts, thus throwing some light on this edition, and of the physical characteristics of the manuscripts and our criteria in transcribing them. We are aware that a detailed description and analysis of the circumstances surrounding the writing of these texts will be given in the second volume of the biography of Louis Althusser.*

A study of the documents and of the evidence gathered so far from his friends enables us to say with certainty that, even if the idea of an autobiography predates it, the writing of *The Future Lasts Forever* was triggered by a brief piece, entitled 'Slight Hunger', written by Claude Sarraute. This appeared in *Le Monde* on March 14th, 1985. Claude Sarraute's article was devoted for the most part to the cannibalistic murder of a young Dutch girl by the Japanese Issei Sagawa and to the success which his book about the crime subsequently enjoyed in Japan. The author was in fact sent back to his own country, having been declared unfit to plead, and he spent a brief period in a French psychiatric hospital. In the course of the article Sarraute referred, in passing, to other 'cases': ' . . . Once we in the media come across the name of someone famous, such as Althusser or Thibault d'Orléans, involved in some juicy trial, we go to town on it. On the other hand, we barely devote a couple of lines to the victim. The guilty party is the one who captures the headlines . . .'.

Following the publication of this article, several of Althusser's friends advised him to protest to the newspaper about this reference to a 'juicy trial'. However, he sided with other friends who, though critical of the approach, took the view that in certain respects Claude Sarraute had put his finger on the crucial and, to him dramatic, issue of the absence of a 'trial', as a consequence of having been declared unfit to plead. On March 19th, 1985, he wrote to one of his closest friends, Dominique Lecourt – though he did not send the letter – saying that he could not 'reappear in public' without first having explained what happened to him, by

* See Yann Moulier Boutang, *Louis Althusser, une biographie*, tome 1, Grasset, 1992.

writing ' . . . a sort of autobiography which would include [his] explanation of the tragedy, the way he had been "treated" by the police, the law and the doctors, and naturally what had caused it'. The desire to write an autobiography was certainly not something new. Already in 1982, for example, when he was released from his first period of confinement following the murder, he wrote a theoretical text on the 'materialism of the encounter' which began: 'I am writing this book in October 1982, having emerged from a three-year period of frightful suffering which, who knows, I may perhaps one day describe if I thought it would throw some light on other events, on the circumstances themselves and what I suffered (psychiatry, etc.). The fact is I strangled my wife, who meant everything to me, during an intense and unforeseeable state of mental confusion, in November 1980. She loved me so much, and since she could not go on living, she wanted to die. Unaware of what I was doing and in a state of confusion, I must have "done what she wanted", which she did not resist and which caused her death.' He then went on to deal with philosophical and political issues and never mentioned these autobiographical allusions again.

In March 1985, having decided to tell that 'story' from his point of view, he wrote to several of his friends abroad, asking them to send any press cuttings about him which had appeared in their country after November 1980. He did the same thing with the French press and also collected or asked his friends to collect a huge number of documents concerning the legal problems associated with the decision to declare someone unfit to plead and with article 64 of the Penal Code of 1838, as well as expert opinion on psychiatric matters. In addition, he asked some of his close friends to let him have their 'diaries' covering these years or to describe certain events to him which he had partially forgotten. He questioned his psychiatrist and psychoanalyst about the treatment he had received, the drugs he had had to take (sometimes he literally 're-typed' their explanations and interpretations). He also accumulated, from odd sheets or diaries he came across, a whole range of facts, incidents, comments, reflections, quotations, and random remarks which were either factual, personal, political, or psychoanalytical. His archive contains all this preparatory material which he used in the writing of *The Future Lasts Forever*.

The writing and typing up of the text probably only took a few weeks, from the end of March to the end of April or the beginning of May, 1985. On May 11th, he gave the (doubtless complete) manuscript to Michelle Loi and on May 30th he typed a revised version of a theoretical text entitled 'Que faire?' On the second page he alludes to the recently completed autobiography as follows: 'I shall abide by one of Machiavelli's fundamental principles which I have commented on at length in my little book *The Future Lasts Forever . . . .*' 'Little' is a figure of speech, since the book contains nearly three hundred pages and, to our knowledge, represents the longest work produced by Althusser, whose published output to date comprises short pieces and collections of articles. On June 15th he was readmitted to hospital at Soisy, as he was on the verge of another acute episode of hypomania.

These appear to have been the dates of composition of *The Future Lasts Forever* – which correspond exactly with the dates of one or two incidents reported in the body of the text (for example: 'Four years ago, a commission was set up by the Mauroy government' (p. 8), and 'Only six months ago, in October '84' (p. 137), and again, 'I am sixty-seven' (p. 319)). Subsequent alterations seem to have been relatively minor ones.

Only a few close friends read the manuscript in its entirety or a significant part of it, and they included Stanislas Breton, Michelle Loi, Sandra Salomon, Paulette Taïeb, André Tosel, Hélène Troizier, and Claudine Normand. It is known, however, that he referred to its existence on a number of occasions in front of several publishers and expressed the desire to see it published, though he did not show them the manuscript or at least the whole thing. Everything suggests that Althusser had taken extreme care to ensure that his manuscript was not widely circulated, which was the opposite of what he usually did with things he had written. There was, for example, no photocopy of it in his archive. One of his friends, André Tosel, said that he was only allowed to read it, in May 1986, at Althusser's home, in his presence, and was not permitted to take notes.

Finally, it is obvious that in writing *The Future Lasts Forever* Althusser drew heavily, particularly for the early chapters on his first autobiography, *The Facts*, of which he had kept two almost identical versions.

The Facts, which forms the second part of the present volume was written in 1976 (the year is referred to on the first page), and almost certainly during the second half of that year. Althusser offered it for publication to Régis Debray, who was to have included it in the second number of a new review, *Ça ira*, the first number of which was published in January 1976, but it never appeared. This autobiography, which was known about by several of Althusser's close friends, has remained unpublished until now.

The original manuscript of *The Future Lasts Forever* comprises three hundred and twenty-three A4 sheets, either green or white, a dozen of which bear the École normale supérieure letterhead. Most of them have been clipped together in a series of numbered 'folders', corresponding in the main to the different chapters. With the exception of a few entirely handwritten pages, all the rest were typed by Louis Althusser himself – which was his usual practice. The foreword, however, both in its original form (which appears in the manuscript) and final version, were typed by Paulette Taïeb on another machine.

On the handwritten title page Althusser had written *The Future Lasts Forever*, followed by a subtitle which had been crossed out, *Brief History of a Murderer*, and another title, *From Darkness to Dawn*, which had also been crossed out. This alludes to a first version of the introduction, of which nine typed pages remain, which ends in mid-sentence.

Many of the typewritten pages of *The Future Lasts Forever* carry numerous corrections and additions between lines or in the margins, and sometimes on the back of a page. When these changes rendered the manuscript almost illegible, Althusser retyped it and made further corrections. He kept the original corrected version of the first seventy-one pages in a separate folder apart, that is, from the foreword and the two introductory pages describing the murder (Chapter I). With this exception, which enables us to study the variants (minimal, as it happens) from one typed version to the next, Althusser's archive contained just one original copy of the text.

It should also be noted that Althusser sometimes slipped small, white sheets of paper with the École normale letterhead and a reference to the page in question between the pages of his manuscript, containing a question or a more or less succinct remark, indicating his desire ultimately to come back to the particular phrase or point he wished to develop. In several other places a mark in the margin, usually in felt-tip pen, suggested he was not entirely happy with the text and that he was considering making certain corrections.

We also learn from the manuscript that its author had envisaged several different arrangements of the text, including four alternative page numberings. This related mainly to the second part, though we were unable to determine completely the different versions to which these various page numberings would have given rise. The manuscript in the form in which we found it, and in which it is published here, was arranged by the author in successive chapters, each bearing a Roman numeral. (There was one unimportant omission at the beginning, which led us to number twenty-two instead of twenty-one chapters. This corresponded to the pagination of the final version of the manuscript from 1 to 276, which did not include one or two inversions and several additions for which the author provided often precise instructions.) This is the version we have used for the present edition.

Finally, we should point out that this edition of *The Future Lasts Forever* does not include two chapters entitled 'Machiavelli' and 'Spinoza', which Althusser in the end omitted* and replaced with the 'summary' to be found on pages 215–20. The same thing is true of the second part[†] of the chapter devoted to political analyses, the future of the Left in France and the situation of the Communist Party (Chapter XIX here). It appears that Althusser wished to include these pages in another work, *La véritable tradition matérialiste*. Apart from these three chapters, which amounted to sixty-one sheets contained in a file bearing this title, there are no more precise details about this projected and unfinished book. These pages, in particular the two chapters on Machiavelli and Spinoza, may be published later on.

We took the decision to publish *The Future Lasts Forever* with almost no references to variants, except for those few additions in the margin where the author failed to alter the text sufficiently and which we give as footnotes, referring researchers

* From 'Before turning to Marx himself' to 'We have not yet, I believe, explored all the implications of this piece of political thinking, the first of its kind and sadly without a sequel.'
† After ' . . . which some would have certainly criticised it for' (p. 241).

to the dossier of material Althusser collected and to the manuscript. All other specific editorial details (underlinings, switching of paragraphs, additions to the text, etc.) conform to what Althusser himself set down, and only minor, standard corrections of such things as the agreement of tenses, punctuation and the first names of people referred to have been made. Errors of fact and wrong dates have been left. However, in one or two places the addition of a word or phrase has been thought necessary, and indicated in brackets, to make the text read better.

The manuscript of *The Facts*, on the other hand, is a typescript with very few corrections or additions. The limited number of variants relate essentially to the order of the opening paragraphs. Louis Althusser kept just two photocopies of the manuscript, which correspond to the two very similar versions of the text.

We are publishing the second version here, though it is clear that various drafts must have existed since, in a letter to Sandra Salomon written during the summer of 1976, Althusser tells her: 'I shall be able to . . . rewrite my "autobiography", which will be considerably expanded so as to include real memories and other imagined ones (my meetings with Pope John XXIII and De Gaulle) and above all an analysis of things I recount. I shall put all the documents together in an annexe. Are you in agreement? It will offer a view of politics from the inside as well as from the outside which will enable me to say some controversial things . . . .'

Our editorial decision not to submerge these two autobiographies under a welter of supposedly illuminating footnotes, other than on the one or two rare occasions where the meaning was compromised, has to do essentially with the nature of the two texts. They should not be read, any more than Rousseau's *Confessions* or the *Mémoires* of the Cardinal de Retz, as biography. In an initial draft of the preface to *The Future Lasts Forever*, entitled 'Two words', Althusser made it clear he had no intention of describing his childhood or the members of his family as they actually were, but wanted to recreate the picture he had gradually built up: 'I shall describe only how I saw them, what I felt, knowing full well that, as with all psychological perceptions, what they may have been like has always-already been invested with meaning in the phantasy projections which were the product of my anxieties.'

7

Thus what he has told us is the story of his affects and phantasies. We are plunged into phantasy, in the full sense of that word as it existed at the time of Montaigne: that of delusion, and even hallucination. 'I intend to stick closely to the facts throughout this succession of memories by association; but hallucinations are also facts,' he wrote in *The Future Lasts Forever*.

This leads us to the most powerfully unusual feature of these texts. They are deliberately projected in two different registers. *The Facts* belongs to the comic and *The Future Lasts Forever* to the tragic mode, situating them outside the scope of binary criteria such as truth and falsehood, which biography is obliged to delineate.* Are we therefore in the realm of fiction, and thus within the enclosed, imaginary symbolic system of the text, which refers only to itself? In a sense yes, and the highly wrought nature of these manuscripts ought really to lead us at a later stage to evaluate the texts as entities in themselves, as one might any literary work. And yet they cannot be read like a Céline novel or a Borgès story, to cite two authors Althusser liked to refer to.

If we enter the realm of phantasy and hallucination with these two texts, it is because the subject-matter is madness and this offers their author the only possibility of defining himself as a madman and murderer, but at the same time as a philosopher and communist. We are brought face to face with a powerful representation of madness, as opposed to what we are given in such 'nosographic documents' as Freud's *Psycho-Analytic Notes on a Case of Paranoia [Dr Schreber]* and Pierre Rivière's *Moi, Pierre Rivière, ayant égorgé ma mère, ma soeur, ma femme*, introduced by Michel Foucault, in the sense that we come to understand how a highly intelligent intellectual and professional philosopher actually experienced madness. We are also made aware of the fact that he was classified as mentally ill by the psychiatric establishment, relying on its methods of analysis. Thus this piece of autobiographical evidence, the core of which existed already in *The Facts*, is an indispensable document to set alongside Michel Foucault's *Madness and Civilization: A History of Insanity in the Age of Reason*. Written by someone who, as a result of being declared

* See Yann Moulier Boutang's *Louis Althusser, une biographie*, tome I, *op. cit.*, for a discussion of the discrepancies, slips, and gaps in the two autobiographies when compared with Althusser's actual life.

unfit to plead, was deprived of his status as a philosopher, *The Future Lasts Forever*, which is an inextricable tangle of facts and phantasies, brings out in relation to a person of flesh and blood, no doubt in an experimental way, what Foucault had tried to establish: the fragile balance between madness and reason. How does thought coexist with madness, without simply being a hostage or succumbing to the awful urge to scratch away at it constantly? How is it that such a story can move into the realm of madness, yet its author remain so aware? How does one come to terms with the author of a book of this kind? Can the 'case of Althusser' be left to the doctors, the judges, and those who have views about the separation of public morality and private desire? Through these two texts presenting the story of his life, he has doubtless escaped them and achieved his own posthumous destiny.

In that sense these two autobiographical works naturally and unquestionably occupy a most important place in Althusser's work as a whole. Only as a result of being read by countless readers who will interpret them quite differently will we discover just what impact they will have on his other writings and the way they are viewed. At this stage, it is impossible to anticipate the nature and scope of that impact.

> *Olivier Corpet*
> *Yann Moulier Boutang*

We should like to thank all those who have helped us in the preparation of this volume and especially François Boddaert, Louis Althusser's heir, who took the decision to publish these texts and who has constantly shown his confidence in us. We should also like to thank Régis Debray, Sandra Salomon, Paulette Taïeb, Michelle Loi, Dominique Lecourt, André Tosel, Stanislas Breton, Hélène Troizier, Fernanda Navarro, Gabriel Albiac, and Jean-Pierre Salgas for the documents and valuable information they have given us and for thus ensuring that the two texts were prepared under the most favourable conditions. They can, however, in no way be held responsible for the outcome. That responsibility is entirely ours. Our thanks also go to those who helped us at IMEC and in particular to Sandrine Samson who has been responsible for classifying the major part of the Althusser Archive.

THE FUTURE LASTS FOREVER

1985

People will probably be shocked that I have chosen not to remain silent, given what I did and that it was thought I benefited from being declared unfit to plead.

Had I not benefited from this decision, I would have had to appear in court and answer charges.

This book represents the response I would otherwise have been obliged to give. All I ask is that I be allowed to give it now as I would have been compelled to in those circumstances.

I realise, of course, that what I am attempting to express here conforms neither to the nature nor the rules of a court appearance. The fact that I was not and never will be tried in due and proper manner does, however, lead me to wonder if what I have to say will not render me more vulnerable to the judgement the public is free to make. But this is what I wish to happen. It is my fate, in seeking to allay one fear, to arouse countless others.

I

What follows, down to the last detail, is my precise memory of those events, for ever engraved on my mind through all my suffering. I shall describe what happened – between two zones of darkness, the unknown one from which I was emerging and the one I was about to enter. Here is the scene of the murder just as I experienced it.

Suddenly I was up and in my dressing-gown at the foot of the bed in my flat at the École normale. The grey light of a November morning – it was almost nine o'clock on Sunday the sixteenth – filtered through the tall window to the left, on to the end of the bed. The window was framed by a pair of very old Empire red curtains which had hung there a long time, tattered with age and burnt by the sun.

Hélène, also in a dressing-gown, lay before me on her back.

Her pelvis was resting on the edge of the bed, her legs dangled on the carpet.

Kneeling beside her, leaning across her body, I was massaging her neck. I would often silently massage the nape of her neck and her back. I had learnt the technique as a prisoner-of-war from little Clerc, a professional footballer who was an expert at all sorts of things.

But on this occasion I was massaging the front of her neck. I pressed my thumbs into the hollow at the top of her breastbone and then, still pressing, slowly moved them both, one to the left, the other to the right, up towards her ears where the flesh was hard. I continued massaging her in a V-shape. The muscles in my forearms began to feel very tired; I was aware that they always did when I was massaging.

Hélène's face was calm and motionless; her eyes were open and staring at the ceiling.

Suddenly, I was terror-struck. Her eyes stared interminably, and

I noticed the tip of her tongue was showing between her teeth and lips, strange and still.

I had seen dead bodies before, of course, but never in my life looked into the face of someone who had been strangled. Yet I knew she had been strangled. But how? I stood up and screamed: 'I've strangled Hélène!'

In a state of total panic, I rushed out of the flat and ran full pelt down the narrow staircase with its iron handrail into the front courtyard enclosed by tall iron gates. I kept running towards the sick-bay where I knew I would find Dr Étienne who lived on the first floor. As it was a Sunday and the École was half empty and people were still asleep, I met no one. I climbed the stairs four at a time, still screaming: 'I've strangled Hélène!'

I knocked violently on the doctor's door. He opened it at last, also wearing a dressing-gown; he looked bewildered. I kept on screaming that I had strangled Hélène and pulled him by the collar of his dressing-gown insisting he come and see her, otherwise I would burn the École down. Étienne did not believe me, saying, 'It's impossible.'

We hurried back down and then, all at once, the two of us were standing over Hélène. Her eyes were staring as before and the tip of her tongue was still visible between her lips and teeth. Étienne felt her heart and pulse and said: 'There's nothing to be done. It's too late.' I said: 'Can't she be revived?' 'No.'

At that point Étienne asked me to excuse him for a moment or two and left me alone. Later I realised he must have telephoned the Director, the hospital, the police station, and so on. I waited, shaking incessantly.

The long, worn-out curtains hung in tatters on each side of the window – the one on the right brushing against the bottom of the bed. I recalled seeing our friend Jacques Martin in his tiny bedroom in the Sixteenth District. He was found dead one day in August 1964 and had been stretched out on his bed for several days. On his chest lay the long stem of a scarlet rose. It was a silent message from beyond the grave to the two of us who had been his friends for twenty years, a reminder of Beloyannis. At that moment I took a ribbon of curtain and without tearing it placed it diagonally across Hélène's chest, from her right shoulder to her left breast.

Étienne returned, and from that point on everything was confused. I seem to remember him giving me an injection and following him back through my office where someone (I do not know who) was removing books I had borrowed from the École library. Étienne spoke about hospital. I sank into darkness. I 'woke up' in Sainte-Anne's Hospital, I am not sure when.

II

I hope my readers will forgive me. I am writing this book principally for my friends, and for myself if that is possible. My reasons will soon become clear.

A long time after the drama occurred, I learnt that two of my close friends (doubtless not the only ones) had not wanted me to be declared unfit to plead,* a decision based on the medico-legal opinions expressed by three experts at Sainte-Anne's in the week following Hélène's death. They would have preferred my case to come to court. Unfortunately, it was a pious wish on their part.

I was in no fit state to take part in legal proceedings on account of my serious mental state (confusion and hallucinations). The examining magistrate who visited me could not get me to say a word. What is more, I no longer enjoyed my freedom or my civic rights as I was automatically committed and under supervision on the orders of the Prefect of Police. Deprived of all choice, I was in fact the victim of an official procedure I could not escape and to which I therefore had to submit.

Such a procedure has its obvious advantages. It protects the accused, who is judged not to be responsible for his actions. But it conceals powerful disadvantages which are less obvious.

Certainly, after such a long and trying experience, I am surprised by my own understanding attitude towards my friends! When I speak of that trying experience, I refer not just to the period of confinement but to my life since then and what I clearly see I shall be condemned to for the rest of my days, if I do not intervene *personally* and *publicly* to offer my own testimony. So many people, with the best or worst of motives, have risked speaking out or remaining silent on my behalf! Any individual who is

---

* Althusser was granted a '*non-lieu*', literally 'no grounds', on the basis of the psychiatrists' reports. In other words, he was declared unfit to plead (Translator's note).

18

declared unfit to plead is destined to be placed beneath a tomb-stone of silence.

The grounds on which I was declared unfit to plead in February 1981 are summed up in the famous article 64 of the 1838 version of the Penal Code; an article which is still in force despite thirty-two fruitless attempts to reform it. Four years ago, a commission was set up by the Mauroy government to look into this delicate matter, which is inextricably bound up with a whole range of administrative, judicial, and penal powers linked to the science, ideology, and practice of psychiatry as it affects internment. The commission no longer meets. It appears it came up with nothing better.

The Penal Code, at least since 1838, makes a distinction between someone held *not to be responsible*; a criminal who has committed an act while suffering from 'dementia' or 'under duress'; and an individual who is quite simply held *to be responsible*, because he is recognised as being 'normal'.

In the case of someone held responsible, a straightforward procedure is set in motion. The person is brought before the court and there is a debate *in public*. The *Public Prosecutor*, representing the interests of society, together with witnesses, lawyers for the defence and for the prosecution, who speak in open court, as well as the defendant himself, who gives his own personal account of what happened, all confront each other. The entire proceedings, which take place *in public*, conclude with the secret deliberations of the jury, which gives its verdict publicly either for an acquittal or for a sentence of imprisonment. In the latter case, the convicted criminal is given a finite term of imprisonment and in this way is 'supposed' to pay his debt to society and thereby 'purge' his crime.

On the other hand, if someone is held *not to be responsible in juridico-legal terms*, he is denied the whole procedure of a public, confrontational court appearance. Above all else, such a decision directly condemns the murderer to a period of confinement in a psychiatric hospital. In this case, too, society is 'protected' from the criminal, but for an indefinite length of time, and he is supposed to receive the psychiatric help necessitated by the fact that he is 'mentally ill'.

If the murderer is acquitted after a public trial, he can return home with his head held high (in principle at least, since the public may be indignant at his acquittal and make its feelings known. In this sort of scandal there are always those knowing individuals who are ready to voice general disquiet).

If he is sent to prison or confined in a psychiatric hospital, the criminal or murderer disappears from society; for a *specific* period (which can be reduced) if he has been sentenced by a court; for an *indefinite* period in the case of someone held on psychiatric grounds. His position is, however, made worse to the extent that he is considered lacking in sound judgement and therefore deprived of his freedom to make decisions. So the murderer who is committed to hospital may lose the judicial right to speak in his own name. This is entrusted by the prefect to a 'guardian' (a legal figure), who signs and acts on his behalf, whereas a person convicted in the ordinary way only loses that right 'in relation to his crime'.

Because the murderer or criminal is considered *dangerous*, both to himself (he may commit suicide) and to society (he may reoffend), the danger is removed by his being imprisoned or committed. To underline this point it is worth noting that a number of psychiatric hospitals still resemble prisons, despite recent progress. Security measures or means of restraint exist in these places for those who are 'dangerous' (manic and violent), such as deep ditches and barbed wire, actual 'straitjackets' or their 'chemical' equivalent, which bring back unpleasant memories. The means of restraint are often worse than those found in many prisons.

It is not surprising the general public should view the two sorts of institution as indistinguishable, given the similar conditions which prevail for those who are imprisoned and those who are committed. In any case, the normal punishment for murder is imprisonment or confinement in a hospital. With the exception of emergency – in other words, acute cases which are a separate issue – hospitalisation is not without its ill effects, both on the patient, who often gets much worse, and the doctor, who is forced to live in an enclosed world. He is 'supposed to know' everything about the patient and often has a close and disturbing relationship with him, which he all too often controls by affecting insensitivity or showing increasing aggression.

But that is not all. The public at large readily takes the view that the criminal or murderer, who is a potential recidivist and therefore permanently 'dangerous', should be kept away from society indefinitely – *even for life*. That is why, among the many indignant voices raised, some stir up social anxiety and guilt for political ends. They claim to be concerned for the security of people and their property and take issue with the policy of allowing 'good conduct' prisoners out on parole before the end of their sentence. That is why the argument in favour of 'life imprisonment' is heard so often, not just as a substitute for the death penalty but also as the 'natural' sanction for a whole range of particularly odious crimes relating to the safety of 'children, the elderly, and police officers'. In these circumstances, how could the 'insane', judged almost more 'dangerous' because more 'unpredictable' than the common criminal, not arouse the same apprehensions? After all, he shares the fate of the 'sane' but guilty person, in being locked away as a natural consequence of his condition.

There is, however, more to it than that, since the insane person committed to hospital as a result of being declared unfit to plead is exposed to numerous other, widely held prejudices.

In the vast majority of cases the person found guilty by the court would be given a specific sentence: two years, five years, twenty years. Moreover, it is understood that a life sentence, up to now at least, may well be reduced. During the period of his imprisonment, the criminal is believed to be 'paying his debt to society'. Once this 'debt' has been paid, he is free to pick up the threads of his life without, in principle, owing anyone an explanation. I say 'in principle' because the reality of his situation is not that simple. It does not immediately coincide with his position in law – witness, for example, the widespread confusion between the *accused* (presumed innocent until proved guilty) and the *guilty*, the lingering scandal in the local and national press, the rumours surrounding the accusation which the media go on spreading for a long time without considering the consequences on the grounds they are providing information. All these rumours can have a harmful and long-lasting effect both on the innocent person who is acquitted and on the condemned criminal who has 'fairly and squarely' served his sentence. In the end, though, one also has to say that the ideology of the 'debt' and of the 'debt paid' to society is loaded in favour of the convicted person who has served his sentence and, to a certain extent, even protects the criminal who has been set free. Furthermore, the law gives him the right to challenge any accusation not related to 'that for which he was tried'. The criminal who is going straight or someone granted an amnesty can sue for defamation when his criminal past is held against him. One can think of thousands of examples. The sentence 'expunges' the crime, and the erstwhile criminal, aided by time, isolation, and a lack of publicity, can begin to live again. This happens, thank heavens, in many cases.

The situation of the 'insane' murderer is not quite the same. When he is committed, it is obviously for an *unlimited period*, even if it is known or should be that *in principle all acute states are transient*. Yet it is a fact that doctors are frequently, if not always, incapable of offering even an approximate time-scale for their prognosis of a cure, even for the acutely ill. What is more, the initial 'diagnosis' constantly changes because, in psychiatry, there is only ever *evolving* diagnosis. Only the changing state of the patient allows the diagnosis to be determined and therefore modified. As a consequence, of course, treatment and prognosis are also determined and modified.

Now, the commonly held view, fostered by a certain section of the press which never distinguishes between the 'madness' of acute but transient states of mind and 'mental illness' with which one is permanently afflicted, is that the mad person must of course be mentally ill. In saying this, it is obviously implied that they will be permanently ill and, as a consequence, should be committed for life: *Lebenstodt*, as the German press so aptly puts it.

As long as he is confined in a hospital, the person who is mentally ill obviously goes on living, unless he commits suicide; but in the silence and isolation of the asylum. For those who do not visit him, it is as if he were lying dead under a tombstone; but who indeed does visit him? Since he is not really dead, however, and since, if he is well known, his death has not been announced (the death of someone unknown counts for nothing), he slowly becomes one of the living dead or, rather, neither dead nor alive; unable to give any sign of life, except to a few close friends and those concerned about him (which is a rare occurrence, since very few inmates *ever receive visitors*; as I have observed with my own eyes at Sainte-Anne's and elsewhere!). In addition, he cannot make his voice heard outside the hospital. I would venture to say he comes into the same category as those victims of world wars and disasters who are reported *missing*.

If I speak of this strange situation it is because I have experienced it and to a certain extent experience it still. Even though I have been out of psychiatric hospital for two years, I am still a *missing person* for the public who have heard of me. I am neither alive nor dead and, though I have not been buried, I am 'bodiless'. I am simply *missing*, which was Foucault's splendid definition of madness.

In contrast with someone who has died and whose death marks the end of the life of an individual who is then buried, a missing person runs the curious risk of reappearing as large as life (as happened in my case). (Foucault referred to such a person as reappearing 'in the bright sunshine of Polish liberty', when he felt he was cured.) It is important to recognise – and can be observed every day – that the peculiar status of a *missing person who may reappear* gives rise to a sense of unease and disquiet in relation to him. This is because the public has a secret dread: the mere absence of a criminal or murderer who has been committed does not put an end to his social existence. It also involves a sense of anguish about death and the threat of it, which is an inescapable fear. As far as the public is concerned, the matter should be permanently resolved by confinement; the gnawing and diffuse sense of disquiet which accompanies its secret and insistent dread is reinforced by the fear that the confinement will not be permanent. If the 'disturbed' patient does return to normal life, even with the support of competent doctors, public opinion has to try to find a way of reconciling this unexpected and extremely awkward fact and the original shock of the murder itself, which is reawakened by the return of the criminal who claims to be 'cured'. This is especially common in cases of acute mania. Is he not likely to do something else? Reoffend? There are so many examples! Can someone who was 'insane' become 'normal' again? And if so, then *was he not normal at the time of the crime?* In the hidden, blind consciousness of the public, blinded by a spontaneous (yet developed) ideology of crime, of death, of 'lifelong debt', of the 'disturbed person' seen as both dangerous and unpredictable, the trial which never took place is indeed about to begin, and the murderer who was declared unfit to plead will again be denied the right to explain his actions, as he was in the first place.

This brings us necessarily to the following strange paradox. Someone accused of a crime who is not declared unfit to plead has, of course, to undergo the great ordeal of a court appearance. But the case for the prosecution and for the defence, as well as any personal explanation of what happened, are made *publicly*. In these 'adversarial' proceedings, the accused murderer can at least count in law on public testimony, a *public presentation* of the case for the defence, and a *public hearing* of the arguments of the prosecution. Above all, he has the right and inestimable privilege of giving, *in his own name and on his own behalf*, an account of his life, the murder he committed, and his future. Whether he is acquitted or condemned, he has at least had the chance to *give this account of himself in public*, and the press is expected, in good conscience, to publish it as well as the outcome of the trial, which legally and again publicly brings the proceedings to a conclusion. If he believes himself to have been convicted unjustly, the murderer can proclaim his innocence, and it is a known fact that public protest of this kind has in several important cases led to a retrial and the acquittal of the accused. Committees are at liberty to defend him publicly. Thus in a variety of ways he neither stands alone nor is without public support. The eighteenth-century jurist, Beccaria, like Kant, took the view that the introduction of public trial and debate provided the ultimate guarantee for the accused.

I regret to say this is not exactly what happens in the case of a murderer declared unfit to plead. There are two factors, rigorously upheld both in law and in the actual conduct of the proceedings, which deny him any right to offer an explanation of his behaviour in public: on the one hand, the fact of his confinement and the concomitant nullification of his legal status and, on the other, medical confidentiality.

What does the public learn? It learns, via the press, that a crime has been committed and the result of the autopsy (the victim died as a consequence of strangulation; that is all). Subsequently, several months later, the public is informed that the person has been declared unfit to plead, under article 64, without further comment.

The public will learn nothing of the details, the arguments, and secret medico-legal evidence compiled in the intervening period by experts appointed by the authorities. It will be entirely ignorant of the (provisional) diagnosis arising from the deliberations of these experts and the initial clinical observations of the doctors. It will learn nothing of their assessments, of their diagnosis and prognosis throughout the period of the patient's confinement, nothing of the treatment prescribed, nothing of the terrible difficulties the doctors often have to face and the agonising impasses which sometimes confront them while they continue to put a brave face on things. Naturally, it will know nothing of the reactions of the murderer who is 'not guilty'; of his desperate efforts to try to understand and explain the reasons, both distant and immediate, for the tragedy into which he has literally been plunged in his madness and delirium. And when he comes out of hospital (if he does ...), the public will know nothing of his state of mind, of the reasons for his being set free, of the terrible 'transitional' period which he has to face, usually alone even if not in isolation, and of the slow, painful progress which imperceptibly, step by step, will enable him to survive and to begin living again.

I have referred to public opinion (to its ideology, that is) and to the public itself, though the two terms do not refer to the same thing. This does not matter, since the public rarely remains uncontaminated by public opinion; that is to say, by a certain prevailing ideology about crime, death, people disappearing and then strangely coming back to life again. It is an ideology which brings into play a whole medico-legal and penal apparatus, as well as the principles and institutions pertaining to each of them.

I would also like to speak about those who are close to the individual concerned, such as family and friends and, where appropriate, about acquaintances too. Those close friends, who have themselves lived through the tragedy in their own way and have been unable to explain it if it has overwhelmed them, will be torn between the simple fact of the appalling tragedy and its exploitation as scandal by a certain section of the press, and their own affection for the murderer whom they know well and often (if not always) love. Torn as they are, they are unable to equate the image they have of their relation or friend with that of the murderer he has become. They too in their bewilderment seek an explanation which no one provides, and when a doctor is bold enough to put forward a hypothesis, it strikes them as lamentable:

'Words, nothing but words.' And who could they turn to in their quest for an initial explanation of the inexplicable, if not to the doctors caring for the patient? They enter the realm of 'psychiatric expertise', which is reinforced by professional secrecy; the world of people who are bound to silence by their code of practice and who often appear sure of themselves in an attempt to overcome their feelings of uncertainty, their anguish even, and to project on to others their own inner distress (this happens frequently).

Very often, in the most serious and intense cases, which are also potentially the most threatening (as was my own case), a strange dialectic comes into play between the anxiety of the patient, which quickly spreads to the doctor and nurses, and that of his close friends. The doctor has to 'hold firm' in the face of his own anguish, that of the 'caring team' and that of the patient's close friends. But it is not easy to make a pretence of 'holding firm'. Nothing is less reassuring to the patient and those close to him than the doctor's visible and obvious struggle against what often appears to him to be a possibly irreversible condition. Thus there looms in the doctor's mind and in the expectations of those close to the patient, though for different reasons, the idea that he may be *permanently committed*.

And though the patient may well return to normal life and manage to settle down, through great personal effort and by over-coming real or imaginary obstacles in his path; and though he may do this with the constant and unswerving support of his friends (as happened in my case), they will still remain deeply worried that he may never get over it. At certain moments they feel sure he will not. Even at the hospital it might cross their mind that he could 'do it again'. He might kill someone else, despite all the protective measures taken, and certainly fall ill again. They will worry that he may have to be taken back into hospital in an acutely disturbed state from which he might not recover. Even if he did manage to get well again, what would be the cost? Would he not be deeply scarred by the tragedy and its consequences? Might he not be a broken man (there are so many!) or plunge helplessly into some deeply dangerous mania which neither he nor anyone else could control?

An even more serious issue is how to reconcile my own expla-nation with that sketched by each and every individual in an attempt to comprehend in some measure the murder of a woman they may not have known well but of whom they have formed an opinion based on a few surface details of her nature and temperament (people cannot easily come to terms with the woman friend of a friend). There will be as many opinions about the murder as there are individuals, since everyone will have his or her own 'interpretation' after the event, as a way of bearing the unbearable and comprehending it. How indeed do they reconcile their private thoughts about the tragedy with the personal 'explanations' and confidences offered by their friend, which are for the most part only his troubled attempts to grope, from within the dark night of his 'madness', towards the light of an unattainable clarity?

His friends are in a very difficult situation. They have their own observations and remember details about the period before the tragedy and his extremely long stay in hospital. The patient himself has forgotten them, suffering as he does from a profound yet protective state of amnesia. Thus they know more than he does about various episodes, except for the tragic event itself. They are reluctant to tell their friend what they know for fear of arousing the terrible anguish he experienced at the time of the event and immediately following it. Above all, they may wish to keep from him the malign comments of certain sections of the press (especially if he is someone 'well known'), as well as the reactions of other people and perhaps in particular the silence of certain close friends. Each of them has done his utmost to forget everything (an impossible attempt). In addition, each knows that were he to disclose his own secret thoughts, he would, by provoking a reaction in his friend, put at risk not just their friendship but the bonds binding them all. It is not merely the fate of their friend which is at stake but their friendship of the whole group.

That is why I have decided to explain my own actions publicly, since other people have spoken for me up to now and the judicial process denied me a public hearing.

First and foremost, I am doing it for my friends and for myself too, if that is possible, to remove the weight of the tombstone which lies over me. I wish to free myself without seeking anyone else's help or advice; to free myself from the circumstances [in which I found myself] as a result of my extremely serious state of mind (on two occasions my doctors believed I was actually dying). I want to free myself from the murder and above all from the dubious effects of having been declared unfit to plead, which I could not challenge in law or do anything about. I had to survive and learn to live beneath the oppressive weight of that declaration, which was like a wall of silence, or as if I were dead in the eyes of the public.

These are some of the negative effects of being declared unfit to plead, and why I decided to give my own account of the dramatic events I have lived through. All I want to do is to lift the tombstone under which that declaration buried me, which would have smothered me for life, and to give everyone the facts I have at my disposal.

People will, of course, believe me when I say my intention is to be as *objective* as humanly possible. I have no desire to reveal only subjective thoughts and feelings. I have therefore taken care to question at some length the doctors who looked after me, not just while I was confined in the hospital, but well before and afterwards too. I was also careful to consult the numerous friends who took a close interest in what happened to me, not only when I was in hospital but for a long time before that (two of them kept a daily log from July 1980 to July 1982). I also consulted specialists in pharmacology and medical biology on important points. Naturally, I read most of the articles which appeared in the press at the time of my wife's murder, in France and in other countries where I am known. I could see that the press behaved very 'properly', with a few rare exceptions (their motives being clearly political). Thus I did what no one else has either wanted or been able to do before: I gathered together and collated all the available 'information' as if it related to someone else, and looked at it in the light of my own experience and vice versa. I then took a conscious decision to explain my own actions publicly, and to assume responsibility for what I was doing.

I have deliberately sought to avoid all controversy. You will, of course, accept that I speak for no one but myself.

People have said to me: 'You will bring the whole affair to life again. It would be better to remain silent and not stir things up.' Others have said: 'The only solution is to remain silent and put up with things as they are. You won't change the way society thinks by what you say. It's too rigid.' I do not accept these warnings. I have no reason to think 'my explanation of events' will revive the extraordinary controversy surrounding my affair. On the contrary, I believe I am not only ready to give a reasonably clear account of myself but I can also get others to reflect upon a concrete case. No one before me has made such a critical confession (apart, that is, from Pierre Rivière, whose admirable confession Foucault published, and doubtless many more whose confessions no editor wanted to take for philosophical or political reasons). I lived through an experience of the most acute and terrifying nature which I cannot fully comprehend since it raises a number of legal, penal, medical, analytical, institutional, and ultimately ideological and social questions. In the end, it has to do with structures which may perhaps interest some of our contemporaries and help them to understand recent major debates about the penal code, psychoanalysis, psychiatry, the issue of locking people away on psychiatric grounds, and the relationship between these things in the minds of doctors who cannot escape the conditions and effects of social institutions of all kinds.

Alas, I am no Rousseau. But in planning to write about myself and the dramatic events I lived through and live with still, I often thought about his unprecedented boldness. Not that I would ever claim as he did at the beginning of the *Confessions*: 'I am embarking on something which has never been done before.' Certainly not. But I can in all honesty subscribe to the following declaration of his: 'I shall say openly what I did, what I thought, what I was.' I would simply add: 'What I understood or believed I understood, what I no longer altogether control, but what I have become.'

I give notice that what follows is not a diary, not my memoirs, not an autobiography. In discarding everything else, I simply wanted to remember those emotional experiences which had an impact on me and helped shape my life; my life as I see it and as others may, I think, see it too.

I shall sometimes describe things in the order in which they happened and sometimes anticipate or recall certain moments. My aim is not to confuse matters; on the contrary, I wish to highlight the crucial and marked similarity of those emotional experiences which occurred at different points in my life and made me what I am.

This seemed to me to be the obvious way of proceeding. Everyone must judge the results for themselves. Similarly, they can judge the powerful role that certain violent organisations have played in my life. I used to refer to these as the Ideological State Apparatuses, and I am surprised I have been unable to do without them in understanding what happened to me.

III

I was born at 4.30 a.m. on October 16th, 1918, in a forestry house in the Bois de Boulogne, a district of Birmandreïs some fifteen kilometres from Algiers.

I am told that my grandfather, Pierre Berger, ran out to fetch a Russian woman doctor, known to my grandmother, who lived in the upper part of town. It appears that this rough, jovial, warm-hearted woman came up to our house, delivered me, and, seeing my large head, assured my mother: 'This one is different!' For a long time, various versions of this remark were to haunt me. When I was approaching adolescence, I recall my first cousin and my sister repeating: 'Louis is an oddball.'

My father had been absent for nine months when I arrived; initially at the front and then simply because he had to stay on in France after he was demobbed. So, for the first six months, I had no father to watch over me and, until March 1919, I lived with just my mother and my maternal grandfather and grandmother.

Both my grandparents were the children of poor peasants from near Fours in the Morvan region of the Nièvre. When they were young, they both sang in church on Sundays; my grandfather, young Pierre Berger, with the other village lads in the gallery at the back of the church above the main door, near the bell-rope. My grandmother, young Madeleine Nectoux, sat with the girls near the chancel. Madeleine attended the convent school, and it was the nuns who arranged her marriage, having decided that Pierre Berger was a decent chap and that he sang well. He was small, stocky, and slightly withdrawn, but a handsome fellow with his newly grown moustache. The wedding took place without any fuss as was the custom at the time in that part of the country. But neither my grandfather's nor my grandmother's parents had enough land to set the young couple up on their own. Jules Ferry was in power at the time and French colonialism was at its height.

My grandfather, who was born near forests and never wanted to leave them, dreamed of becoming a forester in Madagascar! Madeleine had different ideas. Even before they were married she had made her views quite clear: 'You can be a forester, but you're not going further than Algeria, otherwise I won't marry you!' This was the first time my grandfather gave in to her, but it was not the last. My grandmother was a capable woman who knew what she wanted, yet she was always calm and measured in what she said and in the decisions she took. Throughout their life, she was the stabilising influence.

That was how the Bergers came to leave France and how my grandfather became a forester in the wildest and most remote mountain region of Algeria. The names came back to me again during the Sixties, when they became key hiding-places and battle-grounds for the Algerian resistance.

My grandfather's health was ruined by the endless treks he made on horseback, by day and night. He was liked by both the Arabs and Berbers. His job was to protect the forests from goats which stood on their hind legs and ate the young shoots but, especially, to fight the fires that would have destroyed the trees. Another of his jobs was to map out roads over difficult terrain and to supervise their construction. One night, when the Chréa plateau was under snow, he set off into the mountains alone and on foot to help a team of Swedes who had gone out and got lost. My grandfather managed to find them, no one ever knew how, and brought them back exhausted after three days and nights to his own house. He was decorated for this act of devotion to duty, and I still have the medal.

Whenever he went off on treks or was at work, my grandmother stayed on her own, day and night, in their isolated house in the forest. I mention this in particular since it is important. My grandparents went straight from the countryside of the Morvan, with its traditional peasant sociability, to those wild and remote forests of Algeria. For nearly forty years they lived almost entirely on their own, even after their two daughters were born. The only people they could mix with were the Arabs and Berbers they met in the different places where they lived, and the 'bosses' of the Algerian Woods and Forests Agency who made irregular inspections (once a year). One of these individuals, a certain M. de

Peyrimoff, kept a fine thoroughbred horse for his own personal use, which my grandfather fed, groomed, and took care of. Apart from these contacts they made the occasional rare excursion to a nearby village or a distant town. That was all.

My grandfather was always on the go, either out on his rounds or preparing to set off. He never let up for a moment, and was a great worrier, constantly grousing. When he was away, often for several days and nights, my grandmother was left alone. On numerous occasions she told me about the 'Marguerite' uprising, when she was alone with her two daughters in their house in the forest. There was a chance that the fiery Arab troops would pass very close to where they were and, though the local people liked my grandfather, there was every reason to be fearful since these troops were from another region some way away. The night of the greatest danger my grandmother did not sleep a wink, although her two young daughters (one of whom was to become my mother) slept peacefully by her side. She sat with a loaded rifle across her knees the whole time. She told me: 'There were two bullets in it for my daughters and a third nearby for me.' She stayed there until morning; the uprising took place some distance from the house.

I am recounting this screen-memory, told me by my grandmother a long time after the event, because it has remained one of my childhood terrors.

Another memory that makes me shudder was also told me by my grandmother. It occurred in a different forestry house in the Zaccar mountains, a long way from the nearest town of Blida. My future mother and her sister, who were about six and four at the time, were playing in a wide, fast-flowing stream of fresh water which ran along a concrete channel above ground. A little further on the water plunged into a sump and disappeared completely from sight. My mother fell into the water, was swept away by the current, and at the very moment she was about to disappear down the sump, my grandmother ran to save her, catching her by the hair.

As a child my head was filled with the fear of people being killed; moreover, in describing these dramatic incidents to me, my grandmother was talking about my own mother and the fact that she might have died. For a long time, naturally (though there was some ambivalence), the thought of it made me tremble, as if unconsciously I had wanted it to happen.

I do not know how my mother and her younger sister were able to pursue their studies, isolated as they were. I imagine my grandmother took care of these things. Then the war came and my grandfather was mobilised. He remained where he was, however, as M. de Peyrimoff simply had him moved for his final posting to the fine forestry house in the Bois de Boulogne overlooking the city of Algiers. The house was much less isolated and the work was not as hard. But they were still fifteen kilometres from the city and had to walk four kilometres to reach the tramway (at a place called Colonne-Voirol) which took them right into Government Square in the heart of the city and quite close to Bab-el-Oued, its noisy streets teeming with poor white settlers (French, Spanish, Maltese, Lebanese, and other Mediterranean people who spoke 'Sabir'). My grandfather and grandmother only went down into the town on very rare occasions, and it was on one of these visits that they met a minor civil servant called Althusser in the local offices of the Woods and Forests Agency. He was married with two sons, Charles, the elder, and Louis.

They too were a family of expatriates who had recently arrived! I never knew my grandfather Althusser, but my grandmother, whom I did know, was an extraordinary woman. She stood as stiff as a ramrod, spoke brusquely, and had a most unyielding nature. I saw very little of her because my father did not like her much. Their feelings about each other were mutual; she did not care much for us either.

Another bitter memory is the fact that, in 1871 after the war between Napoleon III and Bismarck, the Althussers chose France and, like many Alsatians who wished to remain French, they were literally 'deported' to Algeria by the government of the day.

Once my grandfather Berger had been posted to the Bois de Boulogne, my mother (Lucienne) and her sister (Juliette) could go to school at Colonne-Voirol. My mother was a model pupil, well behaved and virtuous in a way children no longer are, and as respectful of her teachers as she was of her own mother. My aunt, on the other hand, was the capricious member of the family; the only one, though heaven knows why.

The Bergers and the Althussers saw each other from time to

time. On a Sunday the Althussers would sometimes 'go up' to the forestry house and, as their respective children were growing up and relatively well matched in age (that is to say, the girls were much younger than the boys, the importance of which will become apparent later on), the parents agreed they should marry. I do not know why, but Louis, the younger boy, was paired with Lucienne, and Charles, the elder, with Juliette. *In fact I know quite well*; it was because their natural affinity was obvious from the start. Louis too was a very good scholar, very well behaved and of unblemished character, and he also enjoyed poetry and literature. He was preparing to take the entrance exam to the École normale supérieure of Saint-Cloud. My father, the elder of the two, had just passed his school certificate and my paternal grandmother decided he should start work as a messenger boy in a bank. My grandfather had no say in the decision. The truth is, they did not have enough money to educate both sons and my paternal grandmother detested her elder son Charles. He was just thirteen when she sent him out to work.

I have two memories of this impossible grandmother of mine, one of which is rather amusing yet highly significant. It came from my father, who often talked to me about the incident at Fashoda. When the threat of war between France and England was announced over some insignificant stronghold in Africa, my paternal grandmother wasted no time in ordering my father to go out to buy sixty pounds of beans. This was a sensible precaution against starvation, as dried beans keep well (except for the 'charençon' variety) and are as nourishing as meat. She asked him to get forty pounds of sugar as well. I have often thought about those dried beans since I discovered they formed the staple diet in the poor countries of Latin America. I have always enjoyed stuffing myself with the large, red Italian ones (and I get that from my maternal grandfather in the Morvan). I once offered a dish of them to Franca (the wonderful young Sicilian woman I later fell madly in love with, though she did not make her feelings known) in an attempt to win her affection.

On another occasion (this is one of my own memories and it is not at all funny), I was with my terrible grandmother in a flat which looked out on to the avenue beside the sea, where a march-past of troops was taking place one July 14th under a blazing sun.

All the boats in the port were draped in flags. I do not know why we were in this flat, which was much too grand for us. I disliked kissing my grandmother because she was a rather masculine woman with a moustache and hair all over her face which prickled, and she never smiled or was at all friendly. After the troops had gone, she produced a cheap tennis racket as a present for me (I was beginning to play tennis with my family). The only thing I noticed was that my grandmother's back was as stiff as a ramrod, just like the wretched handle of my racket. I felt a sense of repulsion. There was no doubt about it, I could not bear masculine women who were incapable of showing affection and giving a present in the ordinary way.

Then the war came. My mother enjoyed Louis's company (she was really only an adolescent when she met him; sixteen by the time she had got to know him. He was the first male friend she had had). Like him, she loved studying, since above all it involved the mind rather than the body, and she also enjoyed being taught and supervised by teachers who were full of goodness and conviction. Thus they had a deep understanding of each other. Each was as sensible and as pure in heart – especially as pure – as the other. Both lived in the same realm of speculation and lofty ideas, far removed from any concern with that dangerous 'thing', the body. They soon began to share their pure passion and disembodied dreams. Later in life I made the following terrible remark to a friend who then quoted it back to me: '*The trouble is, there are bodies and, worse still, sexual organs.*'

In the family, Louis and Lucienne were thought of as engaged, and soon they were. When Charles and Louis went off to war, Charles into the artillery and Louis into what was to become the air corps, my mother kept up an innocent and continuous correspondence with Louis. She always kept a bundle of sealed letters which intrigued me. From time to time the brothers would come home on leave either together or alone. My father showed everyone photos of the huge long-range guns, and he was always standing in front of them.

One day in 1917, my father turned up alone at the forestry house in the Bois de Boulogne and told the Berger family that his brother Louis had been killed while serving as an observer in a plane over Verdun. Then Charles took my mother aside in the large garden and ended up by proposing that 'he should take Louis's place and marry her'. (I heard this from Aunt Juliette on numerous occasions.) After all, my mother was young, beautiful, and desirable, and my father truly loved his brother Louis. I am sure he expressed himself as tactfully as possible. My mother was, of course, shattered by the news of Louis's death, whom she loved deeply in her own way, and she was also taken aback by the unexpected nature of Charles's proposal. It meant, however, that the two families would still come together and the parents were bound to agree. She was the same person I later came to know, a well-behaved, virtuous, submissive, and respectful woman, whose only thoughts were those she had shared with Louis. She accepted Charles.

The church wedding was fixed for February 1918, during one of Charles's periods of leave. In the intervening year, my mother became a teacher in a primary school close to Galland Park in Algiers. There, she met men she could listen to and with whom she could still have chaste conversations, as she had done with Louis. They belonged to that great generation of teachers, men of conscience with a sense of mission and professional responsibility, who were a good deal older than she (some of them could have been her father), and who showed her every respect as a young girl. For the first time in her life she had formed her own circle of acquaintances, whom she was pleased to know and meet, but never outside school hours. Then, one day, my father came back from the front and they were married.

My mother always kept the details of this frightful marriage from me. Obviously I have no personal memories of it, but my aunt, my mother's younger sister, talked to me a great deal about it on numerous occasions. There is surely a reason why these belated accounts struck me so forcibly. I must have coloured them with my own personal sense of horror and linked them with that whole succession of violent emotional shocks that were to affect me in a similar way. I shall come to these in due course.

Once the wedding had taken place, my father spent a few days with my mother before returning to the front. My mother, it seems, was left with three appalling memories of that period: one was of being sexually violated by her brutal husband; another was of seeing all her savings frittered away by him in a single evening of eating and drinking (my father's behaviour was surely understandable given that he was returning to the front and perhaps going to his death. He was indeed a very sensual man, having already had a number of affairs as a bachelor – how dreadful! – and even a mistress called Louise (that Christian name) whom he had simply dropped when he got married without saying a word to her. It was again my aunt who referred to this impecunious and mysterious young woman as someone the family never mentioned). Finally, my father decided without further ado that my mother should at once give up her job as a teacher, and, therefore, the world she had chosen for herself. She would be having children, and besides he wanted her to be at home just for him.

Thereupon, he went back to the front, leaving my mother robbed, raped, and shattered; physically brutalised, deprived of the savings she had patiently accumulated (something in reserve, one never knows – sex and money are closely linked here), and cut off from the life she had begun to make for herself and to enjoy. My reason for giving these details is because they have almost certainly helped to shape *after the event*, and so to confirm and reinforce in me unconsciously, the image I have of *a martyred mother, bleeding like a wound*. The mother who existed in my mind was associated with memories (also reported long after the events) and with incidents involving an early death (miraculously avoided). She was to become a suffering figure, condemned to a life of pain which she paraded in a reproachful way, and a martyr to her husband in her own home, her wounds clearly visible. She revealed herself to be a masochist but also dreadfully sadistic, both with regard to my father who had taken Louis's place (and was thus associated with his death) and to me (since she could not help wanting me dead, as the Louis she loved was dead). Confronted with her terrible pain, I constantly experienced a huge and profound sense of anguish, and an urge to devote myself to her service, body and soul, as an act of oblation in order to save myself from an imaginary sense of guilt and her from martyrdom and from her husband. I had the unshakeable conviction that this was the supreme mission and meaning of my life.

Furthermore, because of her husband's decision, my mother

found herself alone again and unable to do anything about it. Together we shared that solitude.

When I was born, I was christened Louis. I know it only too well. For a long time, Louis was a name I literally detested. It was too short, had only one vowel and ended in the sharp 'ee' sound which offended me (bear this in mind when I later come on to my phantasy of the stake). Doubtless it also said yes a little too readily on my behalf, and I rebelled against this '*yes*', which corresponded to my mother's desire rather than to mine. Above all, it contained the sound of the third person pronoun ('*lui*'), which deprived me of any personality of my own, summoning as it did an anonymous other. It referred to my uncle, the man who stood behind me: '*Lui*' *was Louis*. It was him my mother loved, not me.

This name was chosen by my father, in memory of his brother Louis who had died in the skies over Verdun, but above all by my mother, to remind her of the Louis she had loved and never stopped loving throughout her whole life.

IV

I have two kinds of memories of the time we spent in Algiers (until 1930) which are unbearably yet fortunately dissimilar. There are those involving my parents, our family life, and the school I attended and those involving my maternal grandparents during the period they were living in the forestry house in the Bois de Boulogne.

My earliest memory of my father (which is so 'precocious' it must surely be a screen-memory created after the event) relates to the very moment of his return from France, six months after the war ended. This is what I saw or believed I saw. My mother, whose half-exposed breasts disgusted me and made me feel ashamed, was looking radiant as she held me on her knee. The downstairs door, which gave on to the large garden and revealed the vastness of the sea and sky, suddenly opened and there in the doorway appeared a very tall, slender figure, the spring air wafting around him. In the clouds high above his head could be seen the long black cigar shape of Dix-Mude, the German Zeppelin which had been handed over to France by way of reparations and which was about to burst into flames and plunge into the sea. I do not know when or indeed how I came to recompose this scene, in which my father appeared in the too obviously symbolic context of a castastrophe involving sex and death. But even if it was created after the event, the association certainly occupied an important place in the sequence of things which made an early impression on me.

My father was a tall man (just over six feet) with a long, handsome face, a thin, finely chiselled nose (like that of a Roman emperor) and a little moustache which remained unchanged until his death. He had a high forehead which suggested intelligence and malice. He was, in fact, extremely intelligent, and not only in a practical way. He proved his abilities in his job, climbing the ladder within the Algerian Bank which he entered as a simple messenger-boy with only a school certificate. It was subsequently taken over by the Union Bank of Paris and then by the Northern Credit Bank. He finished up as general manager of the Moroccan branches of the Algerian Bank, then went on to become manager of the important Marseille office after a double stint as a senior executive in Marseille and deputy-manager in Lyon. His competence and understanding of financial and business matters, not to mention the techniques and organisation of production (he loved visiting businesses with which the bank was involved and having all the details explained to him) were much appreciated by his superiors in Paris – hence the succession of postings and promotions. This meant that our little family had to move house a number of times (between Algiers, Marseille, Casablanca, and Lyon), which my mother bemoaned quite openly to all and sundry. This was something else she constantly complained about and which made my life a misery.

My father was fundamentally very authoritarian and totally independent, even, perhaps especially, in relation to his family. He made it clear from the start what his responsibilities were and also those of his wife: she exercised authority in the home and over the children, but that was all. He had his job, looked after money matters, and concerned himself with the wider world. On these issues he was wholly unwilling to compromise. But he never took any initiative in the home or on the subject of our education. In these spheres my mother reigned supreme. On the other hand, he never talked at home about either his job or about friends he had outside the family (except for two we got to know, one of whom took us in his car to Chréa where there was snow). My father began to talk about things just six months before his death, in the little house at Viroflay to which he had retired. I ought to explain that I then felt sufficiently bold to ask him certain questions, albeit rather late in the day! Anyway, he felt his end was drawing near, that he was becoming 'decrepit' as he put it. The first thing he told me was that he had long known what to expect in the bank.

When he was in Lyon during the early days of the Vichy government (until 1942), he refused to join an association of bankers which supported the National Revolution. Similarly, in Morocco, when General Juin swore he would get Mohammed V 'to eat straw', my father, the most senior person in the bank in Morocco, rather conspicuously just kept quiet, which did not go unnoticed, even though bank managers as a group paid court to the Resident General. When he retired, he was sufficiently competent, experienced, and qualified for the general management in Paris to have invited him to join their staff – something they usually did and which would have been in their own interest. 'I knew they wouldn't do it in my case. I didn't belong as I hadn't been to the École Polytechnique, nor was I a Protestant or married to one of their daughters.' They simply thanked him and nothing more. Yet he was so competent and had such breadth of vision. When I questioned him that day about the economic and financial situation, he gave me a remarkable overview not only of economic and financial matters but also of political affairs as well, though he was a very old man and in physical decline. He still had a clear mind and astounded me with his intelligence and insight and his understanding of social problems and conflicts. I had lived with this man quite unaware of the qualities he possessed! But throughout his life he never talked about himself, and I had never dared question him or get him to tell me anything. In any case, I am not sure he would have responded. I have to confess that for a long time I hated my father for causing my mother's suffering, which, as a martyr, I took upon myself for us both.

Yet on one occasion in Marseille after the war, when I went to collect him at his office, some colleagues came in with documents for him to look at. He had the reputation of always being decisive. After slowly looking through the documents without saying a word, he looked up and made a few comments to the two men who stood waiting. He then muttered something that was hard to make out and totally incomprehensible to me. His colleagues left the room without asking a single question. 'But they didn't understand a thing!' – 'Don't worry, they will.' Thus, quite by chance, I discovered how my father ran his bank. The impression I had gained was confirmed much later by one of his former colleagues whom I met in Paris: 'We hardly ever understood what your father was saying. Frequently, we walked out without daring to ask him to repeat what he had said' – 'So what happened then?' – 'It was up to us to do as we thought.' That was how my father 'ran things' – without ever making anything clear, which was perhaps a way of allowing his colleagues to make decisions which they knew had been approved without being clearly defined. Doubtless they knew their job; doubtless he had long since got them used to his ways; doubtless they knew my father well enough to understand his drift. Even his chauffeur did not always understand him when it was a question of taking a new route! Thus my father had created a good-natured if authoritarian persona for himself. And because his mutterings were so difficult to understand, his employees had learnt to anticipate his almost unintelligible decisions, even if it meant being firmly ticked off. It was a hard school of 'man management', which not even Machiavelli would have dreamt up. Yet it was astonishingly successful. Former colleagues of my father whom I met after his death confirmed what I knew of his strange behaviour and its consequences. They had not forgotten him and spoke admiringly, almost devotedly, of him. There was no one like him. He was an 'oddball'.

I never knew to what extent conscious deliberation or inner uncertainty and indeed distress even entered into my father's relationship with other people, if not with himself. Though he had abilities and was intelligent, he had to come to terms with his deep discomfort at expressing himself in front of others and with the fact that he was reserved by nature rather than on principle, which reflected his profoundly taciturn character. An authoritarian figure, given to occasional violent outbursts, he was at the same time paralysed by an inability to reveal himself to others when called upon to speak. His fear made him reserved and prevented him from expressing clearly the decisions he had taken. He also had a strong and tacit belief in the value of reticence, which came from his humble background. It was seemingly this quiet reserve which meant he was the only person both in Lyon and Casablanca not to go along either with his social superiors or with the authorities of the day; which just goes to show how deeply embedded class conflicts and differences can be.

My reason for dwelling on this subject at such length is because my father behaved in exactly the same way towards us. Admittedly he had decided that my mother should have sole charge of the house, the children's education, and daily needs, and related things such as clothes, holidays, the theatre, music, etc. His mumbled interventions were extremely rare and only ever expressions of irritation. We knew at least that he was angry but we never knew why. He truly worshipped my mother in the role to which he had confined her. Occasionally, he liked to refer to her as 'the dynamic Mme Althusser!', especially in front of other people, choosing the word which had been used to describe him by his boss in Algiers, M. Rongier, whom he revered. In contrast to my father, my mother never stopped talking. She did so unrestrainedly, with reckless and childlike spontaneity and, to my great surprise (and shame), my father let her have her own way in public. He never said anything to my sister and me. But instead of giving us a sense of freedom to do as we wished, he terrified us with his unfathomable silence; at least he terrified me.

For a start, he was big and strong, and I was impressed by his forcefulness. I knew he kept his service revolver in a cupboard and was afraid he might use it one day; like the night in Algiers when he started raging, shouting, and banging saucepans, and then got out his gun because the people in the flat next door were making a row. I was trembling in case it ended in a physical confrontation and shots were fired. Whether by luck or because they took fright, silence was restored almost immediately.

Frequently during the night he would let out the most terrible howls in his sleep, like a wolf that was out hunting or had been cornered. They went on and on with unbearable intensity, and we hid at the bottom of our beds. My mother could never waken him from his nightmares. For us, or for me at least, night-time was terrifying, and I constantly dreaded those unbearable shrieks of his which I have never forgotten. Later on, when I vehemently defended my martyred mother against him and provoked him more than he could bear, he would jump up from the table before the end of the meal uttering the one word '*Fautré!*', and disappear out into the night, slamming the door behind him. We were immediately overcome with a terrible sense of anguish, or I was at least. He had abandoned my mother, abandoned us (my mother appeared indifferent). Had he gone for good? Would he come back or had he disappeared for ever? I never discovered what he did on these occasions. He probably walked the streets in the dark. But each time, after what seemed to me an endless wait, he would return and go to bed alone without saying a word. I kept wondering what he said to my mother, the martyr, or whether he spoke to her at all. I thought him incapable of saying anything.

Both before and after each outburst he would silently and conspicuously sulk, incapable of behaving in any other way towards us. Then it would pass.

But that was only one aspect of his character. When he was among friends (the few we actually knew) and no longer preoccupied with work, he revealed a biting and irresistible sense of irony. He played with people and made fun of them, producing endless witty, provocative, and teasing remarks which almost always carried sexual overtones. He was incredibly inventive in this respect, forcing those listening to him to join in the laughter which at the same time reflected his uneasiness. He was too powerful for anyone else ever to have the last word. No one, especially my mother, was allowed to take part in the game or could withstand his attack. It was doubtless another form of defence, to avoid having to say what he thought or wanted, perhaps because he did not really know what he wanted, seeking merely to disguise his deep-seated unease and indecisiveness behind a transparent mask of unrestrained irony. He particularly enjoyed playing this game with the wives of different friends, and what a performance it was! I suffered for my mother, watching him flirt with them so 'scandalously'. He was especially roused by the wife of one of his colleagues at the office, one of the few friends we knew. Her name was Suzy, a radiant and extremely beautiful woman, who knew how good-looking she was and loved him making advances. My father would go on to the attack in front of all of us and engage in an endless erotic joust that would make Suzy dissolve into a state of laughter and confusion which she enjoyed. I suffered in silence on my mother's behalf and because he did not live up to my expectations of him.

This powerful and profoundly sensual man loved wine and red meat as much as he loved women. Then one day, when we lived in Marseille, my mother became besotted with the ideas of a certain Dr Omo – another pure spirit who appealed to her in her naïvety. He owned a fine country house in the northern district of the town where the gardens were full of flowers. There he grew the vegetables he needed for his diet and preached strict vegetarianism (selling little jars under his own name at rather inflated prices). So my mother decided off her own bat to put my sister and me, as well as herself, on a purely vegetarian diet –

which lasted six whole years! My father made no objection, but insisted on having his rare steak every day. We ate cabbage, chestnuts, and a mixture of almonds and honey which was conspicuously prepared in front of him, as he calmly cut up his steak, to register our collective disapproval. I used to cheek him and attack him quite vehemently. He never made any response, except sometimes to utter his customary riposte: '*Fautré*!'

There were, of course, times when my father wanted me to side with him. He occasionally took me to the sports stadium, where he liked to get in without paying under the knowing gaze of a bank employee who supplemented his income by looking after the entrance money. I was fascinated by his skill at 'working these fiddles'. I would never even have dared think of doing it myself, having had the fundamental principles of honesty and virtue instilled into me by my mother and my teachers. One dreadful memory I recall of his bad example concerns a visit we made to some tennis courts. As usual, my father entered without paying, but I was behind him and could not get in. So he just left me. Subsequently, however, I must have made an effort to acquire his skill of entering without paying. He would go in, I would follow behind, and we would then watch the match together. There was always a rowdy atmosphere and on two occasions at Saint-Eugène I remember shots being fired in the crowd. Always shots! (how symbolic . . .). I shook with fear, thinking they were meant for me.

I have one horrible memory of this period. We were learning about the Crusades in school, about towns being plundered and burnt and their inhabitants put to the sword. The streets were running with blood and many of the native people were also impaled. I constantly visualised one of them, his body supported only by the stake which had gone in through his anus and was slowly going up through his stomach until it reached his heart. It was only then that he died, in terrible agony, with blood running down the stake and on down his legs to the ground. It was terrifying; because it was me who was being pierced by the stake (perhaps by the dead Louis who was always *behind* me). I have another memory from this period which I must have got from a book. A victim was trapped inside an iron maiden, which was covered from top to bottom with hard, sharp points. Slowly they pierced his eyes, his skull, and his heart. Again, I was the one inside the iron maiden. What a slow and frightful death! For a long time it made me shudder and I would dream about it at night. You may or may not believe me, but neither here nor elsewhere have I any intention of engaging in 'self-analysis'. I shall leave that to those clever people who like to indulge in 'analytical theory' worthy of their private obsessions and phantasies. I am simply recording the various emotional experiences which marked me for life, both the earliest ones and those which occurred subsequently and were linked to them.

On one unique occasion, my father, who had returned from the war with countless photos of his artillery division in which he was always to be seen standing in front of their huge long-range guns, took me to the army firing-range at Kouba. He made me pick up and aim a heavy rifle. I felt an enormous kick on my shoulder and fell over backwards with the noise of the explosion, which I found unbearable. In the distance people were waving flags to indicate that I had missed the target. I was perhaps nine years old at the time. My father was proud of me. As always, I was terrified.

But when, at a later date, I passed the 'scholarship' exam for the *lycée* in 1929 (coming well down the list although I was a good student), my father asked me what I would like as a present. Without hesitation, I replied: 'A nine-millimetre rifle from the Arms and Cycle Company in Saint-Étienne', whose catalogue I used to pore over (with so many things that I had never had or even seen, to fill me with raging). I got my rifle without any fuss, as well as some cartridges and bullets. My mother disapproved, but my father did not question my choice for a second. One day I was to use it for a very strange purpose.

From a very early age I was extremely good at aiming at things: throwing stones at empty tins and also hitting objects with a catapult. I tried to shoot birds but always missed, except on one occasion when I stalked the hens that were pecking up seeds in my grandfather's field at Bois-de-Velle. I took aim at a handsome red cockerel which was near the hedge, though I was some distance from it (twenty metres or so). I fired my catapult and was really scared when I hit it right in the eye and saw it jump with pain, jab its beak up and down violently, and then run away squawking. My heart went on pounding for several hours.

This is what happened when I got my rifle. At first I used it just to fire at cardboard targets, which I was good at. One day, however, we were at a remote place way up in the hills called Les Raves, a property my father had decided it was a good idea to buy. I was roaming in the woods, my rifle in my hands, looking for some bird or other to shoot at. Suddenly I spotted a turtledove and fired. It fell to the ground and I looked everywhere for it in the dry bracken. In the end I became convinced I had missed it, that it had pretended to fall and thus escaped. I went on my way and suddenly, without consciously thinking about it and certainly without knowing why, the idea came to me that I could try to kill myself. I pressed the barrel of the rifle against my stomach and was about to pull the trigger when I was restrained by an uneasy feeling, though I will never know why. I opened the breech, and there was a bullet. How had it got there? I had not loaded it. I never knew how it happened. Instantly, I came out in a cold sweat, shook all over, and had to lie on the ground for a considerable time before returning to the farm in a very reflective frame of mind. Once again, death was a reality, but this time it had been my own death.

I am not sure what makes me associate this memory with a subsequent one which aroused similar feelings of total panic. My mother and I had left our flat in the rue Sébastopol in Marseille and taken a short-cut down a little street with high walls on both sides. In the distance, on the right-hand pavement, we noticed a man and two women. The two women were shrieking and violently lashing out at each other. One was on the ground and the other was dragging her by the hair. The man stood motionless, watching what was happening but doing nothing to intervene. As we passed them, he warned us quite calmly: 'Be careful; she has a revolver!' My mother walked stiffly by, looking straight ahead, not wishing to see or hear anything and completely indifferent to what was going on. She showed no emotion and never said a word to me about the drama we had witnessed. It was clear to me I should have intervened. But I was a coward. The relationship between my mother and me, my mother and death, my father and death, myself and death, must have been an unusual one. It was

only considerably later that I came to understand these relationships, when I was undergoing analysis.

Did I really have a father? Certainly I bore his name and he
was there. But, in another sense, I did not. After all, he never once
intervened in my life to steer me in any particular direction, nor
did he reveal anything to me of his own life which might have
given me some idea about self-defence, schoolboy fights, and, later
on, about virility. Here again, it was my mother's duty to fill me
in on this subject, despite her horror at anything to do with
sexuality. At the same time, my father was clearly but quietly
wanting me to side with him in his practice of fiddling things
and later on over his allusions to my relationships with women.
Naturally, he never wanted to hear anything about the women I
knew nor about what I did. But whenever I was going out he
made the same remark which invited neither comment nor reply:
'Make her happy!' Her? My mother simply remained silent.

He doubtless thought he had made my mother happy! It will
already have become clear, however, that this was hardly the case.
Basically, my father was too intelligent to have *the slightest illusion*
on that score. My mother, who was eleven years younger than my
father, was a very beautiful woman in her youth. She always
remained a child, moving straight from the protective care of
her parents to that of her husband, without having acquired any
experience of life, of men, or of women. The only fond memories
she cherished eternally were of Louis, to whom she had been
engaged and who died in an aeroplane, and of the teachers she got
to know during her brief career, brutally cut short by my father.
She also had a girl friend of her own age in Algiers, as innocent
as herself, who became a doctor and whose life was cruelly cut
short by tuberculosis. She was called Georgette. Naturally, when
my sister was born, my mother named her Georgette after her
dead friend. Another dead person's name.

My mother was on the small side, blonde, with regular features
and beautiful breasts, which I can picture in my mind's eye, or
rather from photos, with a kind of repulsion. She certainly loved
me very deeply. I was her first-born, a boy, and she was proud
of me. When my sister was born, I was entrusted with the task of
looking after her all the time, of making a fuss of her and, later
on, of holding her hand and taking care when we crossed the road.

49

Later still, I was expected to keep a watchful eye on her on all occasions. This I did most faithfully and to the best of my ability, both as a child and as an adolescent, called upon to play an adult's role, a father's role even (my father had a soft spot for her which I found disgusting. I openly suspected him of behaving incestuously when he took her on his knee in what to me was a quite obscene manner). The task with which I was solemnly entrusted must have been overwhelming for a young child and even for an adolescent.

My mother constantly reminded me that my sister was delicate (like her no doubt) because she was a girl, and I recall another obscene memory which horrified and shocked me deeply. It took place in Marseille when my naked sister was being given a bath by my mother and I, also naked, was waiting my turn. I can still hear my mother saying: 'Do you see, your sister is a delicate creature and much more exposed to germs than a boy' – and showing me to make her point she went on: 'You've only got *two holes*, but *she has got three.*' I was deeply ashamed of my mother for being so brutally intrusive as to make sexual comparisons between us.

I realise now that my mother was literally assailed by phobias. She was afraid of everything: of being late, of not having (enough) money, of draughts (she always had a sore throat, as I did too until I went off to do my military service and got away from her). She had a great fear of germs and of catching them, of crowds and the noise they made, of neighbours, of accidents whether in the street or elsewhere, and especially of having dealings with dangerous or dubious people which might go wrong. Let us be frank and say that what she feared above all was sex, robbery, and rape; she was afraid of being physically violated, of her body no longer being intact; a dubious notion indeed since this had already happened.

I have another memory of her, which surpasses everything in its horror and obscenity. It is definitely not a screen-memory, overlaid with a subsequent emotional charge, but one which dates from when I was thirteen or fourteen. As such, it is isolated and extremely precise, without a single added detail. It is probable, likely even, that it was reinforced after the event by incidents of a similar nature, but they only served to accentuate the truly appalling sense of shame and indignation I felt at the time.

I was nearly thirteen and we were living in Marseille. For some weeks, with considerable satisfaction, I had registered an acute, burning sensation of pleasure at night in my sexual organs, followed by an agreeable feeling of relief. In the morning I noticed large, dull stains on the sheets. It does not much matter whether I was aware that I was having wet dreams, since I knew quite well it had something to do with my sexual organs. One morning I had got up as usual and was having coffee in the kitchen when my mother came in looking solemn and serious and said: 'Come with me, son.' She took me into my bedroom, pulled back the blankets in front of me, and pointed to the large, dull, dry stains on my sheets. She gazed at me for a moment or two with a restrained look of pride on her face, which suggested that something momentous had occurred. Feeling it was her duty to measure up to the occasion, she declared: 'Now you are a man, my son!'

I was overcome with shame and an unbearable sense of rebellion. My mother had dared to grub around in my sheets, and had invaded my privacy, the most intimate part of my naked body, in other words, my sexual organs, just as if she had looked into my pants or grabbed hold of my penis to show it off (as if it belonged to her!); and she had a horror of sex. Added to this, she had forced herself (which I strongly sensed), as if it were her duty, to point it out and comment on it in such an *obscene* manner. Instead of coming to terms with it myself, she did it for me, for the man I had become long before she realised it, and for which I owed her nothing. What I felt at the time and still feel is that I was utterly degraded, morally speaking, and that her behaviour was obscene. It was truly a form of rape and castration. I had been raped and castrated by my mother, who felt she had been raped by my father (but that was her affair, not mine). *Family fate* was indeed inescapable. But the horror of what happened was intensified by the fact that my mother perpetrated this obscenity and behaved so unnaturally in considering it to be her duty (whereas it should have been my father who did it). I went out without saying a word, slamming the door behind me, and wandered the streets feeling confused and enormously angry.

My body and my freedom were subjected to my mother's phobias. I longed to play football with the poor kids I could see from our fourth-floor flat in the rue Sébastopol as they romped around

on a large piece of waste-ground. I was forbidden to play football!
'You shouldn't mix with that sort of people, and you might break
your leg!' I longed for the company of children of my own age,
to make friends with them so that I would no longer be alone but
would be accepted and recognised as one of them. We would have
talked, swapped marbles, even had fights, and I would have learnt
from them all the things I did not know. That was my dream. But
I had no friends. It was forbidden.

When we were in Algiers, I had to cross only one quiet road
to get to the local school, three hundred yards or so from where
we lived (in the rue Station-Sanitaire). But my mother hired an
Algerian maid to take me there. We always arrived at school too
early, so that I would not be late (another of my mother's phobias).
The French and Algerian boys would be playing marbles against
the wall or running around together quite freely, making a lot of
noise. I arrived looking rather prim, since that was how I had
been taught to behave, accompanied by our Moorish maid who
never said a word. Deep down I was ashamed and felt I would be
despised for being privileged and rich (in fact, we were poor at
the time). Instead of waiting outside until the school opened,
former colleagues of my mother had arranged for me to wait in
the playground until the teachers arrived. One of these teachers,
a lean, mild-mannered man, would invariably stop and ask me,
though I never knew why, 'Louis, what is the fruit of the beech
tree called?' I gave him the answer he had taught me and he would
pat me on the cheek and go on his way. Ten minutes later, the
other kids came running and shouting into the playground just as
lessons were about to start. I was no longer on my own, but there
was now no chance of joining in with them. I found this (daily)
ritual unbearable and was ashamed of being a teacher's 'pet', just
so that my mother would not worry about all the risks I ran when
I was in the streets: meeting the wrong sort of people, catching
germs, etc.

Another vivid memory concerns a game of marbles that took
place during playtime with a boy who was much younger than
me. Since I was very good at the game, I always won, and on this
occasion I got all the little boy's marbles. He was terribly keen to
keep just one, but that was cheating. All of a sudden, I slapped
his face, though I could not explain the reason for my violent

outburst. He ran off and I went after him, wanting to take back what I had done, the pain I had caused him. Clearly, I could not bear fighting.

Since I am in the process of recalling vivid memories of this period, here is another one. I was in class with the very good teacher who really liked me. He was at the blackboard with his back to us. At that moment the boy sitting just behind me let out a fart. The teacher turned round with a reproachful and disappointed look on his face and said: 'You, Louis....' I was so convinced it was me who had farted, I did not reply. I was totally ashamed, as if I were truly guilty. In desperation I told my mother about it, as she had been trained by this teacher, knew him well, and liked him a lot. 'Are you sure it wasn't you who (she could not bring herself to say the word) did this dreadful thing? He's such a nice man, he couldn't have made a mistake.' No comment!

My mother loved me deeply, but it was only much later, in the light of my analysis, that I came to understand how. Both in her presence and away from her, I always had the overwhelming feeling that I did not exist in or for myself. I always felt there had been a mistake, and that it was not really me she loved or was even looking at. I am in no way blaming her in saying this; the poor woman came to terms as best she could with what had happened to her. She had had a child and could not help calling him Louis after the man she had loved and loved still in her heart, and who had died. When she looked at me, it was not me she saw, but *another person*, the *other* Louis, who was not me but whose name I had been given and who had died in the skies over Verdun, those pure skies which belonged to the past but which were ever present. He stood behind me, in some infinite and imaginary sky which was for ever marked by his death. It was as if she looked through me. I disappeared under her gaze, which reached out beyond me, beyond death to recapture the face of another Louis who was not and never would be me. I am reconstructing what I experienced and the way I understood it. One can philosophise about death and explore it in literary terms as much as one likes: death, which is an integral part of social reality in which it is 'inverted', just like money, does not always assume the same form in reality as it does in phantasy. In my case, death represented a man my mother loved more than anyone else, more than me. In her 'love' for me, something chilled and marked me from earliest childhood and determined my fate for a very long time. It was not a phantasy but the very *reality* of my life. That is how phantasy becomes real for each individual.

Later, when I was an adolescent living in Larochemillay with my maternal grandparents, I wanted to be called Jacques, like my godson who was the son of sensual Suzy Pascal. I am perhaps reading a little too much into the phonemes of the signifier – but the 'J' of Jacques is a spurt (or sperm), the dark 'a' (Jacques) the same as in my father's name Charles, the '*ques*' obviously a *tail*; and Jacques is like the Jacquerie, a secret peasant revolt my grandfather told me about at the time.

Anyway, from earliest childhood I bore the name of a man who still lived and was loved in my mother's thoughts: it was *a dead man's name*.

V

It is perhaps possible now to piece together and understand the contradictions, or rather the ambivalence, of the life to which I was condemned from my earliest years.

On the one hand, like all breast-fed babies I had physical, physiological, and erotic contact with my mother's body. She suckled me and bestowed on me the warmth of her body, her skin, her hands, her face, her voice. I was intimately and erotically attached to my mother and loved her as every healthy, lively child loves its mother.

But I knew early on (children are unbelievably perceptive about things which adults fail to see, though such perceptions are certainly not conscious) that my mother whom I loved with all my heart loved someone else through and beyond me, using my physical presence to remind her of a person who was absent, or rather seeing his presence through my absence. It was only *later* I discovered this person had been *dead* a long time. Who can say when this 'actually occurred'? Obviously, my own views on the matter were determined 'after the event' through the effects they had on me. These were repeated over and over in various highly intense emotional experiences; patterns which were inescapable and never changed. How therefore could I make my mother love me, since it wasn't actually me she loved? I was doomed to be merely a pale reflection, that of a dead man, perhaps even a dead person myself. Clearly, the only means I had of escaping this 'contradiction' or ambivalence was to *seduce* my mother (as one might seduce a stranger one met) so that she would look at me and love me for myself. I wanted to seduce her not just as little boys are commonly said to want to 'sleep with their mothers', as Diderot pointed out. In my case it was something much deeper, because I sought to win my mother's affection in order that I might become the person she loved, who was for ever beyond me and sanctified by death. I would *seduce her by fulfilling her desire.*

It was both a possible and an impossible task. After all, I was not the paragon of goodness and purity my mother wanted me to be. The further I pursued this aim, the more I experienced various aspects of my own desire, including violent ones; especially the basic desire of not living in a phantasy world of death but rather of living for myself, of simply existing in my own body, which my mother so despised (just like the Louis she loved) because it disgusted her.

The image I have preserved of myself as a young boy is of a thin, indolent creature with narrow shoulders which would never be very manly. I had a pallid face, dominated by an over-large forehead, and looked lost as I stood alone on the white path of some huge, empty park. I wasn't a boy at all, but a feeble little girl.

That image, as clear as a screen-memory, was to haunt me for a long time, and its effects will in due course become clear. By some miracle I came across a small photograph among my father's papers after his death which provided some tangible evidence in support of it.

There I am, standing on one of the great wide paths in Galland Park, Algiers, close to where we lived. I really was a thin, frail, and pallid little boy, who seemed not to have any shoulders. My over-large forehead was crowned with a pale-coloured hat. At the end of my out-stretched arm was a minute little dog (it belonged to Suzy's husband, M. Pascal) which looked very lively and was tugging at its lead. I was alone with the little dog; there was no one else to be seen on the deserted paths. One might say that the fact of my being alone was of no significance and that M. Pascal had simply waited until everyone else had gone. Though he may have chosen to take a photo of me on my own, that image of me alone joined together in my memory the reality and phantasy of my loneliness and vulnerability.

I was indeed *totally alone* in Algiers, as I would be for much of the time in Marseille and Lyon, and later still terribly alone after Hélène's death. I had *no* real playmate, even among those I mixed with under supervision in the playground, Arabs, French, Spanish, and Lebanese. My mother was so intent on preventing us (herself) from having any contact with dubious acquaintances, keeping us away from germs and impulses which might have led to goodness knows what! I really mean *no playmate* and therefore, *a fortiori, no friend*. When I went into the first form at the Lycée Lyautey in Algiers after leaving primary school, I didn't have a single friend in the playground. Worse still, I remember the rich boys being very smart, haughty, disdainful, and cynical, and wanting to have nothing at all to do with me. They were picked up from school in magnificent, chauffeur-driven sports cars (including a splendid Voisin). The only company I had was at home, a voluble mother and a silent father. Apart from that, I ate, slept, and did my lessons and homework; dutifully and 'willingly'.

I was a model pupil at primary school and my teachers liked me. But in the first year at the *lycée*, I felt lost and was thoroughly mediocre, despite my efforts. It was only when I got to Marseille (1930–36) and then Lyon (1936–39, where I prepared the entrance exam for the École normale) that I was top of my class. Because of my mother, I joined the scouts in Marseille and naturally became a patrol leader, appointed by a chaplain who was too clever to be an honest man. He realised it was my sense of guilt which led me to accept the first responsibility that came my way. I was good, too good, and pure, too pure, just as my mother wished me to be. I can honestly say I fulfilled my mother's wishes by being totally pure – and for a long time too, until I was twenty-nine!

Indeed, I fulfilled her wishes and expectations of the other Louis; what she had longed for from time immemorial (the unconscious is not bound by time) – *and I did it to seduce her*. I strove for goodness, purity, virtue, a pure intellect, a disembodied state, academic success, and to crown it all a 'literary' career (my father would have preferred me to go to the École Polytechnique, something I discovered later, though he never let it be known). To accomplish all this, I was to go to the École normale supérieure, not at Saint-Cloud where Uncle Louis was to have gone, but the one in the rue d'Ulm. Then I became a well-known intellectual who fiercely refused to 'dirty his hands' in the media (what purity!) and got my name on the cover of a few books which my mother proudly read. I was an established philosopher.

Did I really succeed in seducing my mother? Yes and no. Yes, inasmuch as she was happy and extremely proud because she recognised in me the fulfilment of her desires. No, because in seducing her I always had the impression I was not myself, that I didn't really exist, that my existence depended solely *on pretence*, indeed was a pretence. The artifice of seduction was bound up with *deception* (it is a short step from artifice to deception), and I therefore felt that I had not truly won her heart, but only artificially and deceitfully seduced her.

Everything was artifice yet I still had my own desires; or, if you like, to put things at their simplest, my own desire, which could not be realised. I wanted to live my own life, to join the kids who played football on the waste ground, to mix with French and Arab boys at primary school, to play in the parks and woods with other kids I might meet, boys and *girls*, whom my mother would *never let me join* 'because we didn't know their parents', even if they were only two feet away or sitting on the same seat. I was forbidden to talk to them, since we didn't know who or what they might be!! Even though I grumbled inwardly at what she said, I always went along with it. I existed only through my mother's desires, never my own, which remained inaccessible.

Another significant memory I have is of being in the Bois de Boulogne forest with my mother and sister, near an aloe tree which had a huge spike on it (yet another sort of stake). A woman came by with two children, a boy and a girl. I don't know why my mother gave in, but we started to play together. Not for long, however! I never knew what came over me, but I suddenly slapped the little girl and said: 'You're a nincompoop!' (I had read this word in a book and it seemed full of meaning, though I wasn't sure what.) You can imagine my mother's reaction: she immediately dragged us off without saying a word. It was yet another sudden violent act on my part, like the one in the school playground. But this time the victim was a little girl. I don't recall feeling any sense of shame or desire to say I was sorry. 'That' at least was something!

I was torn, but helpless in the face of my mother's desire and my own inner conflict. I did everything she wished. I held my sister's hand and helped her cross the road, because it was so dangerous. On the way home from school I bought two little '*pains au chocolat*' with the exact money my mother gave me, never having had any pocket money (until I was eighteen!), because *I*

might have been robbed and also because one never knew what
nasty or useless thing a child might buy. Her excessive thriftiness
was combined with a fear of eating contaminated food and the
danger of being robbed. At home I performed my duties like a
good boy and was present at meal times. Subsequently, the only
excursion I ever made in Algiers, taking my sister's hand, as always,
was to the flat of a thin, languid pair who seemed disembodied
and otherworldly. They were not husband and wife but brother
and sister (like us), both unmarried and living together permanently. My mother had placed her total trust in them (on account
of their manifest purity). My sister took piano lessons and I learnt
the violin, so that the two of us could also play together later as
brother and sister. I could do nothing to escape these constraints.
How would I have done so, given the way I was? As a result I
developed a strong dislike of music, which was later reinforced by
having to go with my mother to weekly classical concerts in
Marseille (my father never came)! But don't worry, I truly enjoy
playing the piano now (on which, as you will discover, I improvise,
never having taken lessons). What indeed could I have done to
avoid these musical and other impositions? There was no one
outside I could turn to, and certainly not to my father at home.
The only friends I knew were the very occasional ones my father
introduced us to. Actually, there was only one, M. Pascal, who
was a colleague at work and a subordinate of his. He was going
thin on top, was as soft as butter, and always gave in to his wife,
the vivacious Suzy.

The year my sister caught chickenpox (as a child she was always
ill), my mother asked the Pascals if I could stay with them so that
I would not catch it (yet again that fear of contagion). Thus I got
to know the funny ways of this childless couple in their own cosy
little nest. Suzy was a splendid and voluptuous woman whose
breasts were always on display and she had a warm air of authority
about her. M. Pascal, I discovered, led a humdrum life, following
his wife around just like the little dog he took to the park on a
lead. When I was in bed I always had the same nightmare: a long
creature slowly appeared from the top of the cupboard, a long,
headless snake (castrated?), a sort of giant earthworm, and came
down towards me. I woke up screaming. Suzy came running and
clasped me to her ample bosom. I calmed down.

One morning I awoke late. I realised M. Pascal had left for work. I got up and went quietly towards the door of the kitchen, where I could hear Suzy doing some chores (making coffee or washing up?). I am not sure how, but *I knew she was standing naked* in her kitchen. Impelled by an irresistible desire and quite sure nothing would happen (you will discover why), I opened the door and gazed at her for a long time. I had never seen a woman's naked body, her breasts, belly, pubic hair, and fascinating buttocks. Was it the attraction of forbidden fruit (I must have been about ten) or the sensual delight of her ample figure? My enjoyment lasted quite a while. Then she spotted me and far from scolding me, drew me towards her, held me against her breasts and between her warm thighs and kissed me. Nothing was ever said about it subsequently. But I never forgot that moment of intense and incomparable 'fusion'.

The following year, when my sister caught scarlet fever (ill as always), my mother sent me to my maternal grandparents, so that on this occasion too I would avoid catching it. They had 'retired' and gone back to their native Morvan.

VI

Those dear grandparents! My grandmother was slim and upright, had honest, pale-blue eyes, and was always on the go, though she did things at her own pace. She behaved generously towards everyone, especially me. She was also extremely fond of me without making a show of it and provided a haven of peace and calm to all and sundry. Without her my grandfather would never have survived his exhausting labours in the forests of Algeria. She brought up her daughters according to her own principles of health and virtue so that they became fine young women who were both upright and pure. My grandfather, a tense and anxious person, was always muttering and moaning under his moustache and peaked cap, yet he was as kind as could be. They were my real family, my only family, my only friends in the world.

You must realise that the vast open spaces where I lived with them, or went to join them, were exhilarating to a child who until then had been cooped up alone in a tiny flat in urban surroundings. More likely it was being with them and the fact that they loved me as I loved them which transformed the houses, woods, and fields where they lived into a childhood paradise.

To begin with, before my grandfather retired and went back to his native Morvan, their home was the forestry house in the Bois de Boulogne, looking out over the whole of Algiers, then the little house at Larochemillay (Nièvre) with its garden and the fields of Bois-de-Velle.

I have a vivid memory of the forestry house in the Bois de Boulogne, hidden away in its vast garden. The rooms were low-ceilinged and cool. I also discovered a dark, mysterious wash-house where water was always running, and some stables which had a marvellous smell of horse dung, bedding straw, and the glistening, sweaty aroma of two splendid thoroughbreds, whose smooth flanks quivered with energy. My grandfather and I looked after these fine animals, which the directors of the company rode for pleasure. I still think horses are the finest-looking creatures in the world, infinitely more handsome than the handsomest human beings. One night these animals made a terrific din but I was not alarmed. It was probably people stealing chickens, who were scared off by the horses, which were more vigilant than dogs.

Twenty metres from the house there was a long, raised tank, and when someone lifted me right up, I could see strange, pale, red, green, and violet-coloured fish slowly disappearing under long, waving strands of black weed. At a later date, when I was reading Lorca, I came across them again; those supple, fish-like thighs of an adulterous woman going off to the river: fish seen in the reeds which parted as they slipped through.

There were beds of marvellous flowers at the forestry house (anemones, freesias with their erotic, overpowering perfume, shy, pink cyclamen surrounded by dark green leaves, like the delicate rose of Simone de Bandol's sexual organs which I was to see later on). At Easter, my sister and I would hunt there for sugar eggs which had been hidden for us and were often already nibbled by ants. Each Sunday my father used to bring home a bunch of gigantic, multi-coloured gladioli which he gave to a 'very beautiful young woman' with a Belgian name when we were not around. We never saw her. There was also a huge vegetable garden full of Japanese medlars. These medlars produced pale-yellow, oval fruit, each containing, side by side, a couple of brown seeds. They were hard, smooth, and shiny and looked like a man's balls (though at the time I was obviously not consciously aware of that!), and I experienced a strange sense of pleasure as I fondled them over and over. My young Aunt Juliette, the individualist of the family, climbed the trees like a goat to pick them off the branches and hand them down to me below as I stood looking up at the interesting things she had under her skirt. As the fruit melted in my mouth, releasing its slippery seeds, how I enjoyed its sweet-tasting juice. But the same fruits were always better when I picked them off the ground, where they had begun to rot in the burning sun and were tainted with the harsh, bitter scent of the earth! Further on there was a smaller tank which I could look into, full of clear, running water (a spring?), and right at the end of the garden, behind some tall, dark cypresses, a dozen beehives in a row. They were visited frequently by a former teacher, a Breton, called M. Keruet, who wore a straw hat but never gloves or a veil because the bees were his friends. That certainly was not the case with everybody. One day, because my grandfather was anxious and agitated and had gone a little too near, they in turn became anxious and agitated and swarmed all over his face. What saved him was that he made a mad dash to the large tank and plunged straight in. Curiously, I was not the least bit afraid on that occasion.

Most important of all was the huge, round carob tree which stood at the bottom of the garden on the left. Its long, smooth, dark pods fascinated me (and I would have loved to have tasted them, but my mother had forbidden it!). For me, the tree was an unexpected and isolated observation post; from there I could see the enormous city sprawled out languidly beneath me in the sunshine, stretching as far as the eye could see. Everything looked minute; the streets, the squares, the buildings, and the port where huge ships with funnels lay motionless at anchor and hundreds of small craft were constantly on the move, slowly criss-crossing each other. Far away, on the pale, smooth sea I first saw a few wisps of smoke on the horizon, then gradually masts and a hull. These ships, which appeared motionless as they made their desperately slow progress, belonged to the Marseilles–Algiers service. If I were patient enough, I would finally see them come alongside at one of the few empty berths after an infinite succession of careful manoeuvres. I knew one of them was called the *Charles-Roux* (there had been so many *Général-Chanzys* and similar things); Charles like my father (I firmly believed at the time that all children took the name Charles when they grew up and that there were nothing but Charles!). I imagined that it ran along on wheels under its hull and was surprised that no one else seemed aware of this.

I also went out with my grandfather into the woods. What a sense of freedom I had! With him, there were never any dangers and nothing was forbidden. How happy I was! Though he was such a 'grumbler', considered by everyone to be so impossible (like Hélène later on), he talked to me quietly like an equal. He pointed out the different trees and plants and told me all about them. I was especially fascinated by the countless eucalyptuses; I liked feeling the scaliness of their bark, long tubes of which would suddenly come crashing down from the tops of their trunks and hang like limp arms or pieces of rag (the rags I later used to enjoy wearing, or the long, red, tattered curtains which hung in my bedroom at the École normale). I also liked their long, smooth leaves, which were curved and pointed and changed with the seasons from dark green to blood red. Their flower-fruit had delicate pollen and the overwhelming scent of a 'druggist's remedy'. Finding the wild pink cyclamen hidden among its dark leaves was to discover it anew, as one had to pull back the protective outer layer to reveal its intimate fleshy pink. There was wild asparagus, as stiff as a man's penis, that I liked munching raw straight from the ground. Then there were terrible aloes, covered with prickly thorns, which occasionally (once every ten years?) thrust a huge spike up into the air at the end of which a flower slowly opened that no one could reach!

I felt free and fulfilled and was intensely happy in the company of my grandfather and grandmother, even when my parents were there too. Their forest home, its garden and huge woods were a paradise to me.

There was quite often a bit of a drama on our way there. At the top of the wood, right next to the dirt road along which we walked (for four kilometres), stood a tall white house which was lived in by a serving captain, M. Lemaître (that name . . .), his wife, his grown-up son of twenty, and their little daughter. It was always Sunday, my father's day off and the day on which M. Lemaître too was off duty. When we went up to the forestry house, he was always at home with his family, but frequently terrible scenes erupted between father and son. The son was expected to study in his bedroom and when he refused his father locked him in. That is what happened on this particular Sunday. The captain, who was in an awful rage, explained why his son was not around. Suddenly, we heard the terrible noise of splintering wood: the son was smashing down his bedroom door. He came out yelling and disappeared into the woods. His father hurriedly went indoors, took out his revolver, and chased after him. Another scene involving a violent father, shouting and brandishing a revolver! On this occasion, however, a violent son was challenging his father's violence. His mother remained silent. In the background, their young daughter, Madeleine, was sitting on the bottom step of the second staircase, her face bathed in tears. I was deeply moved and went and sat beside her, took her in my arms and started to comfort her. I had the impression it was an enormous act of pity and self-denial on my part, as if I had discovered once more (after the experience with my mother) a new and definitive purpose in life, that I had a mission to which I could devote myself: that of saving this young martyr. No one except me took any notice of her, which increased my sense of elation. The son returned, his father behind him holding the revolver in his hand. He locked him in another bedroom, and we left this violent and distressing family scene for the calm of the forestry house nearby. I was again very frightened but, how can I put it, I also experienced a sort of joyful pleasure in having taken little Madeleine in my arms (that was my grandmother's name too. Ah! these names . . . Lacan was right to stress the role of 'signifiers', since Freud had written of people having hallucinations about *names*).

I was very struck by the fact that my grandfather, who never stopped moaning and groaning about everything with everyone else albeit quietly and through his moustache, behaved quite differently towards me. In fact I never for a moment feared he would abandon me. If he happened to fall silent when I was with him, I never had a sense of anguish (which was not the case with my mother or father!). For he only fell silent in order to talk to me. Each time it was to point out and explain the wonders of the forest which I was not yet aware of. Rather than ask anything of me, he continued to shower me with gifts and surprises. That is how I first came to realise what it is like when someone loves you. The impression I had on each occasion was of receiving something without being expected to give anything in return. This proved to me that I existed in my own right. He also showed me the high brick walls protecting the residence of Queen Ranavalo, whom one never saw, and which bordered the grounds of the forestry house. Later on I learnt that the French troops who invaded Madagascar in the heyday of colonial expansion had captured the queen and forcibly confined her in this residence overlooking Algiers, where she was closely guarded. Similarly, at a later date in Blida I was to meet a huge, bespectacled black man always protected by a large umbrella (there were picture postcards of him) who held out his hand to all the passers-by with the greeting: 'Friends, you are all friends!' His name was Béhanzin and he was the former Emperor of Dahomey, who had also been banished to Algeria. The situation seemed strange to me; it was doubtless my first lesson in politics.

VII

When my grandfather retired – in 1925, I believe – that was the end of the forestry house and all its wonders (I never saw it again).

My grandparents then went back to Morvan, where they originally came from, and bought a small house at Larochemillay, a little village fifteen kilometres from Château-Chinon and eleven from Luzy, in a hilly and wooded region. Other wonders lay in store for me. It was of course a long way from Algiers, but we spent endless summers there, usually without my father who remained at work in Algiers. First, we had to make the sea crossing, in one of those slow, uncomfortable ships called *Governor General something or other* which provided the service. Just the smell of the gangways and cabins, covered in what looked like a thick layer of grease that stank of vomit, made me feel sea-sick even before we sailed. I was always sick, as were my mother and sister, but never my father.

We had a brief glimpse of the port at Marseille, 'la Joliette', found our luggage, put up with the anxieties of our mother (that we might be robbed!), and then boarded the train. Ah, the train! The smell of steam trains puffing out great plumes of smoke, the smooth chattering of the connecting rods, the long bursts on the whistle as you sped along (why? you wondered. Probably a level-crossing). Then, as you arrived at a station or were leaving one, there was the endless and reassuring noise of the wheels gripping the rails, interspersed with the regular and comforting bump of the buffers. When every carriage was properly hitched and all was in order, we set off. My mother constantly worried we would have an accident. Not me. A landscape that was unknown to me flashed past the windows. We ate on our laps, once my mother had got out all the food from the bag which she had prepared beforehand in Algiers. We never discovered the splendours of the restaurant car; we always economised!

At Chagny we had to take the branch line to Nevers. So we changed trains (making sure we had all the luggage!) and climbed into a much more antiquated carriage, pulled by a slow and wheezing engine. But we were getting closer to 'home'. I quickly got to know and recognise the stations and, as we laboured along, I tried hard to spot the first wild strawberries growing among the grass on the banks close to the line. I was looking forward to eating them. Were they already ripe? I wondered. Finally, we reached the end of our journey at Millay, an insignificant little station where our adventures really began.

A small horse-drawn trap was waiting for us outside the station. It was raining very heavily on our first visit which meant we saw nothing, but we were protected by the canvas hood as we huddled together for warmth. Usually, however, we arrived in brilliant sunshine. M. Ducreux, who was to become mayor of Laroche in 1936, defeating the count, drove his fine bay mare gently along. Her powerful hindquarters rapidly began to froth with sweat, and I observed with considerable interest the fleshy opening at her rear end. We climbed for six kilometres before reaching the plateau of the Bois-de-Velle from where we looked out on to a vast landscape of densely wooded mountains (there were oak, chestnut, beech, ash, and hornbeam, not to mention the hazels and willows). Then there was a long, gentle descent which the mare took at her customary trot, and finally we reached the village. After a steep climb up a rough track, past the village school (built of granite), we were suddenly at 'the house' where my grandmother stood erect in the doorway.

This house wasn't very big, but it had two huge, cool cellars and a large attic which was more or less habitable, full of novels by Delly, cut out of *Le Petit Echo de la Mode* which my grandmother always read. There were lean-to sheds for rabbits, a big wired-in chicken-run where the poultry wandered slowly and contentedly around, always on the look-out, and a smart concrete tank to collect the rainwater. (Sometimes the cats fell in and drowned, much to my alarm (yet more deaths) – what drama!) Above all, it had a beautiful, sloping garden with a fine view of one of the highest mountains in Morvan: the Touleur. At that time there was neither running water nor electricity, so we had to go to fetch water in buckets from two old girls who lived opposite.

We had oil lamps that gave a lovely glow, especially when you went from one bedroom to another *carrying the lamp with you* and the shadows moved, often disconcertingly, across the walls. It made me feel safe, carrying my own lamp!

My grandfather subsequently had a proper well dug after consulting a water diviner who, twig in hand, determined there was water close to the large pear tree and estimated the depth of it. Believe it or not, the well was dug by hand right through a layer of pink granite! The work demanded strength and precision. Holes were made for charges which were set off, and then the blocks of stone had to be removed. After that new charge holes were made with a crow bar. Water was discovered at the exact depth predicted by the diviner. From that time I had a great respect for those who possessed the skill of finding water with a hazel twig. I was to feel the same respect at a much later date for 'M. Rocard senior', the director of the physics laboratory at the École normale and the father of Michel Rocard (who was a stranger to me and apparently to his 'father' as well). He did strange experiments in the field of magnetism, walking around the grounds of the École on Sundays when there was no one to see him. He carried his twig everywhere: on his bicycle, in cars, and even in aeroplanes! On his own initiative, this legendary figure equipped the physics laboratory at the École (opened in 1936 but without equipment) by going round German laboratories and large factories and loading all the stuff he needed into army lorries he had borrowed from his chief the day after French troops first crossed into Germany. This meant that the laboratory, which was one of the foremost in France (where the future Nobel prizewinner, Louis Kastler, worked), had what it needed to function properly. M. Rocard senior was also thought to be the 'father of the French atomic bomb', which was never confirmed or denied; but the title or pseudo-title was enough to attract the political hostility of most of the students. Rocard was the first in the world to perfect a system of detecting atomic explosions on the basis of their dissemination by the earth's crust and using triangulation; the waves being registered the instant they arrived. (He built a number of quite comfortable small houses in about twenty places, most of them in inaccessible parts of France; he once invited Dr Étienne – much to his astonishment – but not me.) At the time, he knew that an explosion had taken place, even underground, a quarter of an hour before the Americans and was in his modest way more than a little proud of the fact. I admired his talent for skulduggery: he knew how to get round most of the restrictions imposed by the administration, which he despised. He also scandalised those who ran the École because he kept a secret fund which enabled him, a physicist, to pay throughout 1967 for a part-time typist to produce my lectures for science students! I have never forgotten his genuine cunning, his ingenuity, his boldness, his total lack of prejudice, and his generosity. M. Rocard senior, who was deaf or sometimes pretended to be and whose smallest gestures and inflexions were imitated by his assistants (so it happened to him too!), mumbled like my father when he told people what to do and was a past-master at 'working fiddles', which went well beyond my father's more timid activities. Though he was never aware of it, he was truly a second father to me after my grandfather.

Once the well was dug, my grandfather had a metal cover made for the rim, and fifty centimetres above that we erected a small zinc canopy to protect the opening. At a certain season of the year, all day long and all night, tiny, bright-red pears would fall from a great height and strike the canopy from time to time with an abrupt ping that could be heard even from the house (though it was fifty metres away and we were indoors). You could not cut these pears with a knife, but my grandmother made marvellous jam with them which I have never come across anywhere else. The pear tree was at least thirty metres tall. Beyond it, on the other side of the hedge and across a rough path, rose the high walls of the playground surrounding the village school. We heard the sharp clatter of the children's clogs when they arrived and went home, shouting loudly to one another, and the noisy games they played before lessons started. Then, suddenly, there was silence as they lined up, the sound of the teacher clapping his hands, followed by the noise of their clogs as they hurried up the little staircase. Then all would be quiet as lessons began.

Nearby, on a high mound, stood the cemetery (where my grandparents lie buried beneath a grey, granite tombstone), two or three weedy fir trees, and beyond it, along a muddy track, the wretched hovel of the 'poor' (there was a whole family; a woman who was deformed by endless pregnancies, a crippled old man, and numerous children, all living in one stinking room). Further on, there was a level bit of road before the woods which one entered alongside a wonderful spring beneath some mistletoe, known as the 'fountain of Love', and a wash-house much frequented by women. One day, when I was out with my mother, I discovered a whole patch of young boletus mushrooms near the entrance to the woods, but she did not like the look of them. The caps of these mushrooms, which were rare in that area, stuck straight up in the air like erect penises. The whole process had no rhyme or reason, yet to me it was fascinating though my mother remained unaware and completely indifferent (at least in appearance). I realise only too well why this memory remained such a powerful one: at the time I didn't know what my own sexual organ was for, but I was aware I had one. I remember later on as an adolescent during the few months I spent with my grandparents, which I shall come to, I happened to be walking alone at the bottom of the garden where no one could see me. My penis was quite stiff beneath the black school overall I was wearing, and I kept on fondling it without attempting to do anything else, the pleasure far outweighing any sense of shame that I was doing something wrong. At the time I knew nothing of the delights of masturbation, which I discovered by chance one night when I was a prisoner-of-war at the age of twenty-seven! I was so overcome with emotion that I fainted.

The woods, which were mostly hilly and had a great variety of trees, were fed by clear springs and streams with crayfish and frogs in them (they also contained a lot of beautiful ferns and broom, and sometimes a farmhouse in a clearing). Though quite steep, they were great, peaceful woods where the sunlight flickered gently through the leaves. They were very different from the woods in Algeria. Nevertheless, my grandfather, a native of the Morvan region, initiated me as he had done before. He taught me how to cut the right sort of chestnut branches (which released their sap in a delicate but powerful stream) for the framework of a peasant basket and then showed me how to make one in his cellar. He also showed me the thin willow stems you needed to weave between the curved framework. He taught me everything, about ponds, frogs, crayfish, but also about the whole region, and the people we met. He would always stop and chat to them in the local dialect.

In those days the Morvan was an extremely poor region. People lived almost entirely on what they made from rearing white Charolais cattle, lots of pigs, . . . and children; they fostered numerous children in care. In addition, they grew a quantity of potatoes, a little wheat, some rye, some buckwheat (which did very well when planted between the chestnut trees), some chestnuts, game, including wild boar in the winter, a bit of fruit, and that was it.

The church, lacking both charm and elegance, was of recent construction and stood on a knoll within the village. In front of it was the usual frightful war-memorial commemorating those who had died in the 1914–18 war. It was covered with a host of names, to which list would later be added, as elsewhere, those who died between 1939 and 1945, the names of a few individuals who had been deported, and the victims of the wars in Vietnam and Algeria; a sad toll which brought home clearly the extent to which wars decimated the youth of the countryside. A veteran of the 1914–18 war was in charge of the church. He said mass, at which I served as an altar boy, and taught the catechism class, which I later attended, in a tiny room heated in winter by a little wood-burning stove which became red hot. This priest, who had seen it all before, was exceedingly indulgent; he was easy going, broad-minded about sin and especially sexual desire and even sexual activity; he was without morbid curiosity in the confessional, always put children at their ease, and was always chewing on the same pipe he had had in the trenches. He too was the good 'father' figure.

He handled things well, given that the count still exercised absolute aristocratic authority in the district. The count's tall château, dating from the XVIIth century, was hidden behind huge, age-old trees. He owned an enormous amount of land, including two thirds of the commune, of which he was the mayor by right, and he kept the peasant farmers under his thumb, most of whom paid him in kind. A free school for girls was maintained by him and controlled by his wife, the countess – an aristocratic woman with a benign face whom I saw only once in the splendid surroundings of her home where the furniture glowed with age. At the time, a quarrel was raging between the supporters of the count and those of the local schoolmaster, who was also a most generous man, it has to be said. But this was only to be expected, an aspect of the social system. The priest, who was a decent chap and politically shrewd, behaved in such a way that he did not have an enemy in the place.

My grandfather told me all about these things when we roamed the woods together or when I helped him in the garden which was full of low-growing strawberries and goodness knows how many different kinds of fruit tree, not to mention the sorrel which tasted so bitter on my tongue that I have never forgotten it. (Later on, when I was at the École, I once wanted to offer the Châtelets pike with sorrel, which they still talk about. I tried to buy sorrel in the rue Mouffetard and asked all the vegetable and herb-sellers. None of them had it, and I got the same reply – thirty times over: 'If we had some, we wouldn't be here!') My grandfather taught me how to sow seeds, how to plant out, how to weed, how to graft fruit trees, and even how to make compost behind the lavatory which collected all the piss and shit from the house. The lavatory was very small, with no window, and your face was right against the door when it was shut. I sat there on the wooden seat for hours on end with a Delly novel in my hand, my trousers down, sniffing the delightful odour it gave off of piss and shit, earth and rotten leaves; the piss and shit of men and women alike. Growing right over the lavatory was a big, bushy elder tree, but I was forbidden to eat the fruit by my mother (she said it was terribly poisonous!). I discovered later that the Germans made a delicious soup with it. I was intoxicated by the heady perfume of the elderflowers, mingled with piss, shit, and rich earth.

My grandfather even taught me how to kill a rabbit with a downward blow on the back of the neck and how to chop off a duck's head with a billhook on a block of wood. The duck would go on running around for several minutes. With him, I was never afraid. But when my grandmother poked long, pointed scissors down a chicken's throat in order to cut its carotid artery, it was horrible, and I felt ashamed to see her do such a thing.

Everything gave me enormous pleasure, but I should point out that it was summertime and once the holidays were over we had to return to Algiers. Yet there were still more surprises and greater happiness to come.

One day, my grandmother, my mother, my sister, and I set out for Fours, where my maternal great-grandmother, Mère Nectoux, lived. She had long been widowed and lived completely alone in one room with her cow. She was another terribly erect, dry old stick, and silent as well, apart from the odd interjection in an ancient dialect which I did not understand. One incident I remember which struck me forcibly occurred near the little river where she took her docile, lumbering cow to graze. I was playing with the multi-coloured dragonflies which were flitting from flower to flower (especially the highly scented 'meadow flowers'). All of a sudden, I noticed my great-grandmother, who never let go of her great gnarled stick (which she used for walking and on the cow), behaving in a very strange manner. She was standing bolt upright and did not say a word as a loud spurting noise issued from beneath her long black skirt. A clear stream ran past her feet. It took me a little while to 'realise' that she was peeing standing up, under her skirt, without squatting down as women usually do, and that therefore she didn't have any knickers on. I was astounded to discover there were women-men, unashamed of their sexuality, who went ahead and pissed in front of everybody, without shame or modesty, and without giving any warning whatsoever! What a revelation! Though she was kind to me, it was all rather confusing. This woman turned out to be a man, and what a man, sleeping with her cow, looking after it, pissing like a man in front of everyone, but without opening her flies and pulling out her cock, and without hiding behind a tree to do it! But she was also a woman, because she didn't have a man's cock, and showed she loved me albeit in a rather severe fashion, yet with the contained tenderness of a good mother. She was nothing like my father's mother. This surprising episode inspired no fear but it did leave me puzzling about it for a long time. As might have been expected, my mother saw nothing and never mentioned it. How unaware she was of everything which affected me.

When, early in September 1928 (I must have been ten or eleven), my sister contracted scarlet fever (this child was always being ill, thus protecting herself by seeking refuge as best she could in physical ill health), my mother took all the measures which seemed right to her, given her phobia about contagion. She consulted my grandparents and then asked if I would mind not returning to Algiers but remaining in Larochemillay and spending the whole year there. As you can imagine, I did not mind at all. There is no question that what I did not yet recognise as my mother's phobias could have – and how! – their positive side – a trick of the psyche.

Obviously a whole year necessarily meant spending the school year in the local village school. I have already pointed out that it was only a stone's throw from the house. The man in charge, M. Boucher, was gentle, firm, and warm-hearted, wholly acceptable to my mother who liked conscientious people and was therefore reassured by him. I wore clogs, so as not to be different from everyone else and also the compulsory black overall. Thus equipped, I joined those peasant children I had heard playing noisily in the school yard, year after year, and longed to be with. From our front door, I heard them climbing slowly up the hill or running down the steep, rough track past the house. I could hear their cheery voices as they called out and barged each other around, and the constant clatter of their clogs in the background. In the countryside at that time, leather shoes were too expensive and marvellous, shiny clogs were made by local craftsmen (I myself had a go at carving some out of blocks of wood with wonderful tools – sharp 'gouges' which were easy to handle). They were hard on the feet and rubbed your Achilles' tendon at first, but you quickly got used to them and they protected you from the cold and from the heat, because wood is a bad conductor of heat and cold – which is not the case with leather.

When I entered the school I was faced with an unknown world and, first and foremost, with the language spoken by the country boys. The dialect of the Morvan included quite unexpected combinations of vowels and consonants, the regular distortion of vowels and diphthongs (by sustained heavy stress on the phonemes), and all sorts of turns of phrase and expressions that I did not recognise. It was certainly not the language of the classroom, where our teacher taught us the classic pronunciation and the French of the Île-de-France. The dialect was a second, different language, a foreign language, their native tongue which they spoke during playtime and in the street; it was the language of everyday life. It was the first foreign language I learnt (since there had been no opportunity for me to learn colloquial Arabic, as I was forbidden by my mother to play in the streets, though she had begun to learn 'literary' Arabic). I simply had to get used to it.

I set about learning this dialect with great enthusiasm and did so quickly and readily, which didn't surprise me in the least since the change of language was both fascinating and easy for me. Much later I had occasion to learn to speak a little Polish (a language which is so difficult to pronounce, yet my pronunciation was such that I passed for a native Pole), the German as spoken in the camps, and also literary German, and of course *lycée* English which I pronounced with a splendid but provocatively American accent that I picked up goodness knows where, probably from the radio. I got a kick out of that (to the great annoyance of my English teacher. It was yet another means for me to acquire *my own* language, teaching myself accent and expressions as a way of distancing myself from the example and authority of my teachers). I learnt these languages so easily that I decided I must 'have a gift', as they say, for foreign languages. A gift! You might as well say that it is the sleep-inducing properties of opium which make you sleep. My hostility to the notion of people having gifts dates from that time (a hostility that pleased Lucien Sève, who fought against the idea for a long time and rightly so, but with quite different arguments from mine, and much more political I have to admit!). Much later, I came to the conclusion that my learning of languages, and specifically my exact pronunciation of the phonemes of foreign languages, to the extent that it was not clear where I was from, must have come *both* from my desire to imitate *and* therefore to seduce, but *also* at the same time from a simple wish to do it well. It was all part of what I called a sort of *physical education of the muscles*, an agreeable coordination of the muscles of the tongue, the teeth, the tongue itself, the vocal cords, and the muscles controlling the mouth. In fact I was very good at 'using' all the muscles of my body. I could get hold of stones with my toes and even throw them, as well as pick up various objects from the ground and put them in my hands or on a table. I very quickly learnt to 'wiggle my ears' in all directions and even to move each one independently of the other (my greatest party-piece with other children) and I could juggle a football better than anyone (except with my head which seemed to me too big and too vulnerable). I even invented tricks with my foot, the sole, the heel, my knees, and back flicks that I later saw done by experienced players.

I was subsequently to make the following curious observation: in doing things I had been taught by my parents (such as playing tennis, swimming, riding a bike which I learnt 'within the family'), I had managed to develop techniques all on my own which my parents could not have taught me (and I had done so by sheer determination). Thus, when my father served at tennis he did so by bringing the racket right down and slicing the ball. A waste of energy! Having spent a long time watching real players and looking at photos of Lacoste and Tilden, I taught myself to serve as people serve now, with a twirl of the racket behind the shoulder which means that the maximum power is transferred to the ball, and I became very skilled at it. My father could only do the breast-stroke, but he loved swimming on his back which he did in a rather unusual way, not using his arms or his legs, but by sculling with his two hands held close to his sides (he moved quite fast like this). He also took great care to keep both his head and his toes out of the water with the result that he was easily recognisable at a distance on account of his unusual style. He used to laugh about it. Again, having observed real swimmers and looked at photos, I thought about it and then taught myself to dive, that is to say I first learnt to hold my head under water as long as possible by holding my breath (how daring I was, keeping my head under water! My mother said it was dangerous and that I might drown!). Finally, once I had coordinated holding my breath with the movement of my legs and feet, I taught myself to do the crawl. In this instance I neither imitated nor tried to seduce anyone, except in so far as I sought to astound people with my achievement. You have to believe it was a point of honour with me at the time to distinguish my own techniques visibly and effectively from those of the family, and if not yet to 'have my own thoughts in my own body' at least to seek to take charge of my own body for myself according to my own desires. In this way I began to break free of the rules and norms set by the family.

That is how I came to learn the Morvan dialect with such ease and with a great sense of pleasure. Soon I was indistinguishable from the local boys. None the less, for some time I was made to feel quite forcibly I was not one of them. When the first snow fell and covered the playground, I remember a very painful session as they pelted me in the face with snowballs. I can still see the wretched little tree where I fell unconscious, as their blows rained down on me. The teacher, wisely, did not intervene. I got my come-uppance but without feeling upset about it and they had some fun and their revenge. Then, gradually, I felt them begin to accept me. How happy I was!

I still remember with some emotion my last class in the Morvan when they granted me the special privilege of choosing the game I wanted to play during the last playtime. I chose prisoners' base because I found the surprise element of chasing people really exciting. And my team won.

'They' referred essentially to the leader of the gang who ran things. He was a tough, stocky, red-faced boy with black hair called Marcel Perraudin who was vaguely and distantly related to my grandparents. He had incredible vitality, and like so many peasants he died later in the war. Someone else I knew who died. At the beginning, he kept on tormenting me quite mercilessly, and I have to admit I was frightened of him, since I was neither as strong nor as daring as he and was scared stiff of physical fights. It was the same old fear that I might injure myself. In fact, I have *never once* got involved in a physical fight in my life.

The boys did not just play physical games, though one of their favourite pastimes was for a group of them to jump out on some lad who they happened to catch alone, throw him to the ground in a shady corner of a field, hold him down, then open his flies and pull out his cock. At which point they would all run off yelling at the tops of their voices. I suffered this fate – although I tried to fight them off of course – with a strange sense of pleasure. There was also a boy of unknown parentage at the school who was in care. He was extremely intelligent and we vied with each other to be top of the class. He was pallid and frail like me, and it was rumoured he played at 'mothers and fathers' in the long grass of the countess's grounds with a girl who went to the convent and was herself in care. One day when some of them were talking about this in front of me, I spoke up rather peremptorily and said it was impossible since they were not old enough! I made out I knew what I was talking about on sexual matters, though I was only expressing my mother's fears and prejudices. Two years later, I learnt that this brilliant but sickly boy had died of tuberculosis.

Another figure who had a tragic destiny: someone else who died and who was pale and fragile like me.

I remember the terrible winter of 1928–29, when the thermometer dropped to thirty-five degrees below freezing at Larochemillay and all the ponds and rivers froze, even the water in the kitchen bucket though it stood by the hot stove. Everything was covered in a thick silent blanket of snow. The birds stopped singing, and all you saw of them was the star-like marks of their feet in the snow. I remember my delight at painting a snow scene for school, tucked up in the warm, and how I loved the snow which covered everything. To me it was the ultimate protection, withdrawing into the sheltered warmth of the house, so that I was secure from all external danger – even the world outside was safe and peaceful under its covering of snow. And I was absolutely certain that beneath this same delicate covering, which brought silence and peace, no harm would befall me. Outside and in were equally safe.

May I add one detail? I was not called Louis Althusser at school, as it was too complicated, but Pierre Berger; my grandfather's name! It suited me down to the ground.

My grandfather continued to teach me all about life and work on the land. When he bought just over four acres of land at Bois-de-Velle together with two dilapidated cottages where he stored his tools, he showed me how to sow wheat, rye, oats, buckwheat, clover, and lucerne, how to cut them with a hook and scythe, and how to make sheaves and then tie them with chestnut twigs or plaited straw, which needed a deft flick of the wrist. He taught me how to turn the clover and lucerne with a fork or a rake when the sun was hot, how to make nice round heaps and then hoist them at arm's length (what a weight they were!) on to a cart belonging to a neighbour who came to collect them from the field.

My grandfather carted his wheat, oats, and rye to the only threshing machine in the whole district which went round to different farms. All the friends and neighbours were gathered in turn for this great event. Only once did my grandfather take me along. I was astonished by the threshing machine, an enormous, complicated, and deafening wooden structure, the moving parts of which kept up an inexplicable clickety-clack. It was driven by a steam engine attached by a long leather belt which was dangerous as it frequently 'jumped off'. It was a most impressive spectacle. From high on the carts sheaves were tossed down with a fork on to the top of the machine. Two men stood there, covered in dust, ready to untie them and quickly feed them into the ever-open mouth of the wooden machine which swallowed them up and crushed the straw in an infernal din.

The air was thick and unbreathable with oat and wheat chaff and men were coughing, spitting, constantly swearing, and shouting to make themselves heard above the infernal racket. It was strangely dark in broad daylight and the men moved around like ghosts with red scarves tied round their necks. Low down at one end of the machine, the grain 'flowed' like a murmuring though silent stream into the sacks which were held by hand. The straw was chucked out at the top of the machine, the stalks broken and stripped of their grain. It was then made into rough bales. The whole threshing area was filled with the wonderfully thick smell of coal, smoke, spurts of water, oil, grain, and jute sacking, as well as that of the men and their sweat. My grandfather attempted to explain above the din how the different parts of the machine worked, and I stood beside him as *his* wheat flowed into *his* sacks. What a sense of splendour and communion I felt, confronted by the marvel of labour and its rewards!

At midday everyone stopped work and an extraordinary silence descended as the noise suddenly stopped. The smell of the men and their sweat then filled the large farm kitchen where the cheery farmer's wife served a generous meal. At rest as at work the men treated one another like brothers, slapping each other on the back, shouting things out across the length of the room, laughing, swearing, and making obscene remarks.

I wandered freely among these men who were exhausted yet elated by their work and all the shouting. No one spoke to me or paid me any particular attention; it was as if I were one of them. I was convinced that one day I would become a man like them.

Then, with the help of the wine which flowed freely into large glasses and down open throats, the first artless murmurings of a song were heard. It started haltingly, tentatively, seemed to go wrong and lose its way only to break out finally in an exultant cacophony of sound. It was an old song of peasant struggle and revolt (a song of the *Jacquerie* – reminiscent of the name Jacques

I wished had been mine), in which nobles and priests were harshly criticised. Suddenly there I was in the company of real men breathing in the smell of sweat, meat, wine, and sexuality. Then they were vying with each other to offer me a glassful of wine to the accompaniment of ribald jokes: was the lad goin' to drenk it? be ye man or not? I had never touched a drop of wine in my life (my mother said it was dangerous especially at my age – I was twelve!), but I drank a little and was applauded. Then the singing welled up again. At one end of the huge table my grandfather smiled at me.

Faced with the truth, I now have to make a painful confession. I was not inside the great kitchen and therefore did not experience the wine-drinking and the chaotic singing at first hand (though I certainly heard it from outside just as I did the election as mayor of M. Ducreux in place of the count, which took place in 1936 in the crowded town hall). I dreamt it, that is to say I simply had an intense desire for it to be real. It certainly could have happened, but for the sake of truth I have to accept and present it for what it was in my memory: a sort of hallucination of my intense desire.

I intend to stick closely to the facts throughout this succession of memories by association; but hallucinations are also facts.

VIII

In 1930, when I was twelve, my father was transferred by the bank to Marseille as a senior executive. We went to live at 38 rue Sébastopol, in the Quatre-Chemins district, and naturally I was sent to the Lycée Saint-Charles which was quite close. Louis, Charles, Simone: some names certainly are 'destinies', as Spinoza said in his treatise on Hebrew grammar. Spinoza!

At home, life went on as before; I was completely solitary. The *lycée* was a continuing adventure. I entered the second form and made a niche for myself, soon becoming one of the best in the class by being as good and as studious as ever. I spent my whole life between the *lycée* (a fine though ancient building which looked over the city on one side) and, on the other, the railway line leading to the central station: Saint-Charles. I have always loved a 'terminus' where the trains stop at enormous buffers because they cannot go any further. The yard where we did gymnastics looked on to the railway line. The good thing about gym was that we only did a few exercises and then the teacher would give up and let us play football. We picked sides at random and I was put in the forwards. On this occasion we won because we had a goalkeeper called Paul who dived as if he had been doing it all his life. He and I talked to each other, got on well together, and a remarkable friendship quickly began to develop.

Paul was not as clever at school as I was and never would be, but he had something I lacked. Though he was not tall, he was sturdy, with broad shoulders and strong hands, and above all he was very brave. My mother realised I had made friends with someone and found out who his parents were. His father was in business, his mother an amiable woman, and as they were a respectable Catholic family, I was given the green light. Our friendship strengthened when my mother made me join the scouts. Paul joined too, which was a further guarantee. I was even allowed to visit Paul's home. The building where he lived with his parents also served as a base for his father's goods: raisins, almonds, pine nuts, etc., the smell of which I still recall.

It was love at first sight. We became inseparable companions and were soon making plans together. Paul wrote poems in the style of Albert Samain and I followed suit, thinking we would create a poetry review that would take the world by storm. When we went our separate ways, and even while we were still in Marseille, we kept up an exhilarating correspondence; a true lovers' correspondence.

For quite some time in the second and third years, I was literally persecuted by a great big, tough, red-headed boy called Guichard. He was 'working class', his speech, habits, and attitudes were 'coarse', or seemed so to me. He enjoyed being crude, did not give a damn for the monitors, teachers, deputy-head, and head, indeed for all figures of authority, and appeared to detest all bright pupils and me in particular. I felt he continually tried to provoke me, whereas I doubtless provoked him unwittingly by my good behaviour – as I realised much later. He urged me, challenged me even, to fight him. The thought of fighting someone as big as a man did not appeal to me at all, and I was truly scared, fearing I would come out of it with *long-term injuries to my body*, if not half dead. Then he appeared to become less aggressive, though I could not understand why. I soon did however. Despite his extreme 'modesty' (a magic word for us), Paul confided to me one day that he had fought Guichard in the street with his bare hands. He had done so on my behalf, to defend my name and without telling me about it in advance. I was very relieved at having avoided the risk myself, and my love for Paul grew stronger than ever.

We were both 'patrol leaders', he of the 'Tigers' and me of the 'Lynx'. The leader of our troop, a man called Pélorson, nicknamed Pélo, was small and a glib talker, which meant he got on well with the chaplain, who had a large nose with hair growing out of it. Pélo, the old devil, boasted openly that he was a womaniser, which seemed totally incongruous to me in a Catholic organisation dedicated to pure living.

In the summer, the whole troop went off for long camping expeditions in the Alps.

On one particular occasion we were camping near Allos in a

beautiful meadow looking down on the valleys. Like everyone else, Paul and I had constructed tiny stone walls around our tents, marking our 'territory', in front of which was a tall archway built of slender birch poles.

It seemed as if everything would go well. However, there was a young lad in my patrol, who was older than me but poor, puny, and utterly useless. He had not been well brought up like me, but spoke and behaved in a 'crude' fashion and aggressively refused to obey me, though it was his 'duty' to do so. Burdened with such a heavy responsibility, I constantly attempted to get him to 'see reason'. Yet in the end he too wanted to fight me. For once, I was far and away the stronger, but he answered me back with insults, threats, and obscene and provocative remarks. Things reached such a pitch between me and this boy that I ended up despairing of my authority and sank into a sort of depression, the first I experienced in my life, I suppose. As my friend Paul was also feeling unwell, for some reason, possibly with a stomach upset, Pélo decided to remove us for the time being to the shelter of a lofty barn on an abandoned farm, five hundred yards away. Our food was brought to us. We stayed there alone, alone at last, tenderly entwined in our mutual anguish and crying over our fate. I remember very clearly having an erection as we hugged each other; that was all that happened but the unexpected erection was a most pleasurable experience.

The same thing happened during what was referred to as the 'first-class expedition', a test which enabled us to win a special badge and earn promotion. In our case (we were still inseparable) it involved covering a considerable distance on foot in the country-side and hills around Marseille, carrying rucksacks, and carefully noting everything we saw: the state of the tracks, the landscape, the flora and fauna, the people we met, the remarks made by the 'natives', etc. Our parents saw us off with due solemnity, united as they were by the double blessing of Pélo and the chaplain. We set off together into the countryside and it was not long before it began to get dark. Where would we sleep? We had a tent with us, but it was beginning to rain so we looked for shelter, which we found in a very tiny village by knocking on the local priest's door. He unlocked the little parish theatre, and we lay down in each other's arms under our blankets, possibly as a way of keeping warm but really out of love and affection. Again I felt myself having an erection. The same thing happened the next day at noon when Paul started to have terrible stomach pains as we were going through a gorge. He was writhing about on the ground, and to comfort him I again took him in my arms. Once more I felt the same unfulfilled pleasure in the pit of my warm stomach (innocent that I was, I did not know it could be satisfied and was only to discover it by chance at the age of twenty-seven when I was a prisoner-of-war!). We could not complete our 'expedition' and returned to Marseille in a car which came to collect us, ashamed and exhausted.

One might have thought I was destined to become a homosexual without my suspecting it, but that was certainly not the case. Alongside the boys' troop there was a parallel troop of girls, led by 'guiders'. One of them was a girl with dark hair who was too tall for my taste, but she had a striking, classic profile and fascinated me because she was so stunningly beautiful. Paul fell in love with her and naturally confided in me. They declared their love one night at a 'camp fire' which they kept feeding with branches. The flames of the fire and of their love rose together into the dark night sky.

From that point on I devoted myself wholeheartedly to this love by proxy, as if I loved the girl myself. They were to marry much later, during the war, at Luynes, the village Paul's father came from where the two of us had spent exhilarating holidays alone together. I played the harmonium during the mass, improvising in my own fashion. The profile and the beauty of this girl marked me for life, and I mean *for life*, as you will realise in due course.

One summer, one of my father's colleagues, who owned a villa at Bandol, rented us the upper floor. My father remained at work in Marseille, but my mother, my sister, and I went there to stay. Shortly afterwards, the colleague's wife and her two daughters moved in on the ground floor. The elder daughter, Simone, struck me the moment I saw her; she had the same profile and the same beauty as the girl Paul loved and was also dark but shorter, *exactly* what I wanted. I developed a violent passion for her. I thought up all sorts of ruses just to meet her, like holding one handle of a basket as she held the other in the presence of both our mothers.

I even taught her the rudiments of the crawl, holding her with both hands under her breasts and her stomach. Finally, I accompanied her ('chaperoned' by her younger sister which my mother insisted on) high into the Madrague, ten kilometres from Bandol, up a steep hill with the fine sand slipping beneath our feet. I melted with desire for her. Though I lacked the courage to caress her (her little sister was always on the look-out, but even had she not been there I doubt if I would have dared to do anything of the sort), I discovered one day that I could at least sprinkle handfuls of sand slowly between her breasts. The sand ran down her stomach and fell in a curve around her pubis. Simone then stood up, opened her legs, and pulled the crotch of her swimming costume so that the sand dropped to the ground. For a split second I caught sight of the bare tops of her magnificent thighs, a profusion of black hair, and, most important of all, the pink slit of her vagina: cyclamen pink.

My mother soon became aware of my innocent yet violent passion. She took me aside and had the audacity to say to me: you are eighteen and Simone nineteen and, given the difference in your ages, it is quite unthinkable and immoral that anything should happen between you. It was not 'acceptable'! In any case, you are much too young to be in love!

Worse was to come one extremely hot afternoon. I knew that Simone went swimming on a beach towards the Madrague. I jumped on my racing bicycle and was about to set off to meet her when my mother suddenly emerged from the house. Where are you going? I knew she knew. There was no question now of my meeting Simone. My reaction, though neither conscious nor deliberate, was instantaneous; I pointed *in the completely opposite direction to where I longed to go* and told my mother: 'I am going to La Ciotat!' I remember clearly pedalling along in an absolute rage, sobbing as I went in a state of total revolt.

From that point on, two episodes were fused in my memory: the one when I felt raped ('you are a man now, my son') and the other when I was forbidden to see Simone. They combined with the feeling of disgust and repulsion I had as a child, or projected back on to childhood in my memory, at the sight of my mother's breasts, white neck, and frizzy blonde hair. They were obscene. My feelings of repulsion and hatred were visceral. How could she respond to my desires in that way? I said 'from that point'. Unconsciously, that was certainly true, but not consciously. It was only considerably later, in the well-known deferred action of key emotional experiences, during my analysis, that I came to a clear understanding of the affinity of those episodes and the way I had reconstructed them.

The whole time we were in Marseille, I maintained my academic success. Two of us vied for the honour of coming top of the class. The other boy, a stocky lad with an unprepossessing face, whose name was Vieilledent, was very good at maths (whereas I, in accordance with 'my mother's wishes', was rather mediocre at it). Old teeth/old houses (Althusser: *alte Haüser* in the dialect of Alsace); we were a strange pair. I remember he tried to get me to enrol one day in the youth movement of Colonel de la Rocque, but I was not interested. It was certainly not a question of political conscience, rather one of prudence. In this I resembled my father.

I got my own back on Vieilledent in the purely literary subjects. My memory of my final year remains very sharp and was later to form the basis of an important insight into the structure of my psyche. We had a remarkable literature teacher called M. Richard, a tall, thin man, who was delicate and always sickly. He had a long, pale face, also dwarfed by a great high forehead, and suffered constantly from a sore throat which was always muffled in woollen scarves (as my mother's and mine of course were at the time). A man of infinite gentleness and refinement, manifestly pure minded too and free of all temptations of the body and the physical world, he resembled the combined image of my mother and myself (the thought has just occurred to me as I write these words). He introduced us to the great writers and poets of history and with such warmth, sympathy, and success! I identified with him completely (I was almost bound to), immediately began to imitate his handwriting, adopt his turns of phrase, his tastes, his judgements. I even imitated his voice and his gentle way of speaking. In my essays I gave him a mirror image of his own character. He recognised my qualities at once. Which ones exactly? Certainly, I was a good pupil and very sensitive, motivated I may say by a constant concern to do well. I subsequently realised there were other things involved.

Initially I identified with him for the reasons I have just given, which were linked to my own image of myself, to that of my mother, and beyond them to the image of my dead uncle Louis. It was M. Richard who later persuaded me to study for the entrance exam to the École normale supérieure in the rue d'Ulm, unknown to my parents, even to my mother. In fact I came to realise that he represented a positive image of the mother I loved and who loved me. He was a real person with whom I could achieve that spiritual 'fusion' which accorded with my mother's desire for me, but which her 'repulsive' being made impossible.

For a long time, however (even at the beginning of my analysis), I believed I played at being a loving and obedient son with him, seeing him as a good father, because in that situation my role in relation to him was that of 'father's father'; an expression which appealed to me for a long time and seemingly explained the nature of my emotions. It was a way of sorting out paradoxically my relationship with my absent father, by giving myself an imaginary father yet behaving as if I were in fact his father.

Indeed, on repeated occasions I found myself in the same emotional situation and had the feeling that I was behaving towards my teachers as if I were their teacher; if not with the aim of teaching them, at least with that of taking them in hand. I seemed to feel most strongly that it was up to me to keep an eye on, to censure, and even to control my father's behaviour especially towards my mother and my sister.

Sadly, this beautiful construction, though accurate at one level, turned out to be wholly one-sided. I came to realise, very late in the day, that I had overlooked the most important element: *my own artifice*, the imitation of my teacher's voice, his gestures, his writing, his turns of phrase, his mannerisms, which not only gave me power over him but existence in my own right. In short, *seeming to be* what I could not be was *a fundamental deception*. I was without a body, having failed to take control of my own, and was therefore denied my own sexuality. Thus I came to understand (but so late!) that I only resorted to deception, in exactly the same way as someone might 'work a fiddle' to get into a sports ground (my father), in order to *seduce* my teacher and get him to like me precisely by practising that deception. What do I mean by this? Having no authentic existence of my own, doubting myself to the point of believing I was insensitive, and feeling I was incapable of sustaining an emotional relationship with anyone, I was reduced to *making myself loved* in order to exist and at the same time thus reduced to practising artifice, seduction, and deception to love others (since loving others calls forth love in return). I resorted to seduction, using the convolutions of artifice; ultimately I was an impostor.

Since I did not really exist, I was simply a creature of artifice, a non-being, a dead person who could only love and be loved by means of artifice and deception which mimicked those whose love I sought and whom I tried to love by seducing them.

Inside, I was no more than someone consciously adept at orchestrating his muscles, and unconsciously and diabolically adept at seducing and manipulating other people, at least those whose love I sought. Via this false love, I looked to them for recognition of an existence I constantly doubted with a terrible sense of gnawing anguish, which I only became conscious of when my attempts at seduction failed.

I became aware of the 'truth' of this compulsion only recently while reflecting on the following strange incident. I was a very good pupil, destined by my teachers to have a great intellectual future. That is why my primary schoolteacher entered me for a national 'scholarship' exam, thinking I would come somewhere near the top. In fact, I was among the last. There was consternation! Similarly, M. Richard and the other teachers each entered me for their discipline in the competitive exam for secondary schoolchildren and I sat the same exam in my final year. Despite my dazzling ability, as my teachers saw it, I failed to achieve the slightest distinction on any occasion. Again, there was consternation! My only explanation now for these disappointing results was that I had managed to maintain a relationship with my teachers whereby I identified with them and therefore seduced them to such an extent that they deceived themselves as to my true worth.

Having assumed the role of 'father's father', or rather of 'mother's father', with them, that is to say having truly seduced them by imitating their character and mannerisms, they saw themselves in me so clearly that they projected either their own idea of themselves or the idea they unconsciously sustained of their own unfulfilled ambitions and hopes. Hence my failure when I was judged by those whom I had not been able to seduce! So, all my artifice, which had been directed *ad hominem* and was only effective in the seductive relationship I had secretly managed to maintain with them, no longer worked but was a complete disaster. Yet more consternation! It was to trouble me for a long time, failing as I did to understand 'just how long it takes to understand'.

IX

When the bank posted my father to Lyon, it involved another change of scene, a renewed sense of exile and suffering for my tearful mother, and for me a transfer to the Lycée du Parc where I joined the class preparing the entrance exam to 'Normal sup.'

The preparation lasted three or even four years. The younger students were in '*hypokhâgne*' and the others in *khâgne*.*

I was literally lost. I knew no one and was confronted by boys who had already acquired all the tricks and affectations, kept up the group traditions, and indulged in hero-worship of those 'old boys' who had got in to the École normale supérieure (there were very few in this provincial town). I found the loneliness extremely hard to bear, and what made things a great deal more difficult was that I was convinced *I knew nothing*, absolutely nothing, that everything lay ahead and there was no one to help me.

At the time I kept a diary (recommended to me by Guitton whom I will come to in a moment), and each day started a new page by summoning the 'will to power', an expression I had picked up somewhere and which gave me the resolve to escape from the void I was in and to assert myself by means of a hollow will which could not take the place of what nature had given me. Beneath this entry appeared long declarations of love for Simone which I never had the courage to send to her. 'It is not the done thing', my aunt said when I asked her if I could at least send Simone a book of poetry without a letter. She had been my only hope.

The first teacher who astonished me was Jean Guitton. He was thirty, had just left the École normale, possessed a great brain (the 'dome of Rome') in a puny little body. He radiated kindness, intelligence, and suavity but a sort of malice as well which always caught us on the wrong foot. He was a strong Christian, a disciple

* *Hypokhâgne* is the first-year and *khâgne* the second-year class preparing the entrance exam to the École normale supérieure (Translator's note).

of Chevalier, Cardinal Newman, and Cardinal Mercier, and devoted his entire philosophy course to an explanation of the way in which Christianity had challenged him and become part of his being through different systems of thought. He was to devote himself to a career as special adviser to Pope John XXIII and Pope Paul VI. He considered Hélène and me to be 'saints' and proved it, after Jean Dutourd's article about Hélène's death had appeared, by interrupting a television programme to declare that he had complete faith in me and would stand by me through thick and thin. I am infinitely grateful to him for what was quite simply a *public act of courage*.

He quickly set us the title for an oral presentation though I cannot remember the subject. I did not know how to 'construct a presentation' and knew very little about philosophy (our teacher in Marseille had been poor). I launched into a Lamartinian piece full of lyrical lamentations lacking both reasoned argument and rigour. I earned a stern seven out of twenty and the brief *ad hoc* comment: '*completely off the point*'. I was devastated by this first bad mark which plunged me into deeper gloom.

Soon after that we were set our first written essay. We wrote it in a large classroom where the older boys worked together after lessons. They were old hands and knew all the tricks of the trade. Guitton had given us the subject: '*Reality and fiction*'. I was struggling in vain to get a few vague ideas together in my head and again feeling completely lost when one of the older boys came up with some sheets of paper in his hand. 'Here, have these. They might help you. Anyway, they're on the same subject.'

It was true; Guitton must have set the same subject the previous year and the older boy mischievously gave me Guitton's own fair copy. I was certainly filled with shame but my despair was even greater. Without a moment's hesitation I took the teacher's fair copy, retained most of it (the overall plan, the development of the ideas, and the conclusion), and reworked it as best I could in my own way – in other words, what I had managed to grasp of Guitton's approach, including his style of writing. When Guitton gave the essays back to us in class, he seemed quite amazed and showered me with sincere praise. How had I made such progress in such a short time! I came top with seventeen out of twenty.

As far as I was concerned, I had quite simply copied out Guitton's version; I had cheated, worked a fiddle and plagiarised his text. It was a supreme act of deception and artifice to win his favour. I was astounded; he could not have failed to see what I had done! Had he set a trap for me? I believed he knew everything and wanted to keep it from me out of generosity. But when, perhaps thirty years later, he again spoke admiringly of that exceptional essay of mine and I told him the truth, he was even more astonished. Not for one moment had he suspected my deception and did not want to believe it!

As I suggested before, a teacher does not dislike seeing his own image projected back at him and often does not even recognise it. This is doubtless because of the conscious/unconscious pleasure he derives from recognising himself in a chosen pupil.

What personal benefit did I derive from this? Of course there was the advantage of immediately being promoted to the top of the class, of enjoying at last the respect of my young friends – above all that of the senior boys – and of being accepted as one of the class. But at what price! I still suffer from the sense of having practised a real deception. I already suspected I was only able to exist through artifice, by adopting characteristics which were not my own. This time, however, I could not even claim that the artifice was my own creation. It involved *deception* and *theft*, which clearly showed I only existed as a consequence of real deceit in relation to my true nature, by unscrupulously plagiarising the ideas, argument, and expressions of my teacher, someone I wanted to be noticed by in order to pretend to seduce him. If guilt is involved, the sense of non-existence ceases to be a technical problem and becomes a moral one. Henceforth, my feeling was not simply one of non-existence but of *guilt that I did not exist*.

Naturally, I took advantage of this; not only because Guitton singled me out and thereafter developed feelings of pure affection and fraternal admiration for me. I was his *alter ego*. He confided in me about his work and even took me to Paris where I had to condemn materialism in philosophical terms (with the help of Ravaisson) in front of an audience of nuns. Actually, Guitton himself developed my argument which he found a little dry.

Guitton, who was an admirable teacher if not a great philosopher, certainly taught me two genuine scholarly virtues, which were later to play a large part in my success: first, to strive for the greatest possible clarity when writing and, secondly, the art (artifice as always) of constructing and expounding an argument on any essay subject, *a priori* and as if by pure deduction, which was coherent and convincing. If I was successful in the competitive exam for the École normale and then in my philosophy exams for the *agrégation*, it was essentially due to him. What he inculcated in me (without my having to work them out laboriously for myself) was an awareness not of arbitrary devices but rather of the ones which would enable me to achieve a reputation at the highest level within the university (I may have been an impostor, but there was no other way for me then).

From that point on, the view I had of the university was as unflattering and disrespectful as the one I had of myself. It never changed, which, you will realise, was both a help and a hindrance to me.

Guitton only stayed a year and told us when he was leaving that his replacement would be a certain M. Labannière. The following year saw the arrival of Jean Lacroix. Guitton had come and gone like a whirlwind.

I carried on using with Lacroix the tricks I had learnt from Guitton. Lacroix was a man of integrity, a 'Personalist' Catholic, a friend of Mounier's, and a philosopher who knew a great deal about the history of philosophy. I still came top in philosophy, but thanks to him I also began to learn something about the subject. Lacroix had married a young woman who belonged to the most exclusive set of the Lyon bourgeoisie. These people thought he was the Devil incarnate and treated him as such. He neither belonged to the same social class as them nor shared their reactionary ideas. In the context of such an exclusive and trying milieu, and especially in Lyon, Lacroix proved himself to be a very courageous man, joining the Resistance and after the war supporting numerous good causes.

The most amazing man who taught us in *khâgne* was the history teacher, Joseph Hours, whom we referred to affectionately as 'Père Hours'.* He thoroughly detested Guitton, whom he called not a man but a woman or, worse still, a 'mother'. Oh! My mother . . . Short, thick-set, and with a face and moustache like Laval's, Hours

* A homonym in French for 'Father Bear' (Translator's note).

was politically very committed and founded *L'Aube* with Georges Bidault. An unusual characteristic of this convinced Catholic was his Jacobin and naturally Gallican attitude, which meant he was fiercely opposed to the European party's ultramontane policy which was seen by him as the legacy of the Holy Roman Empire. He never minded expressing out loud and in class his views on the political situation in France (and did so even more forcefully when one visited him at home, a privilege I slowly gained). I remember him saying to me in 1937: 'The French bourgeoisie has such a hatred of the Popular Front that even now it would prefer Hitler. Hitler will attack and the French bourgeoisie will choose defeat to escape the Popular Front.' I have simply quoted this one remark, but it was supported by a detailed analysis of social and political forces and of the personality and career of politicians whose behaviour he studied closely. He particularly singled out Maurice Thorez as one of the best and pinned all his hopes not on the privileged but on the 'ordinary people of France', of whom he wrote a brief *History* – doubtless in the tradition of Michelet. My earliest views on politics and the risks involved, as well as on communism which for me meant Thorez, came from 'Père Hours'. There was something about him physically and about his constant grumbling which reminded me of my grandfather, who died around that time, leaving my grandmother on her own in the house at Larochemillay where she lived for another twenty years.

It was during the same period that I set out to implement a grand scheme which I personally had devised. The Church had just launched what were referred to as the Catholic Action Movements in response to the growth of socialism. It was not one general movement, rather a series of movements aimed at different 'socio-professional' groups: the Christian Agricultural Youth Movement for farm workers, the Christian Workers' Youth Movement for young workers, and a Student Christian Movement. There was no Student Christian 'circle' in the Lycée du Parc, so I decided to create one and therefore tried to find a chaplain, as we could not decently do without such a figure. Following someone's advice, though I cannot remember whose it was, I climbed up to Fourvière one day and knocked on the door of a young Jesuit, Father Varillon, a tall thin man with a huge straight nose. He agreed to come and from that day on attended our meetings, which brought together for the most part the senior students, including therefore my own class. Here again I had assumed certain responsibilities, but for the first time I had done so *alone*. 'The will to power!' We occasionally went on retreats to a Trappist monastery at Dombes, which was a hundred kilometres from Lyon and surrounded by large ponds. We were welcomed by the only monk who was allowed to talk – what a chatterbox! – and entered in silence the vast buildings which stank of polish and old soap. We slept in cells and were wakened several times during the night by the bell that summoned us to the various services which we attended. I was fascinated by the monastic life, devoted to chastity, manual labour, and silence. This triple vow suited me quite well. Later in life I often thought that withdrawing permanently into a monastery would have solved all my insoluble problems. To disappear into anonymity has always been my one true calling, and still is, despite, and in opposition to, the notoriety I have achieved, which causes me terrible suffering. We also held our own meetings as a group within the monastery, and I remember being charged with the task of giving a short talk on the virtue of 'meditation'. I expressed myself with such suppressed exaltation and pious conviction, and with such an excessive spirit of 'mystical union' that all my friends were carried away by my emotion. For the first time I discovered the powerful and contagious effect of my eloquence, but in putting it across I realised I resorted spontaneously to another kind of artifice. In fact the rhythm of my speech was excessive, as were the pathos and suppressed emotion I wanted my friends to be caught up in and to share. I still had the same nostalgic desire for 'union'. It was as if, to believe what I was saying and to make others believe it, I found it necessary to 'gild the lily', to become more emphatic in my language and emotions than the situation warranted. In succumbing to such excess, I would be moved to tears, believing it was necessary for me to cry, to display such exaggerated emotion to carry my listeners with me, and above all to believe in it myself. I only came to understand much later the meaning of this strange attitude of mine. I was first made aware of it when a very dear friend said to me one day: 'I don't like it when you exaggerate' (with her especially, of course). It is true that my love for her was marked by an excessive desire for union which she was perfectly aware of. The same friend, who was without doubt extremely perceptive, also made a most telling remark about me, which I will comment on at the appropriate moment: 'What I don't like about you is that you are determined to destroy yourself.' I had not yet realised that the tendency to exaggerate, let us call it the tendency to paranoia, and a suicidal tendency were one and the same thing.

I passed the entrance exam to the École normale in July/August 1939, but was called up in September, and therefore did not take up my place until six years later, in October 1945.

X

I was called up in Issoire, with a group of Reserve Cadet Officers belonging to the horse-drawn artillery. And so I became acquainted with other wretched reservists in the French army, the night guards, and also the heavy draught horses which had been requisitioned, not to mention the stables, where a small and splendid dark-haired girl with that famous profile tried her hardest to get me to sleep with her in the straw. Naturally, I repelled her advances. We discovered the jolly little ways of our flashy warrant-officer, Courbon de Casteljaloux, and I made some very good friends, of whom, sadly, only one survived.

We stayed in Issoire until the spring of 1940, dragging out our training during the 'phoney war'. Guitton, who was at staff headquarters in Clermont, sometimes came to see me. I was very frightened of war, not so much of being killed as of being *wounded*, but as I was still a believer I had found a prayer that sent me peacefully to sleep: 'Oh God, may your will be done!'

In May 1940 they asked for volunteers for the air force. I declined. It was too dangerous (my uncle Louis had died in an aeroplane). I have already mentioned how scared I was of getting into fights, fearing I would be injured or rather that I would *damage* my fragile body. My mates went off to seek adventure and I was on my own again. I had made my choice . . . . Then, a bit later, for some unknown reason, I too was threatened with having to join the air force. I *pretended* that I was ill and before the doctor came to see me I tried to produce a false reading on the thermometer by rubbing it hard against my leg. Again I cheated dishonourably, though nothing happened, as I recall. The doctor came but did not select me.

My father had been called up at the same time and was really happy to be back with the heavy artillery in the Alps above Menton. This time they found themselves in concrete bunkers, which were quite cushy, and he wined and dined extremely well in the much improved officers' mess. From time to time they fired a few shells at an Italian port, just 'to keep up their morale'. But it was not very serious.

My mother left Lyon and went to live with her grandmother in the Morvan. At last she was alone! And then something quite wonderful happened. She became town clerk and had to deal with numerous local problems, which were greatly increased by the exodus of May/June 1940. She coped admirably, without the slightest health problems. As she was no longer subject to her husband's authority, she could at last do as she wished and she was happy. All her illnesses disappeared.

When I visit her now in her nursing home, she scarcely recognises me, but claims to be very happy. Her health is excellent despite her advancing years and she refuses to be called Mme Althusser. She refers to herself by her maiden name, *Lucienne Berger*, and that is that. The issue has been resolved, but just sixty years too late!

In March or April 1940 we were sent to Vannes where the pace of our training quickened. There was a final exam, and I naturally came last. Father Dubarle, who is now very ill, came top. If he reads this, I would like him to know I have never forgotten him and that I read his splendid books on Hegel.

Hordes of German troops were arriving. Paul Reynaud announced that we would fight in our 'Breton stronghold', but one after another the towns were declared 'open', including Vannes. Our officers [were] under the command of that scheming traitor General Lebleu who, fearing we might be or become 'communists', prevented us from moving towards the Loire, which was still in French hands at Nantes, and from there heading south. He kept us holed up in our barracks, *guarded by our own side*, even when the German tanks arrived. 'If you abandon your posts, you will be considered deserters and shot!'

The Germans were clever, telling us we would be freed in a week, a fortnight, then a month, and they threatened us with reprisals on our families if we escaped. During three whole months there were thousands of occasions on which we could easily have escaped from poorly guarded French camps. The food and Red Cross lorries entered freely and offered us the means of getting out of the camp. We were too naïve, thinking it was not done to escape under cover of the Red Cross. Personally I was not brave enough, and I was not the only one.

Finally, a long convoy of cattle trucks took four days and nights ferrying us to northern Germany, to a huge camp at Sandbostel amid sand and heathland. There for the first time we saw, behind electrified barbed wire, Russian prisoners who were almost naked even though it was already intensely cold. They were emaciated and deathly pale and they begged for bread which we threw them from our own meagre rations.

A young student from Brive kept me company throughout the journey. We pissed into the same bottle. He was the only friend I had. He told me amazing stories about girls he met in the park near the *lycée*. There was one in particular which moved me to tears: 'We would put our hands up the girls' skirts from behind without warning, just like that! One day, I had my hand up a girl's skirt and she turned round reproachfully and complained: "Why didn't you tell me you loved me?"'

I and several mates who were also students were then sent with three hundred other French prisoners, almost all of them peasants from Normandy, to a gigantic *Luftwaffe* base where various private firms were building huge underground storage tanks for fuel, making money at our expense. Despite the comradeship among the prisoners, it was a very tough year. We were starving hungry and they made us do forced labour in the coldest weather (down to minus forty that year). Our only respite came in the evenings which we spent in our huge, intensely heated huts or dormitories where we got the stoves red hot by feeding them with peat blocks. Sunday was wonderful; we were allowed to rest and given a meatball covered in gravy!

All my student friends contracted tuberculosis and were sent home. Again, I found myself alone. I stood up to it very well and I liked the peasants from Normandy with whom I worked. Some of them could not help being over-zealous in order to show the 'Jerries' how hard we work in France. We students did as little as possible and our comrades from Normandy disapproved of us. They were quite ready to accuse us of 'sabotage'!

Some of the men I got to know there seemed to me quite extraordinary, especially Sacha Simon, a famous journalist who worked for *L'Est républicain* and who never stopped telling stories about sex which I found staggering. He had masturbated two women at once under the table-cloth at some important function: 'It was dead easy, just what they wanted.' Since then I have heard a great many more; in particular the adventures of a friend of mine who was an international government official and whose one ambition in life was to get senior officers in the Red Army to ejaculate under the table. One of them even suffered a seizure as a result of the emotional excitement. Since then, she has 'banged' the vast majority of presidents of the Republic, as well as several bishops and cardinals. Her ultimate goal, as yet unfulfilled I believe, is the Pope. How she would laugh and laugh about it!

One day I fell ill, from a kidney complaint apparently, and to my astonishment I was taken in a very comfortable German ambulance to the camp hospital which was a day's journey away. This was done on the orders of the French doctor at our camp, Lieutenant Zeghers, whom I later met again at the main camp. I spent a week there and was then transferred to the said camp, Schleswig, Stalag XA. My number, with lots of zeros, was 70670. It suited me. I continued to do hard physical labour, unloading coal wagons, etc.

It felt totally natural doing physical work, and I especially enjoyed the comradeship of my peasant friends, having grown used to being with people like them since childhood.

There were several contingents of Poles who, having arrived first, made sure they ran things in the camp. They had a low opinion of the French as they had 'been traitors' in 1939. There were also a number of podgy Belgians, all of whom were regular, non-commissioned officers, among them a flautist and an actor who played women's roles in the theatre. Finally there were the wretched 'Serbs', several of whom hanged themselves from the ends of their beds.

Officially, according to the Geneva Convention of 1929, each nationality should have had a representative who liaised with the German authorities, someone 'trustworthy' who was chosen by his comrades. The first of these, a man called Cerutti – a car-dealer in Switzerland – had been automatically chosen by the Germans, no doubt because he spoke German very well. For a time I was 'assigned to' the camp hospital, where I became an expert on injections, which personally never hurt me (almost the opposite) when I had to have them (the opposite of the stake!). I was under the supervision of Dr Zeghers, who looked as neat as ever in his spotless uniform. I had learnt a little German and was therefore quickly appointed 'chief nurse'. As had happened previously in the scout patrol and then at the Lycée Saint-Charles, I again found myself confronted by a huge, loud-mouthed Parisian who spoke slang and would not accept 'orders' from me. He wanted to punch my head in. I backed off, swallowing my pride.

This ordeal lasted until, one day, the Germans repatriated 'their' trustworthy prisoner as a reward for his behaviour. As Hitler had granted Pétain and France the 'privilege' at Montoire (contrary to the Geneva Convention) of being the 'guardian' of its own prisoners, and as Pétain took advantage of this 'agreement' to send French officers into the camps who were collaborators so that they would push the ideas of the National Revolution and create countless Pétain Appreciation Societies, the Germans agreed that the new trusty should be elected. However, they presented their own candidate: the president of the Pétain Appreciation Society, a blue-blooded and wonderfully handsome young man.

Unfortunately they had overlooked the argumentative nature of ordinary Frenchmen! A vast, clandestine electoral campaign got underway within the space of two days, inspired by a Parisian dental technician who was an anarchist given to speaking his mind in no uncertain terms. He assisted the pathetic dental officer who dribbled constantly, a frightful sight, and spent his time openly tossing squares of chocolate to the unfortunate Ukrainian women in the adjacent camp, some ten metres away, so that they would open their thick thighs. The dental officer would then masturbate as he stood looking at their naked fannies. The whole camp knew about this, and those who felt like it turned up for the daily spectacle.

A man called Robert Daël, who was greatly liked in the camp, was triumphantly elected.

The first thing he did was to appoint the president of the Pétain Appreciation Society, the Germans' chosen man, as his assistant. As a consequence Daël was subjected to a great wave of criticism, but he did not respond. A month later, however, having reassured the Germans with this skilful manoeuvre, he negotiated the immediate repatriation of the president which was just what the latter wanted. Then we understood. And I began to understand what a man of action really was.

One day, Daël summoned me to his 'office' along with the architect Mailly and several others, and I saw at first hand what he could do. Showing firmness, and speaking a rather halting and unlikely German of his own concoction, he took over from the Germans total control of the foodstuffs, clothes, and shoes sent from France and put a stop to the wholesale looting on the part of the camp authorities; and all this within the space of a few days.

He obtained a lorry [through the good offices] of Pétain, which enabled him to distribute the *Liebesgaben* sent from France to the smallest outposts where they had never set eyes on any gift before, let alone seen the trusty from the main camp! I sometimes accompanied him on his rounds. I so admired him for the incredible way he cheeked the German who kept an eye on him, immediately bribing him with a couple of bars of chocolate. I also admired his warmth towards his fellow prisoners, who had felt totally abandoned until he came along.

I understood then what it was to act in a way that respected principles without applying them simplistically. One had to come to terms with the imponderables of the situation, of the men and the things that mattered to them, and of the enemy. This called for all sorts of human resources other than clear and strict moral principles.

The first and most important result of all this was that it gave me a completely new approach to my fear of artifice. I began to realise that resorting to artifice, subterfuge, and other such practices was not merely to engage in deception. They could have beneficial effects on the person who used them and on other people, as long as one knew what one wanted and overcame any sense of guilt one might have. In short, one had to be free, which is something I learnt in the course of analysis. Without knowing it at the time and never having perceived the slightest parallel with that obsessive fear of artifice which was part of my nature – and though I only came to realise it much later – I worked my way towards the rules laid down by the only man – and I mean the *only* man – who thought about the prerequisites and the forms of action – albeit exclusively in the sphere of politics. He was the man who largely anticipated the discoveries of Freud, *long before his time*, and some day I hope to demonstrate this. His name was Machiavelli. At that time, however, I was a long way from understanding all this.

What I also discovered during my captivity [was*] how much I enjoyed living with people other than my father and mother and away from the world (without any outside) of books, the classroom, and the family flat. In short, I was free from that most *frightful, appalling, and horrifying of all the ideological State apparatuses*, in a nation where the State exists, namely the *family. Do you hear what I am saying, Robert Fossaert, and you too Gramsci from the depths of your dreadful tomb?* May I say that even in Lyon, for three whole years – from the age of eighteen till I was twenty-one! – *I knew absolutely no one* apart from my friends in *khâgne* and my teachers. And the sole reason for that was an awful combination of fear, upbringing, respect, timidity, and guilt which was instilled into me by none other than my own parents, who were themselves trapped in the same ideological structure which was dreadful for my mother and for my father, however it might have appeared. They did it in order to instil in me as a small child the supreme values prevailing in the society in which I was growing up: absolute respect for absolute authority and above all for the State, which since Marx and Lenin we have come to recognise, thank God, as a terrible 'machine' in the service not of the dominant class which never holds power alone (yes Fossaert, yes Gramsci), but of several classes constituting a 'power bloc', as Sorel so aptly termed it at a time when there was such widespread theoretical and political indifference in France. But how long will even the most informed and intelligent people allow themselves to be deluded by something even more blind and blinding than that dreadful deaf fish of the unconscious, which Freud trawled up from the very depths of the seas in his long net? How much longer will they fail to recognise the blinding evidence of the true nature of the *Family* as an ideological State apparatus? Does one now have to point out that, in addition to the three

* The author's inclusion of a lengthy digression on the family, not included in the first version of this chapter, led us in this and the following paragraph to make two slight changes which appear in brackets and which make the development of his argument more coherent (Editors' note).

great narcissistic wounds inflicted on Humanity (that of Galileo, that of Darwin, and that of the unconscious), there is a fourth and even graver one which no one wishes to have revealed (since from time immemorial the family has been the very site of the *sacred* and therefore of *power* and of *religion*)? It is an irrefutable fact that the Family is the most powerful ideological State apparatus.

In captivity I came into contact [moreover] with a whole other world outside the hallowed family: with mature men who could at least be said to have gained by being liberated *from their families* as they were now free adults. The peasants from Normandy, the lower middle-class Belgians, the Polish regular non-commissioned officers who talked endlessly of the gargantuan meals they enjoyed in peacetime, and of their sexual exploits and obsessions down to the most crude and intimate details; all of them taught me in some way what it was to be adult and sexually liberated. On the other hand, they were 'alienated' inasmuch as they were neither economically, nor socially, nor politically, nor ideologically liberated (that is to say, in terms other than those used by Feuerbach and Hegel, either exploiters or the exploited, oppressors or the oppressed, indoctrinators or the indoctrinated!). What discoveries did I make in this new world? My obsession with always wanting to have *something in reserve*. That was crucial to my understanding of myself.

The first year, when we were given just two hundred and fifty grammes of black bread and fifty grammes of black sausage and no more, I had a panic fear that I would run out of food and so I cut a piece of bread and a slice of black pudding every day and put them under my mattress. They were my precious reserves; just in case!

But when I had to leave my first unit, all that I found under my mattress was a pile of food that had *gone bad*. I had lost all my reserves by trying to save them. The truth, the reality of my desire to keep some reserves was there to be seen, touched, smelled, and tasted: *a rotting heap*! Yet I was unable to draw the lesson from this painful experience during the next sixty years! In the better times that followed, I continued to build up reserves, first of bread, biscuits, chocolate, sugar, shoes (I still have around a hundred pairs in my cupboards today!), clothes too, and of course *money*, the most important thing of all to have in reserve.

Marx pointed this out, though a number of others had already done so, Locke most forcefully of all (for Locke, money was in fact *the only commodity which was imperishable . . .*). Unlike all other goods which are perishable, money stands out as being different in this respect. Later still I had reserves of friends and ultimately of *women*. Why? Simply because I did not want to run the risk of finding myself *alone one day without a woman*, if by any chance one of my women friends left me or died. This did happen on numerous occasions, and if I always kept *a reserve of women* in addition to Hélène, it was to ensure that, if by chance Hélène abandoned me or died, I would never for a single instant find myself alone. I know only too well this awful compulsion of mine caused a great deal of suffering to 'my' women, and especially to Hélène. One of my women friends recently told me, and how right she was *on that occasion*: 'You certainly know how to use your friends (referring to men rather than women), but you don't respect them.' Her remark took me aback at the time (four months ago) and gave me something to think about, but I missed the point.

Quite naturally, this compulsion of mine to have reserves of all kinds was in my mind related to my mother's phobias and in particular her totally irrational obsession to cut down on all her expenses and to amass savings. This she did for no better reason than to be prepared for whatever might possibly befall her in the future, *above all a robbery.*

Like all the women of her generation (and of her mother's generation too), my mother hid her money beneath her skirts, at least when she went out or was travelling, which meant *as close as possible to her sexual organs*, as if she had to protect both in every way she could against unsavoury people and the threat they posed. And certainly for a long time I was no freer in my sexual than in my spending habits. It was a way of living constantly in the same present, never having the courage or rather the simple freedom to face the future (without a prior guarantee of reserves) other than as an accumulation of the past, which was supposed to produce its own exorbitant interest.

I finally succeeded in truly freeing myself of this obsession two months ago, and without any doubt it proved to be one of the hardest tasks of my whole life. In a moment I will explain why and how I achieved it.

I now feel I know for certain that one is not really alive unless one spends, takes risks, and therefore has surprises, and that surprises and spending (freely rather than for profit, which is the only possible definition of communism) are not simply a part of all life but constitute the ultimate truth of life itself, in its *Ereignis*, its surging forth, its very happening, as Heidegger has argued so well.

So that now, when I visit my mother, who picked up something called amoebic dysentery when she was in Morocco and has lived ever since with a dread of stomach disorders, I stuff her with large and very expensive chocolates from Hédiard's. She would never have behaved like this in the past nor allowed me to do so. Indeed, she would have strictly forbidden it, so far as both she and I were concerned. Now she pounces on the chocolates from Hédiard's without even asking how much they cost, and for someone who was so afraid of amoebae (it is a known fact that you are strongly advised not to eat chocolates if you have amoebae), she feels not the slightest twinge either in her stomach or elsewhere nor any of the countless imaginary ills which necessitated twice-daily visits from assorted doctors plus incredible remedies, both medicinal and dietary, when my father was alive. She now greedily devours my chocolates without the slightest ill effects!

One can thus be totally cured of an incredible range of phobias *without recourse to an analyst*. For example, the death of her husband was all that was required for Mme Althusser to become again Lucienne Berger and for order to be restored. Perhaps desire and freedom were not restored to her but pleasure certainly was and the pleasure principle is, according to Freud, linked with the libido, what believers call the Holy Spirit (and my mother was always a firm believer).

To live just in the present! We did not know, of course, that our captivity would last for five years, but day by day, month by month, time passed, especially after June 21st, 1941, when fighting started on the Eastern Front, raising all our hopes. In actual fact I have to admit I began to feel quite at home as a prisoner (I was genuinely comfortable because I felt genuinely secure under the protection of German guards and behind barbed wire). I was untroubled by my parents and I confess that I found life easy because I enjoyed the comradeship of real men and I was happy because I was well protected. We were behind barbed wire, watched over by armed guards and subjected to the vexations of roll-calls, searches, fatigues. We were very hungry during the first and last years, yet how can I explain it, I felt secure and protected from all danger simply because I was a prisoner.

I never seriously thought of escaping, despite the example of several friends who tried their luck as many as six times. One of them, a marvellous chap called Clerc, was tiny (four feet eleven), yet he was a first-class footballer who headed the ball with incomparable skill despite his size and had won the French Cup in 1932 with Cannes, the team he played for. On the other hand, I dreamed up a way of escaping to which I subsequently gave a great deal of thought.

Having noticed that the Germans alerted all the police and troops within a very wide radius once they realised one of us had escaped, which usually resulted in the capture of the daring individual concerned, I decided the surest way of escaping would be to *let them believe someone had escaped*, wait until the general alert was over which never lasted more than three or four weeks, and then escape *after that*. What I therefore had to do was *disappear* from the camp (I must have had a vocation for 'disappearing'!), and let them think I had gone, before actually going once the alert was past. To do this, I did not actually have to escape, but simply disappear, in other words hide within the camp itself (which was not impossible) and only then vanish into thin air, when all the measures adopted for the alert had been dropped (three weeks later). In essence I had found a way of escaping from the camp *without actually leaving* and of remaining a prisoner in order to escape! Though I perfected my plan, I did not carry it out, but simply prided myself on the fact that I had found 'the solution'. Having proved that I could do it, there was no need to put it into practice. I have often thought since that the 'solution' came from deep within me, combining a fear of danger and the absolute need for security to produce a fictitious act of bravery. If my friend Rancière had known about this 'episode' when he reproached me at a much later date for criticising the

Communist Party in order to remain within it, I believe it would have given him food for thought.

Protection! Yes, I was protected in the camp, and because of it I allowed myself to commit several acts of daring. Initially I was protected by Dr Zeghers and then by Daël. Daël, who was six feet six inches tall and as affectionate as a woman towards me (the real mother I never had), was also a 'real man' and capable of confronting danger and the Germans without the slightest fear (like the real father I never had). I felt quite safe with him and under his fond protection I reproduced the same old pattern of obsessional behaviour. Being sheltered by him, I became his adviser on all matters, including his daring schemes, thereby turning myself once again into a 'father's father' (as I had previously been with Zeghers), and also at the same time a 'mother's father', which enabled me once more to resolve in my own way the loneliness and contradiction in my life of never having had a real mother and father. I am fully aware, too, that I was, again in my own way, very much 'in love' with him. On our return to France, we parted in Paris, but I soon had news of him. He told me what pleasure it gave him to hear 'the sound of a woman's heels on the pavement as she held his arm and they walked together around town'. This made me terribly unhappy because I was jealous. I wrote to him from Morocco, where I had rejoined my parents, begging him *never to get married*. Though he gave me his word, he did not keep it, and I was left to suffer.

My own personal 'acts of daring' fell flat. When, later on in the Stalag, I forged the writing and the stamps on my military pass, turning it into a forged *nurse's* pass (because at that time the Germans were repatriating nurses), and then pretended I had found it in a parcel sent from France which was being opened by an old sentry who was almost blind (the operation could not have been easier), *I happened to overlook* a document signed by General Lebleu which listed me, along with all the reserve cadet officers from Vannes, as 'part of that contingent'. What is more, there were only two pages left in my pass, as I had torn out all the others in case they compromised me! Only two pages, yet I had made an 'oversight' of that magnitude! The German captain handed me back my documents with a knowing smile. How could I have overlooked that paper, given that my pass contained only two pages? It certainly suggests that unconsciously I did not wish to leave the camp – it is the only possible explanation. And though I might suggest *to* Daël all sorts of daring schemes, some completely crazy, I was quite incapable of carrying out a single real one myself. Clearly I had no desire to escape from captivity as it suited me down to the ground, and this could only be explained in terms of some more compelling force than my conscience or my carefully thought-out plans. I had a row with the German doctor one day, but when he summoned me to appear before him, all I could do was stammer pathetically, watched in silence by the whole of the Polish medical staff who were sizing me up, or rather trying to assess the extent of my apparent claims and my boldness as a rebel. I was locked up for a month in one of the cells where the wretched Russian prisoners were rotting away.

Finally, the Allies got closer. The guards were given two hours to think about their situation and then disappeared into the night. It was an incredible period of freedom and revelry, during which the prisoners went hunting and looking for women; but I remained aloof. The English had still not arrived. So I thought up the idea (oh so daring!) of going out to meet them and persuaded Daël to go along with it. Like me, he had given up his role as a trusted inmate but, to the astonishment of the Germans, we had both refused enforced repatriation. I got hold of a car and a driver and we set off clandestinely towards Hamburg and Bremen in the south. In Hamburg we were 'taken prisoner' by the English but managed to escape by the skin of our teeth thanks to the brilliance of our driver, though we then had to turn back because the roads were blocked. We returned to the camp and were widely condemned by our friends who were unwilling to forgive us for having 'cleared off'. The person who felt it the most was undoubtedly the camp chaplain, 'the little priest Poirier'. We were fond of him and he was fond of us too. He was particularly sad that this initiative had destroyed the comradeship in the camp. On the one occasion I had tried to get Daël to go along with *one of my daring plans*, it had gone completely wrong. Clearly I was not cut out to be a man of action or a brave adventurer.

One final point; it was in the camp that I first heard about Marxism from a Parisian lawyer who was passing through. I also made the acquaintance of one lone communist.

This man, whose name was *Pierre Courrèges*, appeared in the camp during the final months, having spent a year in a unit for incorrigible prisoners at Ravensbrück under a very tough regime. Daël had ceased to be a trusty for some considerable time and a tall, rather colourless individual, an undertaker by profession, had replaced him. Simultaneously, certain irregularities or compromises which had existed previously began to resurface. Not on a large scale however. Though no one asked him to do so, Courrèges intervened off his own bat and in the cause of honesty and fraternity. The effect was incredible. He was straightforward, direct, warm, and natural and seemed capable of talking and acting quite effortlessly. His presence alone transformed the camp and we were totally astonished by him. All the accommodations and semi-compromises with the Germans disappeared overnight and we felt an atmosphere in the camp which had not existed since Daël's 'reign'. This surprising change had been brought about by *one single* individual acting *on his own*, a man who was certainly 'different from the rest', another 'oddball' (communists are 'different', a propaganda theme I became familiar with later on). Thus I began to have great respect for militant communists. At the same time I realised one could act differently from Daël, that other approaches were possible, other forms of action, and that the possession of certain skills was of secondary importance when one's actions were motivated by genuine 'principles'. There was no need to resort either to 'sharp practice' or trickery. Courrèges was an astonishing man and he gave me my first practical lesson in communism! I have met him since in Paris, and he is still the same warm person, though he is just an ordinary man like everyone else. But I did not believe then that he could be an ordinary man.

At any rate, those who imagined it was Hélène who converted me to communism should know it was Courrèges.

The English arrived at last, and we were flown back to Paris. I went to see Jean Baillou, the secretary of the École normale, and was feeling so desperate that I said straight out to him: 'I can speak German (I had learnt it while I was a prisoner), a little Polish (*idem*) and the English I learnt at school. Please, I beg you, find me a job.' He replied: 'Go back to your parents first, and we'll see what can be done later on.' I passed myself off as an officer (the first piece of *sharp practice* I had engaged in which succeeded, and yet another deception) and on that basis was put on a direct flight to Casablanca, where my father had been posted in 1942. My parents did what they could to make me feel welcome. My father, who had a company car, took me on a quick tour of a few Moroccan towns. At the time my parents were very friendly with just one couple, the Ardouvins. They were a totally ill-assorted pair; M. Ardouvin was tiny and bent and he worked for the Moroccan railways. He was a former classmate of my father who still gave him a rough time. Mme Ardouvin was tall, rather good-looking, and an intellectual who taught French in a private school. She was a warm-hearted woman, greatly liked by my mother, with whom she could discuss scholarly things, literature and poetry. My father still behaved in exactly the same way and was full of mischief and good humour. He never stopped teasing them and bombarding them with his jokes. But I met *no one* else for three months. My mother was ill; she had become a hypochondriac, had stomach troubles and goodness knows what else besides. My one concern, heaven knows why, was that I might have caught venereal disease. I consulted ten military doctors, who declared me to be in good health, yet each time I was convinced they were hiding something. I found myself in a completely closed world, far from the comradeship of the prison camp, far from Daël whom I thought about constantly, and on the edge of depression. I am not sure how I managed to escape it, but it was probably due to the fact that I quickly returned to France. I was clear-sighted enough at least to conclude during those two months that I had to help my sister to escape her dead-end existence (she had interrupted her studies to become a nurse in a children's ward and to care for those who were badly wounded in the air-raids on Casablanca). Thus I devoted myself to her, won over my mother who 'entrusted' her to my care – it was the same old story – and we set off together in an old tub which only progressed by moving in semi-circles, stopping and restarting. We spent four days and nights at sea in this stinking boat before reaching Marseille. I found my sister a room in Paris and at last entered the École.

It was a disaster! I knew no one (I was the only person in my year to have been taken prisoner, but anyway, coming from the provinces, I would have known no one in my year even in 1939).

I felt irremediably old and overtaken by events. I no longer knew what I had previously learnt and came from a wholly different world from that of the university. This sense of coming from a 'different world' and the feeling of being a complete stranger among university people, of not sharing their ways and lifestyle, always stayed with me. What is more, I never established a personal relationship with anyone at the university, except for Jean-Toussaint Desanti and Georges Canguilhem, and you will discover why. The reason I later presented a thesis relating to the research I was doing at the time was because I was pressed into it by Bernard Rousset, president of the University of Amiens, who wanted a 'Parisian', 'who had achieved a certain fame' (Heine) to give a little publicity to Amiens. So I was completely alone; to add to that I felt ill (I was still sexually obsessed and had persistent eye problems – actually I was seeing spots – which made me fear I was going blind) and had no idea where I was going. At an earlier stage I would have liked to have done history, influenced no doubt by 'Père Hours' and the fact that I was already interested in politics. But I was hesitant about committing myself to it now (I no longer had a good memory, or that is what I thought). I therefore settled for philosophy and told myself that all I needed was the ability to write a proper essay. My ignorance would not matter and I would cope.

The doctor at the École, young Dr Étienne, took me into the sick-bay as a way of protecting me, though he did not believe there was anything wrong with my eyes (how right he was!). I occupied a small room at the end of the corridor on the first floor, next to that of a native of Lyon,* Pierre Moussa, whom I got to know. My sister, the only person I knew in Paris, was the first to visit me in this tiny room. She washed my socks and made tea for me. I had written her lyrical, semi-love letters from the time I was first taken prisoner, giving her some sort of special significance, no doubt so as not to have to write to my parents, to whom I had nothing to say. My only explanation for this is that it

---

* The author made the following hand-written note in the margin without relating it to the main body of the text: 'Hélène, who knew him in Lyon, had very strong views about him, as did my father when he was visited by him in Casablanca, slyly pulling his leg and telling him yarns (one could be sure of my father's discretion and savage sense of humour)' (Editors' note).

represented a form of displacement. It was there too that I made the acquaintance of Georges Lesèvre, known as Séveranne, who also hailed from Lyon and who had heard of my local 'fame' (direct from Lacroix and Hours), as usually happened in the provinces where few people in *khâgne* passed the exam to the École. His entry to the École was also delayed due to his long involvement with the Resistance where he had known Hélène well, as I was to discover later. But knowing one man, whose past exploits and ease of manner made me feel inferior, was not much comfort.

I wanted to have a relationship with a woman, but I do not remember how I set about it. I do however remember taking dancing lessons for a while with a rather stiff girl in a filthy night club in Montparnasse in preparation for the ball at the École . . . where I knew there would be students from the École normale for women at Sèvres. On the night of the ball in 1945, I noticed a face with that same profile which had haunted me for such a long time. It belonged to a small, charming girl who was as silent as me and with whom I danced briefly. Immediately I began to have incredible amorous phantasies about her. Her name was Angeline, for which I dreamt up countless variants: Angel, 'Angelette', Ameline, 'Amelinette', 'Ronsardelette' . . . . I saw her a number of times, wrote to her, and, in a state of some elation, resolved to think only of her, until the day she shared my feelings. However, her parents made it clear to her that it was out of the question. In the meantime, Lesèvre had got me to go on a trip to Czechoslovakia, under the auspices of the Republican Youth Movement (in fact they were communists), presided over by Herriot. Lesèvre was a communist and had access to all sorts of people, including numerous members of the Resistance he knew. Beside the River Vltava in Prague, which was half dried up and stinking, I realised that Nicole, one of the girls in the group, had fallen in love with me. I was so scared I could not even touch her. I really wanted to be in love with a girl, but I could not bear her being in love with me. As you can see, I experienced the same old repulsion.

It was then that I met Hélène.

XI

One evening in December '46 when Paris was covered in snow, Lesèvre invited me to visit his mother in her apartment at the top of the rue Lepic. She was in a sorry state, having just returned from deportation. I can still picture Lesèvre and me crossing the snow-covered pont de la Concorde, with him talking non-stop about his mother. Then he said to me: 'You'll meet Hélène, a very good friend of mine. She's slightly crazy, but she has a quite extraordinary understanding of politics and a generous nature.' Slightly crazy? What could this possibly mean given that he also sang her praises? 'We'll meet her at the entrance to the Métro at the bottom of the rue Lepic.'

Indeed, she was already there, waiting for us in the snow. She was very small and all wrapped up in a coat, so much so she was hardly visible. We were introduced and immediately set off up the rue Lepic on the icy pavement. My first instinctive gesture was to take her arm so that she would not fall and to help her up the hill. But I also slid my hand towards hers. It was cold and I clasped it in mine, which was warm. I never knew why I did this (or rather, I know only too well. It represented an impossible appeal for love, coupled with my usual display of pathos and my liking for exaggerated gestures). We climbed the hill in silence.

I have painful memories of that evening. A huge log fire was burning in the grate. Mme Lesèvre was pleased to see her son again and made us very welcome. She was a tall woman, totally emaciated by what she had been through, gaunt and almost like a shadow. She did not smile at all. She spoke slowly, choosing her words to recall the stirring memories she had of the Resistance and the 'sinister' nightmare of deportation. The deportation camps were nothing like the prisoner-of-war camps I had been in, nor were they like the conditions which Georges and Hélène had experienced in the Resistance. One could not even begin to *imagine* what they were like. Georges never said much about his exploits in the Alps and in Lyon itself. I had heard people talking about deportees, but this was the first time I had met one, and a woman at that, who remained upright and resolute in the face of her suffering. I remember I was wearing a badly cut, tight, brown jacket that someone had flogged me in Paris when I returned from captivity (being careful with money, I had not bought another one). Later on, Hélène often referred to that coat and what she felt at the time seeing me so badly dressed, like a gawky adolescent who was completely indifferent to the way he looked, or a ghost from beyond.

In fact I wore dull, off-the-peg clothes for a long time, which were never altered or properly finished.* I did this to save money and because I took a delight in pretending I was impoverished, like the little Arabs I knew in childhood or the prisoners in the camp. I remember I said very little that evening, just a few things about the Spanish Civil War, memories of 'Père Hours' and also of my grandmother, who, when I was reading Malraux's novel *L'Espoir* to her one day at Larochemillay, could not help showing her feelings: 'The poor things!' Hélène listened attentively to what Mme Lesèvre had to say and to my few remarks about politics, but said little herself. She said nothing about her own poverty, about her friends who had been executed by the Nazis during the war, or about the desperate state of distress she was in. I did however detect a certain unfathomable suffering and sense of loneliness and thought I understood after the event (though it was not true, as I have said) why I took her hand in the rue Lepic. From that moment on I was filled with a powerful desire to serve her: to save her and help her live! Throughout our life together, right to the very end, I never abandoned this supreme mission which gave my life its meaning until the final moment.

Try to imagine our meeting. We were two extremely lonely people, both in the depths of despair. Having met quite by chance,

---

* The following remark written in the margin was not linked to the main body of the text by the author: 'never made-to-measure (too expensive) until I was taught to dress with a certain style by the extremely beautiful and affectionate Claire, the first woman I had an affair with while I was with Hélène. Hélène always gave her great credit for this' (Editors' note).

we realised we were kindred spirits, sharing the same sense of anguish, of suffering, of loneliness, and the same desperate longing.

Gradually I discovered her background. She was born of a Jewish family, by the name of Rytmann from the borders of Russia and Poland, who had fled the pogroms. She herself was born in France in the Eighteenth District, near the rue Ordener, and used to play in the gutter with other children from the same street. She had dreadful memories of her mother. Since she had no milk, she never offered her daughter the breast and never held her in her arms. She hated her because she had wanted a son, and this savage, dark-skinned girl upset all her hopes and plans. As a mother, she never showed her the least affection, only hatred. Hélène, who like any child wanted to be loved by her mother, was in fact denied everything; the warmth of her body and her milk as well as the little signs and gestures of loving kindness. But she identified irrevocably with this frightful woman who hated her and with the dreadful image the mother had of her daughter. She saw herself as an object of hatred because she had been rejected, as a savage, dark, and rebellious little creature who could not be got round and who was always in a violent temper (her only defence). Her mother's hate-filled image of her as a little girl, a small, dark creature, violently aggressive and fighting for its survival, was overlaid with the image she had of her mother as a frightful, malevolent woman, and together they formed the basis of Hélène's terrifying phantasy about herself which lasted throughout her life, right to the end. She had an uncontrollable fear that she too would always be a frightful, shrewish woman, totally unjust and violent, spreading hurt all around her, and unable ever to curb the terrible excesses to which she was driven by a force more powerful than she was.

Here again, it cannot be argued that Hélène could in any way claim to be an exact and objective mirror-image of her real mother or to reflect her conscious intentions, and therefore by definition her unconscious intentions. All one can say is that her original phantasy was not arbitrary, but linked to real 'signs' through which her mother's unconscious and 'willed' desires (her implacable desires) revealed themselves. It is true that as a child Hélène was puny, dark, and given to rages. But rages . . . . Thus, something quite real was expressed, if only through her memory, which

literally prevented Hélène from *living*; so terrible was her fear of
only ever being a frightful and malevolent woman, incapable
of being loved – because she certainly knew how to love others!
I do not think I have witnessed in any other woman a similar
capacity for love, which was no phantasy, but real, as she proved
to me!

On the other hand, she had good memories of her father. This
gentle, attentive man had a little greengrocery business in the
Eighteenth District. In the local Jewish community he was considered a 'wise man'. People came to seek his advice and he was
always prepared to help his neighbour. His one passion was horses
(him as well). He ended up buying one and looked after it with
his daughter. Her father's trust and affection in sharing these
tasks with her gave Hélène great pleasure. But she could never
understand how her father put up with his wife, other than by
showing extreme patience. They soon left the Eighteenth District
for a little house in the Chevreuse valley. And it was there that
tragedy struck.

Her father developed cancer. Hélène's sister and brothers, it
seems, led their own separate lives and took little interest in their
parents. Hélène, who was ten or eleven years old, spent months
and months alone at her father's bedside, comforting and caring
for him, her mother having off-loaded total responsibility on to
the bad daughter. Kind Doctor Delcroix, a genuine, warm, and
thoughtful person whom Hélène liked, was of course there to
help her. Isolated and weighed down with responsibility that was
enough to crush a child, he was the only person she could turn
to. Unfortunately, when the young girl was confiding in him one
day, the good Doctor began to feel inside her pants and play with
her sexual organs. It was as if her one friend in the world had
abandoned her. Not only did she continue to look after her father,
she was the one to whom Dr Delcroix turned to administer the
final large dose of morphine during his final, painful moments. It
was as if this frightful child had killed the father she loved and
who loved her.

A year later, her mother also contracted cancer, and it was the
same situation all over again. Hélène was the one who watched
over and nursed a mother who detested her. Again, during the
final moments of her life, Dr Delcroix prescribed a fatal injection,

and Hélène administered it. The frightful child also killed the mother who detested her. At the age of thirteen!

I am not too clear about what happened subsequently, but Hélène managed to find a job on her own, to earn her living in a small way, to read and even follow a few courses at the Sorbonne, where she listened to Albert Mathiez, among others, whom she often spoke of. At the Sorbonne she met her first real friend, who accepted her for what she was, since she was able to detect behind the wild outbursts an incomparable intelligence and generosity of spirit. Her name was Émilie. She was a philosopher with a passionate interest in Spinoza and Hegel and also a communist. One day she went to the Soviet Union to pursue her studies, was ultimately detained in Siberia, thrown into a dungeon, and in the end executed with a bullet through the back of her head. Hélène only learnt about this last detail in the 1950s. Though she was not a philosopher herself (she had wanted to be a historian), Hélène had learnt from Émilie and remembered the vital importance of philosophy in politics. That is why she understood me when we met and why we got to know each other better.

Hélène joined the Communist Party in the Thirties and as a young woman became extremely militant in the Fifteenth District. This was near the Citroën factory (Javel), where there was such repression that union and political activity could only be organised outside the workplace. She acquired an exceptional reputation, standing firm against all who challenged her, facing the insults and ridicule of fascist opponents, in order to sell *L'Humanité* every day to the Citroën workers. She became extremely popular with them, and a formidable opponent to those who belonged to the fascist leagues, such was her determination and courage. It was there she made friends with those exceptional militants Eugène Hénaff (Gégène), with whom she was genuinely in love, Jean-Pierre Timbaud, and also Jean-Pierre Michels, who was subsequently to become deputy for the Fifteenth District. These two were both executed at Châteaubriant. She also got to know and became a close friend of Paul Vaillant-Couturier at *L'Humanité* as well as André Marty (though she was not as close to him). She was impressed by the latter's 'fantastic eloquence' and 'swinish character'. She took part in the street battles against the fascists on February 9th, 1936, alongside her worker comrades who had been mobilised by their union and by the Party. It was the time of Maurice Thorez: 'Let our voices be heard, we don't want dummies in the Party!' She even met Jacques Duclos on one occasion and beat him at billiards in a café: 'Fortune favours the innocent!' commented Duclos, mockingly.

It was during this period that the one passion in her life began to develop: her passion *for the 'working class'*. It was a genuine, total, demanding, and, in certain respects, mythical passion, yet it gave her effective protection against another myth: that which surrounded those who led the working class and their organisation. Not once in her life or in front of me did she ever confuse the two things. On the contrary, the moment came after 1968 when she said quite openly that 'the Party had betrayed the working class' and she could no longer understand why I remained a member. As far as my books were concerned, she kept saying 'they showed the "true worth" of the working class', and that is why she approved and valued them. The only thing that mattered to her in politics was the working class, its virtues, resources, and revolutionary courage.

Lastly, may I in this connection lay to rest once and for all a personal myth about Hélène and me which has become widespread even among some of my friends (though certainly not the closest): *Hélène never applied the slightest pressure on me* either in the realm of philosophy or of politics. The pressure came not from her but rather from Pierre Courrèges, from Séveranne and his friends, and then from my own experiences of unions at the École normale where I clashed with the socialists and even managed to defeat them for the leadership of our union. It also came from Jean-Toussaint Desanti and Tran Duc Thao, both philosophers and communists, who taught at the École normale and whose courses I followed after the *agrégation*. She *never* suggested I should make the slightest change of emphasis in any of my manuscripts, which I naturally gave her to read. In her judgement, she lacked the necessary competence both in philosophy and political theory, as she did not know *Das Kapital*. On the other hand, she had incomparable experience of both the Party and political action. She contented herself with approving what I did and would only intervene to suggest changes which might reinforce or soften a particular phrase. Ill-informed people have tried to suggest there was a basis for conflict between us on these matters, whereas we had a perfect understanding. She discovered echoes of her own experience of practical politics in what I wrote. When she talked to me about those experiences, she provided living confirmation of what I was about to write.

Our personal difficulties stemmed from something quite different, as will be seen.

When I got to know her in 1946, I quickly discovered that not only had she lost all her friends, including an extraordinary priest, Father Larue, whom she knew in the Resistance in Lyon and fell madly in love with and who was executed by the Nazis at Montluc at the very end of 1944, but also that a daring plan involving irregular soldiers could have freed him and all the prisoners in Montluc, had it not been *forbidden by the Party and the government's representative in Lyon*, Yves Farge, who had been appointed by De Gaulle. Hélène reproached herself throughout her life, as if it had been her fault, for not having persuaded those responsible to intervene in time to try to free the members of the Resistance who were being held hostage by the Nazis in Montluc. Father Larue (a small square in Fourvière now bears his name) understood her and loved her deeply. Their miraculous relationship filled her with great joy and elation, but now he was dead, and for ever after she would reproach herself that she had been unable to save him.

I also discovered that she was living in poverty, having lost all contact with the Party, which had gone underground in 1939. During the war, unable to re-establish that contact and having broken with Jean Renoir, who left France for America and whom she had assisted on a number of films without ever allowing her name to figure in the credits (she also knew Françoise Giroud, maliciously referred to as 'black pudding' on account of her size), she joined an important Resistance organisation ('Libération-Sud', I believe, though I am not sure). At the same time, in order to get information, money, and arms from Switzerland into France, she became the French representative for Skira, which meant she met and became acquainted with the greatest painters of the day. Through Jean and Marcou Ballard, her friends who worked for the *Cahiers du Sud* in Marseille and who entertained or gave refuge to numerous writers and members of the Resistance, she also got to know the greatest names in French literature of the period. That is how she knew Malraux so well and became a close friend of Éluard and Aragon, neither of whom had been able to renew their links with the clandestine Party, because of the Draconian security measures in force. She also got to know Lacan very well. He confided in her endlessly as they strolled late into the night along the promenade des Anglais in Nice where he lived with Sylvia. On one occasion Lacan made the following remark, later confirmed by my own analyst who was unaware of Lacan's opinion: 'You would have made an exceptional analyst!' Due no doubt to the fact that she was extraordinarily good at 'listening' and had astonishing insights.

But in 1945 not a single one of these relationships with friends and lovers was still intact. In due course I will explain why. So when I met her she was utterly destitute and was surviving by selling a few original editions of works by Malraux, Aragon, and Éluard. She was living in a squalid attic room on the top floor of a hotel on the place Saint-Sulpice.

It was there that she invited me to visit her after our meeting at the Lesèvres. One thing is certain, if she had not called me, nothing would have happened between us. I drank her tea and she said something about my jacket (I was still wearing it) which had made such an impression on her. She even made a few passing remarks about my face and forehead which she found 'handsome'. We went out into the square and sat on a bench. As she was about to leave, she stood up and with her right hand softly stroked my fair hair without saying a word. But I understood only too well. I was overcome by feelings of terror and repulsion. I could not bear the smell of her skin which I found disgusting.

It was she who called me from time to time. Lesèvre and I then went off on our travels in central Europe. I was still courting Angéline and Nicole was still in love with me, though I was not at all in love with her. I went on a university trip to Rome to meet the Pope, organised by Father Charles whose deliberate and popularity-seeking vulgarity appalled me. He was chaplain at the École and I got him thrown out on the basis of certain irrefutable arguments I presented. He is now in Montmartre and has probably never forgiven me for what I did – that is if he still remembers it, being a person who quickly forgets things, not wishing to learn what a dishonest priest *he is*. I was still a believer at the time. I wrote two articles about that trip for some daily paper or other. It was not long after Italy had suffered enormous destruction. Our train slowly crossed endless wooden bridges, suspended in mid-air at a dizzying height, which shook as we went over them. After reaching Rome in the dark, we recited the Creed together. The visit was impressive and extremely moving. We were received by the Pope (Pius XII) in a group, but he had a word or two for each of us, asking questions in the most improbable French. He asked me if I was at the École normale – yes – and whether I was doing arts or science – arts. Well, be a good Christian, a good teacher – and, above all (above all!) a good citizen! That 'above all' summed up Pius XII. Then he gave me his blessing. I realise I have not exactly lived up to his expectations.

It was in February 1947 that the first great drama began to develop. I was still courting Angéline and since I had taken the initiative in this affair, I felt I had the advantage. I still saw Hélène from time to time, but she had taken the initiative, rather than me, which was something of a problem. Then I had not just the idea of introducing Angéline to Hélène but an irresistible urge to do so. It would not be the last time I behaved so provocatively or got into similar difficulties. But I was then very far from suspecting the real motivation for my preposterous idea: the irresistible desire to win Hélène's approval of the person I had fallen in love with, not her as it happened but someone else.

I invited them to tea in my little room in the sick-bay. I was nearly thirty, Hélène was thirty-eight, and Angéline was twenty. I do not recall what was said, but I remember clearly that we ended up talking about Sophocles. Angéline defended some view or other concerning high tragedy, which was doubtless very scholarly, but I had no views at all and just listened. Gradually, Hélène began to criticise Angéline's arguments, at first putting forward serious points quite dispassionately, but as Angéline countered them, Hélène's face and voice began to change. She became more and more severe and intransigent, brusque even, and ended up by creating a sort of 'scene' which was hurtful and affected Angéline deeply, causing her to burst into tears. (It was the first such scene but not the last, unfortunately, which I was to witness.) I was terrified by Hélène's violent outburst which I did not understand (why had Angéline challenged her perfectly reasonable arguments?) and in the face of which I was helpless. Angéline left and I remained silent. I realised Hélène could stand neither the girl nor the scenario I had forced her to take part in, or rather the provocation to which I had subjected her. It was clear too that my relationship with Angéline was at an end, shattered. I never saw her again. Hélène had thus entered my life in an eruption of violence, but not against me.

The 'drama' began to gather pace a few days later when Hélène kissed me while sitting beside me on the bed, still in my little room in the sick-bay. I had never kissed a woman (though I was thirty!), and certainly never been kissed by one. Desire welled up within me and we made love on the bed. It was new, thrilling, exhilarating, and violent. When she left, I was plunged into a profound state of anguish from which I could not escape.

I telephoned Hélène the next day to tell her very firmly I would never make love with her again. But it was too late. The sense of anguish would not go away, indeed it got more unbearable with each passing day. I need hardly say it was not my Christian principles which were at stake. It was something wholly different! A far more violent and deep-seated feeling of repulsion gripped me, which was much more powerful than my own will and my attempts to regain my moral and religious principles. The days passed and I began to sink into a state of intense depression. I had gone through difficult periods before, as for example when my patrol was at Allos, when I was a prisoner, or when I was in Casablanca. But they were wholly different and had barely lasted a few days, a few hours even, and then everything had been all right. I tried to cling on as best I could and to rely on my friend Dr Étienne; but things became impossible and every day I sank a little deeper into a terrifying void, unable to do anything about it. Rapidly, my state of anguish ceased to have any specific cause. It was what specialists refer to, I believe, as 'neurotic as opposed to objective anxiety'.

Hélène was very worried and advised me to consult a specialist. We made an appointment with Pierre Mâle, the great psychiatrist and analyst of his day, who questioned me for a long time and came to the conclusion I was suffering from 'dementia praecox'(!).

As a result, he immediately gave orders for me to be admitted to Saint-Anne's Hospital.

I was put in Esquirol ward, a huge communal ward, and immediately cut off from the outside world as I was strictly forbidden to have any visitors, and that included Hélène. I stayed there several months and I have never forgotten the appalling experience. I was in the care of a woman psychiatrist. She was doubtless affected by the fact that I was young, by what I had gone through, and also perhaps because I was a philosopher and an intellectual. She was ready to believe I loved her, certain that she loved me and would 'save' me through her love. Naturally, she thought it was Hélène's fault that I was ill (she was the first but not the last to think this). I do not know what I was prescribed, but my condition deteriorated markedly. Thanks to Hélène's ingenuity, I had found a way of communicating with her. A minute window in the toilets on the first floor looked out on to the external world. I do not know how she managed it, but Hélène often appeared beneath this window around one o'clock, though she had not visited me once in the ward. Thus I managed to communicate with her from a distance without too much difficulty. My feeling was that the people in the hospital did not understand me, whereas she thought they were going about things the wrong way (especially the woman psychiatrist with her terrible 'love') and that I had to break the vicious circle in which I was permanently caught (dementia praecox!). We agreed she should try to contact Julian Ajuriaguerra, whom I had met on one occasion when he came to talk at the École at the invitation of Georges Gusdorf. It was extremely difficult, and still is, for another doctor to be accepted by the hospital staff and certainly to intervene, especially as he was still a Spanish immigrant. I do not know how he managed it, but he turned up one day in the huge communal ward. I followed him into an office and was able to discuss things with him. He concluded I was not suffering from dementia praecox but from profound melancholia. He recommended shock treatment, which had only recently been introduced but which was proving successful in such cases. The psychiatrist agreed to this. I suffered approximately twenty-four shocks, one every two days, in the huge communal ward. A thick-set man with a moustache would appear carrying a large electrical box. On account of an uncanny and striking resemblance, including even his walk and mockingly silent air, he was nicknamed 'Stalin' by the patients. He calmly set up his equipment on each bed (at least thirty of us received shock treatment) and began turning the handle in front of all the rest who were awaiting their fate. The patient immediately suffered alarming convulsions. But what made it particularly dramatic was that we could see Stalin approaching from some way off. One after the other, his victims displayed convulsive and uncoordinated movements, yet he would move on to the next without waiting for the previous patient to recover. There was a risk of breaking a bone (especially in the legs), and you had to bite on a towel so that you would not damage your tongue; in my case it was always the same filthy old towel. For years afterwards I still had the vile and terrifying taste of that unspeakably awful, shapeless towel in my mouth, which heralded 'a little death'. I watched what happened to those near me, and then it was my turn. Stalin approached, still without saying a word, and put the band over my head. I clenched my teeth and prepared to die. I felt a sort of flash and then nothing more. I woke up shortly afterwards, always wondering where I was and what had happened to me (to my great despair, I only slept for a couple of minutes though I longed to lose myself in sleep, whereas almost all the others slept for hours on end, even for half a day!). The longer it went on, the more my fear (of dying) increased. In the end, it became unbearable. I tried to refuse the ceremonial execution as forcefully as I could, but they strapped me firmly to the bed.

I would like to mention one little incident, which says a great deal about the atmosphere in the hospital, the way they saw the inmates, and the total failure of the psychiatrists to believe anything a patient said. As I could not sleep at all and had no ear-plugs, I decided to make myself some out of breadcrumbs, which was all that was available. But small balls of bread pushed into the ears immediately started to go bad (obviously, they are not held by the strong, flexible cotton wrapping used in real ear-plugs) and sticky crumbs went down the auditory passage right to the ear-drum. The disintegration of the balls caused me unspeakable agony, unbearable headaches, and pains in the throat. I kept mentioning this to the doctors, but they would not believe me, thinking I was delirious. *For three weeks, I repeat, three whole weeks* they refused to let me be examined by an ear, nose, and throat specialist. I suffered agonies. Here again, Ajuria* had to intervene to convince them, and after three weeks of terrible suffering I was finally taken to an ear, nose, and throat specialist who took only a second or two to get the bits of bread out, and the pain was gone. I received not one word of regret or apology from the psychiatrists!

All things considered, the treatment recommended by Ajuria slowly did me good, and after another long period without shock treatment and several months after going into Esquirol ward, I felt better. Though I was still shaky, I was less anxious and I left hospital. Hélène was waiting for me at the gate. I was overjoyed!

She took me to a tiny little room in another hotel where a wretched chamber-maid had stolen all her things, but that did not matter. For her the theft hardly counted beside me – and what she had done for me. I only discovered this much later, not from her as she said not a word about it, but from one of her friends. The consequence of our one sexual encounter was that Hélène had become pregnant and then gone to England to have an abortion so that I would not suffer renewed depression, since I had already expressed such intense horror at having physically made love to her. Would anyone else have made such a sacrifice? Even now I am overwhelmed with emotion both physically and mentally. [So] there was Vera, her oldest living friend. She was very tall, dark-haired, and beautiful and she came from a family of Russian aristocrats. Hélène made light not only of the theft but of everything else as well and was more welcoming than ever. I felt immense affection for her as I took her in my arms, convinced that, had it not been for her, I would have stayed in hospital, perhaps for ever.

Hélène, together with Jacques Martin (whom I was beginning to get to know), found a convalescent home for me at Combloux which took in students who were tired or convalescing. The peace and the splendour of the mountains, which I have loved since my scouting days, and the thoughtfulness of the Assathianys were just what I needed. They were the couple who ran the home, and they did so with much enthusiasm, tact, and extreme devotion, while at the same time allowing everyone the greatest freedom. I was

* The diminutive of Ajuriaguerra (Editors' note).

also surprised to meet a marvellous, unknown group of Hungarian musicians, called the Vegh Quartet, who were resting, as well as young men and women of my own age. We indulged in all sorts of pastimes, including amorous ones. I very quickly spotted a small, dark-haired girl called Simone (that name again). She was good-looking (though she did not quite have the profile I liked) and seemed a most interesting person. I pursued her in a violently provocative manner and called her Léonie. Nothing serious happened, but we were very close during the three weeks I was there and became friends for life, until the day only six months ago, in October 1984, when she went out of my life, leaving the following message: 'You certainly know how to use your friends, but you have no respect for them.' She had indeed 'hit the nail on the head'.

I left Combloux fully recovered and went to stay at a youth hostel near Saint-Rémy-de-Provence, where Hélène was to join me. She still had no money and had to hitch-hike to get there. One driver tried to rape her (as an adolescent, near Chevreuse, when she was looking after her dying father, she had been attacked by four young louts who had made their intentions only too clear. She had managed to see them off by swinging her handbag round and round on the end of its long strap like a windmill, but whenever she spoke of this incident she did so with the same terror in her voice. As I listened, I secretly thought that, unlike her, I could not have conceived of putting up a fight because deep down I was a coward). But there she was. She loved me and I loved her too and was immensely proud of her. Spring was in the air, in the countryside, in the woods and vineyards, and in our hearts, and we were going to make love upstairs in a farmhouse nearby, where they gave us milk, bread, butter, and olives (I was not in the least bit fearful, on the contrary!). The farmers complained about the noise we made during our love-making. I have to admit I went at it with a will, displaying the same kind of violence and passion as my father. My reason for recalling all these details is that, one day, the youth hostel was suddenly filled with a group of young people, boys and girls, who looked scruffy but were extremely cheerful and amusing (until then we had had it to ourselves). We got to know each other, and I even prepared an extraordinary fish soup one day which Hélène talked about long afterwards. I never liked classic recipes, preferring what I call 'culinary experimentation', which enabled me to be extraordinarily inventive. Compared with what I did, classic dishes or even those created by the greatest chefs lacked imagination. 'By chance' I had singled out a dark-haired girl in the group with the celebrated profile, and she seemed to enjoy my advances as we walked to a quiet lake where we swam side by side in silence (I still have some photos). It was pretty incredible all the same! For months I had been in the most hellish depression I had ever experienced, and Hélène had rescued me; we were together again, elated by love and springtime; I made love to her freely and without anxiety, yet all it needed was for a couple of girls to turn up, like Simone (when I was without Hélène at Combloux) and Suzanne, when we were together at Saint-Rémy, for me openly to make advances in front of Hélène to some casual acquaintance I hardly knew, but who clearly aroused something deep inside me. It was partly the girls themselves, but beyond them a particular image of a girl, and beyond that the irrepressible desire to experience with them something which was lacking in my relationship with Hélène (though in neither case was it fulfilled). What was it? The same situation was to be repeated throughout my life. I recently discovered that intense sexual excitement is one of the major symptoms of hypomania, which *can* follow any depression. At the time I was incapable of grasping any underlying reasons. Naturally, my amorous antics did not escape Hélène's notice and she was hurt by them. Yet she made not the slightest complaints nor did she display any of the violence she had done with Angéline. Did I thus have her approval? It is clear that is what I sought.

Suzanne soon departed with her friends and we spent several genuinely happy, carefree, and exhilarating months in the Midi. I arranged to take Hélène to the village of Puyloubier, which I had good reasons for wanting to get to know and love, as it was the birthplace of my friend Paul's marvellous fiancée and wife. A unique spot, it was at the foot of mont Saint-Victoire, which had the appearance of a gigantic flower, its rocky form constantly alive and changing colour, and it overlooked the great plain of Flers with its jagged backdrop of the mont Sainte-Baume. In the distance you could also see the spires of the abbey of Saint-Maximin. A little way out of the village, we came across a couple of retired minor civil servants who agreed to put us up for next to nothing. When we got up in the morning, exhausted by our nights of passionate love-making, we went down to the terrace as the sun was rising and Mme Delpit brought us a typical Provençal breakfast: coffee, milk, goats' cheese, raw artichokes, honey, cream, and black olives. How delicious it all was and how happy we were in the bright sunshine of those peaceful May mornings.

On one occasion, some time later, when Hélène was expecting me at the Delpits, I took the train from Paris as far as Cavaillon, having put my racing bike in the guard's van. When I got there, I jumped on my bike and, in a state of great excitement (unlike my bicycle ride at Bandol), set off to find the love of my life who was still forty kilometres away. She was waiting for me on the little dirt track which led to the village, having seen me coming some way off. I was exhausted, but this time I did not cry, except perhaps with joy. At last I had my revenge on my mother! I was a man.

I was truly proud of the fact. However, Hélène was still as poor as ever. When, with my help, she found a tiny attic room belonging to a well-known geography professor at the Sorbonne, Jean Dresch, high up in a fine old building in what had been the Val-de-Grâce, I used to visit her at all hours of the day and night, especially the night, and would leave very early in the morning, around four o'clock. How cheerful and proud I was listening to the sound of my footsteps echoing down the deserted rue Saint-Jacques. My body was light and exultant and the whole world looked beautiful as the first rays of the sun caressed the walls of the École. I walked slowly in. All the students were still asleep. Never in their lives or in their hearts had they known a love like mine! I would not have changed my supreme good fortune, my treasure, my love, my joy, for anything in the world.

I have to say my pride was justified. It is possible, probable, that my friends had relationships with women which they had carefully sought or effortlessly found among their student acquaintances. (Men and women from the Écoles normales quite often went out together and then got married. They kept things in the family, within their own university world; the world I hated at least as much as Hélène did, but her reasons for hating it were more justified than mine, given that she had always been an outsider.) I enjoyed the unrivalled privilege of loving (and being loved) by a woman who was quite outstanding! It was of no importance that she was quite a bit older than me – the difference in our ages was not an issue for us – but rather that she had a clear mind, a generous nature, great courage, and had such vast and varied experience of the world. She knew the most important painters and writers of her day and had been active in the Resistance to the extent of being given important military responsibilities (even though she was a woman, she behaved like a man, as Lesèvre himself recognised). She played an exceptionally heroic role, displaying exemplary and astonishing courage for a frizzy-haired little Jewess, whose Jewish nose was recognisable at a hundred yards. She had foiled a number of attempts to capture her, including one in a train from Lyon to Paris when she was recognised as a Jew and arrested by the Gestapo who were checking papers. She had enough on her to warrant her immediate execution and was only saved by her coolness and the fact that she was bold enough to stand up to the Nazi officer whom she left stammering. She told this story as if it were something quite straightforward and with the same calmness she had displayed at the time. In short, she was an exceptional woman (at least that was my feeling about her, and one which was shared by all her comrades in the Resistance; by Lesèvre and others who had been in *khâgne* in Lyon with whom she had worked, and by *all* those who subsequently got to know her during our long life together). She was infinitely superior to me and did me an enormous favour by introducing me to a world I did not know. I expected nothing of her and did not even ask what she thought of me. Hers was a world I had only dreamt of in the isolation of the prisoner-of-war camp, a world of solidarity and of struggle, a world of reasoned action based on high fraternal principles, a world of courage. I felt so impoverished and cowardly, retreating in the face of all physical danger for fear of getting hurt. I had never fought anyone, nor could I ever have done so, on account of my hopeless cowardice. But she used to say to me: 'If you had not been taken prisoner, you would have joined the Resistance, and you would almost certainly have been killed, executed like so many others. Thank God that being in prison meant you were saved for me!' I shuddered at the thought of the mortal danger I had escaped, certain in the knowledge I would never have had the strength or the courage to face the physical and life-threatening risks of clandestine armed struggle. I had never fired a single shot and had been terribly frightened by military weapons since childhood. My immediate reaction was to run when confronted by the slightest danger, but she introduced me to a whole other world and had confidence in me! And suddenly, thanks to her, I was not only the equal of all the fighters she had known, but also infinitely superior to the other poor students at the École whose youthfulness and knowledge had overwhelmed me and who had made me feel incredibly old, so old in fact that I seemed to be denied any sense of youthfulness – I who had enjoyed no youth. Now I felt younger than anyone had ever done before – and I went on feeling young, imagining myself to be younger than my analyst, for example, though he was my exact contemporary. Even the other day or last week a woman doctor of thirty asked me quite straightforwardly for my date of birth and was surprised when I told her it was October 16th, 1918. That cannot be right, she said, you must mean 1938! You must mean 1938! It is true, I did look young thanks to my beloved Hélène.

Subjectively, I was convinced of my own youthfulness – it had after all been recognised – and, gradually, I began to understand the reasons for this. If at last I was young at heart, felt so young, it was because Hélène was for me a good mother and also a good father. She was older than me, had acquired a totally different experience of life, yet she loved me as a mother loves a child, her miraculous child, and at the same time like a good father in that she introduced me, quite simply, to the real world, that vast arena I had never been able to enter (except on false pretences, except when I was a prisoner). Through her desire for me she also initiated me, pathetic creature that I was, into my role as a man, into my virility. She loved me as a woman loves a man! We truly made love like a man and a woman, whereas my friends had not reached maturity and were still – I was convinced – fumbling around in their pathetic love affairs with their fellow students. After so much suffering and as if to prove I truly loved her, I had come to like her womanly smell, whereas previously I could not bear it, just as I had been unable to bear my mother's smell. Not only had I become a man, I was a changed man, capable of really loving someone, a woman even, and the one whose smell I had at first found disgusting!

Someone who had recently become a friend and had been in Germany on compulsory labour service, not from political conviction – he favoured the communists – but out of intellectual curiosity, was Jacques Martin; he understood me, understood us both. He was a homosexual and though warm-hearted was an unhappy and somewhat distant person due to his latent schizophrenia; he none the less became a valued friend. I could ask him anything, unlike my fellow students at the École to whom I was ashamed to reveal my ignorance (I genuinely believed I knew nothing, had never known anything, or had forgotten what I had learnt). Martin responded to me like the real brother I had never had. His parents had literally abandoned him, leaving him to fend for himself. His father, a chemist, was a terrifying man who never opened his mouth in his son's presence, but his mother, who had been dead a long time, had left him a little money. I do not know how he managed to live on it. Michel Foucault was as friendly towards him as I was and, like me, often gave him sums of money. There came a time, however, when he had no money left and little hope of getting any (his sister, whom he was very fond of but who took little interest in him, lived some way away in Melun, where she too was a chemist, I believe). He ended up by committing suicide during the summer of 1964 in the wretched room he rented from an old lady in the Sixteenth District. He died alone one appalling August day. I was in Italy at the time, caught up in the excitement of a new love affair which I will talk about later. For a long time I felt utterly ashamed and reproached myself for having failed him at the crucial moment by not giving him enough money just to survive. I must admit I had little money and spent it mainly on Hélène. What is more, I still had a terrible obsession with saving which prevented me from giving much away. But I had given Jacques a lot of money. All I could say when his sister asked if I had lent him money (in fact I had given him nearly three hundred thousand old francs, more than Foucault) was: no, nothing. But what a pathetic response that was, when I think that I might have saved his life! Anyhow, it was the only money I never regretted having spent even though I got nothing for it. With Jacques Martin's death, suicide became part of our lives and there was no way we could ever alter that fact. Sadly, it was something that stayed in my memory.

Jacques Martin not only helped me, and helped us both, with his trusting and uncompromising affection, he also helped me to find someone in the profession whose 'skill' might be of use to me. This may seem strange today, but at the time, students like me, who were impoverished and not well-informed, though we might have heard of psychoanalysis, did not know a single analyst whom we could contact nor how to find one. One day Jacques found out from a mutual friend who had attempted suicide several times (yet another suicide, albeit unsuccessful) about the existence of a therapist who did analysis 'under hypnosis'. He was a decent, likeable man, with a pot-belly and a slightly rustic air, who agreed to treat Martin and took me on as well. For twelve years, I repeat twelve years, I was 'treated' by him, which meant that he gave me supportive therapy. In our eyes he had a great deal of prestige (he ended up treating the whole family, my mother, my sister, and many other close friends) since he told us he was personally acquainted with certain Soviet doctors, though this remained something of a mystery. They sent him phials of 'Bogomolev's serum' which were supposed to work wonders 'in almost all cases'. For instance, my sister, who had married a solid young working-class Parisian, was able to have the baby she had longed for. Though her husband expressed himself mostly in slang and had an undoubtedly crude streak, he was completely frank and honest in a 'common' sort of way. My father, of course, could not stand him. I was in love with a Jewess and my sister had married a working-class man whom my father considered 'vulgar' or very ordinary. His wishes had received the two-fingered salute. He retaliated by refusing to meet either Hélène or Yves. My instinctive response was to postpone my decision to marry Hélène until *a year after my father's death* (a paltry posthumous consolation for him), and my sister ended up getting a divorce, though she kept her ex-husband's name, Boddaert. Like my mother, she too did not wish to be known by the name of Althusser. She obtained a legal separation from her husband and settled in the Midi, after a lot of psychological problems which I helped her with as best I could – that is, with a mixture of devotion and ignorance. We lived twenty kilometres apart, but constantly visited and telephoned each other. Thanks to the doctor (?) I mentioned, she had a son called François whom she lives for and who really loves her, though from afar. (He lives in Argenteuil, where he obtained the post of deputy town-clerk on account of his abilities and serious-mindedness.)

I was so overwhelmed by Hélène's love for me, by the wonderful privilege of knowing her, of loving her, and of sharing my life with her that I tried my hardest to return that love, as a sort of *offering*, as I had done with my mother. It was impossible for me to see my mother as anything other than a martyr to my father, like an open, living wound. I have already mentioned how I always took her part, at the risk of openly confronting my father and driving him out. It could be said that the risk was imaginary since my anger never resulted in violence, unlike young Lemaître in the Bois de Boulogne in Algeria. I only ever flouted his authority within the tacitly accepted bounds of family conventions, even though I did so constantly and with some force. Yet I never stormed out (as in the prisoner-of-war camp I never summoned up the courage to leave the family, to escape this circle of Hell, as my dearest friend did; it would have meant abandoning my mother to her terrible ordeal). He was the one who took off! Until he returned, I, at least, and possibly all of us, were plunged into a state of unbearable anguish. That is why I always flew to my mother's aid, or at least wished to do so, as one might have come to the aid of a real martyr. I rushed to do the washing-up, which I felt was the worst form of torture for her (why was this?) and, strange as it may seem, though perhaps understandably, I very quickly came to take an intense and perverse delight in doing it. I was the only one who swept up, made the beds, did the cooking, which I also tried to spare her, laid and cleared the table. They were visible and obvious acts of reproach addressed to my father, who was unashamedly lazy – my sister did not give a damn. Thus it was that I became a truly domesticated individual, like a pale and slender girl (my screen-image in the park). I felt at the time that I was certainly lacking something as far as virility was concerned. I was not a boy and definitely not a man; more of a housewife. I behaved in a similar way with Hélène, but the situation was quite different!

I knew her when she was in the depths of despair and in the

most appalling destitution. 'Appalling' was a word she frequently used and went on using right up to her death. The word still makes me shudder when I hear another friend of mine using it obsessively. It is true that Hélène's own life was appalling. She had lost everything, her close and distant friends who had been executed during the war, the unfaithful Renoir, as well as Hénaff and Father Larue, the one man she loved before she met me. In the end she had lost all contact with the Party. One could scarcely say she was housed, living as she did in 'appalling' attic rooms in tough and dubious surroundings. She had no job and therefore no money and had to make what she could by selling her few precious books and typing the essays of other students at the École for next to nothing (after doing mine). I got her this work, though I felt a little ashamed at doing so. Did I offer her any help? I certainly tried to help her all I could, but in the beginning I only received twenty francs' 'scholarship' myself from the École; that is until Maurice Caveing and I obtained a salary for ourselves and all the other students via the illegal union we had set up. I did not dare ask my father for a penny, since I was very anxious to conceal from him my 'needs' and what sort of woman I loved and was consorting with. Since she was Jewish, he would have been bound to see her as someone who was after money. Were not all Jews like this? In addition, I was terribly afraid of being without money, without savings, as I have already pointed out. You can imagine therefore how I accounted for every penny I spent, even though I wished to show how generous I was. I still remember the day I bought a little metal wood-burning stove so that Hélène would not feel too cold in her maid's room in the Val-de-Grâce. It was so poorly made it was dangerous and scarcely gave out any heat. That was my supreme gesture of devotion and of generosity, and how pathetic it was. It is true I had no money or made out I had none so that the sums I gave would appear more generous.

Perhaps everything turned on this; at any rate it was what I subsequently came to think. Here are my reasons.

I have said I felt incapable of loving, that I could not respond to others and to the love they so generously showed me. This was true of the women I knew and even of my men friends. It seems that my mother's impersonal love, directed not towards me but through me to someone who was dead, made it impossible for me to exist in my own right or in relation to another person, especially if that other person was a woman. I felt powerless or impotent in the full sense of the word; I was incapable of love, but first and foremost I felt impotent in myself, physically. It was as if I had been deprived of my physical and psychological being. If a part of you is removed, thus permanently denying you your wholeness as a person, you can legitimately refer to it as a form of amputation, of castration therefore.

And while I am on the subject, I would like to return to the extraordinarily powerful phantasy I had when I was released from the prisoner-of-war camp and went home to my parents in Morocco. I was convinced I had contracted a sexually transmitted disease and, as a result, would never really be able to use my sexual organs. In the same 'train' of associations and memories (and I have a very precise memory in this case), I recall being extremely anxious about an apparently common phenomenon, the Latin name of which is *phimosis*, which literally poisoned my life during the years we were in Algiers and Marseille (Latin enables one to refer to a number of immodest things . . .). I spent a lot of time pulling my foreskin without being able to uncover my glans. I had what are referred to as 'discharges', from under my foreskin, which from then on kept worrying me. I thought there was something seriously wrong with my penis, making it impossible for me to have a full erection and to ejaculate, even though I was not ill. I endlessly pulled at my foreskin, which was painful and achieved nothing. One day my mother informed my father and locked us both in the lavatory. For a whole hour, in total darkness (we left the light off for the sake of decency or perhaps from fear), my father tried in vain to release my foreskin. Naturally, not a word was spoken! My problem persisted for years and I became totally convinced that, in this respect at least, I was simply not normal. It was as if I was missing something, which meant I did not have a proper man's penis, and never would; or perhaps something had been removed (by whom?). My mother, of course. You will recall, she had literally 'interfered with me'.

Why have I dwelt on this example? Because it is symbolic and is not confined to my own specific case, but concerns everyone. How does one define the ability to love? An individual must have a sense of wholeness as a being and of his 'potency', though not merely for the sake of pleasure or from an excess of narcissism. On the contrary, he must be capable of giving fully, positively, and without weakness. In the same way, to be loved is to be capable of being seen and accepted as a free agent in one's giving, so that the gift is 'transmitted', or finds its way, to the other and elicits in response another act of giving from deep within. Being loved is precisely the free exchange of the gift of love. But if one is to be the free 'subject' and 'object' of this exchange, one must, as it were, be able to initiate it. One has to begin by giving wholeheartedly, if one wishes to receive a similar or even greater love in return (this exchange is quite the opposite of a utilitarian calculation). Obviously one needs to be an entirely free agent if one is to do this, with one's physical and spiritual integrity undamaged. To put it bluntly, one must not have been 'castrated' but be in full possession of one's potency (think of Spinoza); nothing must have been cut away, otherwise one is doomed to some form of hollow and illusory compensation.

But I had been castrated by my mother, ten if not twenty times, a victim of that same compulsion of hers, the vain attempt to control her own fear of castration, of being robbed (having her possessions or her savings cut away), or raped (having her own body torn open). Yes, I was castrated by her, especially when she claimed to make me a gift of my own sexuality, an appalling gesture which I experienced as rape on her part, as the theft or violation of my own sexuality. By 'interfering with me' she acted against my deepest wishes, against my desire to keep my sexual organs *for myself* and no one else, and especially not for her, which was the ultimate obscenity. As a consequence, I felt incapable of love because I had been *intruded upon, violated* in the most intense area of my life. How could you even claim to love when the most intimate area of your life, your deepest desires, your innermost being, had been intruded upon? Those were the feelings I always had with Hélène as a result of my mother's attack upon my privacy. I felt like a man (a man? that is putting it too strongly) who was incapable of the least expression of genuine love towards her, and because of her towards anyone else. I was turned in upon myself and what I have described as my lack of sensitivity. My lack of sensitivity? In fact it was my mother's insensitivity which astonished me in Morocco when she refused to go to the aid of her dying mother on the pretext that she had a stomach bug or something of the kind. So, when my grandmother suffered a fatal heart attack, it was I who went to the church in the Morvan very early one cold morning to receive her body. My lack of sensitivity? Again it was my mother's insensitivity, silently expressed, which impelled me not to visit Simone but to set off on my bicycle for La Ciotat in a rage. My lack of sensitivity? Again, it was hers I witnessed when, without a trace of emotion, she coolly kissed my dead father's forehead, made a simple sign of the cross as she knelt down, and then got up and left the room. My lack of sensitivity? Again it was hers when my friends Paul and Many, the only ones who knew her, went to see her in her isolated little house at Viroflay to tell her, after a great deal of careful thought, that Hélène was dead and that I had killed her. She simply took them round the garden, without saying a word and as if nothing had happened, her mind clearly on other things. Sadly, I know only too well what they were. My lack of sensitivity? Hers, when, having overcome all her phobias once she was on her own and had given up the name Mme Althusser to revert to her maiden name of Berger, she pounced on the special chocolates I took her without the slightest worry about the amoebic dysentery or her other stomach complaints! Goodness knows, perhaps I am being too hard on her! She was upright, she hid nothing, she displayed no violence towards anyone, she was warm (to the few friends she had), she clearly loved us to the best of her ability, and she alone had to think of 'good' ways of giving us a good upbring-ing (music, concerts, the classical theatre, the scouts). The poor woman did what she could for what she considered to be our happiness as well as her own, nothing more, nothing less. Though she thought she was doing right, in following the example set by her quietly fearful mother and anxious father in the wild and isolated forests of Algeria, she in fact contributed to my unhap-piness.

It is not surprising that I came to acquire the same awful feeling of insensitivity, the feeling that I too was incapable of truly loving another person; nor is it surprising that I projected all this on to Hélène, another unhappy soul whose suffering was visible and who also seemed (to me) like a martyr, an open wound. It was my, our, destiny to have fulfilled my mother's desires to such an extent that I was never (up to the present day) capable of 'refashioning' myself in order that I might offer Hélène by way of love something other than the artifice, the frightful caricature I inherited from my mother. I certainly loved Hélène with all my heart. I felt exhilarated and proud, wholeheartedly devoted to her, yet how could I free myself, a prisoner of the solitude to which I seemed doomed, doubtless not without lapses and secret reservations? How could I respond to her anguish when she said to me in bed and elsewhere: say something to me! which meant *give* me what I need so that I can rid myself of the terrible anguish of being permanently alone and a frightful shrew who cannot possibly find a love to equal mine?

No one in the world can respond to that cry of anguish: say something to me! when what is meant is *give me everything*, let me for once feel that I exist! so that I can stifle the anguish of not really existing in your eyes, as part of your life; the anguish of merely being a passing whim, of being inadequate to the task of permanently restoring your wholeness of being so that you can love! I myself knew only too well, as did Hélène, what remained unspoken behind this pathetic appeal: Hélène's extravagant fear that she was a wicked woman, a *frightful* mother, and a vicious shrew who hurt the one who loved her or who sought to love her. Her powerlessness to love was matched by her fierce, obstinate, and violent refusal to be loved because she did not merit it, because basically she was just a horrid little animal, all claws and prickles, full of anger and courage. To all appearances, which are so readily accepted (because it is so much easier!), we were a sado-masochistic couple, incapable of breaking the vicious circle of our own dramatic anger, hatred, and mutual destructiveness.

This explains our 'appalling' marital 'scenes' which horrified or disgusted our friends (depending on their nature) when they witnessed them with a feeling of helplessness. Like my father, Hélène would storm out and slam the door, her face as white as a sheet or a block of marble. I would run after her, suffering terrible pangs of anguish at being abandoned by her often for days on end and often without my having done anything at all. What, for example, had I done when I took her by plane to Portugal after the peaceful revolution? She had a hysterical outburst in a restaurant where we had been taken by some Portuguese friends because the streets of Lisbon were *too steep*. So I had to take her to a quiet spot up in the lofty castle and wait for her to calm down. Similarly, what had I done in Grenada when, for no apparent reason, she refused a friend's offer to take us to the Alcazar? We did not need him! She made a terrible 'scene'. Again, what had I done in Greece when she refused – and did so in advance – the hospitality of a wonderful meal of welcome which was traditionally offered by petit-bourgeois families? Doubtless I had not really done anything in these situations, but sadly I have to acknowledge that, too often, I upset her and provoked her by probing too much in order to discover whether or not she was really in agreement.

The same thing was true of my 'entanglements with women'. I always felt the need to have various 'women in reserve' alongside Hélène and to seek her explicit approval of my involvement. Doubtless I 'needed' these women as erotic extras, to supply what poor Hélène herself could not give me: a youthful body which had not suffered and that profile which I endlessly dreamt of finding. These were things I needed to satisfy my flawed desire, proof that I was capable of physical desire for an ordinary, desirable woman alongside a father-mother figure. But, until recently, I could never embark on anything without her explicit approval.

Thus, unconsciously, I realised a form of 'synthesis', a supreme achievement. I fell in love with women who were to my liking but who lived sufficiently far away and therefore posed no ultimate threat. One lived in Switzerland (Claire) and the other in Italy (Franca), therefore at a distance which I had not consciously contrived but which meant I saw them only intermittently (if I was with them for more than three days I regularly, in other words unconsciously, became bored and fed up, though both Claire and Franca were exceptionally beautiful and fine women). The geographical precautions I had taken did not, however, exempt me from the customary ceremonies of approbation and protection. When I met Franca, in August 1974, I at once invited Hélène to meet her on the fifteenth. They got on very well, but a few months later there were several painful episodes in which I was torn between Hélène and Franca. There were also numerous telegrams and telephone calls between Panarea (a Sicilian island) and Paris, Bertinori and Paris, Venice and Paris, which only led to more deceitful and provocative acts on my part and a worsening of the situation.

But things came to a head when my 'women friends' broached the subject, either directly or indirectly, of my living with them and having a child. The matter was raised by Claire when we were on a bank beside a road in the forest of Rambouillet. She spoke of the little 'Julien' we both wanted so much and suggested living with me – so she too had 'designs on me'. I fell immediately into a state of depression. It was even worse in the case of thirty-six-year-old Franca, a magnificent Italian lady, who had despaired of ever loving anyone again. She turned up in Paris one day on the pretext of following a course given by Lévi-Strauss, whom she had translated in her own country, and telephoned me to say she had arrived and that I was free to do what I liked with her. She even came to see me at my place, which she thought was awful, and got in by climbing through the window. It was all too clear. I immediately became ill and was extremely depressed. She also had had 'designs' on me.

My successive depressions were not all caused by the same thing. They were, however, strange depressions, in that once I had been taken into hospital I calmed down almost immediately, as if the maternal protection of the hospital, isolation, and the 'overwhelming' nature of my depression were sufficient to satisfy my desire not to be abandoned against my wishes and to be protected from everything. I might even describe them as fortunate depressions, since they sheltered me from the outside world and gave me ultimate security as I did not have to fight, even against my own desire. It had no effect at all when my analysts kept repeating they were neurotic, atypical, and 'bogus depressions'. As they usually only lasted a very short time (a fortnight to three weeks), and as they miraculously ceased once I was put in hospital, despite the awful anticipation of them occurring (which was worse and lasted longer than the depression itself), I was not greatly troubled by them. My work and my plans were scarcely affected, and I often came out of hospital in a hypomanic state which made everything seem extremely easy and appeared to resolve all my own difficulties and those of others as well. I did considerably more work and easily caught up with the supposed backlog. They simply became part of my somewhat turbulent life.

My analyst, whom I consulted on a regular basis, enlightened me about one aspect of my depressions that I had obviously not suspected myself. He told me that depression made one all-powerful. Strictly speaking, that is unquestionably true. One withdraws from the world and 'takes refuge' in illness, away from all immediate and active concerns; one is protected within the white walls of one's hospital bedroom, where attentive nurses and a doctor give you maternal care (the very marked regression which accompanies all depression turns you into a little child; though, far from being abandoned, you give way to the deep, reassuring feeling that you will never again be abandoned). You submit to the comic fetishism of drug treatment which in fact only *shortens* the process of getting out of depression, as you are aware, and which makes you feel calm and enables you to sleep. Without doing anything or having to give something in return, everyone is at your beck and call: doctors, nurses, those who love and visit you. With nothing to fear from the outside world, you are all-powerful like a child with various loving mothers. You can imagine how much this theoretical explanation appealed to someone like me who felt impotent, that he did not really exist (other than through artifice and deceit). Now I discovered I wielded the sort of power I had only ever dreamt of. It was not difficult to move from that position to one where I believed I only ever fell ill and wanted to go into hospital in those circumstances (I literally begged to be allowed to go in). This is indeed true. But when would I be able to enjoy this all-powerful role in real life? In fact the possibility arose when I was in an excited, hypomanic state immediately after a depression (though it did not always occur, it did so more and more frequently). I went very rapidly from a state of depression to one of hypomania, which sometimes took the form of extremely violent and real mania. In that state I truly felt all-powerful, in the face of the outside world, my friends, my plans, my own problems and those of others. Everything seemed and was incredibly easy. I soared above all difficulties, my own and those of others, and set about solving other people's problems, sometimes with success, even though they had not asked me to. I rushed into things which they considered extremely dangerous (both for me and for them) and which frightened them. But I was unconcerned by their objections and took no notice of them, totally convinced that I was master of the situation, of every situation, and on one occasion at least almost on a world scale, and why should I not have been? I remember one awful remark I made around 1967 that unfortunately I have never been able to forget: 'We are in the process of becoming hegemonic . . .'. Everyone will be aware there was a huge element of aggression which came out in that incredible facility and pretentiousness of mine, or was released rather in the excitement, a symptom of the phantasy of my impotence and therefore of my depression. It was in fact a defence mechanism turned against my depression and the phantasies concerning my impotence which fed that depression. How true Freud had been, as had Spinoza, in claiming that ambivalence was prevalent in all cases. It was certainly true so far as I was concerned. My fear of being totally impotent and my desire to be all-powerful, my megalomania, were two aspects of the same phenomenon: the desire to possess *what I lacked which would make me a man*, at once whole and free, and which I was terrified I did not have. I was haunted alternately by the same dual phantasy (hence its ambivalence) in the unreal nature of my all-powerfulness when I was depressed and in the megalomaniac all-powerfulness of the manic state.

Furthermore, if I examine the conscious 'themes' of my depressions, I can classify them under three headings (I suffered at least fifteen depressions from 1947 to 1980, all of them short, except the first and the last, and none of them had any 'professional' consequences, far from it. I would like to thank those in charge at the École who were very understanding and never made me take sick leave as, after each depression, I worked twenty times harder). The first heading relates to my fear of being abandoned (by Hélène, my analyst, or one of my male or female friends); the second to my fear of being asked for love which felt like a threat that I might be 'the victim of someone's advances' or, more broadly, that someone might have 'designs on me', clearly not my designs. I will return to this. Thirdly, I feared being revealed to the world at large for what I really was, a worthless person who only existed through artifice and deceit. I was afraid I would be roundly condemned and that to my shame this would become public knowledge.

I think everyone will have realised why my fear of being abandoned provoked such anguish that I became depressed. To the fear of being abandoned by my mother was added the old fear caused by my father's disappearances at night, reactivated when Hélène stormed out violently, which was something I could not bear. To me they were like death threats (and you know how active my involvement was with death). This 'over determination' left me in a state of terror, unable to do anything. I simply had to abandon myself to my 'fate', succumb to my desires, live out my true destiny, cease to exist, disappear from the world, in short, go into hospital, but with the perverse idea at the back of my mind that I was taking refuge in illness where there was no further risk of being abandoned by anyone. Since it was publicly and officially acknowledged I was ill, I tyrannically demanded and obtained everyone's attention. I repeated this pattern of behaviour, in a most extreme form, in the final phases of my most serious and lengthy depression in Sainte-Anne's Hospital and especially at Soisy. I shall return to this.

XII

I also experienced extreme anguish and repulsion at the idea (and in situations which made me think) that someone wanted to 'get their hands on me'. What I feared above all was scheming women. Clearly, there were obvious associations with the traumas, the attacks, the violations even, involving my mother, whose aggressive behaviour carried with it the threat of castration. If a woman offered to live with me (which implied, therefore, that Hélène might abandon me, though I did not feel she ever would have done such a thing), I became terrified and sank into depression. This may surprise a number of my friends, but *I never felt that Hélène meant to get her hands on me like a castrating mother-figure.* It was, on the other hand, the impression I always had when my 'extra-marital' friends exceeded the limits I imposed (by taking advantage of situations or choosing them unconsciously). By their behaviour they risked depriving me of Hélène, by forcing her to abandon me (something I realise only too clearly now). I did everything I could to protect myself against such a crazy and dangerous threat. Obviously, I fiercely resisted any such offer which felt like 'an unbearable assault upon my person' (by immediately falling ill). As a precaution, I even resorted on occasion to insane remarks and ripostes (actually it is what I always did in one form or another). For example, I once replied to a young woman who wrote declaring her love, which I had been aware of for some time: 'I detest being loved!', which was completely untrue but which signified: I detest anyone taking *the initiative* in this respect, 'getting their hands on me'. I found it unacceptable that anyone should take such an initiative, which was mine alone to take and no one else's. I am referring of course to myself personally as an individual and not as a philosopher – in relation to my mad desire to love, of which I felt, knew even, I was incapable.

In a violent exchange (on my part) with my analyst, I one day referred to a more general variant of this refusal of mine to accept any initiative from a woman as a feeling of repugnance towards anyone who had 'views about me'. In this case I referred not only to women but also to men as well, and above all to him, my analyst. I did not properly realise at the time that he represented the 'ideal mother figure', a woman, indeed the most important woman of all. I must make clear that I never felt Hélène had 'views about me', since she was so ready to accept me as I was, respecting my own desires. Desire is, in fact, the fundamental issue here, as it was in my previous remarks. I had been so much under the influence of my mother's desire, to the extent that I felt it could only be fulfilled in opposition to my own. Thus I finally began to claim the right to my own desire in order not to have to put up with someone else, whoever it might be, imposing his desire and his 'views' about me as if they were mine (even though I was incapable of realising that desire, indeed experienced only the lack of it; the feeling it had been amputated, was dead). Having broadened the issue to this extent, I would add that my claim (albeit impossible) to fulfil my own desire was at the heart of my fiercely independent line both as a philosopher and in the Party and also explains my independent attitude towards my closest friends, despite the fact that I was very good at getting them to agree with me, in other words to bend their opinions towards my own. This trait or 'shortcoming' did not, I think, escape them, and I often made them suffer dearly for it. It may even partly explain the reaction of the friend whose remark I have already quoted: 'You know how to use your friends, but you have no respect for them.' It is certainly true that I have benefited positively from this independence (I now see its negative origins), which helped shape the 'personality' I have. It is yet another example of my ambivalent nature, and must have been the cause of other depressions.

However, my most vivid phantasy fear – the fear of the impossible phantasy situation where I was expected to appear all-powerful though I was nothing of the kind – is the third 'factor' which caused several of my depressions and, in particular, the dramatic one which occurred in the autumn of 1965. I was in a state of euphoria, having just published *Pour Marx* and *Lire 'Le Capital'* in October. But then I became obsessed with the terrifying thought that these texts would expose me completely to the public at large as I really was, namely a trickster and a deceiver and nothing more, a philosopher who knew almost nothing about the history of philosophy or about Marx (though I had certainly made a close study of his early work, I had only seriously studied Book 1 of *Capital* in 1964 when I took a seminar which resulted in *Lire 'Le Capital'*). As a 'philosopher', I felt I had become part of some arbitrary construction, which was totally remote from Marx himself. Raymond Aron, who had praise heaped upon him even by the Trotskyists when he died, was not altogether wrong in referring to 'imaginary Marxism' both in my case and that of Sartre but, as always, he totally failed to understand the significance of what he was saying – when he actually had something important to say – though I have no comment to make about his other work. In short, what I feared was a catastrophic, public refutation of my position. Because I was afraid of such a catastrophe (or wanted it to happen, since fear and desire go insidiously hand in hand), I precipitated this catastrophe by 'having' a spectacular depression. It was serious enough as far as I was concerned, though my analyst was not deceived.

I had known my analyst for some little time and would now like to say something about him. People would find it strange were I to remain silent about the decisive role he played in my life, if only because, even at the professional level and among a number of his friends and mine, he was the object of severe criticism after Hélène's death. It even seems that a petition criticising his 'methods', signed by several 'heterodox' practitioners, some belonging to his own school, was sent to *Le Monde*. Thanks to the intervention of a former student of mine, Dominique Dhombres, it was not printed. 'They' can buy him a few drinks now (or when he gets back from Moscow)!

I was advised to consult him by Nicole, who became a dear friend though she had so many phobias I was paralysed by them. I began to suspect that the treatment I was receiving from my first therapist, though very supportive, was not genuine analysis and was having no real analytic effect. He was a generous man who helped me at moments of difficulty and was always prepared to give me advice and the medication I needed for my condition and to get me into psychiatric hospitals or clinics (Epinay, Meudon, etc.). I wrote out my dreams for him or revealed them under hypnosis, which I greatly enjoyed, and he commented on them at length, pointing out the 'positive elements' as well as the 'negative' ones. I understood some things, but he intervened at least once in my personal life when I was in hospital, telling Franca, who had sought his opinion: 'What occurred between you two wasn't serious, it was just a holiday romance.' And on another occasion when I was in hospital at La Vallée-aux-Loups (a former residence of Chateaubriand) and being looked after by an old lady, one of the two daughters of Plekhanov, I made a serious attempt on my life with a horrible long knife. This was because my therapist had delayed getting me the shock treatment which I had been violently clamouring for as I was in an indescribably distressed state. So, Nicole advised me to see a proper analyst, 'someone sufficiently broad shouldered to take you on'. I remember her exact words, probably not by chance. After all, I might have thought of my friend Paul who really did have broad-enough shoulders to do battle on my behalf.

I saw my analyst several times before the summer of 1965 and he finally agreed to take me on for regular sessions of 'analysis', *but face to face*. He subsequently explained on several occasions that I was so burdened with anxiety that he felt I could not have coped with the couch, and the even greater anxiety of not being able to see him, not to mention his silence. In fact, looking at him, seeing all his facial expressions and listening to his often immediate if not direct response to my questions, I was certainly reassured. He was there, in front of me, *visibly* attentive and that was particularly reassuring. At the same time, I discovered (and observed) that face-to-face analysis is much more difficult for the analyst than one conducted with the patient lying on a couch, since he has to control his facial expressions especially when silent. He cannot simply breathe quietly, comfortably installed behind the patient, and take refuge in his pipe and armchair or by riffling through his diary.

When my books appeared in October, I had such an attack of panic that I talked only of trying to destroy them (but how?) and then finally of destroying myself, the radical and ultimate solution. This was the terrible situation with which my analyst was confronted. I have often thought since of so many analysts who do not intervene at all in such situations, out of respect for the so-called 'letter' of the analytical law, and who refuse to act as psychiatrists or doctors and thereby to give their patient the narcissistic satisfaction of helping him (not only to find a clinic but even a psychiatrist). The simple explanation is that they do not want anyone, either within or outside the profession, to blame them for not intervening should the patient kill himself. A very dear friend of mine who was undergoing analysis committed suicide in 1982 without his analyst apparently having intervened to provide the least 'support' (I say apparently because I may be ill-informed, though I know of other cases which cannot be disputed, and from Lacan himself). My analyst saw me every day in 1965 and right to the end, keeping me 'at arm's length' (he told me later he too must have been slightly 'hypomanic', thinking he could get me over my difficulties). Faced with my repeated threats of suicide, he finally gave in to my pressure and agreed to have me taken into hospital. He specified: 'A hospital I know well, at Soisy, where we use our own methods.' He even indicated that he would take me there himself (to be quite sure, I suppose). He came to collect me at the École in his car and I can still see my old friend Dr Étienne rushing to the gate so that he could talk to this old chap at some length. My analyst seemed to listen to him but said very little. I have always thought, and certain clues make me think I was right, that Dr Étienne gave him his personal interpretation of the situation: that it was Hélène's fault I was ill. This facile, comforting version of events was later to be 'rumoured' more widely, though *very little* among my closest friends. There was a good reason for this. They *actually* knew Hélène, and they also knew (though only a small number of them) that we were not the classic 'sado-masochistic' couple, which was often such a fatal combination.

I was admitted to the splendid modern hospital at Soisy, its buildings dotted around a huge park. I made a great deal of fuss in an attempt to get a sleep cure, believing it would work wonders (yet another Soviet myth). My wishes were partially satisfied as I was made to sleep a little during the day. I quickly calmed down (which surprised me) and was fully restored and discharged after a month. Subsequently, I nearly always subjected my analyst to the same pressure, as I could not bear him ignoring me in my state of anxiety. Thus he found himself caught up in something which already had a long history and, even though he eventually left the decision entirely to me as to whether or not I should go into hospital, it was always through him that the decision was made, at least *which* hospital I should enter; whether to go to Soisy or to Vésinet, which was run by friends of his, and where he could 'follow my progress' through them. Each Sunday morning my analyst would arrive at Vésinet in his car. I was astounded by his devotion, and all the more so when I learnt after my first period in hospital, that he charged me the same for this special visit, involving a long car journey, as he did for my normal sessions (just recall how important money matters were to me – and to analysts!). My father still gave me no help, though he could easily have done so at the time, and I did not ask him for any. On each occasion I was overwhelmed to the point of tears as I greeted my analyst, like a little child with its mother.

Later still, towards 1974–75, things became complicated. Hélène, whose emotional troubles were now obvious, agreed to begin analysis with a woman. She visited her once a week for about a year and a half for face-to-face analysis and then abruptly gave it up following an incident, of which I only heard her version. Her analyst had alluded to a classic Freudian theme (relating to face-to-face analysis) and Hélène's response was that she knew nothing about it (in actual fact she had no theoretical knowledge of analysis). To which her analyst retorted: 'That's impossible, *you're lying!*' (Hélène's general knowledge was such that her analyst legitimately assumed she knew the term, but 'knowingly' refused to acknowledge it, if I might put it that way.)

As you can imagine, Hélène was distraught at being abandoned in this terrible fashion, and I was even more distraught. I urged my analyst, with suicidal insistence, to find a solution. He then agreed to have a face-to-face therapy session with her once a week (which is what I was really hoping for). That is how he came to 'assume responsibility', so to speak, for the two of us at the same time, something extremely rare in the profession though not without precedent (Lacan frequently adopted the same approach). After Hélène's death, grave suspicions were voiced both in the profession and by a number of our friends concerning his conduct.

One of them even referred to a 'circle of Hell', an 'eternal triangle', a 'total impasse' which could only lead to tragedy. It is true my analyst always said I was an 'atypical' case, similarly Hélène and the two of us together (but isn't every case?), and that an atypical case demanded an atypical solution. Though it did not strictly conform to classic norms, it was not entirely ruled out, as long as one knew what one was doing, strategically and tactically, in relation to the 'case'.

I always had the feeling afterwards that I pressured my analyst so much by blackmailing him with the threat of abandoning analysis or committing suicide, that once he became involved with me in 1965, he was reluctantly forced to keep it going while waiting for the relationship to become sufficiently relaxed for him to extricate both himself and me. But that depended on the way my therapy evolved, therefore in the final analysis on me. And this is exactly what happened. The strategy adopted by my analyst was proved right in the event.

Several times when I was in a hypomanic state after a depression, I had the feeling my analyst had been successful. In these miraculous circumstances I even invented a metaphor representing the end of analysis. Analysis is like a heavy lorry full of fine sand. Slowly, the hydraulic system raises the back so that it will empty. At first nothing falls out, then gradually a few grains, and finally the whole load slides to the ground in one go. The metaphor is too neat, reflects too obviously what I wanted to happen. I had to learn the hard way that it was not like that. I told my analyst with absolute conviction and total gratitude: 'This time, you've done it!' And each time I recall his silence, not of tacit agreement but full of vague foreboding he could not disguise, despite his best endeavours to avoid 'counter-transference'. I even remember a gesture of his which disgusted me at the end of one these sessions when I was to be 'liberated'. As I was leaving in a state of total euphoria, the last thing I remember seeing through the half-open door was him waving his hand up and down, as if to say: go easy, and then repeating this gesture several times. I was disgusted and had a violent set-to with him. 'Either you think I've got into a hypomanic state for unconscious reasons I can't control, and if so how do you expect me to control them, and what right have you to advise me to take care when you know I can't? Or you believe

I am capable of controlling myself and thus everything depends on me, in which case your gesture seems pointless. Finally, what right have you to suggest how I should behave since your intervention is "against all the rules of analysis" in my "case" as in any other?' Strictly speaking, I was in the right. I never asked him for his opinion on this issue, which I found so hurtful. Doubtless I was wrong.

During the great phase of violent arguments with my analyst, which lasted several months around 1976–77, I roundly and vigorously condemned him for always having 'views about me' and not treating me simply as an ordinary person, but rather as someone well-known, which I was, and with too much consideration. I reproached him for having confessed my books were 'the only works of philosophy he understood', for being friendly towards me, and letting me know he liked me, both of which were analytically suspect. In essence, I reproached him because he could not control his own *counter-transference in my case* and I wrote a supposedly theoretical piece about counter-transference (for his benefit) which I sent him. I developed a fairly cogent argument to the effect that it was not transference but counter-transference which came into play from the outset. He read it and then coolly pointed out this had been known for a long time. I was terribly hurt and this added to my feeling of animosity towards him. But I did not think I could be the source of the complicity I felt existed between us, nor did I think I had either wanted it, caused it, or brought it about as part of some gigantic attempt to seduce him. At the time I did not realise I had done everything in my power to seduce men and women alike and have them at my mercy, by continuous provocation. Had my analyst really given in or was it simply the impression I had? I cannot say, but I am revealing all my weapons, or rather my pitiful weaknesses, along with the memories of my most vivid traumas.

Seduction and provocation; the two naturally went together. With the women I met during these hypomanic states, I was immediately and irresistibly seductive and successful. After ten minutes to half an hour of good-humoured advances, the thing was in the bag. Each time I wanted something, I took the initiative, as for example when I held Hélène's hand, though the consequences were terribly embarrassing and the fear that I had put myself in an awkward position or let myself be trapped in one filled me with anxiety.

Of course I compensated for these rash and crazy advances and the anxiety they caused by 'going over the top', by investing emotionally in the situation and convincing myself I was really and madly in love. Thus I created an image of the woman I had met that was powerful enough to sustain my excessive passion. Until very recently, which I will come to, I have always sought to live out my actual relationships with women at an exaggeratedly intense and passionate level. It was my own personal way, albeit a rather strange one, of feeling I was 'in control' of the situation, or rather in supreme control of a situation that was in fact beyond my control and, given the way I was 'made', would remain beyond my effective control. I should have accepted the women I fancied just as they were and myself as well, without any 'exaggeration', a word I got from a woman who became extremely dear to me and who was the first to see my failings and to tell me what they were to my face without the slightest hesitation: 'The one thing I don't like about you is that you want to destroy yourself.'

Certainly, exaggeration and excess both involve provocation. You cannot talk to a woman as if you were madly and passionately in love without unconsciously wanting her to measure up to this love in her being, her gestures, her feelings, and her sexual behaviour. Yet I was divided. On the one hand I looked forward to great confessions of love and tenderness from the women I was pursuing; on the other, I was terribly afraid of their anticipated show of affection. I feared I would be at their mercy, having lost the initiative, and paled at the awful thought of falling into their clutches.

Things followed a similar course with Hélène yet they were also different. I was never afraid she would get her hands on me or that she had 'views about me'. We shared a sense of communion, of kinship which averted any such danger. And though I constantly provoked her, I think I made her realise my provocations were of a different order. I always wanted her to meet my new women friends as soon as possible so that she would give me her approval like the good mother I never had. But Hélène never felt in the least like a good mother and thought of herself rather as a frightful person and a shrew. You can imagine her reaction. At first she was patient and thoughtful, then gradually she turned critical and in the end suddenly became dogmatic and abrupt (and since initially she had been patient and tolerant I did not understand what was happening). It was not so much that she was jealous (she wanted me to be 'free' and was, I believe, deeply sincere, respecting my every wish and need, and even my quirky ways). But once that initial tolerance had vanished, she became so obviously obsessed with her terrible phantasy of being a shrew that she succumbed to my unbelievable provocation and behaved in accordance with her innermost fears. It was yet another example of ambivalence. Afterwards, she would reproach herself bitterly and tell me constantly I could do as I wished, but on one condition: that *I did not talk to her* about my love affairs. But I seemed incapable of following this obvious and sensible advice which she calmly and rationally offered. Every time I felt compelled to go to rub her nose in it. We owned a very beautiful house at Gordes, an old farmhouse we bought for next to nothing, which we restored to the original splendour, and which surpassed everything in the area. I arranged for my most recent women friends to visit it, in order, as always, to gain Hélène's approval. Only once did things turn out really well, and that was with the one woman friend who understood me.

My compulsion to provoke Hélène was obviously more pronounced in my hypomanic states. As everything seemed and indeed was so superficially easy, I dreamt up other ways of being provocative besides these perverse introductions. Hélène suffered dreadfully, having come to realise from experience that my hypomanic states boded ill. She knew I would plunge back into a depressed state with all its attendant suffering both for me and for her. What is more, she felt personally and directly threatened by my incredible behaviour (I now realise she was right). I had a devilish imagination. On one occasion I spent a whole month in Brittany systematically engaging in a new sport: shoplifting, which I naturally found very easy. Each time I proudly showed her my varied and increasing spoils and described in detail my infallible methods. Indeed, they were. At the same time I chased after girls on the beach and from time to time, having quickly got round them, I took them home for her to admire and approve. It was also during this period that I had the idea of committing the perfect bank robbery and of stealing an atomic submarine (which again I considered foolproof). You can understand how terrified she was, knowing that I was quite likely to do something but not how far I might go. Because of me, she was insecure and in a state of total panic. Just imagine what it must have been like!

On two occasions I put her through even more appalling suffering. The first was serious but clearly unlikely to come to anything.

We were dining one evening with some friends, together with a couple we had not met before. I do not know what came over me (or rather I know only too well), but I started to make advances and all sorts of declarations and provocative suggestions to the beautiful young woman I did not know. At a certain point I suddenly proposed we could and should make love there and then on the table in front of the others. My advances had been such that this seemed the obvious conclusion. Mercifully, the young woman defended herself admirably and skilfully evaded my suggestion.

On another occasion we were staying in the house of some friends in Saint-Tropez while they were away. I had invited a political friend of mine to visit us. He came with a very attractive young woman, whom I immediately went after. I gave my friend a manuscript of mine to read. During a meal, in front of Hélène and the friend, the same scene took place all over again. Obviously nothing happened on the table, but I did take the girl aside and started to stroke her breasts, her stomach, and her fanny. Though slightly startled, she let me do it, because of what I had said. Then I suggested we go to a little beach which was normally deserted and which was totally deserted on that particular day because the Mistral was blowing strongly and the sea was rough. Meanwhile, my friend was back at the house reading my manuscript. When we were on the beach, and in front of Hélène who could not swim, I asked the young woman to get undressed and then the two of us went into the raging sea in the nude. Hélène was already screaming with fear. We swam out a little and almost made love in the water. I saw Hélène completely panic-stricken running along the beach shouting. We went further out into the waves but as we turned to come back we realised we were caught in a strong current which was carrying us even further out. It took a couple of hours of incredible effort before we got back to the shore. This young woman saved my life as she was a better swimmer than me and helped me when I was floundering. When we reached the beach, Hélène had disappeared. The nearest houses were several kilometres away across rugged hills and the only lifeboat was a long way off at Saint-Tropez. Had Hélène, in desperation, gone to seek help? After hunting far and wide, I found her at the water's edge but some distance from the beach. She was unrecognisable, completely hunched up and trembling with hysteria, her face ravaged like that of an old woman and bathed in tears. I tried to take her in my arms and comfort her, to tell her the nightmare was over and I was safe. It was to no avail; she neither saw nor listened to me. Finally, after goodness knows how long, she spoke and told me in violent terms to go away: 'You're vile! It's finished between us! I never want to see you again! I can't bear living with you any longer! You're a coward and a bastard, a bastard, just bugger off!' I signalled to the young woman to leave and I never saw her again. It took a good two hours before Hélène finally agreed to come back to the house with me, still crying and shaking. We did not mention this horrible incident again, though deep down she almost certainly never forgave me. One thing is certain, it was no way to treat another human being. I came to realise that what she really feared was not my drowning in the waves but something much worse: that she would die on the spot because of my horrible and insanely provocative behaviour.

The fact is: for the first time my own death and hers were fused. They were *one and the same death* – the cause might be different but the end product would be the same.

I cannot tell you how much I was struck by Hélène's face the first time I saw it and how it haunts me still. She had a strange beauty. She was not exactly beautiful, but her features had such intensity, such depth and life; they could change in a flash from an expression of complete openness to one suggesting she had totally closed in upon herself, that I was both dazzled and disconcerted. A friend who knew her well told me he came to understand her when he read a line of Trakl's: '*Schmerz versteinert die Schwelle* (Pain petrifies the threshold)', adding that in Hélène's case it ought to read: '*Schmerz versteinert das Gesicht* (Pain petrifies her face).' Her whole face and the hollows of her cheeks were marked and lined by the endless pain of being alive, by her long and terrible 'negative struggle', as well as the personal and class battles in which she had engaged in the labour movement and the Resistance. All her friends were dead, including Hénaff whom she had been fond of, Timbaud, Michels, Father Larue whom she had truly loved; all of them executed by the Nazis. As a result, her face bore the marks of death and despair. Her own appalling past had become petrified. She was what she had been, '*Wesen ist was gewesen ist*: Essence is what has been' (Hegel). When this same friend quotes Trakl and Hegel, it is her I see; that poor little face with its look of self-absorbed suffering which would suddenly radiate joy, in what her friends called her 'genius for admiration' (a remark made by her philosopher friend Émilie who was executed by the NKVD in Siberia). No one could match her enthusiasm where other people were concerned and her generosity knew no bounds, especially towards children, who adored her. 'The genius for admiration' was a phrase of Balzac's, who remarked: '*The genius for admiration, for understanding is something which makes an ordinary man the equal of a great poet.*' Through her ability to listen, her understanding of the human heart, and her genius for understanding she was indeed the equal of the greatest who lived, and God knows she was loved by many of them as a friend!

Yet that face which revealed such openness would harden into a mask of intense pain, as her suffering welled up from the depths of her being. It looked like a block of mute, white stone, featureless, expressionless, and dull-eyed. Time and time again, those who did not really know her cruelly considered her to be as awful as she feared she was, judging her on the basis of a few superficial characteristics. After a while, sometimes a minute or two, often a few hours and even a day or two (which was awful but infrequent), her face once more began to radiate joy. It was a dreadful ordeal for her and for those close to her and especially for me, suddenly seeing myself abandoned. For a long time I had feelings of guilt over her dramatic change of expression and tone of voice, as my mother doubtless did at having betrayed Louis, the love of her life, when she married Charles.

Hélène's voice always sounded as she looked: incredibly warm and pleasant, always deep and varied like a man's, and even when she was silent she seemed receptive (Lacan realised she was a better listener than most); but then suddenly it became hard, uncommunicative, muffled, and in the end fell totally silent. Apart from her fear of being a terrible shrew, what was it that brought that physical look of horror to her face? I have never exactly understood the deep-seated reason for the terrifying, dramatic, yet dazzling transformation which took place. Doubtless it, too, was caused by feelings of extreme anguish that she did not exist, that she was already dead and buried beneath a great sepulchral slab of incomprehension.

When she was 'open', she was extremely funny. She had an extraordinary talent for telling stories, and the softness of her laugh was irresistible. She was equally celebrated among her friends for her prodigious talent as a letter-writer. I have never read such lively letters, which were as unpredictable as the course of a new-born river on its rocky bed. Her style was daringly inventive, and when I later came to read Joyce, whom she greatly enjoyed, I felt her language was infinitely more inventive than his! Naturally, no one will believe me. But those to whom she continued to write [knew it to be true], like her friend Véra, currently in Cambridge, who said this to me recently on the phone.

But what moved me more than anything were her hands, which never changed. They had been fashioned by work and bore the marks of hard physical labour, yet her touch had a wonderful tenderness which betrayed her heartbreak and helplessness. They were the hands of a poor, wretched old woman who had nothing and no one to turn to, yet who found it in her heart to go on giving. I was filled with such sorrow at the suffering engraved on them. I have often wept into these hands and they have often made me weep, though I never told her why. I feared it would cause her pain.

Hélène, my Hélène . . .

XIII*

I know you are waiting for me to talk about philosophy, politics, my position within the Party, and my books, how they were received; to reveal those who liked them and those who were implacably opposed to them. But I do not intend to discuss these totally objective matters in a systematic manner because the information is available to anyone who does not have it already, just by reading what I have written (a vast number of books published in many different countries). You can however rest assured that I only ever trot out the same old themes which can be counted on the fingers of one hand.

However, what I do owe the reader, because I owe it to myself, is a clarification of the subjective roots of my specific attachments: my job as Professor of Philosophy at the École normale supérieure, philosophy itself, politics, the Party, my books, and the impact they had. What I really want to discuss therefore is how I came to invest and inscribe my objective, public activities with my subjective phantasies (this is not a matter of lucid reflection but something obscure and largely unconscious).

I will, of course, go straight to the *essentials* and steer clear of the sort of anecdotes and personal observations which seem to be expected in current autobiographical writing (a sign of unprecedented literary decadence).

The first fact or sign is that I never left the École. It is true, I entered six years later than anticipated, but I only left on November 16th, 1980. Since then, I have never been back, not even for a passing visit.

* The author included five pages at the start of this chapter, which were probably typed after the main body of the text, but had failed to make the whole thing cohere. As a consequence, there were several repetitions or variants of the same incidents and the chapter as a whole did not read very well. For this reason, we decided to keep to the original version (Editors' note).

I obtained my diploma, having written a thesis for Bachelard on Hegel's notion of content, using the false quotation, 'One content is better than two', whose author I did not know, and also the following: 'The concept is necessary since it is freedom', which was an idea of René Clair who was talking about 'work' rather than the concept, though, if one believes Hegel's 'work of the negative', it amounts *strictly to the same thing*. I adopted a very precious style in writing it (which I had acquired when I was in *khâgne* in Lyon and copied in particular from my 'seniors', Georges Parain, Xavier de Christen, and Serge Chambrillon, all of them royalists – followers of the Comte de Paris rather than the frightful Maurras – and refined writers who adored Giraudoux, and whose tastes I shared at the time). I wrote my thesis at Larochemillay, where I was welcomed by my grandmother after my long depression in 1947. Though I had not warned her in advance, I took Hélène with me and she spent her time at the 'old house' typing the pages of my text as I wrote them.* My grandmother gave her a warm welcome, as I had expected. She was fully aware of the nature of our relationship and accepted it as a matter of course, in spite of her principles. How generous she was!

I do not think Bachelard read my thesis as he was very busy. One of the major themes I discussed was the 'circularity of content.' He simply objected that it might have been better to use the term 'circulation' instead, but I disagreed. That was all he said. Our lecturers at the École at that time were Desanti, a little Corsican, who was '(already) battling on', a phrase of his which was very apt, and Maurice Merleau-Ponty. The latter, whose courses we followed with interest (the only course I followed, apart from the rather repetitive classes given by Desanti, who remained a very Husserlian Marxist), suggested that Jacques Martin, Jean Deprun, and I should publish our theses, before he had even read them. We all refused rather haughtily. I came second in the *agrégation* in 1948, having taken Spinoza's use of the Latin word *solum* to mean the sun! Deprun came first, which he richly

---

* The author added the following comment in the margin without linking it to the text: 'with a dish of grilled potatoes beside her which she had cooked herself: meaning she was not invited to dine at my grandmother's table' (Editors' note).

deserved after his failure the previous year; a punishment for the absolute effrontery of speaking without notes at his oral.

I should point out that in both the written and oral exams I knew very little about most of the topics I dealt with. But I did know how to 'construct' an essay and suitably disguise my ignorance by arguing *a priori* whatever the subject. I also structured my arguments the way one should in a good university essay, suspending theoretical judgement where appropriate, as had been instilled into me by Jean Guitton.

'Old Mother Poré' was just an ordinary secretary at the École, but she had kept it going throughout the tough war years and even under Albert Pauphilet after the Liberation. She practically ran the whole establishment single-handed, and I had got into her good books (my love of older women as well as my seductive charms). Everyone, including that totally idle, negligent Parisian, Pauphilet, got something from her. She knew everything and everybody. You must believe me when I say she liked me because, when Georges Gusdorf left in July 1948, she suggested to the Director that I take his place, and he, quite naturally, went along with this.

That is how I came to take over Gusdorf's rather cramped quarters (a small room with a mock-Louis XV desk on the ground floor) as well as his functions. I got rid of the Louis XV desk and replaced it with a fine, old, grey oak table from the library. The duties of a philosophy tutor [*caïman*] were somewhat ill-defined. We had to 'look after the philosophers', though Gusdorf paid very little attention to us. He had produced his thesis (*La Découverte de soi*, based on a study of private diaries while he was a prisoner, which he simply read out to us instead of giving us lectures! One day we sent him a letter supposedly from the Director of the Palais de la Découverte which said: 'Nothing connected with discovery is foreign to us . . .'). He continued to polish up his thesis in the hope of obtaining a university post, which he did in Strasbourg. I tried to improve on what he had done, which was not difficult. First, I gave a course on Plato, which kept me busy for two years, then I moved on to other writers. Above all I got my students, who quickly became friends, to do rhetorical exercises, which were invaluable. Merleau had told us that, fundamentally, the *agrégation* was 'an exercise in communication' based on a minimum of required knowledge. Thanks to Guitton, I had been convinced of this for a long time. But I took the message to heart and instituted a rather personal way of correcting students' essays. I wrote very little in the margin, other than to correct obvious mistakes and to put a long line without comment indicating approval or a + showing I liked what I had read. However, I typed out one, two, or more pages of comments, depending on how much I had to say, drawing attention to the good points in the student's essay and above all suggesting how *he could and should have constructed it so as to make his argument (whatever it was) as forceful as possible.* I never told anyone to adopt a line of thought which was not his own and to have done otherwise would have been folly. This was a principle of mine which I always stuck to out of simple respect for the individuality of each student. On this basis I never tried to instil anything into anyone, contrary to the idiocies put around by a few journalists looking for a 'scoop'.

In my early years at the École I took a warm and maternal interest in my protégés, nurturing and watching over them, to the extent of organising a rest period at Royaumont which I shared with them, between the written and oral exams for the *agrégation*. Subsequently, I became a little more reserved, though I still took an interest when they were having problems and in helping them to shape their own thought processes.

I rapidly became Secretary of the École, attending all the meetings concerned with the running of the place, advising the directors on numerous issues, often 'getting' them to take important decisions which are still visible in the bricks and mortar of the building and in a number of organisational practices. I played an especially important role in the interval between directors. This was only to be expected as I was there permanently, whereas directors died or gave up their post (Hyppolite, for example, moved on to the Collège de France).

What did the École mean to me? Very quickly, in fact from the outset, it was really a 'womblike' place, where I felt warm and at home and was protected from the outside world. I had no reason to leave it in order to meet people as they dropped by or came to see me, especially when I became well-known. In essence it had a maternal ambiance, was like an *amniotic* fluid.

Then one fine day Gusdorf's cramped flat was turned over to

architects who had been given the green light by the ministry (after an improbable delay, though I never discovered whose initiative it was). They began to enlarge it, adding a huge reading room for the students. I felt very comfortable there and was ready to welcome Hélène. She moved in with me because she was living in a new flat near Montparnasse and could not bear the howling of two puppies left alone all day while their master was at work. She had been unable to get him to do anything about it for the sake of his neighbours. (This gives one [some idea] of the vigilance of caretakers and the police for whom such things were a routine matter . . . .) Again I 'saved' Hélène. This was around 1970, before we were married.

And so life went on. The doctor and the sick-bay were close at hand, the services of the École were available (the plumber, the carpenter, the electrician, and so on), as was the library (which I scarcely ever visited much to the surprise of Mlle Kretzoïet and M. and Mme Boulez, the discreet parents of the composer), the refectory which some days I went to, the rooms of the philosophy students, and of Jacques Derrida and Bernard Pautrat when they were appointed as colleagues. There was also a post office nearby and a tobacconist, in fact everything I needed, within easy reach. It lasted for thirty-two years! Thirty-two years of ascetic and semi-monastic seclusion (my dream of long ago . . .) and protection. When Hélène came to live with me, it certainly complicated my female relationships, but I had her there as well beside me.

The huge task I set myself, as an act of 'oblation' (still that same task of saving a bleeding mother-figure), was to get her accepted by my friends, most of them my former students. It was not at all easy. The age gap between them, her intense dislike of the university world, not to mention her prickly nature, which soon became well-known, did not help. Often I was successful but at the cost of what felt like great self-denial; and always with an uneasy feeling, as if it was entirely up to me to overcome for both of us the fear of her sudden changes of mood. Here again I have now come to realise (actually I have realised for some time) that I must have in some way 'induced' in my friends the very judgement I feared they would make about her (as I had done in Dr Étienne's case). By anticipating their possible reaction, I behaved somehow 'guiltily', seeking in advance their forgiveness of the two of us. And I was able actually to observe the harmful effects of my attitude. Hélène had her failings, but when one really got to know her, as Lesèvre and all her famous friends had done in the past, when one got beyond first impressions which were often a product of her reputation, one discovered an exceptionally intelligent, intuitive, courageous, and generous woman. All the people she worked with, who appreciated her as a person and recognised her true worth, were unanimous in their support of that view. Yet the greatest friends she made through work she made herself, without any help from me. For once she owed nothing to me and I did not have to intervene to 'save' her from the awful fate of being a frightful woman.

You can see the terrible contradiction in which I became embroiled on my own account as a result of my compulsions and fearful phantasies. I say embroiled on my own account because, in attempting to 'save' her (she had practically no other male friend), I *gave* her my friends. But I could do this only by inducing and reinforcing in them the image I feared they had of her, but which I in fact carried within me as a kind of curse. It 'worked' on a few rare occasions, albeit sometimes with major hiccups, and then only with former students of mine, such as Étienne Balibar, Pierre Macherey, Régis Debray, Robert Linhart and Dominique Lecourt, and also Franca, when she could engage in a real exchange of ideas and experiences, or when it simply involved a calm and creative emotional relationship. With others it was often a disaster, which I dwelt on privately and with a sense of guilt and shame. One of the most important undertakings of my life with Hélène thus resulted in painful misunderstanding which I constantly, though vainly, strove to repair. My successive failures reinforced my prejudice and fear which not surprisingly reinforced my doubts about my real manhood and my capacity to love a woman and be of help to her in her life.

Anyway, I carried out my duties as a philosophy teacher and felt more and more that I was a philosopher, despite all my misgivings.

In fact my philosophical knowledge of texts was rather limited. I was very familiar with Descartes and Malebranche, knew a little Spinoza, nothing about Aristotle, the Sophists and the Stoics, quite a lot about Plato and Pascal, nothing about Kant, a bit about Hegel, and finally a few passages of Marx which I had studied closely. My way of picking up and then really getting to know philosophy was legendary: I used to enjoy saying it was all done by 'hearsay' (the first confused form of knowledge according to Spinoza). I learnt from Jacques Martin, who was cleverer than me, by gleaning certain phrases in passing from my friends, and lastly from the seminar papers and essays of my own students. In the end, I naturally made it a point of honour and boasted that 'I learnt by hearsay'. This distinguished me quite markedly from all my university friends who were much better informed than me, and I used to repeat it by way of paradox and provocation, to arouse astonishment, incredulity, and admiration (!) in other people, to my great embarrassment and pride.

I had another particular ability. Starting from a simple turn of phrase, I thought I could work out (what an illusion!), if not the specific ideas of an author or a book I had not read, at least their general drift or direction. I obviously had certain intuitive powers as well as a definite ability for seeing connections, or a capacity for establishing theoretical *oppositions*, which enabled me to reconstruct what I took to be an author's ideas on the basis of the authors to whom he was opposed. I proceeded spontaneously by drawing contrasts and distinctions, subsequently elaborating a theory to support this.

The phantasy I had about my own complete autonomy and my desire to be combative while at the same time feeling totally safe were thus exploited to the full in these practices of mine. In addition, through my practical experience of and my liking for politics, I had a keen and intuitive understanding of the 'conjuncture' and its consequences. This was another theme about which I later developed a theory, because at the heart of a given theoretical conjuncture it is possible to discern what the philosophical oppositions and connections are. To what did I owe my acute awareness of the 'conjuncture', if not to my extreme sensitivity to 'situations' of irreconcilable conflict which I had experienced since childhood? To this can be added another instinctive conviction of mine that philosophy operates at a distance, in a void (mine!) like Aristotle's Unmoved Mover, something I rediscovered in the analytic situation (a theme to which Sacha Nacht drew attention in a brief and striking statement). So I was a philosopher and as such operating at a distance, from my refuge within the École, and away from the university world which I never liked nor had much to do with. I got on with my work on my own, without any help from my peers, without recourse to libraries. I worked in the sort of isolation I had long grown used to and which became an underlying principle of my thought and behaviour. Operating at a distance was also a way of operating without being directly involved, always as a number two (I was an adviser, an *éminence grise* to Daël and the directors of the École), both protected and aggressive, but sheltered by that protection. Clearly, I was still quietly obsessed with the idea of being 'the master's master', but in fact the masters from whom I kept my distance, a situation which I found to my liking, were the very ones who protected that distance. I still found myself in that perverse relationship, not so much of 'father's father' but of mother to my supposed master, thereby imposing on him as an intermediary the task of fulfilling my own alienated desire via his own.

In reality it is only now that I have become aware of these things (writing makes one reflect); at the time I behaved quite differently. A writer's striking phrase which I remembered (from one of his texts) or one that I picked up listening to a student or a friend were to me the equivalent of taking *soundings* from a body of philosophical thinking. We all know that test *borings* are made deep into the earth to try to discover oil. Narrow borers go deep into the substrata and are brought back up with what are known as core samples, which give precise details of the composition of the various layers of earth and enable those using them to detect oil itself or earth impregnated with oil and what lies immediately above and below it. I see now quite clearly that I proceeded in exactly the same way as a philosopher. Phrases I came across or picked up were like 'philosophical core samples', on the basis of which I was easily able to determine (using analytical methods) what the deeper levels of a particular philosophy were. Then, and only then, was I able to read the text from which the sample came. Thus I read a limited number of texts extremely closely, and naturally as rigorously as I could, without knowing in advance any semantic or syntagmatic details. As a matter of curiosity I was never able to penetrate a single text by Freud or his commentators (which is doubtless highly significant, though the significance escapes me and perhaps always will), despite all my psychoanalytical samples and personal experience (as analysand)! He remains a closed book to me. My best woman friend always tells me it is just as well and that I am completely hopeless at the theory of analysis. She is absolutely right. What matters in analysis is not the theory but the *practice* (a fundamentally materialist and Marxist principle).

From the beginning I felt my attitude towards philosophy as such was irreversibly and profoundly critical, destructive even. This was due to the influence of my friend Jacques Martin and of Marx's *The German Ideology*. My involvement in politics reinforced this attitude, as did my subsequent reading of Lenin, who was so hard on 'professors of philosophy' (see my little book *Lénine et la philosophie*, which contains the only public lecture I have ever given in France, which was quite a challenge. Jean Wahl invited Jacques Derrida and me to address the Philosophical Society). My talk caused a minor uproar but enabled me to make the acquaintance of an astonishing philosopher and theologian, Father Breton, who became one of my closest friends.

XIV

I tried to reconcile my radical criticism of philosophy as ideologically fraudulent (my objective: never to tell myself stories,
which is the only 'definition' of materialism I have ever subscribed
to) with my experience as a practising philosopher, and initially
came up with definitions such as 'Philosophy represents the
science of politics and the politics of science', and then subsequently ' "In the last instance", philosophy represents class
struggle in theory'. I still cling rigidly to the second of these
definitions, which naturally caused a scandal. On the basis of my
conception of materialism, I constructed a whole philosophical
system as if it had no object (in the sense that a science has
objects), but was rather a practical and polemical affair, and I
began to develop a practical and polemical view of philosophy,
based on a model of political thought I was working out at the
same time. I put forward theses in opposition to existing theses,
this *Kampfplatz* (Kant) echoing in the theoretical sphere the social,
political and ideological class struggle. It is clear, at any rate, that
though I had no knowledge of Gramsci at the time, I established
a close link between philosophy and politics, an unexpected synthesis of the political lessons of 'père Hours' and my own specifically philosophical studies.

What was I seeking to achieve in such an undertaking? I have
no intention of discussing the objective consequences in the realm
of theory. Others have done so and it is not for me to offer a
judgement in this respect. All I seek to do is to elucidate if possible
the deep-seated, personal motives, both conscious and especially
unconscious, which underpinned this whole undertaking beneath
its outward and visible form.

At the heart of it, without doubt, was what I have referred to
as the fulfilment of 'my mother's desire' in a particularly pure and
perfect, that is to say, abstract and ascetic form. Objectively I had

indeed become a pure-minded student of the École normale, an academic, and above all the author of a body of philosophical work which was abstract and impersonal, but passionately concerned with the self. At the same time I had succeeded in combining 'my mother's desire' with my own desire, that of living in the outside world,* of having a social and political life. This combination was discernible in my successive definitions of philosophy, thus of my own activities, but *in the pure realm of thought*. What was I in fact doing in the sphere of politics, if not engaging in pure political theory? Georges Marchais was of course wrong when he spoke subsequently of 'intellectuals behind their desks', as if that were true in my case. The implications of his remark were however not entirely wrong, and all those, including opponents of the Communist Party, who constantly criticised me for being a pure philosopher, looking down with disdain from my theoretical ivory tower on the practical realities of politics, were not entirely wide of the mark as far as I was concerned (they included Jean-Paul Enthoven, who on one occasion wrote of a dedication of mine to Waldeck-Rochet[†] that 'I still sounded like a model pupil').

But this does not entirely explain my profound rapport with philosophy and with my own conception of it (which itself offered some sort of explanation). I was greatly struck and still am by something Marx said to the effect that the philosopher expressed in his concepts (in his conception of philosophy, that is) his 'theoretical relationship with himself'. In addition to what I have just said, what other markedly personal elements was I seeking to express in the way I conceived of and practised philosophy? Some of my readers and friends have noticed in a number of my essays, in particular the little book on Montesquieu and my article on Freud and Lacan, a frequently recurring theme: the fact that the greatest philosophers were *fatherless* and lived out their lives in the solitary realm of their own theory and in the lonely risk they took in relation to the world at large. Bernard Edelmann pointed

* Added in the margin and not linked to the text: 'actively on my own initiative rather than that of anyone else (Hélène, Desanti, Merleau) other than Jacques Martin who helped me like an elder brother (though he was two years younger), but as I wrote in an obituary "twenty years ahead of us"' (Editors' note).
[†] 'For Waldeck-Rochet who admired Spinoza and talked about him at length to me one day in 1966.' Dedication to *Éléments d'autocritique*, Paris, Hachette, 1974 (Editors' note).

this out to me on a number of occasions most perceptively. True, I did not have a father and continued indefinitely to play the role of 'father's father' to give myself the illusion I did have one, or rather to assume the role in relation to myself, since all those I met or who might have acted as fathers were not up to it. I disdainfully placed them beneath me, though my own position was clearly subordinate.

Philosophically speaking, I had to become my own father. But that was only possible if I conferred on myself the essential role of the father: that of dominating and being the *master* in all situations.

That is what I did, following the great tradition in the history of philosophy and adopting for myself the classic claim that philosophy is an all-embracing view of things (Plato: *sunoptikos*), which has been endlessly repeated from Plato right down to Heidegger (in his observations as a negative theologian), and including Descartes, Kant, and Hegel: philosophy thinks *everything*, or rather the conditions of the possibility or impossibility of everything (Kant), whether in relation to God or the individual human being. It is thus master of the Whole and the Remainder (a phrase of Henri Lefèbvre's). Mastery of the Whole, and in the first place of the self, that is to say of its relationship to its object as the Whole, this is what philosophy is about; it is really only 'the philosopher's relationship with himself' (Marx); thus also is the philosopher. But the Whole can be grasped only by thinking which *rigorously* and clearly aims to be comprehensive, and which thus reflects the elements and articulations of the Whole. So I was a clear-minded philosopher who claimed to be rigorous. Echoes of this claim of mine were certainly to be found in the inclinations and expectations of my readers. It undoubtedly struck a chord with their demand for intelligibility, and since my language was one of *mastery*, controlling its own pathos (see, for example, the preface to *Pour Marx* and *Réponse à John Lewis*, etc.), my readers were surely as affected by it as they were by the rigour of my arguments, as mastery had been delegated to them. And of course since all these things hang closely together (not only in my case, given that thought and style are a function of the same 'relationship of the philosopher' with his concepts), this unity of thought, clarity (mastery with total clarity, clarity as a form of mastery, it goes without saying), and language won me a readership that my arguments alone would not have reached profoundly. Thus to my great astonishment, I learnt from Claudine Normand, for example, that I had my own 'style' and was, in my own way, a kind of writer. Of course, I developed a theory of philosophy as mastery both of the self and of the Whole, and of its parts and of the articulation of these parts and, outside the sphere of philosophy proper, mastery at a distance through concepts and through language. Like all philosophers, though I radically criticised this claim (I criticised what to me was a ridiculous notion, the claim to be an omnipotent father-figure), yet I felt I had some responsibility for things which touched on human ideals, and even for the conduct of history in the real world, including whatever claimed to be guiding it to its destiny (a destiny which, as Heidegger put it so well, exists only as an illusion in the collective consciousness and that of politicians), namely politics and politicians. That is why, on a number of occasions, I have ventured into the actual realm of politics, making pronouncements (at some risk, it must be said) about Stalinism, the crisis of Marxism, party congresses, and the way the Party worked (*Ce qui ne peut plus durer dans le Parti communiste français*, 1978). But what philosopher has not succumbed privately, particularly if he will not admit it, and in the case of the major ones often openly, to the temptation of keeping in view what he hopes to change or transform in the world? It is an integral part of philosophy. Heidegger himself said, though only in relation to phenomenology (but it is a mystery why it was just phenomenology) that it aimed to 'change the world'. That is why I criticised Marx's celebrated remark in the *Theses on Feuerbach*: 'The problem is not only to interpret the world, but to change it', pointing out in opposition to him that *all great philosophers* have sought to change the course of history, either to transform the world, or to make it regress, or to preserve and reinforce the status quo so as to avert the threat of changes, perceived as dangerous. On this point I still think I was right, despite Marx's bold and celebrated remark.

You can understand therefore the overwhelming personal responsibility which the philosopher feels he bears. For unlike with the sciences (which are, in my view, all experimental), he has no tools or procedures for verifying things. He must limit himself to putting forward theses without ever being able to verify them himself. He must always anticipate the effects of his philosophical claims without even knowing when or how they will manifest themselves. Obviously, he does not put forward positions arbitrarily but takes into account what he perceives to be the Whole, or believes it to be, and the way it is evolving, and sets them against existing arguments in his own field. As he has always to anticipate and is aware of his historical subjectivity, he finds himself on his own confronted by his perception of the Whole (each person has their own of course) and even more alone when he takes the initiative to put forward new lines of argument, without there being any consensus, since it is his aim to alter some dimension of that consensus. The philosopher leads a lonely life. Descartes did in his heroic and warm retreat, so did Kant as he meditated in his peaceful retreat at Königsberg. Kierkegaard lived out his private, tragic drama and Wittgenstein took refuge in his shepherd's hut in the forests of Norway. I myself, like every other philosopher in the world, was alone in my office, even though I was surrounded by friends; alone with my thoughts, my pretensions, my extraordinary daring. I was alone and wholly responsible, of course, for my acts and their unpredictable consequences, sanctioned only by the ultimate evolution of world history, which had not yet come to pass. I was entirely alone as a philosopher and yet in my *Réponse à John Lewis* I wrote: 'A communist is never alone.' There seems to be a gulf between the two statements, but it is bridgeable if every philosopher truly seeks to 'transform the world' – which he cannot do alone without a genuinely free and democratic communist organisation, having close links with its grass roots and beyond them with other popular mass movements (see the pamphlet I wrote in 1978).

You only have to read my texts to realise that the themes of solitude and responsibility run through them like an obsessive leitmotiv. On so many occasions I have repeated that I simply *intervened* as much in politics as in philosophy, alone against the world – which my adversaries made me aware of for a long time – and at my own risk. I knew I was on my own and that I was running a considerable risk. I was certainly made aware of the fact, but I always knew it in advance. What no one can contradict, who reads what I have written, is that I was always conscious of my absolute isolation when I intervened; that the responsibility for what I was doing was entirely my own; conscious, too, of the risks and perils to which both my isolation and my responsibility exposed me. It will not come as a surprise that a great number of readers recognised that sense of isolation as their own or that they assumed some responsibility in accepting my views and ran certain risks arising from the political consequences of those views. But at least they were not entirely alone in what they did, since I had preceded them and therefore acted as a guarantor and an authority (I was the master of mastery), just because I had taken the initiative first and thus alone.

Yes, in this sphere I alone and no one else took the initiative, as I dreamed of doing in the realm of love. I sometimes boasted (and I know Guitton was hurt by it) that no one was my teacher in philosophy (I said as much in the preface to *Pour Marx*) or even in politics (except Hours, Courrèges, Lesèvre, and Hélène). I was solely responsible for what I did, had finally discovered the field where I could exercise exclusively my own initiative, fulfil my own desires or at any rate the desire of at last having my own desires (desiring a desire is certainly a desire, but only in a formal sense, since it is the empty form of desire, and taking it for the real thing had certainly been my personal drama, from which I had emerged as the victor, in the realm of pure thought). It was as if I had been destined to achieve this by fulfilling the pure desire of my mother, which I had finally come to experience as the negation of that desire.

In these circumstances, how could I not give my thinking the abrupt form of a break or rupture? You will be aware that this is one of the most objectively equivocal themes that has always obsessed me. Equally, how could I escape the need to mark, in the very language of my discourse, the abruptness of this break by the abruptness of abrupt formulations, giving all the appearance of the 'dogmatism' for which I was so reproached? I had a fundamental feeling that by defining itself in terms of the claims it put forward without any possibility of experimental verification, all philosophy was essentially *dogmatic*, a view I expressed in 'Cours de philosophie pour scientifiques' (1967). It put forward its claims as true and was concerned solely with putting them forward. Quite simply, I asserted the truth of what I thought and did (sometimes openly putting forward theses as in *Philosophie et Philosophie spontanée des savants*) as all philosophers before me had done, whether they acknowledged it openly (Saint Thomas, Spinoza, Wittgenstein, etc.) or said nothing about it. When you are aware that you alone are responsible for the isolation needed to express the truth in your arguments, *and* for your truthfulness as a philosopher, *and* for the truthfulness of all philosophy, surely the least you can do as a sign of that *honesty* is to use language in keeping with the nature of your activity, including the way in which you make interventions or interpellate things (think how I made play with interpellation when discussing ideology); and express yourself in the way which conveys directly what you are thinking and doing?

My father gibbered, whereas my mother was clear and aspired to clarity. But the clarity I displayed had the same brusqueness as my father's inner thoughts and blunt interventions. My father called a spade a spade, even when he was silent, and was the sort of man who would suddenly take out his revolver. One day he set about an unfortunate young cyclist who had knocked my sister down in the woods, as if he wanted to kill him. In the end I was bold enough, felt free enough to accept what my father was really like, with his violent refusal to 'tell stories', his wordless brutality, and the fact that he neglected me or at least neither initiated me nor taught me that the world was governed by physical and other forms of struggle and was not ethereal. Had I not finally and truly become my own father, that is to say a man?

It is no good looking for the ultimate and objective meaning of a particular philosophy in an analysis of this kind. Whatever a philosopher's conscious or rather subconscious inner motivation might be, his published philosophy has an entirely *objective reality* and its effect on the world, if it has one, is similarly *objective* and may, thank God, have almost no connection with the inner world I have described. Philosophy, like every other activity come to that, is nothing more than the pure interiority of all the subjectivities in the world, each enclosed in its own solipsism. If I ever doubted this, I was to discover the truth of it in person from the terrible reality of politics, but first from philosophy itself.

XV

Any man who intervenes actively – and, quite rightly, I considered philosophical intervention as a form of action – always does so in a specific conjuncture in order to alter their course. What, then, was the philosophical conjuncture in which I was induced to 'intervene'?

It was in France, which, as always, remained ignorant of all that was happening beyond its borders. I myself was ignorant about everyone, including Carnap, Russell, Frege, and therefore about logical positivism, as well as about Wittgenstein and English analytical philosophy. Somewhat belatedly, I had read Heidegger's *Letter to Jean Beaufret on Humanism*, which influenced my arguments concerning *theoretical* antihumanism in Marx. Thus I was confronted by what was being read in France, in other words Sartre, Merleau-Ponty, Bachelard, and much later on Foucault, and above all Cavaillès and Canguilhem. I also got to know a little about Husserl, whom we discovered via Desanti (a Husserlian Marxist) and Tran Duc Thao, whose thesis I found brilliant. Of Husserl himself, I only ever read his *Cartesian Meditations* and *Crisis*.

I never thought as Sartre did that Marxism could be 'the untranscendable philosophy of our time', for a huge number of reasons which I will one day explain. My major reason still holds good. I have always thought that Sartre, though a brilliant mind and the author of wonderful 'philosophical novels' such as *L'Être et le Néant* and *Critique de la raison dialectique*, never really understood anything of Hegel, Marx, or, needless to say, of Freud. At best, I saw him as one of those post-Cartesian and post-Hegelian 'philosophers of history' whom Marx detested.

I was aware, of course, of how Hegel and Marx had been introduced to the French. Kojevenikov (Kojève), a Russian *émigré* who held an important post at the Ministry of Economic Affairs,

176

had made them known. I went to meet him one day in his minis-terial office to invite him to give a lecture at the École, which he did. A black-haired, dark-skinned man, he was full of infantile and mischievous remarks about theory. I read everything he wrote and rapidly came to the conclusion that he understood absolutely nothing about Hegel and Marx, even though everyone – including Lacan – had listened to him with immense interest before the war. For him, everything centred on the life and death struggle and the End of History to which he ascribed a stupefy-ingly *bureaucratic* content. Though history as class struggle might end, history as such would continue, but only in terms of the routine *administration of things* (long live Saint-Simon!). No doubt it enabled him to bring together his desires as a philosopher and his professional role as a high bureaucrat.

I could not understand how Kojève had so captured the interest of his audience, which included Lacan, Bataille, Queneau, and a good many others, but for the total ignorance of Hegel on the part of the French. On the other hand, I had unbounded admiration for the courageous and erudite work of someone like Hyppolite who, instead of interpreting Hegel, was content to give him his own voice in his admirable translation of the *Phenomenology of Spirit*.

That, then, was the philosophical conjuncture in which I had to 'think'. As I have already said, I wrote a short thesis on Hegel, guided by my friend Jacques Martin who had a wide knowledge of philosophy. It was not hard to see that the French 'Hegelians', disciples of Kojève, *had not understood him at all*. One only had to read Hegel for oneself to realise that. They were all taken up with the master/slave relationship and the total absurdity of a 'dialectic of Nature'. Even Bachelard, to judge from the remark of his which I quoted earlier, had not understood him. Indeed, he made no claim to have done so, never having had the time to read him. *In France at least*, everything about Hegel still had to be understood and explained.

Husserl, on the other hand, had penetrated France to some extent due to Sartre and Merleau. Everyone knows the famous story told by Simone de Beauvoir. Sartre's 'good friend' Raymond Aron had spent the year 1928–29 studying in Berlin, which opened his eyes to the rise of Nazism and where he had also absorbed the rather colourless philosophy and the subjective German sociology of history. On his return to Paris, Aron went to see Sartre and Castor [Simone de Beauvoir] in their usual café, where he found Sartre drinking a large apricot juice. Aron said to him: 'I discovered a philosopher in Germany, my friend, who can explain to you why you are sitting in a café and drinking an apricot juice and why you like doing so.' The philosophy was, of course, that of Husserl and his pre-predicative could account for everything, including apricot juice. It seems Sartre was astounded by what he heard and began to devour Husserl and then the early Heidegger! It is easy to see in his own writing what he borrowed from them: a subjectivist and Cartesian apologia for the subject as opposed to the object and essence, the primacy of existence over essence, etc. But it has little to do with the more profound ideas either of Husserl or of Heidegger, who quickly distanced himself from Sartre. It was more a Cartesian theory of the *cogito* within the framework of a generalised and therefore completely distorted version of phenomenology. Merleau, a philosopher of much greater profundity, was far more faithful to Husserl, especially when he got to know the later works, particularly *Erfahrung und Urteil* and his 'Lectures on time-consciousness'. He gave an excellent commentary on these in his lectures at the École, drawing parallels between the theory of the pre-predicative in the notion of praxis in Husserl and the theory of natural judgement in Malebranche and ideas about the body itself in Maine de Biran and Bergson. It was all very illuminating. In private, Thao told us: 'You are all equal transcendental egos!' He smiled as he said it, but how profoundly true it was!

What Merleau told us about Husserl was extremely illuminating, and in continuing to reflect on his work he returned to that most profound French tradition, spiritualism, though his version of it was particularly subtle and embellished with profound ideas on childhood, Cézanne, Freud, language, silence, as well as Marxist and even Soviet politics (see, for example, *Humanisme et Terreur* and *Les Aventures de la dialectique*). Merleau, in contrast to Sartre, who resembled Voltaire as a philosophical novelist but had the personal intransigence of Rousseau, was a truly great philosopher, the last in France before that giant of a philosopher Derrida, yet he was not in the least illuminating about either Hegel or Marx. In this respect, I think above all of Desanti, who was an extremely competent logician and mathematician (he proved as much in his various books). Each year he began a course on the history of logic, but though he 'battled on' he never got beyond Aristotle. It did not much matter. What mattered as far as I was concerned was that when he began to talk as a philosopher about Marx, it was to consider him straight away in Husserlian terms. And as Husserl had established the splendid category of pre-predicative 'praxis' (the original level of meaning linked to the manipulation of things), our friend Touki (the nickname we gave him) was delighted to discover in Husserl a *meaningful basis* for Marx's notion of praxis. Touki was yet another of those (like Sartre) who claimed to give the original meaning of Marx's own 'philosophy'. Obviously, I did not go along with this, as I had begun to read and understand Marx for myself, thanks to Jacques Martin, and I was indignant about the claims made for the humanistic and seminal nature of the early writings. I never went along with Desanti's Husserlian 'interpretations' of Marx nor with any 'humanist' interpretation either. It is easy to see why. I detested any philosophy which claimed to establish *a priori* any transcendental meaning and truth at a fundamental level, however pre-predicative it might have been. This was not true of Desanti; he just did not have the same dislike as me for the concept of the fundamental and the transcendental.

I began to suspect he was 'toeing the line' when I saw him, following in the footsteps of his fellow Corsican Laurent Casanova, playing with the notions of bourgeois and proletarian science for political ends. This was something I never did. Every time I meet Victor Leduc, an important official for 'intellectuals' in the Party at the time, he reminds me of the position I adopted in discussions at this time: 'You were against the idea of two opposing approaches to science and were almost the only intellectual in the Party to take this view.'

Naturally, the workers did not give a damn about it. All I know is that, to his shame, Touki wrote an implausible theoretical article in *La Nouvelle Critique*, 'laying the basis' (still the same old story) of the theory of two sorts of science as part of the class struggle. He did this 'under orders' and he subsequently admitted as much. No one asked him as a matter of conscience to renounce publicly his whole philosophy and way of thinking. But he did so, without even the excuse of having had to appear before the Local Committee.

But the worst thing of all, for which I cannot forgive him, however, is a television broadcast about himself which he made around 1975. He appeared alone with a nasty, runty little dog (the sort favoured by old ladies) which led him from one statue to another (to pee on them) while Touki kept up a monologue. He referred back to the period of the two sorts of science and how he had been recruited to defend that view. He recounted the story in a comic tone (for which he had a talent), although the whole dreadful business had or might have caused a number of deaths and certainly reduced Marcel Prenant to a shadow of his former self. He was like a drunk telling some trivial story: 'They told us it had to be done, so we did it.' It was unbearable, and he went on in the same vein for ten minutes or so. His monologue was only interrupted when he stopped to call his awful little dog as they walked up and down the broad avenues of the Luxembourg Gardens and by the conspiratorial nods and winks he made to the viewers. It had to be done. Touki has since left the Party and is pursuing his sober career as an academic. Someone told me that recently he had tried to re-examine his Husserlian past. We shall see.

Thus there were too many political and philosophical reasons for me to be inspired by him and to follow his example. This 'twin truth' approach just did not suit me. I could not see how you could be a philosopher, thinking for yourself at the École, and Casanova's poodle in the Party. The unity of theory and practice, crucial to Marxism and for communists (Courrèges!) excluded as far as I was concerned – as far as everyone was concerned come to that – the possibility of twin truths, recalling as it did the practices of the clerics in the eighteenth century, which were so justly criticised by Helvétius and d'Holbach. It was beyond me that a philosopher who claimed to be a Marxist could, from 1945 to 1950, fall short even of the principles of the Enlightenment which, however, I scarcely shared.

That is why, as I have pointed out in the preface to *Pour Marx*, I had no real philosophical mentor, apart from Thao, and he soon left us to return to Vietnam, where in the end he languished as a street sweeper and suffered from ill-health without the medicines he needed (his French friends tried to get some to him). There was also Merleau, but as he was already powerfully attracted by the old, dominant spiritualist tradition, I could not follow him.*

Philosophy in the university was thus divided between this unbelievable French tradition and the so-called neo-Kantian tradition of Brunschvicg. The tradition was founded in institutional terms by Victor Cousin at the beginning of the nineteenth century (see Lucien Sève's interesting first book) and in the work it produced, its official syllabuses, and in the extravagant imaginings of the eclectic school, so firmly challenged by the socialist Pierre Lerous, it 'spawned' figures like Ravaisson, Bergson, Lequier, and recently Ferdinand Alquié. There is no equivalent of this tradition in other countries. It had its 'merits' – what an irony of the dialectic of history – since it saved France, at least until recent years (and the work of Jules Vuillemin and Jacques Bouveresse) from an invasion of Anglo-Saxon logical positivism and English-language analytic philosophy (which, for all that, is extremely interesting). Apart from these two predominant non-French movements, the work of someone like Wittgenstein remained completely unknown to us – as Jacques Vouveresse, Dominique Lecourt, and Argentine Mari have clearly brought home to us. But what value is there in being 'protected' by ignorance or disgust? Machiavelli clearly demonstrated that fortresses are the weak link in a military plan, and Lenin, following on from Goethe, rightly pointed out: '*If you wish to get to know your enemy, you have to enter his terrain.*' It was all pathetic, including even Brunschvicg's neo-Kantianism, which turned Spinoza's thought into the dullest spiritualism; that concerned with consciousness and the mind. Certain texts have, however, now been translated; Nietzsche and now Heidegger have become established figures; Bouveresse has provided us with highly erudite studies of logical positivism; and the work of Wittgenstein, Hegel, and Marx has largely been translated and commented upon. At last, the frontiers are open.

From 1945 to 1960 that was not the case. We had to 'make do' with what we had. There was Descartes, of course, but the interpretations were so spiritualistic, apart from those of Étienne

---

* This sentence, which was partly crossed out by the author, making it ungrammatical and incomprehensible, has been printed in its original version (Editors' note).

Gilson, Emile Bréhier, and also Henri Gouhier. Gouhier engaged in a polemical debate with Alquié, whose interpretation of Descartes was spiritualistic. There was also Marcel Guéroult, a man of erudition who showed not the least indulgence in his reading of different authors. He was the only great historian of the period, whose successors were Jules Vuillemin and Louis Guillermit. But Guéroult was only a great 'commentator' of the works of other writers, and no one suspected he had in his head a *structural* theory of philosophical systems. Vuillemin and Guillermit were practically unkown. I got them to come to the École, but Vuillemin (like Bouveresse, his equally bitter follower) was so full of resentment over his intellectual isolation that he always managed to reduce his student audience to two or three. As a consequence, he came to tell me he was giving up. I had the same strange experience with Bouveresse, though he was much younger. He had been a student of mine, and I kept on inviting him to the École. I am pretty sure it was Bouveresse who accused me (and perhaps still does) of being responsible for the decadence of French philosophy. In his last book he maligned Derrida, a towering figure who, as Hegel had once been, was treated as a 'dead dog' (if he did not actually use the phrase, the sentiment was the same). Even philosophers can rave on quite openly.

I invited Guéroult to the École over a long period, but what a business it was! I had to fetch him and take him back by car. But he was a great hit with the philosophers there. Derrida, who had just been appointed on my recommendation, was isolated and despised in French university circles and was not yet well known at the École. And I was still not sure where he was going.

I felt I had to get involved in philosophy for political and ideological reasons and therefore 'accepted it' as it was with the knowledge I had: a little Hegel, a lot of Descartes, not much Kant, a fair amount of Malebranche, a bit of Bachelard (*Le Nouvel Esprit scientifique*), a great deal of Pascal, a little Rousseau, Spinoza and Bergson, and my bedside book, Bréhier's *L'Histoire de la philosophie*. Naturally, I also knew a fair amount of Marx, the only one who was able to help us dispel the confusion over genres.

So I started working, initially on a few obscure articles which were published in the *Revue de l'Enseignement philosophique* (they were very heavily influenced by dialectical materialism,

although I was careful to distinguish between dialectical materialism and historical materialism, without attributing any theoretical
primacy to the first over the second). I also published an article
on Paul Ricoeur.

Then in 19[6]2, I was given the chance to contribute to *La
Pensée*, in circumstances I have described in the preface to *Pour
Marx*. In fact, it was due to the friendship of Marcel Cornu, who
persistently stood up for me against Georges Cogniot, Maurice
Thorez's secretary at the time. Cogniot, who edited the review,
was in the habit of making cutting comments on all the articles he
received with such violent exclamations as: bloody stupid! idiotic!
absurd! crazy! Try to imagine the scene when the editor came face
to face with the author! Marcel quite simply threatened to resign
over me, which kept Cogniot in check.

However, after my article 'Contradiction et sur-détermination'
had appeared and been virulently attacked by Gilbert Mury in a
piece on 'monism', inspired by Garaudy who was all-powerful at
the time, Cogniot organised a 'theoretical investigation'. This was
held in the 'Henri Langevin' laboratory and presided over by
Orcel, in the presence of the leading lights of *La Pensée* in the
spheres of both politics and philosophy. Compared with the Local
Committee, it was something of a comic performance. It went on
for a month and a half and met every Saturday afternoon. Cogniot
did not intervene, but allowed anyone who wished to challenge
me to have the floor. As usual, I outlined a few things on the
blackboard and answered criticisms. After six weeks of this,
Cogniot began to smile. Basically, I was a product of the École
normale, as he was, and I realised that, even if I had not won him
round, I had at least disarmed him. When the last meeting was
called, after a month and a half, I simply sent a note saying: 'I
believe I have more or less answered you and that those responsible for theory within the Party, who have a great deal on their
plate, would be well advised to put an end to this investigation
and deal with more urgent matters.' I did not attend.

Thanks to Jacques Martin, I at last discovered two thinkers to
whom I owe practically everything. First, Jean Cavaillès, from
whom I took one or two statements ('the criticism not of a dialectic
but of a concept'), and Georges Canguilhem, reputedly an impossible individual, like my grandfather and Hélène. But, like both of

them, he was in fact a wonderfully intelligent and generous person. After considerable prodding by his friends, he finally agreed to apply for a post in higher education. He had written a book about the normal and the pathological inspired by Nietzsche as well as a celebrated article on a certain kind of 'psychology which leads either to the Collège de France or the police force'. In order to be accepted into higher education, he wrote a short thesis on the notion of reflexes, providing evidence for the paradoxical view that the concept of the reflex developed in a vitalist rather than a mechanistic context. He provided textual evidence and incontrovertible proof to support this scandalous view. This gave me an astounding view of the consequences for the sciences of turning prevailing ideologies upside down. I learned several vital lessons from him; first, that the so-called epistemology to which I had appeared to pay so much attention was absurd outside the framework of the history of science; secondly, far from conforming to the logic of the Enlightenment, such a history might have implications for his discoveries on the basis of what he referred to, almost in the same terms as us, as 'scientific ideologies', philosophical representations influencing the development of science, the generation and even the nature of scientific concepts, and often in a wholly paradoxical manner. Such a crucial lesson was not lost on me. I cannot over-emphasise the importance for all of us of Canguilhem's influence. His example led me, led us (Balibar, Macherey, and Lecourt followed him even more closely than I did) away from an idealist approach, which had inspired my earliest theoretical definitions of philosophy as a theory of theoretical practice. In other words, I saw it as a form of scientific practice, an almost positivist concept of philosophy as the 'science of science'; a definition I hastened to rectify in the preface to the Italian edition of *Lire 'Le Capital'* (in 1966). I have not seen him for a very long time. One day, having read my books, he said to me: 'I understand what you wanted to do', but I did not give him a chance to tell me. I know he allowed his students to call for a demonstration, a strike, etc., in May '68. I owe him more than I can say. It was from him I learnt the disconcerting historical cunning of the relationships between ideology and science. He also confirmed me in the thought that epistemology was a variant of the theory of knowledge, the modern version (from Descartes and Kant) of philosophy as Truth, and thus a guarantee of truth. In the last resort, Truth exists only to provide a final guarantee of the established order of things and the moral and political relationships between people.

Thus I finally established my own position as a philosopher, on the *Kampfplatz* where factions were irrevocably opposed to one another. Ultimately, they reflected stances taken within the totality of the class struggle. I forged my own personal philosophy, which, though not without its forebears, was very isolated when looked at in the context of French philosophy, since those who had inspired me, Cavaillès and Canguilhem, were either unknown or unrecognised, if not despised.

When 'structuralism' became the fashionable ideology, with the advantage of breaking with psychologism and historicism, I seemed to go along with it. For we discovered in Marx not the notion of a combinatory (of arbitrary elements) but rather that of a combination of distinct elements fitted to constitute the unity of a mode of production. Furthermore, this structural and objectivist approach meant the demise of 'anthropological' humanism derived from Feuerbach, with which I was extremely familiar, having been the first person in France to translate and edit him, not counting the partial and very mediocre translations of Joseph Roy, who also translated *Das Kapital* badly. From the outset we had insisted on drawing a structural distinction between a *combinatory* (abstract) and a *combination* (concrete), which created the major problem. But did anyone acknowledge it? No one took any notice of the distinction. In structuralist circles I was everywhere accused of defending the unchanging nature of structures within the established order and the impossibility of revolutionary practice, whereas I had more than outlined a theory of conjuncture in relation to Lenin. But this was of no importance, since what they really wanted was to hold up to public ridicule an isolated individual who claimed that Marx had grounded his ideas on the rejection of a philosophical basis in man, in human nature; Marx who had written: 'I start not from man but from the given historical period' and 'Society does not consist of individuals but relationships', etc. I certainly was isolated both politically and philosophically. No one, not even the Party which subscribed to a self-satisfied socialist humanism, was willing to recognise that

only theoretical antihumanism justified genuine, practical humanism. Demagoguery, based on emotion and experience, captured
the mood of the times and was reinforced, if that were possible,
by equivocal leftist attitudes revealed in the enormous upheavals
of '68. No one was interested in theory. Only a few individuals
understood my reasons and objectives. And when the Party abandoned the notion of the dictatorship of the proletariat 'as you
might abandon a dog', nothing happened. Those against me
included not only the band of philosophers who wrote books 'for
man' against Foucault and me (Mikel Dufrenne and others) but
also all the ideologues of the Party as well who made no secret of
their disapproval and who supported me only because they could
not have me expelled (given my notoriety). It was a marvellous
period! I had at last achieved what I wanted: to be right, alone
and against the world!

Actually, I was not quite alone. I derived some comfort from
Lacan. In a sly footnote to an article for the *Revue de l'Enseignement philosophique*, I made the point that just as Marx had rejected
'homo economicus', Lacan had rejected 'homo psychologicus', and
then drew the logical consequences. Lacan called me a few days
later and we had dinner together several times. Naturally, I once
again played the role of 'father's father', especially as he was in a
bad way. I remember the extraordinary cigar he always had in his
mouth and me saying to him by way of a greeting: 'You roll your
own!' (I obviously did not.) In the course of conversation, he
made some disparaging remarks about some of the people he was
analysing, and especially the wives whom he analysed at the same
time as their husbands. I realised he was in a very difficult position
having been threatened with exclusion from Sainte-Anne's Hospital, and so I offered him hospitality at the École. As a result, and
for a good many years from that day on, there were expensive
English cars all over the pavements of the rue d'Ulm on Wed-
nesdays at midday, much to the annoyance of the local inhabitants.
I never went to one of Lacan's seminars. He spoke to a room full
of people which was thick with smoke. It was for this reason that
he was later asked to leave, because the smoke impregnated the
precious books in the library immediately above. Despite severe
warnings from Robert Flacelière, Lacan could never get his audience to refrain from smoking. One day Flacelière was so fed up

with the smoke he gave him his notice. I was ill at the time and away from the École. Lacan telephoned and kept on at Hélène for over an hour to give him my address. At a certain point he said: 'I'm sure I recognise your voice, who are you?' Hélène replied: 'A friend.' And that was all. Lacan had to leave the École, but not without a great deal of protest.

Though I did not see him again (he simply did not need me any more), Lacan remained a sort of distant companion. We even had occasion to make contact via third parties.*

I had long taken the view that there existed everywhere and at all times what Marx called 'the incidental costs of production' or 'expenses', losses without right or reason. Malebranche, I realised, had anticipated this discovery when he referred to 'the sea, the sand, and the highways' on which rain falls to no discernible purpose. I thought about my 'account' of the materialist philosopher, who 'jumps on a moving train' without knowing where it has come from or where it is going. And I thought about 'letters' which, although posted, do not always reach the addressee. One day I happened to read a remark of Lacan's to the effect that: 'A letter always reaches its addressee.' It came as a surprise! But the issue was complicated by a young Hindu doctor who underwent a short analysis with Lacan and was bold enough to ask him at the end: 'You say a letter always reaches its addressee. Althusser, however, says exactly the opposite. What are your views of what he calls his materialist argument?' Lacan thought about it for ten whole minutes and then simply said: 'Althusser isn't a practising analyst.' He was right, of course. Within the framework of transference which forms part of analysis the affective relationship is so structured that no gap exists. As a consequence, any unconscious message which is truly addressed to the unconscious of the other person necessarily gets through. Yet I was not wholly satisfied with my explanation. Lacan was right, but so was I. I also knew full well that it was unfair to accuse him of idealism, because of his materiality of the conception of the signifier. Then I saw a way out of the dilemma. Lacan spoke as a practising analyst and I as a

---

* Following several handwritten notes which do not all appear to be Althusser's, the three following paragraphs had been run together in such a way that the meaning was not always clear. We therefore reverted to the original version where sense dictated it (Editors' note).

practising philosopher. They were two entirely different fields which I could in no way reduce to one another, if I was to remain true to my critique of classic dialectical materialism: neither the philosophical to the analytic domain or to scientific practice, or vice versa. We were therefore both right, but neither of us had perceived clearly the basis of our difference. At any rate, after this I had greater respect for Lacan's clear-sightedness. Despite the ambiguity of some of his vocabulary (empty speech, full speech in his 'Discours de Rome'), he had sensed immediately the difference and pointed to it, without perhaps having fully reflected on it.

Right at the end of his life (when he was terminally ill), our paths crossed again when he made his last public engagement at the Hotel PLM. A very close friend – whom I no longer wanted to meet because of his scandalous behaviour – urged me to go with him to this meeting 'to give him moral support'. However, he neither turned up nor sent a message. I was therefore left on my own. I went into the vast foyer though I did not have a pass, and a young woman came up to me and asked under what auspices I had been invited. I replied: 'In the name of the Holy Spirit otherwise called the Libido.' Then, slowly and ostentatiously, my pipe in my mouth, I crossed the great empty space in front of the audience, which was sitting there in silence. I paused and, still very deliberately, tapped the pipe on the heel of my boot, filled and lit it, walked over to Lacan, and shook his hand at some length. He looked absolutely done in, having just finished reading his long lecture. I showed all the respect I felt towards this great old man, who was dressed like a pierrot in a blue-checked tweed jacket. I then spoke 'on behalf of the analysed' and fiercely criticised the audience for remaining silent. An indignant voice then said: 'Whose couch has this gentleman been lying on?' I went on talking unperturbed. I forget what I said, but I have not forgotten the effect and the silent squirming my intervention provoked. I wanted to continue the discussion after the end of Lacan's speech, but everyone left.

Actually, I had dealings with Lacan at a much earlier date and in dramatic circumstances. One morning, very early, someone rang my bell at the École. It was Lacan. He was in a dreadful state and almost unrecognisable. I hardly dare recount what had happened. He had come to tell me of the suicide of Lucien Sebag, who was undergoing analysis with him, 'before I learnt about it through the rumours which were incriminating him, Lacan, personally'. Lacan had had to give up the analysis, as he had fallen in love with Sebag's daughter Judith. He told me he had 'gone round Paris' explaining the situation to all those he could contact in order to put a stop to the 'accusations of murder and negligence on his part'. He was absolutely panic-stricken and explained how he had been unable to continue Sebag's analysis once he had fallen in love with Judith: 'It was impossible, for technical reasons.' He told me he had, none the less, gone on seeing Sebag every day and had even seen him the previous evening. He had assured him he would visit him at any hour of the day or night if he asked him to and that he had an extremely fast Mercedes. However, Sebag had fired one bullet into his head at midnight and managed to finish himself off with a second around three in the morning. I must admit I did not know what to say to him, though I wanted to ask if he could not have had Sebag taken into hospital for his own safety. He would probably have told me that it was against the analytical 'rules'. At all events, he said nothing about the safety angle of taking someone into hospital. He was still trembling when he left me in the early morning to continue on his rounds. I have often wondered what he would have done in my own case, had I been one of his patients; if he would have left me unsupervised (I constantly wanted to kill myself) so as not to infringe in the slightest way the 'rules' of analysis. My analyst had formerly been Lacan's greatest 'hope', but had left him the day he realised that 'Lacan was totally incapable of listening to anyone'. I wondered, too, what he would have done with Hélène, in the context of his famous 'rules' which neither Freud nor his followers took to be totally rigid, but simply as technical guidelines. He told me when we first met that he had accepted for analysis the wives of several of my former students. This incident gave me a curious insight into the awful conditions of analysis and their famous 'rules'. I hope people will forgive me for reporting in detail what he said, but, as well as the unfortunate Sebag of whom I was very fond and Judith whom I knew quite well (she married a former student of mine, Jacques-Alain Miller), it also concerned me: '*De te fabula narratur.*' This was a tragic 'tale', not just for Sebag but above all for Lacan, whose principal preoccupation was his professional reputation and the scandal which would rebound on him. I hope the analysts who at the time sent a petition to *Le Monde* (which was not published) condemning my analyst's 'methods' will kindly take note of what I have said.

Around 1974 I went to Moscow for an international conference on Hegelian philosophy. I gave my paper in the vast reception hall during the final session but did not attend anything else. I spoke about the young Marx and the underlying reasons for his development. At the end of my talk, which *Pravda* reported – in advance – there was an official silence, but a few students remained behind in the hall to ask me questions such as: What is the proletariat? What is the class struggle? Clearly, they were unaware that these things were discussed. Though I was astonished, I readily understood the reasons for it.

I understood because, during the eight-day conference which I did not attend, my dear friend Merab, a remarkably clever Georgian philosopher who would never have wanted to leave the Soviet Union as his friend Zinoviev had done ('because here at least you see things as they really are, not dressed up'), introduced me to well over a hundred Soviet citizens of different backgrounds. They talked about their country and the real material, political, and intellectual conditions in which they lived. I came to understand a great many things, which were subsequently confirmed by all the serious studies of the USSR I read.

The USSR is different from the usual descriptions we read in this country. Any public involvement in politics is, of course, forbidden and dangerous, but as far as everything else is concerned, what a splendid life they lead! First of all, it is a vast country which has solved the problem of education and illiteracy on a scale unknown even in France. Then, it is a country where the right to work is guaranteed and, I might add, planned and compulsory. Since the workers' pass books have been done away with, there has been an enormous increase in the mobility of labour. Finally, it is a country where the working class is so strong it is respected, and the police never enter factories. The workers find release in alcohol, moonlighting, and in stealing things from collective enterprises for private ones. It is still a two-tier society where people work for the black economy in industry, in teaching, in medicine, and (with official blessing) in the agricultural sector. I have since learnt something I did not know at the time. Workers now set up their own teams and charge enterprises a great deal for their services, in order to catch up on the targets set. You could not imagine it happening here, even with moonlighting, since it is not the 'bosses' in the USSR who set the wages but groups of friends who get together and sell their services to businesses which have fallen behind. I believe K. S. Karol is right. He knows the USSR well, having lived there for a number of years and had extraordinary adventures which he described in a remarkable book. (*Solik: tribulations d'un jeune homme polonais dans la Russie en guerre*). With the rise of new generations desperate for consumer goods, against a background of widespread education, of patriotism fed by the memory of twenty million dead in the 'great patriotic war', and of the total destruction of the peasantry, its traditional way of life, and even its know-how (the peasants are told when to reap and sow on the radio!! – how different from China!!), changes can be patiently and reasonably expected to occur at a slow pace in the USSR. And all this is taking place despite the fact that people are scandalously shut away in prisons and psychiatric hospitals, which also happens in France, though not on the same scale and not always for directly political reasons; but is it fundamentally different? The younger generation, like Gorbachev, must be given a chance; for the first time in the history of the Soviet Union they have their spokesman. Not surprisingly, I found the USSR a philosophical desert. My books had been translated, like all other foreign publications, but they were hidden away in reserve collections in libraries, available only to select specialists who were politically safe. When the Dean of the Faculty of Philosophy took me to Moscow airport, all he could think of saying to me was: 'Say hello from me to the young ladies of Paris!!'

XVI

I imagine you are waiting for me to get on to the subject of politics. There is a great deal I could say, mainly anecdotes about minor matters, but they have little bearing on the subsequent [*après coup*] 'genealogy' of the emotional traumas of my psyche which I am attempting to chart. Anecdotes of that kind are two a penny and saleable, but they do not interest me. I have already said I here only want to record events and memories which have left their mark on me, thereby either helping to shape the structure of my psyche, or above all those which through the effect of [*après coup*] endless subsequent repetitions have reinforced the structure or, as a result of conflicting desires, inflected it in the first place in seemingly strange ways.

At this point I must remind the reader of certain events he already knows about.

The Party played a most important part in resisting Nazi occupation. However, in June 1940, the leadership undeniably adopted an ill-fated line. The Third International, with Stalin's authority, in effect directed all communist parties to do so (including the French party, which was 'controlled' by a delegate from the International, the Czech Fried who was, it seems, a remarkable man to whom Thorez owed a great deal). According to its theory, the war was a purely *imperialist affair* in which the French and the English were opposed to the Germans for purely imperialist reasons. The protagonists should thus be allowed to destroy each other, and the USSR would simply bide its time and then pull the chestnuts out of the fire. It had signed the Nazi–Soviet pact for one very simple reason: long before Munich, the Western democracies were reluctant to honour their signature, clearly from a mixture of fear and fascination for Hitler and by virtue of their celebrated stance, 'better Hitler than the Popular Front'. Nazism was preferable to the Popular Front and *a fortiori* proletarian revolution. We all knew and had proof of what the bourgeoisie was like. The USSR had desperately sought to negotiate to achieve the agreement of the Western democracies after the first great defeat for the workers' movement, in Spain, where it had intervened on a large scale (with arms, planes, and via the International Brigades). But neither Daladier nor Chamberlain had had the 'courage' simply to respect the political and military agreements they had formally entered into. They proved as much when they openly abandoned first the Sudeten and then the rest of Czechoslovakia, though, at the time, there was nothing to prevent them from intervening, as was the case later on in fascist Poland.

The case is demonstrably proven, since the facts are clear, and no serious historian would contest them. Yet despite these historical facts and the profound mistrust to which they gave rise, the USSR went on trying to establish a united front with the Western democracies against Hitler who was becoming more and more wild in his quest for additional living space and especially the rich Ukrainian plains. He was evidently looking eastwards and therefore at territory a long way from France and England. When Hitler's attack on Poland was imminent and the Polish fascist Pilsudski forbade the Red Army to cross its territory to engage the Wehrmacht, the USSR *was obliged* to seek a compromise with Hitler's Reich, given the circumstances and the patent historical cowardice of its Western 'allies'. This led to the famous Nazi–Soviet pact and the inevitable division of Poland. The USSR could not allow the *whole of Poland* to be occupied by Hitler's troops. It was obliged to push its frontier as far as possible and if necessary retake the White Russian lands ceded to Poland at the Treaty of Versailles, which historically it was perfectly justified in doing. Thus it established a forward defensive position in the event of a German attack.

Those were dramatic times for all militants belonging to the international communist movement and their allies. Some left the Party, as Paul Nizan and others did in France. Not surprisingly, they were considered renegades (the word used at the time). For a long time afterwards, the Party made it clear to Rirette Nizan, whom Hélène knew very well, and to her children, what their attitude was. Thorez always refused to meet them. What a way to behave! Like any number of militants, Hélène realised the USSR could not have done otherwise faced with the threat of Hitler and the total political 'cowardice' of the Western democracies. Indeed, what else could she have done? Those bold enough to claim there was an alternative should have the courage to tell us what it was.

Thus the communists were caught up in a strange political situation, and the USSR *seemed not to contradict* the Nazi line which implied that Nazism was fighting against 'international capitalism', though its former line, from well before the Spanish Civil War, constantly proved the opposite. For a while, the decisive factor was Stalin's unbelievable trust of Hitler. He had a deep conviction that Hitler was sincere, that he would keep his word and would not attack the Soviet Union. Hélène, who had had numerous contacts and carefully sifted through documents and testimonies of the period, drew my attention to this surprising though unknown fact very early on. It was subsequently proved to be largely correct. It was also known that Stalin had considerable advance warning of the imminent Nazi attack, and this via numerous channels including Sorge and a number of Soviet spies in Japan as well as from Roosevelt himself. In addition, a German communist deserter crossed the lines at three in the afternoon to warn the Soviets that the German attack on the Soviet Union was to begin the very next morning. He was immediately executed. It is known, too, that Stalin ordered there should be *no response* to the Nazi air attacks which had gone on for many weeks, believing them to be a mistake (*sic*) or simply peaceful military manoeuvres. All this is now well attested. What followed were the familiar catastrophes.

There was total confusion in the Western parties. In France, the International had succeeded in getting Thorez to 'desert', though he was fiercely opposed to it. It was, however, an order and not open to discussion. He was to spend the whole of the war in a tiny village in the Caucasus, with a radio he could not use and totally cut off, especially from France. Duclos took over the leadership of the clandestine French Party (its deputies had been arrested in 1939–40). Initially he defended the theory of the *imperialist war* without recognising that it was simultaneously a 'war of liberation' (a line which was only adopted at a later date). Consequently, orders were given after the defeat not only that contact should be made with the occupying German authorities so that *L'Humanité* might be published again under the editorship of Marcel Cachin, but for something infinitely more serious. The underground leadership of the Party gave firm orders to its militants in positions of responsibility, especially those who were well-known to the masses, those who were union officials, political figures, mayors, etc., to appear quite openly in public and to hold meetings. It was an incredible decision which had the following consequences: leading Party militants such as Hénaff, Timbaud, Michels, and others were identified and arrested by the Germans, taken to Châteaubriand, and later shot. That is how Hélène's greatest friends disappeared and were massacred.

At the same time, a number of militants who were no longer in touch with the Party organised popular resistance in their own locality and on their own initiative, long before de Gaulle's appeal on June 18th. I could mention, for example, Charles Tillon, whom Hélène and I got to know very well thanks to Marcel Cornu. Not only did he organise one of the first Resistance networks in the Midi, when he received orders from the clandestine leadership to follow its line of 'militant pacifism', but he flatly refused to obey them, and was by no means the only French communist to do so. Declared anticommunists are not interested in true facts like these.

In December 1941, the International corrected its official line. The war was no longer simply an imperialist affair but a 'war of liberation'. The whole Party officially joined the Resistance *en masse* and devoted everything to the cause.

When I recall the political attacks made against the Party, either at the time of the German occupation (I have a huge collection of documents illustrating this) or afterwards and even today, by people who adopted the defeatist stance of the French bourgeoisie with deep-seated, almost physical conviction (even if as individuals they remained patriotic), it gives me food for thought. And it is in this context that Mauriac's remark, 'The working class alone remained faithful as a *class* when the country was violated' takes on its full meaning. Because the course of history is determined not by the attitudes of individuals but by class conflict and class positions.

The immediate post-war period, from 1945 to 1947, was marked by the consequences of these very grave events. De Gaulle was in power and there were communist ministers in the government.

The country had to be rebuilt and, if necessary, it was important to know 'how to end a strike'. But the communist ministers were pushed out by the socialist Ramadier under direct pressure from the Americans, and there was a really tough struggle ahead for the Party. As if by chance, this was the moment I chose to join.

It was no time to shilly-shally, given the vehemence of the anticommunist attack and the threat of war. The USSR did not yet have the atomic bomb which had killed so many people in Japan. The mass of the people had to be mobilised on the basis of the Stockholm Appeal.

This was the most urgent struggle. Internal Party issues were not even discussed. Having emerged victorious from the Resistance, its traditions and principles reinforced, having stood the test of time, the Party seemed incapable of being other than it was, for whatever reason. On the contrary, its leadership was 'more royalist than the king' or, in other words, than Stalin (who later placed less emphasis on linguistic definitions) by fiercely and publicly defending the concept of 'two sciences', bourgeois and proletarian. There were countless international incidents (Berlin, Budapest, Prague, etc.) before things began to change slightly even within the Party, and then not much and so belatedly! It seemed not to dawn on anyone (except a few individuals like Boris Souvarine, but who listened to them?) that a party based on the Leninist principles outlined in *What is to be done?*, in other words of *clandestinity*, which it practised so effectively in the Resistance, could or should organise itself differently once it was no longer clandestine.

That is why, objectively, *no form of political intervention was possible within the Party other than a purely theoretical one*; it was even necessary to take the existing accepted theory and direct it against the Party's own use of it. And since the accepted theory no longer had anything to do with Marx, being based on very dangerous absurdities derived from the Soviet, or rather Stalinist, interpretation of dialectical materialism, the only possible course of action was to go back to Marx, to a body of political thought which was fundamentally unchallenged because it was *sacred*, and show that Stalinist dialectical materialism, with all its theoretical, philosophical, ideological, and political consequences, was a total aberration. That is what I attempted to do in my articles for *La Pensée*, subsequently brought together in *Pour Marx*, and, with my students at the École in what became *Lire 'Le Capital'*, both of which were published, I recall, in October 1965. I have pursued the same line of attack ever since, first at a theoretical level then in straight political terms within the Party, to the extent of analysing its incredible internal functioning (*Ce qui ne peut plus durer dans le PCF*, 1978). Then came the tragedy of my life, since when I have ceased to be a card-carrying member. I am a 'communist without a party' (Lenin).

As you know, I have always insisted that my aim was to 'intervene in politics as a philosopher and in philosophy as a politician'. In fact, it would be possible to discern in my political action and experience the precise interplay of my personal phantasies: solitude, responsibility, mastery.

In venturing on an enterprise of theoretical opposition within the Party, I was on my own except for the help of friends who, in the early days, could be counted on the fingers of one hand. I later voiced my political opposition and became more openly critical. Certainly, my phantasy that I was in possession of the truth about the Party and of the practices of its leaders led me on a number of occasions to adopt the role of 'father's father'. I did so, for example, in laying down the law to students in 1964 in an article for *La Nouvelle Critique*. In other words, I allowed myself to be intimidated by the risks stemming from my attitude and by the attacks of the Party leaders, who clearly understood my strategy! Nevertheless, my text, which had the strategic advantage of putting the 'duty' of every communist towards Marxist theory above obedience to the Party, quickly disgusted me and I refrained from including it in *Pour Marx* in 1965. Rancière failed to take the point I was making, but for numerous other readers, including for example Greek students, it was clearly of considerable political value in their situation. (When Rancière vehemently criticised me in *La Leçon d'Althusser*, he largely based his case on this article, as if I had not excluded it from *Pour Marx*, which is my one major complaint against him.) I did so again when I demolished the unfortunate David Kaisergruber ('Sur une erreur politique') in two long articles in *France-Nouvelle*, where I defended auxiliary teachers as 'the proletariat of the education service'. Another example occurred in my meetings with Henri Krasucki, then 'the Party official responsible for intellectual matters', who kept hinting

'Ah! What might we not be able to do, if only we were not confronted by Aragon and Garaudy, who give each other support and are both supported by Thorez!' I was astonished to hear him suggest that just two militants could halt all the Party's initiatives in the intellectual sphere and I rebuked him for it. He did not reply. I was particularly disappointed because the idea of the leading intellectual being a real proletarian and a senior CGT official to boot had filled me with such high hopes. So I knew in advance that I would be sure to learn from him that the Party would definitely not publish my two books (*Pour Marx* and *Lire 'Le Capital'*) under its own imprint and that even the preface to *Pour Marx*, which the courageous and far-sighted Jacques Arnault promised would appear in *La Nouvelle Critique*, of which he was then the editor, would not be allowed to appear. There were further disappointments in store.

When, at a later date, with feelings of great goodwill I came face to face with Waldeck Rochet in his tiny office, yet again I assumed the role of 'father's father', though with a certain tact. At the age of fifteen, when he was an agricultural worker, he had found time and felt the inclination to read Spinoza. We talked about humanism (on a number of occasions I had defended the notion of Marx's theoretical antihumanism) and I asked him: 'What do the workers think about humanism? They don't give a damn! What about the peasants? They don't give a damn! But why then all these speeches in the Party about Marxist humanism? Don't you see, it's a question of speaking the same language as all those intellectuals and socialists. . . . ' I came down to earth with a bump, especially when I heard Waldeck's calm voice murmuring: 'We have to do something for them or they'll leave us.' I was so astonished I did not even dare ask him who 'they' were.

Long after that I talked to Marchais for three whole hours at the Party's headquarters. I got on my high horse on that occasion and told him just what I thought about the way the Party did things, backing it up with lots of details. With Jacques Chambaz by his side, Marchais listened to me during those three hours, hardly saying a word and not contradicting me once. He appeared to listen attentively to what I said, and I did at least respect his apparent desire to learn, which, I was told, came naturally to him. I will not discuss my meetings with Roland Leroy, who played at being a charmer and a liberal though he was doctrinaire at heart, nor my escapade with him at the festival organised by *L'Humanité* where I met Benoît Frachon, who had aged quite a bit, and Aragon, whom I really went for in an aggressive and abusive manner (you will discover why). Nor could I refrain from seeking the limelight during a public debate in which I took the unfortunate Pierre Daix to task politically, something I shall regret to the end of my days. He never forgave me for my Stalinist intervention, the only one in the whole of my political life. Need I add that I did not seek these meetings with leading Party figures, but was personally invited by them as they were anxious to know what I was like and what my ideas were. This was because my articles in *La Nouvelle Critique* and *La Pensée* (where I was openly protected by Marcel Cornu) had had a certain political impact, especially among the students at the École normale who had introduced new forms of training and action in the Young Communists Association. They had outflanked the leadership (Jean Cathala) and then left to form the Association of Young Marxist-Leninists, which was to become very active pre-'68 under the leadership of Robert Linhart, a student at the École for whom Hélène had a soft spot.

It must be obvious that I thus fulfilled my desire to take my own initiatives and to oppose fiercely the Party leadership and its apparatus, but I did so from within the Party itself, under its protection, as it were. In fact I never took up a position where I risked being expelled, except around 1978 and then not really. Even Roger Garaudy did not make me give way after Argenteuil, where he and I were the centre of attention in the debate about cultural matters. The next day he sent me a telegram saying: 'You lost, come and see me.' But I never went to see him. As well as recognising how wide our differences were, I doubtless felt sufficiently confident about my own arguments and position in the Party to ignore him completely, despite his having 'won' at Argenteuil.

I conducted this lively dispute under the protection of the Party and took care never to exceed the limits of its tolerance. But what really mattered to me in this was that I fulfilled my own desires, which had long been repressed or condemned by my family. They were desires I had first experienced at school in Larochemillay and rediscovered during my military service and then in the prison camp; the desire to become involved in the real world, with all sorts of people, and the desire above all to fraternise with the most deprived, the most straightforward, the purest, and the most honest. I wanted the real world, the world of struggle, as my own world. (Though it was very difficult for me, I finally faced up to being clubbed on demonstrations, like the terrifying one against Ridgeway, where we enthusiastically joined forces with the jeering Renault workers, armed with small, filed-down metal placards which were extremely useful in confrontations....) Swallowed up in vast crowds (at marches and meetings), involved in action and struggle, I was at last in my element. I was no longer obsessed with my phantasies about being in control.

I did, however, come directly into conflict with the *repressive apparatus of the Party* in certain circumstances, one of which was serious, the others somewhat comic. It is not only the State which has a repressive apparatus available: every ideological machine, whatever it may be, has one. My reasons for recounting these episodes are still the same: to understand myself more clearly.*

I joined the Party, then, in 1948, at the time of the Stockholm Appeal. I went up and down hundreds of staircases in run-down buildings near the gare d'Austerlitz, knocking on doors. People quite often opened the door but almost always refused to sign the petition I showed them. One day, a beautiful young woman in a négligée (her breasts showing...) opened the door with a smile but impassively refused to sign. As I was going down again, I heard a voice calling me back. She then said: 'After all you're young and handsome and I don't see why I should hurt your feelings.' And she signed. I left her with mixed emotions.

At the time I was wanting once again to 'save' Hélène from despair, from loneliness, and from being abandoned by the Party (yet again – as was always the case – I did everything I could right up to and including her death). In my naïvety, I was unable to understand how the Party and its various organisations could possibly do without the services of such an intelligent, politically astute, and extraordinarily militant woman. As she told me she

---

* We have left out a sentence at this point which provided a link in the first version of the chapter but which the author forgot to remove when he reordered his paragraphs (Editors' note).

had known Paul Éluard, I arranged a meeting with him which involved a great deal of scheming, without her knowing.

A naked woman was asleep on a couch in the room. I addressed Éluard in the familiar *tu* form (as we were comrades . . .), which he did not greatly appreciate. I passionately pleaded Hélène's cause, giving him a lot of details, and asked if he could possibly intervene so that she might be allowed to join the ranks of the 'Femmes françaises' as a militant. All he said by way of reply was: 'Hélène is indeed a remarkable woman and I know her well, but she always needs someone to help her.' That was the end of our discussion. Clearly, not all communists were like Courrèges.

Hélène ended up joining me on the Local Committee of the Peace Movement in the Fifth District. Everything seemed to be going smoothly, she made friends, and I was happy for her. But one day when she was at the movement's headquarters in the rue des Pyramides to collect some posters, she was recognised by a minor Party official who had seen her in Lyon. He reported it to the leadership of the Fifth District Committee and no doubt to Farge as well and this set in motion the most odious proceedings imaginable.

This minor official described how in Lyon 'everyone was aware' that Hélène, known as Sabine, Rytmann, who subsequently took the name Legotien (because she hated her family name and had adopted that of one of the first Jesuits to visit China in response to the wishes of Father Larue), was at one and the same time an agent of the intelligence service and the Gestapo (*sic*). It is true that certain rumours of the kind had spread in Lyon, the origin of which should now be revealed. At the time, Hélène was very friendly with the Aragons and throughout the period of the Resistance often used to bring them things from Switzerland, which were unobtainable in France, in particular silk stockings for Elsa. It so happened on one occasion that the stockings she brought were not quite the right colour or gauge for this very demanding lady. Whereupon Aragon got into a great rage and broke with Hélène. He also began to talk about her as an agent of the intelligence service! In addition, when Lyon was the scene of fighting at the moment of liberation, Hélène was in charge of a group of irregulars who went in for rough justice. They captured a senior Gestapo official, locked him up in the cellars of their building, tortured him, and then summarily executed him. Now Hélène had given strict orders, first that he should be treated the same as all the other prisoners, and secondly that they should take care to keep him alive so that he could be interrogated and the maximum amount of information obtained which would be useful to the Resistance and the young fighters of the French Forces of the Interior. But her irregulars disobeyed her orders. News of this execution spread in Lyon and reached the ears of those close to Cardinal Gerlier, whose attitude had been somewhat dubious during the occupation. One of his assistants, described by the communist militant as a 'whipper-snapper', sought an explanation from Hélène and went on at some length about the methods of torture she 'used' on prisoners held by the irregulars. Obviously it was all false, but it provided an alibi for those close to Gerlier who had a bad conscience. While they were at it, they decided to embroider the story a bit, and so the rumour spread that Hélène was a Gestapo agent.

The Party official's 'revelations' came as a bombshell, or at any rate provided the opportunity they had been waiting for to settle old scores in public. It is a known fact that Hélène, who had been a member of the Party since 1930, had not been able to renew contact with it during the war and that it had refused to take her back after the war. The following incredible story was then put around. Perhaps Hélène had been expelled from the Party in 1939, at the time of the Nazi–Soviet pact, but since the only person who could testify to this was a certain Vital Gaymann, who had turned his back on the Party, it could not become involved in investigations into her past. Meanwhile, Hélène was considered highly suspect by the Party for having been expelled in 1939.

The official's 'revelations' together with the Party's suspicions led to a full-scale trial, conducted by the leadership of the Local Committee, doubtless on the orders of the Party. The trial, during which extremely serious allegations were made against Hélène, lasted a whole week. Though she was allowed (not without a struggle) to call two Resistance friends to testify on her behalf, it was to no avail. Having looked carefully at all the evidence, the committee drafted a firm resolution recommending she be expelled from the Local Committee (though there was nothing in its statutes permitting it to do so or even to set itself up as a tribunal). I still recall the tall silhouette of Jean Dresch who listened without saying a word. I had fought like a tiger when the evidence of the 'whipper-snapper' priest came up. The leadership insisted on referring to him as a simple 'priest' ('so as not to offend the Catholics'). It is the only point which I won. When it came to the vote, everyone raised their hand (Dresch was not there) and, to my shame and astonishment, my own hand went up. I had known it for a long time: I was indeed a coward.

The Party summoned me, and Marcel Auguet, the secretary in charge of 'organisation', notified me of the order that I should break with Hélène. The secretary of the cell at the École, Emmanuel Le Roy Ladurie, took the initiative and the cell as a whole tried to see to its execution. (Le Roy Ladurie at least had the honesty to report this in his book *De Montpellier à Paris* and above all to apologise to Hélène the first time he met her. I would like to emphasise he was the only one of that rotten bunch to apologise or make the slightest gesture.) The most obvious sign that we were under 'surveillance', however, was that everyone shunned us *totally*. All our comrades avoided us in the street, and the only issue on the agenda in our cell was 'to save Althusser'.

Obviously, I refused to comply with their request. And soon afterwards, Hélène and I went off to take refuge in another form of isolation in Cassis where, even if we did not have any friends, at least people did not avoid us. Added to that, we had the consolation of the sea, the wind, and peace and quiet. Hélène displayed admirable courage. She kept telling me: 'History will prove me right.' All the same, we had experienced a proper Moscow-style trial in Paris, and I often thought later that, had we been in the USSR at the time, we would have ended up with a bullet in the back of the head.

Not surprisingly, all this gave me an unusually realistic insight into the leadership and workings of the Party. It related to another experience I had not long after I first joined. I had got the cell to set up a Politzer Circle at the École with the intention of inviting leading politicians and trade unionists to come to talk to us about the history of the workers' movement, and that is how we came to hear Benoît Frachon, Henri Monmousseau, André Marty, and others. But being prudent and disciplined, we agreed to seek the advice of Casanova who was in charge of 'intellectuals'. I went to see him with Desanti who, as a Corsican, had free access to Laurent and who followed his political lead, if he will excuse me saying so, like a little dog. We spent a good hour in the waiting-room with just a thin wooden partition separating us from Casanova's office. For an hour we listened to him shouting and bawling the most incredible insults at someone who said almost nothing. He was going on about proletarian science, a Party slogan at the time, and made the most staggering assertions including something about $2 + 2 = 4$. It seems that this was a 'bourgeois' notion. In the end a man came out absolutely crushed. Desanti told me it was Marcel Prenant. When we entered Casa's office, he started off again on the same furious argument he had just put to Prenant. Having calmed down, he read my notice and gave his approval. What a lesson!

The most surprising thing is that upsets of this kind, especially the first, which was horrible, did not make me depressed. I felt flattened but indignant, and that indignation, together with Hélène's extraordinary courage, certainly kept me going. I was becoming a man.

These early ordeals gave me the strength to fulfil within the Party itself the desire I had to resist and struggle, something I continued to do thereafter. I knew at last what was to be my chosen battleground, but by engaging in struggles within the framework of the Party I received its protection, as I have already said. The attacks on me were endless and intense, but I was tolerated, doubtless from some ulterior motive and because my theoretical interventions attracted a large audience. The situation I found myself in was distinctly advantageous since it satisfied my hitherto ineradicable desire for protection as well as my longing to take part in a struggle which I had so far achieved only through artifice. This time it was serious and became more and more so until the dramatic events of 1980.

XVII

Now I have spoken of the long road which led me to Marx or helped reinforce my belief in his ideas, and having already explained the whole history of my relationship with Marx both in *Pour Marx* (especially the preface) and 'Soutenance d'Amiens', I can be more succinct.

What I can say is this: it was largely *through organisations connected with Catholic Action that I came into contact with the class struggle and therefore Marxism.* But I have already pointed out, I believe, the astonishing quirk of history whereby, through exposure to the 'social question' and the 'social politics of the Church', countless sons of bourgeois and petit-bourgeois parents (including peasants in the Young Christian Agricultural Workers Movement) were introduced to the very thing it was feared they would be attracted to: socialism. In fact the Church, via its chaplains and encyclicals, made their own militants aware of the 'social question', of which most of us were *totally* ignorant. Of course, once we recognised there was a 'social question' and that the remedies proposed were ridiculous, it did not take much, in my case the profound political vision of 'Père Hours', for us to explore what lay behind the woolly-minded slogans of the Catholic Church and rapidly convert to Marxism before joining the Communist Party! This is how tens of thousands of militants from various Christian Youth Movements – students, workers, and agricultural workers – made contact with CGT or Party officials, in most cases through the Resistance. The current mass movement in support of liberation theology can be expected to produce even more important results.

I kept my 'faith' for a long time, until 1947 or thereabouts. It was certainly severely shaken in the prison camp when Daël and I 'took a trip in a van' to visit units in the countryside. As we drove along I caught a passing glimpse of a very young girl sitting silently on some stairs, *her knees close together*, who struck me as unbelievably beautiful. But something has suddenly occurred to me thinking of those 'clasped knees'. I am reminded of the astonishing lessons given by Henri Guillemin, who became our French teacher in Lyon for a whole fortnight in 1936. He got us to read *Atala*, but we skipped over, rather too quickly for his liking, the description of the beautiful young girl's dead body and especially the phrase 'the modesty of her clasped knees'. He became extremely angry, called us 'virgins' and, as no one dared offer an interpretation, in the end he literally shouted at us: 'If her knees are clasped together, it's because no one has forced her legs apart to fuck her! Can't you see she's a virgin? Once someone's been raped, they hold their knees apart!' I have to confess this alleged interpretation, which was more of an 'outburst', gave me something to think about. At any rate, it is possible there was some sort of emotive link between the knees which Guillemin alleged denoted virginity and the clasped knees of the beautiful young German girl I glimpsed. Furthermore, when I was in *khâgne* in Lyon, I had long been disturbed by an illustration in a book of Latin literature depicting lascivious, naked dancers on an Alexandrian bas-relief sculpted in bronze. I was so physically 'aroused' by it that I confided in Father Varillon. He gave me a 'spiel' about art and sublimation. OK.

Anyway, I had the very clear *feeling* I was ceasing to be a believer because of the striking incompatibility between my faith and my sexual desires (I still recall it: as an isolated incident).

Nevertheless I remained a believer until somewhere around 1947 when, with Maurice Caveing, François Ricci, and others, we set up our illegal union and fought to have it officially recognised (a situation not unconnected with my earlier problem of wanting to escape: how to get out of the camp while remaining there – but this time the situation was *reversed* and serious). Together with Hélène I visited 'young Father Montlucard' and the Church Youth Group at Petit-Clamart, though I cannot think why, as I told everyone I met: 'Atheism is the modern form of the Christian religion.' This remark went down well with our group. I wrote a long article about the state of the Church for the group's magazine, which liberation theologians still do me the honour of quoting. For me, Christ was the embodiment of Christianity as revealed in his evangelical 'message' and revolutionary role. Whereas Sartre was very keen on the idea of 'mediation', I came to the conclusion that it was either worthless or the thing itself, and this as a result of less than rigorous thought. If Christ was the mediator or the mediation, then what he mediated was nothingness and therefore *God did not exist.* Etc. Father Breton told me there was a whole history of such ideas in negative theology and among the mystics.

Thus I came to communism through Courrèges and my old friends in Lyon who became Resistance fighters (Lesèvre, etc.). Hélène's dramatic experiences naturally played their part and in no way contradicted or precipitated my own earlier experience.

As I had been a firm believer, I quickly became interested in Feuerbach's *The Essence of Christianity.* I worked on a translation of it for a good many years and though it took a great deal of time I only published a tenth, becaue Feuerbach is a man who constantly repeats himself. It was he who opened my eyes to the early writings of Marx, which I subsequently explored in some detail.

Feuerbach, an astonishing and largely unknown figure, was the real originator of phenomenology (with his theory of the intentionality of the subject–object relationship). He also influenced some of the views of Nietzsche and of Jacob von Uexküll, the extraordinary philosopher-biologist much admired by Canguilhem, who reinterpreted Feuerbach's concept of *Welt* as *Lebenswelt*, etc. I owe a great deal to the close reading of his work. Of course I also read the early works of Marx, which were seen at the time as great treasures which provided the basis for his ideas, and quickly realised they were *wholly Feuerbachian in inspiration,* including the 'break with our erstwhile philosophical conscience' which rapidly leads to *The German Ideology.* Nevertheless, Marx draws certain revolutionary consequences from this in relation to the means of production and the elements which comprise its 'combination'. These are found neither in Feuerbach nor even in Hegel. Having read the early writings, I found his later work much harder going. I had brought the 'young Marx' and the *Economic and Philosophic Manuscripts of 1844* to people's attention in *La Pensée* and introduced the idea of Marx's theoretical antihumanism. I then embarked on the astonishing manuscript of 1858 (the first version of his *Critique of Political Economy*) where

I came across the following striking phrase: 'The anatomy of the ape does not explain that of man, rather human anatomy contains a key to the anatomy of the ape.' This remark is astonishing for two reasons: first, it precludes in advance any teleological interpretation of an evolutionist conception of history. In the second place, it literally anticipates, though clearly in different circumstances, Freud's theory of deferred action [*après coup*], whereby the significance of an earlier affect is recognised only in and via a subsequent one which simultaneously establishes its existence in retrospect and lends it meaning. I later came across the same idea in Canguilhem's powerful critique of the *precursor*.*

As I have already said, I only read *Capital* in 1964–65 for the seminar which was to lead to *Lire 'Le Capital'*. If I remember correctly three individuals, Pierre Macherey, Étienne Balibar, and François Regnault, came to see me in my office in January 1963 to ask if I would help them read Marx's early works. So it was not my initiative which led me to talk about Marx at the École but rather a request on the part of a few students. This initial collaboration gave rise to the Seminar of 1964–65, which we set up in June 1964. Balibar, Macherey, Regnault, Duroux, Miller, and Rancière, etc., were there. Miller was the one with the most fixed ideas on the subject, but he dropped out completely in the course of the year. He was living in a hunting-lodge at Rambouillet with a girl who 'produced', so he said, 'at least one theoretical concept a week'. At any rate, she had just come up with one when I paid Miller a brief visit, as I was passing with Hélène.

We worked on the text of *Capital* during the entire summer of 1965. At the start of the new academic year, it was Rancière, to our great relief, who agreed to sort out the difficulties. He spoke for two hours on three occasions with extreme precision and rigour. I still say that without him nothing would have been possible. You know what happens in these cases. When the first person speaks at such length and in such detail, the others take advantage of it for their own work. This is certainly what I did, and I admit quite openly that on this occasion I owed a great deal

---

* Following handwritten comments not all of which seem to be Althusser's, the two subsequent paragraphs were not very clearly merged, making the text more difficult to read. Wherever sense demanded it, we reverted to the original version in the manuscript (Editors' note).

to Rancière. After his intervention everything was easy because he opened up the debate effectively and in areas to which we were already giving some thought; this was after a talk of mine on Lacan during which Miller intervened to announced a 'conceptual discovery': 'metonymic causality' (otherwise known as the absent cause), which caused quite a stir. The year went by, and Duroux, the cleverest member of our group, did not once open his mouth. But when Miller returned from Rambouillet in June 1965 and read the duplicated pages of the papers people had given, he discovered Rancière had 'stolen' his own concept of 'metonymic causality'. Rancière suffered terribly when charged with this. And is it not the case that concepts belong to everyone? I certainly thought so, but Miller had different ideas. My reason for relating this ridiculous incident is not to put Miller down. After all, youth must have its fling. Furthermore, it seems he began his magisterial course on Lacan this year by solemnly declaring, '*We are not studying Lacan but being studied by him.*' This proves he too was capable of acknowledging someone else had invented and owned a concept. The year ended very badly. By some trick of dialectics Miller accused me rather than Rancière of having stolen his concept of 'metonymic causality'. Happily for him, Rancière was therefore no longer implicated in this frightful business. I alluded to it in *Lire 'Le Capital'*. When I used the term 'metonymic causality', I referred in a footnote to the fact I had borrowed it from Miller, but I immediately changed it to 'structural causality' which no one else had used and was therefore my expression! What a to-do! It does, however, give some idea of what that small world was like. Debray was very struck by it on his return from Bolivia, and my readers must find it astounding.

I recently learnt from Father Breton that the whole question of authorship has a long history. Everyone knows that in the Middle Ages, unlike today, *scientific authorship* was attributed to an individual such as Aristotle. Literary works, on the other hand, were not attributed. Nowadays, exactly the opposite is true. Scientists contribute anonymously to a team effort, and at most, people refer to 'Newton's law' but usually to the 'law of gravity' or, in the case of Einstein, to special or general relativity. Even the most modest work of literature, however, permanently bears its author's name. But Breton discovered from a colleague of his, Father

Chatillon, who was an extremely erudite medievalist, that in a violent controversy with the Averroists Saint Thomas declared his opposition to the impersonality (in other words the 'anonymity') of the individual thinker, arguing very much as follows: all thought is impersonal since it is a product of the intellect as agent. But since all impersonal thought must be thought by a 'thinking being', it necessarily becomes the property of an individual. In law, it should therefore bear this person's name. It had not even crossed my mind that, in the Middle Ages, when, as Foucault told us at Soisy, the law of literary impersonality reigned, Saint Thomas should have established under philosophical law the need for authorship, albeit in the context of his controversy with the Averroists.

None the less, this absurd issue of the 'theft of concepts' touched on a point of principle which concerned me deeply and caused me great anxiety: the question of *anonymity*. Since in my own eyes I did not exist, you will readily understand that I sought to establish the fact of my non-existence through my own anonymity. I used to muse over Heine's remark about a famous critic: '*He was known for his notoriety.*' I liked Foucault's critique of the wholly modern notion of the 'author' and the fact that he personally disappeared by involving himself in militant action on behalf of those in prison, as I did within the obscurity of my Party cell. I liked Foucault's profound modesty, and I know Étienne Balibar appreciated 'more than anything else' the fierce attempt I constantly made to avoid all publicity surrounding my name. I had the reputation of being a recluse, shut away in my old flat at the École which I scarcely ever left. And if I kept up the appearance of being a total recluse it was in order to achieve, if I could, the anonymity I believed was my destiny and which would in addition bring me peace. And in offering this extremely personal record of my life to whoever wishes to read it, I again seek, in a somewhat paradoxical manner, *a definitive state of anonymity*; not the anonymity afforded by the fact I was declared unfit to plead, which was like a tombstone over me, but by publishing all there is to know about me, thus putting an end to further requests for me to be indiscreet. This time journalists and other media people will have had their fill, though you will see that they will not necessarily be satisfied. First, because they will not have done any of it for themselves, and secondly because they will have nothing to add to what I have written; not even a commentary, because I have provided my own!!

Thus, the more philosophy I read and the more I studied Marx, the more I came to realise he had explored major doctrines elaborated by writers who preceded him, such as Epicurus, Spinoza, Hobbes, Machiavelli (partially, in actual fact), Rousseau and Hegel. Whether he did so knowingly, I am not sure. I did, however, become more and more convinced that the philosophy of Hegel and Feuerbach had served both as a basis and an epistemological obstacle to the development and even the formulation of his own concepts (Jacques Bidet offered a rigorous demonstration of this in his recent thesis *Que faire du 'Capital'?*, published by Méridiens-Klinksieck). This naturally led people to ask questions of and about Marx which he himself could not and did not raise. Similarly, we became aware that if we wished to 'think for ourselves' when confronted with the incredible, contemporary 'imagination of history', we, in our turn, had to invent new forms of thought, new concepts – but always in tune with the materialist inspiration of Marx so as to 'avoid telling stories' and to be alert to the novelty and inventiveness of history. I am thinking here of the development of extremely interesting ideas even though they owe nothing to Marx and are believed (?) to be politically anticommunist, and in particular of that most remarkable book by François Furet on the French Revolution. He quite rightly counters the purely ideological tradition which developed at the time of the Revolution, and which Marx described as the 'illusion of politics', with reference to the rule of the Parisian Revolutionary Committees.

These are the things which dominated my dealings with Marx and Marxism. I have since come to realise, as anyone might (and as Marx himself largely did), that the philosophical, if not the scientific, core of Marxism was elaborated long before his day (by Ibn Khaldoun, Montesquieu, etc.), apart, that is, from the woolly and literally untenable labour theory of value which Marx claimed as his one genuinely personal discovery. I shall refer elsewhere to the political aspects of what might appear to have been a purely theoretical venture (so much has been said about our 'theoriticism' and our 'disdain for practice'!!).

XVIII

Only now do I see clearly what my dealings with Marx have been about. And again I am not concerned with the objectivity of what I wrote, nor with the way I related to one or some objective objects, but with how I related to an object as an 'object-choice' [*objectal*], in other words an internal and unconscious object. For the moment I am only concerned with talking about this 'inner' [*objectal*] relationship.

This is how I see things now or, to be more precise, since I began writing this book.

How did I connect with the world that surrounded me in childhood, at once so narrow and so repetitive? And since I lived within my mother's desire, how was I able to relate to that world, once I became aware of it, as she did, not by using my body and hands to touch and work with what already existed, but simply by using my eyes? The eye is passive, removed from the object it observes. It receives an image without having to do anything, without having to approach, make contact or handle whatever it might be (my mother's phobias included dirty hands and dirt in general – and that is why I rather liked dirt). Thus, from Plato and Aristotle to Saint Thomas and beyond, the eye is the speculative organ *par excellence*. As a child I would never have 'felt any little girl's thing' but I was something of a voyeur and remained so for a long time. Distance was a feature of my life: the double distance suggested to me and imposed by my mother. In the first place, there was that distance which protected you from the intentions of others before they could touch you (theft or rape). Then there was the distance separating me from the other Louis whom my mother constantly looked to through me. I was therefore a seeing child, bodiless and bereft of touch, since all contact is physical. I am told I made the following dreadful remark around 1975: 'There are bodies, you know, and they have sexual organs'!

As I felt I had no body, I did not even have to protect myself from physical contact with things or people, and no doubt that is why I was panic-stricken at the thought of fighting, afraid my body (or what I had of one) would be injured in those brief but violent encounters between boys, afraid its illusory wholeness could be breached; I was panic-stricken too about masturbating, an idea which never occurred to me before I was twenty-seven.

I believe, however, that my body felt a deep-seated desire to achieve its own existence. That is why I so wanted to learn to play football. It also explains my considerable skill at exercising all the different muscles in my mouth and throat, my arms and legs (speaking languages, playing football, etc.). These desires were merely latent until I was fortunate enough to get to know my grandfather, first at the forestry house in the Bois de Boulogne but especially in the garden and the fields in the Morvan. I see quite clearly now that this was the exhilarating period of my life when I finally acknowledged and had brought home to me the existence of my body, and when I truly realised its potential. Remember the discoveries I made: the smells, especially of flowers, fruits, and plants, but also of their decay, the heavenly smell of horse dung, the smell of earth and shit in the little wooden privy in the garden under the heavily scented elder tree; the taste of the wild strawberries I hunted for on the banks, the smell of mushrooms, above all the boletus, the smell of hens and of blood; the smell of the cat and the dogs, the smell of chaff, of oil, of spurts of boiling water, of animal and human sweat, of my grandfather's tobacco; the smell of sexual organs, the pungent smell of wine and cloth, the smell of sawdust, the smell of my own sweat when I was physically active; the joy I felt when my muscles responded to my impulses and I was strong enough to lift sheaves high up on to a cart or to pick up logs and branches, just as they had responded to my desire to teach myself to swim, to play tennis well, and ride a bike like a champion. All these things I acquired in the Morvan through the active and kindly presence of my grandfather (whereas my father's violence in Algiers and Marseille filled me with fear rather than providing me with a model).

That is where I began to 'think' with my body, something which remains with me still. It was no longer a question of thinking distantly and passively by merely looking, but 'thinking' actively with my hands, through the unbounded interplay of all my muscles and bodily sensations. When I roamed around my grandfather's field and garden or in the woods, I thought only of turning and working the soil (I was an expert at digging), of lifting potatoes, of scything wheat and barley, of parting the branches of young trees to cut them with my knife. Oh, how I loved cutting young chestnut branches for basket handles with the knife my grandfather gave me, as big and as sharp as his. How I loved cutting withies to make the framework of the basket and how I loved weaving them myself. How I loved cutting up the dry bundles of kindling with a bill-hook or splitting logs with an axe in the musty cellar which smelt of wine.

A whole new life opened up for me, so that instead of simply looking at things speculatively from a distance I felt the thrill of physical exercise, walking in the woods, running, or going on long bicycle rides which involved exhausting climbs. As I have already said, I got the same sense of personal exhilaration from physical labour in the prisoner-of-war camp. It was something permanent and deep-seated which determined the course of my life and enabled me to discover my own true desire rather than my mother's. (She had a holy terror of all physical contact, so obsessed was she with her own bodily 'purity' which she defended in all sorts of ways against any encroachment which spelt danger, relying especially on her countless phobias.) I felt happy at last having my own desires, happy above all in my own body and with the incontrovertible evidence of my physical existence. I had nothing in common with St Thomas Aquinas and the theology which is still governed by the figure of speculative eye, but a great deal in common with St Thomas the Apostle who wanted to touch before he would believe. More than that, I was not content simply to believe in reality because I had touched it, I had to work it and transform it to believe not only in simple reality itself but beyond that in my own existence which I had at last achieved.

When I 'came into contact with' Marxism, I subscribed to it with my body; not simply because it represented the radical critique of all 'speculative' illusions, but because it enabled me to establish a true relationship with plain reality, by way of that same critique of speculative illusions. It further allowed me thereafter to experience the same physical relationship *within thought itself* (both in terms of simple contact but above all by working on social or other dimensions of reality). In Marxism and Marxist *theory* I discovered a system of thought which acknowledged the primacy of the bodily activity, and labour over passive, speculative consciousness and I thought of this relationship as materialism itself. I was fascinated by it and had no difficulty in subscribing to such a point of view which came as no surprise to me because I had already discovered it for myself. In the sphere of pure thought (where, as far as I was concerned, the image of my mother and her desires still prevailed), I at last discovered the primacy of the body and of the hand as the agent of transformation of all matter. This enabled me to eradicate the internal division between my theoretical ideal, derived from my mother's desire, and my own desire which had acknowledged and then realised physically my desire to exist for myself, to have my own true existence. It was not a matter of chance that every category within Marxism was conceived by me in terms of practice, and that I put forward the notion of 'theoretical practice', which enabled me to fulfil my desire for a compromise between speculative, theoretical desire (derived from my mother's desires) and my own desire which was obsessed less with the concept of practices than with my experience of and desire for real practice, for contact with (physical or social) reality, and for its transformation via labour (the worker) and action (politics). Interestingly, the expression 'to think is to produce' is found in Labriola. No one was aware of this fact, but who in France had read Labriola?

In my early writings I was still expressing this compromise in the only way I could through pure thought. Doing the best I could within the terms of this compromise, I was led to formulate that excessively celebrated definition of philosophy as: 'The Theory of theoretical practice' (Cesare Luporini was so affected by that fragile capital letter . . .), but quickly abandoned it as a result of the criticism of Régis Debray and especially Robert Linhart, both of whom really knew what political action was and its primacy. In fact, the reason my friends were able to get me back on the right track so easily was because it corresponded to my own profound and longstanding desires.

Before turning to Marx himself, I ought to talk about the detour I made via Spinoza, Machiavelli, and Rousseau, though it represented in fact a 'royal road' which led me to him. I have already suggested as much without explaining it properly.

What I discovered in Spinoza (as well as the well-known Appendix to *Tractatus* Book I) was a formidable theory of religious ideology, an 'apparatus of thought' which turns the world upside down and takes causes as ends; the whole thing elaborated in terms of its relationship to social subjectivity. What a 'cleansing' operation it proved to be!

What I also discovered in what he called knowledge of the 'first order' was not knowledge as such, and *a fortiori* not a theory of knowledge – a theory of the absolute 'guarantee' of all knowledge, an 'idealist' theory – but a theory of the directly lived world (for me the theory of the first order was quite simply the world, in other words the immediacy of the spontaneous ideology of common sense). Above all, what I found in the *Tractatus Theologico-politicus* was the most striking and, at the same time, the least known example of knowledge of the 'third order'; or at least that is how I saw it. It was the highest form of knowledge, which afforded both unique and universal understanding of an object (though I have to admit this is a somewhat Hegelian reading of Spinoza, it is not in my view a false reading. It was not by chance that Hegel considered Spinoza to be 'the greatest'). The understanding achieved was that of the unique historical individuality of a people, that of the Jewish people (I believe that in his 'third order' Spinoza was aiming at knowledge of all unique and, in its way, universal individuality). I was absolutely fascinated by his theory of the prophets, which reinforced my view that Spinoza had attained an incredible understanding of the nature of ideology. Everyone knows, of course, that the prophets climbed mountains to hear the word of God. What they actually heard was the din of thunder and lightning together with a few words, which they took back, *without having understood them*, to the people awaiting them on the plains. The extraordinary thing is that the people themselves, with their self-consciousness and knowledge, then explained to these deaf, blind prophets the meaning of God's message! They explained it to all of them, except that idiot Daniel who not only failed to understand what God said to him (the lot of all prophets) but even the explanation provided for him! This simply proves that ideology can, in certain cases, and maybe naturally does, remain totally impenetrable to those subjected to it. I was filled with admiration, as I was by Spinoza's conception of the relationship between the religious ideology of the Jewish people and its material existence in the temple, the priests, the sacrifices, the observances, the rituals, etc. Following his example on this point, as well as that of Pascal whom I greatly admired, I was later to insist strongly on the material existence of ideology, not only the material *conditions* of its existence (an idea which is found in Marx as well as in a number of earlier and later writers) but also on the *materiality* of its very existence.

I had not, however, finished with Spinoza. He was a thinker who rejected any theory of knowledge (of either the Cartesian or later, Kantian kind): a writer who rejected the fundamental role of the Cartesian concept of the subjectivity of the *cogito*. He contented himself with putting forward as a fact: 'man thinks', without drawing any transcendental consequences from this. He was also a nominalist, and Marx taught me that nominalism was the royal road to materialism. In fact, it leads only to itself, but I can think of hardly any more profound *form* of materialism than nominalism. Without offering any explanation of the origins of its meaning, Spinoza declared: 'We have a true idea', a 'norm of truth' provided by mathematics – yet another fact offered without any explanation of its transcendental origins. What is more, he was a man who believed in the *facticity* of facts, which was astonishing in a supposedly dogmatic person who deduced the existence of the world from God and his attributes! Nothing could be more materialist than this thought without origin or end. I later took from it my description of history and of truth as a *process without a subject* (providing the origin and basis of all meaning) and without end (without any pre-established eschatological destination); for by refusing to believe in the end as an original cause (by a mirroring of the origin and the end), I truly came to think as a materialist. I employed the following metaphor: an idealist is a man who knows which station the train leaves from and also its destination. He knows it in advance and when he gets on a train, he knows where he is going because the train is taking him there. The materialist, on the other hand, is a man who gets on to a moving train without knowing either where it is coming from or where it is going. I used to enjoy quoting Dietzgen, who anticipated Heidegger, though unknown to him, in saying that philosophy was '*der Holzweg der Holzwege*', the way of ways which led nowhere – knowing also that Hegel had earlier thought up the remarkable image of a 'path which makes its own way', opening up and forging a way through woods and fields. For me, all these ideas were or became closely associated with Spinoza's thought. And I am not referring here to his famous remark: 'the concept of the dog does not bark', which drew a distinction between the concept and its sensible referent, but was on this occasion a central element in the creation of a scientific, conceptual system of thought. What that meant as far as I was concerned was that the concept had to be distinguished from its ideological overlay of 'received experience', such was my theoretical antipathy to Husserlian phenomenology – and especially Husserlian Marxism as represented by Desanti.

What struck me the most, however, was Spinoza's theory of the *body*, of which the *mens* (wrongly translated both by the word soul and the word spirit) is the idea, itself wrongly conveyed by this term. Though we are ignorant of so many of the body's capacities, he thought of it as a *potentia*, both as a force (*fortitudo*) and as an opening on to the world (*generositas*), a disinterested gift. Later on, I came across a startling prefiguration of Freud's concept of the libido in this same theory, as well as of the theory of ambivalence. It was startling inasmuch as Spinoza to give only one example thought that *fear was the same as its opposite hope*, and that both were 'sad passions' and the opposite of the vitally expansive and joyful *conatus* of the body and the soul, which were as inseparable as the lips and the teeth.

You can imagine how positively I responded to his idea of the body since it confirmed my own experience. At first, I had the sense that my body was fragmented, lost, absent, full of excessive fears and hopes. It had then been reconstituted. It was as if I had discovered it by learning all the things of which it was capable as I worked in the fields with my grandfather and then in the prison camp. The discovery that a person could take control of his body and in the process think freely and powerfully, in other words with and in that body; that is to say, the discovery that *the body was capable of thinking* as it realised its full potential really excited me, as it confirmed what I had truly experienced for myself. Hegel was so right when he said you only know what you yourself have *recognised*.

All the same, it took other philosophers as well truly to introduce me to Marx, in the first place the political thinkers of the seventeenth and eighteenth centuries, as I pointed out in my 'Soutenance d'Amiens'. I had planned to go on to write a State doctorate on them. From Hobbes to Rousseau I discovered the same profound idea of a world of conflict in which people and their possessions can be protected without dispute only by the absolute authority of the State (Hobbes) which would put an end to 'the war of all, against all'. This of course prefigures the class struggle and the role of the State which, as everyone knows, Marx declared he did not discover but borrowed from his predecessors and in particular from the French historians of the Restoration, who could hardly be described as 'progressive', and from the English economists, especially Ricardo. He could have gone even further back, to the famous debate between the 'Romanists' and the 'Germanists', not to mention the authors I have referred to. The celebrated Cardinal Ratzinger, who cannot sleep at night because of the class struggle, would do well to improve his mind a little. Rousseau, who conceived of similar social conflict existing in the 'developed' state of nature, had another solution to the problem: the elimination of the State, to be replaced by the direct democracy of the 'contract' expressing the general will 'which never dies'; enough to make you dream that communism might one day exist! But I was also fascinated by Rousseau's Second Discourse and the theory of the illegitimate contract, which he represented as a trick conceived by the rich in their perverse imagination as a way of subjugating the poor. This was yet another ideological theory, but one linked to its social role and causes, in other words to its *hegemonic* function in the class struggle. I consider Rousseau to be the first theorist of hegemony after Machiavelli. There were also his plans to reform the government of Corsica and Poland which, far from suggesting he was Utopian in his thinking, showed him to be a realist who took into account the complexities and traditions of each country and respected the rhythm of time. He revealed exactly the same qualities in his remarkable theory of education, *Émile*, in which he insisted that the natural stages of development should be respected and never anticipated. Again, it was a question of respecting the part time played in a child's development (knowing how to waste time in order to gain it). Lastly, I saw the *Confessions* as a unique example of a form of self-analysis, undertaken without the slightest trace of complacency, in which Rousseau clearly revealed himself in writing about and reflecting on the key events of his childhood and adult life. But most important of all, and for the first time in the history of literature, they dealt with *sexuality* and put forward a splendid theory of the sexual '*supplement*', which Derrida interpreted brilliantly as a metaphor for castration. What I especially liked about him was his radical opposition to the eschatological, rationalist ideology of the Enlightenment 'philosophers' who detested him so much (this, at least, is what he believed in his permanent state of paranoia) and believed that understanding between peoples would be improved as a consequence of intellectual reform, which was a total aberration as far as the real nature of all ideology was concerned. I found the same opposition expressed with uncompromising lucidity in the works of Marx and Freud. Another thing I liked about Rousseau was his radical independence as an individual when he came face to face with the temptations of riches and power, not to mention the immense pleasure he derived from his own self-education, which also meant a great deal to me personally.

Machiavelli was a later discovery, and in my view he went a lot further than Marx on a number of issues, for example in trying to conceive the conditions and kinds of political action in its pure form, that is to say at the conceptual level. What struck me again was the radical manner in which he took account of the chance nature of every conjuncture. In addition, he revealed that what was needed, if Italian national unity was to be achieved, was for a nobody starting with nothing and from nowhere in particular, but outside the framework of an established State, to bring together the fragmented elements of a divided country, without any preconceived notion of unity which might have been formulated in terms of existing political concepts (all of which were bad). We have not yet, I believe, explored all the implications of this piece of political thinking, the first of its kind and sadly without a sequel.

In short, I became a Marxist as a result of all my personal experiences, as well as the things I read and the associations I made. I began to think about Marxism in my own way, though I now realise it was not exactly the way Marx himself thought. I can see that what I essentially tried to do was make Marx's theoretical texts intelligible in themselves and for us as readers, because they were often obscure and contradictory, if not deficient in respect of certain key points. I am also aware I had two driving ambitions in undertaking this task. First and most importantly, I did not want to resort to mere storytelling either about reality itself or the reality of Marx's thought. Thus I sought to distinguish between what I referred to as the ideology (of his youth) and his later thought, which I believed represented 'nature just as it exists without any admixture' (Engels). 'Not to indulge in storytelling' still remains for me the one and only definition of materialism. Secondly, in 'thinking for myself' (a phrase of Kant and taken up by Marx), I tried to make Marx's thought clear and coherent to all who read him in good faith and want to understand his theory. Naturally, it meant that my exposition of Marxist theory took on its own particular form, as a result of which a good many militants and specialists had the feeling I had invented my own view of Marx and an imaginary version of Marxism (Raymond Aron), which was far removed from the real Marx. I willingly accept this, since in fact I suppressed everything which seemed incompatible with his materialist principles as well as the remaining traces of ideology, especially the apologetic categories of the 'dialectic', and even the dialectic itself, which seemed to me to serve only in his famous 'laws' as an apology (justification) after the event for what had happened in the uncertain historical process, and which was used by the Party leadership to justify its decisions. On this issue I have never deviated, and that is why my own version of Marxist theory, which offered a corrective of Marx's own literal thought on a number of issues, brought forth countless attacks from those who clung to the letter of what Marx had written. Yes, I accept I created a Marxist philosophy which was different from the vulgar one, but since it provided the reader with a coherent and intelligible interpretation rather than a contradictory one, I thought I had achieved my objective and 'appropriated' Marx by restoring to him what he required: coherence and intelligibility. Moreover, it was the only possible way of 'breaking' the orthodoxy of the disastrous Second International which had given Stalin free rein.

Without doubt, I 'opened up' a new perspective to many young people at the time. It enabled them to think within the framework of my new presentation of Marx without in any way having to abandon the demands of coherence and intelligibility. It was thus possible to do both him and ourselves a service, by mastering his own thought better than he had done. He, after all, could not help being a prisoner of the theoretical constraints of his day (and of the inevitable contradictions to which they gave rise). Thus Marx became truly our contemporary, and this represented a minor 'intellectual' revolution in the whole conception of Marxist theory. Yet it was not so much these ridiculous innovations to which our opponents took exception but the basic aim we had of distancing ourselves from the literariness of Marx in order to render his own thought intelligible. As far as they were concerned, Marx remained a basically sacred figure, even in his aberrations, the founding father who was beyond reproach. I did not care for sacred father-figures and had for a long time believed that a father was simply a father, basically a rather dubious individual who found it impossible to play his role. Moreover, I had not only become accustomed to playing the role of 'father's father' but also enjoyed doing so, and therefore I found it very easy to think for him, to have the thoughts he should have had.

In addition, by basing my argument on Marx, who was after all the founding father of the Communist Party and their official source of inspiration, I acquired a peculiar position of strength. This made me difficult to attack within the Party when I challenged the official interpretation of Marx which they used to justify their decisions, in other words what was effectively the Party line. What I did in fact was simply to appeal to Marx's thought against various aberrant interpretations, and especially the Soviet ones which served as a source of inspiration to the Party. Even Lucien Sève, who had a very good mind, drew on them for his own ideas and trotted out unlikely, untenable, and outdated formulations on several topics including ontology, the theory of knowledge, the laws of the dialectic as a kind of movement, which was the unique 'attribute' of matter. He did not [spare] me his criticisms and, as I never took the trouble to reply to what he said, he concluded from my silence that I had no objections to make. He went even further, however, by defending the celebrated and spurious dialectic and its laws, which he manipulated at will to justify *a priori* the changing line of the Party, in particular the abandonment of the dictatorship of the proletariat. As André Tosel recently showed in an essay on the ideas of Gramsci and the Italians, he continued, without realising it, to think within the unchanging framework of dialectical materialism (giving primacy to that dreadful term 'dialectical materialism' over all science).

At a time when the leading 'hair-splitting philosophy' – as Marx described the 'decomposition' of Hegelian philosophy – considers Marxism dead and buried, when the craziest ideas based on the most implausible eclecticism and feeble-minded theory are in fashion, under the pretext of so-called 'post-modernism', in which, yet again, 'matter has disappeared', giving way to the 'immateriality' of communication (the latest theoretical concoction which not surprisingly justifies itself on the basis of the impressive evidence of the new technology), I remain profoundly loyal to the materialism which inspired Marx, though without accepting it word for word, which I have never done.

I am an optimist, believing that Marxist thought will survive through thick and thin even if it assumes different forms – which is inevitable in a world undergoing profound change. It will survive for another powerful reason: the feebleness of current theoretical thinking is such that the mere reappearance of those elementary but necessary ingredients of authentic thought – rigour, coherence, and clarity – will, at a certain point, contrast so markedly with prevailing intellectual attitudes that all those who are bewildered by what has happened are bound to be struck by them. That is why, for example, I appreciate the trouble taken by Régis Debray to remind those who wish to pass judgement, of such elementary facts as these: that the period of the Gulag, at least on a massive and dramatic scale, is over in the USSR, that the USSR has more important things to do than think about attacking the West. Admittedly, Debray does not go very far, but by simply reminding people of certain obvious facts in the face of the powerful, prevailing ideology, he performs, what Foucault was fond of calling, a 'cleansing operation'. And what exactly is a cleansing operation? It involves a critical reduction in the layer of ideological notions which are simply taken as given, thus allowing contact with reality 'without extraneous additions'. It is, I concede, a simple and limited operation, but a truly materialist one. My firm belief that we shall emerge from the present intellectual 'desert' is due to the fact that Debray's exceptional and courageous reminder of the true situation, at a time when the best minds are deadened by the prevailing mood of intellectual nullity, may have multiple consequences. When, in a void such as this, someone has the courage to speak out, his voice is heard.

I have, I believe, made it clear I was not sectarian, and it matters little to me whether ideas claim or are believed to be right-wing. I shall always find them interesting, unless they are a lot of hot air, so long as they break through the stifling layer of ideology and bring me face to face with stark reality, as if I were making actual physical contact with it (yet another modality of the existence of the body). This is why, in my view, Marxists are, thankfully, far from being the only ones striving nowadays to discover and tell the truth about reality. Without realising how close they are to the Marxists, many honest people, with real practical experience and conscious of the primacy of practical experience over mere consciousness, are already following them in their quest for the truth. Knowing this, and taking into account differences of style, temperament, and politics, there is reasonable cause for hope.

I am not sure whether humanity will ever experience communism; Marx's eschatological view of things. All I know is this: the inevitable transitional phase of socialism which Marx spoke about is 'a load of crap', as I pointed out in 1978 in Spain and Italy to audiences who were disconcerted by the vehemence of my remarks. In those situations, too, I told a 'story'. Socialism, I said, was like a very wide river that was very dangerous to cross. Soon we would have an enormous sand barge, in the form of political and union organisations, which would hold everyone. But in order to negotiate the eddies, we would need a 'helmsman', namely State power in the hands of revolutionaries. Class domination by the proletariat over all the hired oarsmen in the galleys was a further requirement (wages still exist as does private interest), otherwise domination by the proletariat would be finished. The huge ship would then be launched but the oarsmen would have to be watched during the entire voyage and strict obedience demanded of them. If they failed in their task, they would be replaced at the appropriate time and even punished. If, however, they succeeded in crossing this vast river of shit, then on the horizon would be the shore with sunshine and soft spring breezes. Everyone would disembark; there would no longer be strife between individuals and interest groups as relationships would no longer be those of the market-place. Instead, there would be fruit and flowers in profusion for everyone to gather and enjoy. It would be a time for Spinoza's 'joyful passions' and Beethoven's 'Ode to joy'. I went on to claim that 'oases of communism' already exist, in the 'interstices' of our society (interstices was the word Marx used to describe the early groups of merchants in the ancient world, copying Epicurus's idea of gods on the earth), *where relationships based on the market do not prevail*. I believe the only possible definition of communism – if one day it were to exist in the world – is *the absence of relationships based on the market*, that is to say of exploitative class relations and the domination of the State. In saying this I believe I am being true to Marx's own thought. What is more, I am sure that there already exist in the world today very many groups of people whose human relationships are not based at all on market forces. But how can these interstices of communism be spread to the whole world? No one can foresee that – and it will certainly not come about on the basis of the Soviet model. Will it be through the seizure of State power? Of course, but this would lead to socialism (and State socialism at that, necessarily) which is 'a load of crap'. Will it be through the withering away of the State? Of course, but in a capitalist-imperialist world which appears more solidly based than ever thus rendering the seizure of State power precarious if not illusory, how can one envisage the withering away of the State actually taking place? It certainly will not be through Gaston Defferre's form of decentralisation nor as a result of the idiotic slogans of Reaganite neoliberals or those who model themselves on Chirac. They will simply rid us of the State which is essential if we are to control the hegemony of international bourgeois capitalism. If there is hope, it comes from mass movements which I always considered more important than their political organisations (thanks to Hélène, among others). Certainly, when you look around the world you see mass movements developing which were unknown and not envisaged by Marx (in Latin America, for example, and even within a traditionally reactionary Church in the form of liberation theology, or with the Greens in Germany, or in Holland where they refused to welcome the Pope as he might have wished). But these movements perhaps risk coming under the control of organisations which they cannot do without but which appear not yet to have worked out an adequate form of coordination which avoids hierarchical domination, trapped as they are in a tradition which relies on existing Marxist-socialist models. In this respect I am not optimistic, but I cling to this statement of Marx: at all events, 'history is more imaginative than we are', and anyway we are reduced to 'thinking for ourselves'. But I do not subscribe to the dictum of Sorel, taken up by Gramsci, that what we need is scepticism of the intellect together with optimism of the will. I do not believe in voluntarism in history. I believe, rather, in intellectual lucidity and in the superiority of mass movements over the intellect. On this basis, and since it is not of supreme importance, the intellect can follow the lead set by mass movements, prevent them above all from becoming the victims of past errors and help them to discover truly effective and democratic forms of organisation. If, in spite of everything, we still entertain some hope of helping to inflect the course of history, it will be along these lines and these lines only. At any rate it will not come about as a result of the eschatological visions of a religious ideology with which we are all utterly bored.

But we have now reached politics proper.

XIX

Now the moment has come which everyone, I hope, has waited for like me, the point where I explain not only my earliest emotional experiences, their repetitive nature, and the domination that the phantasy of not existing exerted on all my secondary phantasies, but also the relationship between those emotional experiences and external reality. If, even in the most dramatic dreams and emotional states, the 'subject' is concerned essentially with itself, in other words with internal, unconscious objects which analysts refer to as subjective (in contrast with external objects that are objectively real), the *legitimate* question everyone asks is the following: how could the projections of and investments in these phantasies issue in action and in a body of work (books of philosophy as well as philosophical and political interventions) which were totally objective and had some impact in the real world?

To put it another way, and much more succinctly, how did the *meeting* come about between the ambivalent investment in phantasised object [*objectal*] and objective reality? Rather, how did the two things 'gel', as one says of mayonnaise or ice cream that it thickens, or that a chemical reaction has occurred under the effect of certain catalysts? On this issue I owe myself above all, but also my friends and readers, if not an explanation at least an attempt at an elucidation.

I ought to warn you, therefore, that we are breaking new ground here in dealing with the conjunction of those unconscious phantasies that fuelled my desire, which was, on the one hand, subordinated to the fulfilment of my mother's desire and, on the other, swayed by real and objective data.

I would first like to clarify an issue to which my friend Jacques Rancière has devoted a most penetrating little study (*La Leçon d'Althusser*). Essentially, he reproaches me with having remained within the Communist Party despite my explicit disagreements with it and with having urged and encouraged a number of young intellectuals both in France and abroad not to break with the Party either.

It is more than likely that Rancière's attitude and what he reproaches me with can be both linked to his own inner 'objects', but I cannot, and, even if I could, I would not wish to enter upon an investigation into a personal and intimate area of his life. All I would say is that we were personally very close when we first got to know each other. It is true he quickly came to the conclusion that my position was 'objectively contradictory' when he left the Party. In doing so, he did not betray the cause of the working class but rather set out to discover what its earliest plans, reactions, and aspirations had been. He went on to produce two remarkable books devoted to popular views about the early workers' movement. In practical terms, I do not dispute what he said. Our positions were close but different and his seemed much closer to the apparent logic of my own writings and interventions. Why then did I remain in the Party, with all the consequences that decision had both for me and the young intellectuals I may have influenced if, that is, I did have some influence on people (which, after all, is possible)?

It would be too easy simply to fall back on the things I have expounded at some length about the impressive 'roots' and 'structure' of my unconscious 'subjectivity' (and this is equally the case for Rancière and those who share his views, since, so far as my subjectivity is concerned, I have laid my cards on the table, which means that anyone can explain my behaviour on that basis and define me once and for all). I will now explain why.

First, I had extremely powerful and concrete proof, in that my closest 'followers', my students at the École, under the astonishing leadership of Robert Linhart (to say nothing of Régis Debray who very early on began to map out his own path outside the Party and went on to join Che and his guerilla fighters in Bolivia), having taken over the leadership of the Communist Youth Movement from within, very quickly abandoned it (without my agreement) in order to set up a new organisation, outside the Party. This was the Union of Young Communists, Marxist-Leninist (UYCM-L), which expanded greatly, organised groups in schools, as well as political and theoretical study groups, and then went on to mass action, in particular by founding most of the first Vietnam Committees, which again grew significantly before May '68. The Party was literally outflanked by the students to the extent that, in May '68, as is well known, there were only a handful, and I mean a handful, of communist students (Cathala naturally stayed in his office) taking part in the immense upheavals at the Sorbonne.

The young members of the UJCm-l were not there either. Why? Because they had adopted an apparently rigorous 'line' which was to prove their downfall: they had gone to the factory gates in an attempt to create a unified movement of students and workers. However, it was not the job of extreme left-wing students to go to ask workers to join in the student insurrection in the Latin Quarter but rather that of Party militants. This was the fundamental error made by Linhart and his friends. Apart from a few rare exceptions, workers did not go to the Sorbonne because the Party, which alone had the authority, did not call on them to do so. Such a call might have been appropriate had the Party not thoroughly mistrusted the 'leftist' revolt of the student masses, but rather seized the opportunity, the 'chance' as Machiavelli describes it, to initiate and sustain with all its power and organisational might (above all that of the CGT which had remained faithful since the split of 1948) a strong mass movement capable of attracting not just the working class but large sections of the petite bourgeoisie too, which would have had the strength and the resolve to open the way objectively to a seizure of power and to a revolutionary politics. Is it generally known that Lenin wrote, with reference to the Dreyfus Affair which never gave rise to mass uprisings or to the building of barricades, that the unrest at the time could have produced a real revolution in France if the Workers' Party had not remained aloof from what was happening? In his blind obsession with the notion of 'class against class', Guesde believed that the Dreyfus Affair was a purely 'bourgeois' affair which had nothing to do with the class struggle of the workers. It is true that in 1968 only Paris was really involved in what was happening; the provinces to a lesser extent. Is it possible to create a revolution in the capital alone (of six million inhabitants) in a country with a population of over sixty million?

Yet, in May and June 1968, a lot of workers in a lot of factories believed that revolution was possible, expected it, and were simply waiting for the Party to give its orders in order to bring it about. Everyone knows what happened. The Party, which, as usual, utterly failed to grasp what was happening and was also terrified by the mass movements which it claimed were controlled by leftists (and whose fault was that?), did everything it could in the very violent battles taking place to prevent a coming together of the student battalions and the fervent masses of workers who were conducting the longest strike action ever in world history. The Party even went so far as to organise separate marches. Furthermore, it *organised* the defeat of this mass movement by forcing the CGT (in fact, given the organic links between the two bodies, force was scarcely necessary) to sit down in order to negotiate a peaceful economic settlement and, when the Renault workers declined the offer, to postpone it for a while. They also refused all contact with Mendès at Charléty, when Gaullist authority had all but disappeared, ministers had abandoned their ministries, the bourgeois were leaving the cities and going abroad, taking their money with them. I will give just one example: the French were unable to change their francs into lire, because the Italians would no longer take francs, as *they were worthless*. Lenin repeated on umpteen occasions that, when your opponent really believes the game is up, when things are finished at the top, and the masses are going on to the offensive in the streets, then not only is revolution 'on the cards' but a *revolutionary situation* actually exists.

Out of fear of the masses and fear of losing control (reflecting its permanent obsession with the primacy of organisation over popular movements), the Party did all it could to break the popular movement and channel it into straightforward economic negotiations. In doing this, it no doubt wanted at the same time to respect the apprehension of the Soviet Union (it did not need to be given explicit orders!) which, as part of its global strategy, preferred the conservative security represented by De Gaulle to the unpredictable nature of a mass revolutionary movement. What the Soviet Union feared was that such a revolutionary movement might have served as a pretext for political and even military intervention on the part of the USA (not altogether far-fetched as a possibility), a threat which the USSR could not have challenged.

In this respect it demonstrated just how effectively it could use its power to organise things and impose the appropriate political and ideological discipline. 'The precise moment, the opportunity' (Lenin) 'have to be seized with both hands' (Machiavelli, Lenin, Trotsky, Mao), since they may only last a few hours. Once they had gone, and with them the chance to change the course of history in a revolutionary manner, De Gaulle, who was as politically shrewd as anyone, reappeared on the scene having staged his disappearance, uttered some serious and solemn words on television, dissolved the Chamber of Deputies and called for fresh elections. At that point, the most conservative and reactionary elements of the bourgeoisie, the petite bourgeoisie and the peasantry, long established in France, rallied to the cause after the incredible procession down the Champs-Élysées. It was all over. The extremely long and violent student struggle and the long workers' strike which lasted several months were slowly defeated and both groups engaged in a long and painful retreat. The bourgeoisie took its cruel revenge. There were, of course, the Grenelle agreements (which represented an unprecedented advance on the economic front), but they were achieved at the cost of a revolutionary defeat the like of which had not been seen since the Commune. Those who took part in this popular movement were without doubt routed, above all because of the conservative instincts of the Party machine when confronted with a spontaneous uprising of the masses, but this time (the first in the history of French popular movements) almost without bloodshed. A number of students were badly beaten but not killed (one student was drowned at Flins, two workers were shot in Belfort, and a few others elsewhere). This was achieved 'peacefully' due to the hegemony of bourgeois, imperialist capitalism, the role played by its impressive State apparatus, its control of the media Ideological State Apparatus, and the 'image' of the Nation's Father-Figure, capable of dealing with any eventuality: the theatricality of De Gaulle's performance, his solemn face and voice had a reassuring political effect on the bourgeoisie. But when revolt ends in defeat without workers being massacred, it is not necessarily a good thing for the working class which has no martyrs to mourn or commemorate. The leftists, who understood these things, believed they could 'exploit' the few deaths they had suffered, such as that of the unfortunate Overney, a militant associated with *La Cause du peuple*. I remember what I kept saying to the people around me on the day his impressive and moving funeral took place (two million people carrying flags attended the ceremony in silence, though the Party and the CGT were absent): '*It isn't Overney they are burying today but the politics of leftism.*' Events were very quickly to prove me right.

This simple fact leads me to another point. To claim – as Glucksmann did so outrageously – that an individual, his work, and possible influence were capable of determining decisive political choices on the part of numerous young students and intellectuals (the only ones to be affected) and, stretching logic to its limits, of inspiring mass slaughter, represents a most strange conception of determination, of (personal) ideology, and of history. One would also need to look at what the existence of the Party, its organisation as well as the practical consequences of its economic, political, and ideological line meant or could mean to young bourgeois and petit bourgeois people. I later explained how the Party functioned. If you do not belong to the Party and have no long-term experience of its practices, you can have no real idea of what it is like, and anticommunist books such as those written by Philippe Robrieux do no more than *remind* those who did belong of certain things they either knew or suspected. At the time of Hélène's problems with the Local Committee, Robrieux was the most Stalinist of all the leading figures and the one who was sufficiently nasty to stir things up in my cell over the awful condemnations made at the Local Committee. There is nothing like first-hand experience and those who were never in the Party and who simply read the studies, or rather the aggressive semi-pamphlets produced by an obsessed journalist like Robrieux who had nothing better to write, gain at best a vague and vicarious impression which has no impact on them, unless other things have already done so. In the end, works of this kind tell us nothing except what some people already know from the inside. Others have long since gathered similar information, albeit in somewhat vague terms, from the vast anticommunist campaign, which was earlier strongly reinforced by Solzhenitsyn and latterly by Montand; a campaign which has always been predominant in the bourgeois ideology of this country and is now spreading far and wide.

Furthermore, in the 1950s, the only real and impressive forces of the left were the Communist Party and the CGT, and people had to 'make do' with them. *There was absolutely nothing else to take their place.*

If I did have some 'influence', as Rancière suggested in that little pamphlet of his that I so enjoyed reading because it was basically honest, profoundly sincere, and theoretically and politically acceptable (though only to a certain extent), how exactly did I exert it other than by asking a number of people (but how can one tell how many?) not to leave the Party straightaway but to remain in it? It is my belief that no other organisation in France, I repeat no other organisation in France, was able to offer genuine militants political education and experience equal to that which they could get if they were members of the Party over a long period. I do not claim to have been consciously aware of it, nor do I claim there were not other personal reasons for my remaining in the Party (I have talked about this at some length, but I want now to talk of totally objective facts and consequences). I do not claim either that I was as lucid as Rancière or others (whose motives were very rarely as pure). But it is a fact and represents the line I took. I never wrote anything or campaigned publicly or privately to persuade anyone to remain in the Party and I never publicly or privately disowned or condemned those who left or wanted to leave. The rule I adopted was that each person had to make his own decision. Perhaps I had bad personal reasons for staying or not good enough ones for leaving. The fact is, I remained within the Party, but all my writings show well enough that on fundamental questions, whether philosophical, political, or ideological, as well as on questions to do with the Party line (cf. *Sur le 22e Congrès*), principles relating to matters of practical organisation and the senseless practices of the Party, I was not in agreement with it. And I was the only one, *the only one I repeat, who said it openly within the Party,* and who adopted a line of internal opposition. It had to be done, and I did it. What is more, the leadership was right to suspect me of wanting to inflect the Party line, from within, in a Maoist direction. That certainly bothered them! Doubtless I was something of a 'mythical' figure, but they were sufficiently alarmed to 'place' two students, one from the École the other from the École des Jeunes Filles, on the

National Committee of the Union of Communist Students so that they could inform them directly – as they thought – about my intentions and activities! The question one obviously has to ask is, why?

However, that is not the crucial question, and one has to look beyond France. For my sins, I was also read in other countries and in a wholly different context! Forgive me for pointing it out, but countless philosophers, politicians, and ideologists claimed to be following my lead and moving in the semi-Maoist direction opened up by my writings. Just one example I could give is that of the Chilean, Marta Harnecker, a student of mine who lived in Paris between 1960 and 1965, if I remember correctly, and then returned to Latin America (Cuba) and wrote a brief manual of historical materialism. Believe it or not, ten million copies were published. It was not terribly good but, as there was nothing better, it represented the only basic political and theoretical text available to hundreds of thousands of militants in Latin America, the only work of its kind on the continent. It repeated literally the ideas put forward by Balibar and myself in *Lire 'Le Capital'*, though often they had not been understood. If you are going to analyse the influence an individual and his work had on and in the Party, it is no good limiting yourself to the wretched politics of France. You have to consider what is going on in the rest of the world. Certainly, Latin-American militants knew I was in the Party, but they also knew I had strong leanings towards Maoism (Mao had even granted me an interview, but for reasons to do with 'French politics', I made the stupidest mistake of my life by not going to see him, fearing the political reaction of the Party against me. But what could the Party have done, even supposing that news of my meeting with Mao had become known through an official, published communiqué? I was not really that much of a 'public figure'!).

In these circumstances, does it make any sense to distinguish between home and abroad? You can, on the other hand, limit your concern to France and follow the old tradition of deep-seated provincialism, thus revealing that unbelievable French pretentiousness which is rooted in too long a history of cultural domination, but which is now beginning to give way on all sides . . .

I was extremely conscious of all these things. By remaining in the Party while adopting an openly oppositional stance (the only reasonably serious and coherent position that existed, for which the vast majority of those in opposition for reasons of *temperament* rather than principle never ever forgave me and never will even when they have read this little book), I thought (and I realise it was largely a megalomaniac idea) I would be able to prove, at least in a formal sense, that oppositional action within the Party on a serious political and theoretical basis was possible, and thus that the Party itself could be transformed in the long term. I kept in close touch with all the former communists I knew (those who were expelled or who left after the Soviet intervention in Hungary or the intervention in Czechoslovakia in 1968 – when, as I know for a fact, Waldeck Rochet made desperate and dramatic attempts to intervene and suffered terribly at being literally kicked out of the Soviet Embassy in Paris, an experience from which he never recovered – and so many other notable people who were expelled and became close friends of mine, such as Tillon), and I also had close contacts with those who belonged to all the leftist groups in which there were former students of mine, and even with certain Trotskyists. They were never very kind to me, though I did not ever attack Trotsky, for whom I had great respect (despite his obsession with military sieges and his curious practice of never being on the spot at key moments in Soviet history). As all these people knew what my thoughts were, *and* what I was saying *and* writing (since I never hid my feelings from anyone – only Hélène asked me what the hell I was doing in a Party which had 'betrayed' the working class in '68, and she was quite right), no one could be in any doubt as to what I felt, what my position was, or the 'strategy' behind what I was doing. Presumably I do not have to remind people, for example, that after the drama of the Local Committee I had other reasons than those of Rancière for leaving the Party, and that when I denounced the abandonment of the dictatorship of the proletariat at the Bastille, I was surprised to see a journalist from *L'Humanité*, who had listened to my emotive outburst ('you don't abandon a concept as you might a dog'), writing up his report in the company of Lucien Sève, which he then let me read (there was nothing I wished to change), and which was published the next day in *L'Humanité* in its original form.

Only those I was not close to or who had nothing to do with the left, people who had been expelled as well as certain others who only knew me at second hand, might have had mistaken views about me. In fact, *not a single one* of my former comrades who had been expelled from the Party or left it at a moment of crisis *ever* reproached me with having remained a member. Rancière was the only one who rebuked me publicly and quite a lot of my ex-communist or leftist friends openly told me they deplored the attitude he adopted.

The crucial fact as far as I am concerned, which, I repeat, I did not perceive clearly at the time but somehow instinctively – which was often the case with me – was that being in the Party was by far the best way for militants to gain unrivalled experience and even more importantly political education, as long, that is, as they were not Party officials completely cut off from the outside world. In the first place, you could get to know the Party from the inside and judge it by what it did, comparing its forms of organisation, of leadership, and its often shameless ways of applying pressure, in other words judge its actions by its principles. Did you know that the Party has often put forward a relatively unknown militant from its own ranks or from the CGT as a candidate at an election in a particular constituency, and supported his candidacy on an *extreme right-wing* platform in order to challenge the genuine extreme-right candidate and thereby divide the vote? It happened recently in Antony, but that was by no means a unique example. Did you know that 'ballot-rigging' was common practice in municipalities controlled by the Party? Other parties do exactly the same thing in their municipalities. (Jean-Baptiste Doumeng, that out-and-out supporter of Stalin and the Soviet Union, whom I met a couple of times and who wanted me to explain Gramsci to him, was unquestionably a millionaire and a perfectly law-abiding businessman but, like any real businessman, he sometimes turned things to his own advantage and cheated the taxman! Poor old Doumeng, a target of both *Libération* and *Le Canard Enchaîné*, knew what he was doing and did not give a damn when people criticised him in a roundabout way. 'My conscience is clear', he would say, and it was a hundred times clearer than that of his contemptible and nit-picking critics!) I will not even mention what actually went on in those municipalities, in the so-called offices of architecture and urban planning and in the import-export companies, a large percentage of whose profits went straight into Party funds. If the other parties have kept quiet about these rather dubious activities, it is because they were involved in similar chicanery themselves, though perhaps on a lesser scale and with less risk (they were in charge of the State).

As an active member it was possible to get an extremely clear idea of the Party's practices and of the obvious contradiction between those practices and its theoretical and ideological principles. I brought all this directly to the attention of Marchais in 1978, but not surprisingly he made no comment. What could he have said? After all, he knew more about it than anyone.

But as well as gaining knowledge of the Party, its strengths, and the way it operated (the qualified voting system involving four ballots at the Congress which I denounced publicly in 1978 in *Le Monde* and in a pamphlet which is now unobtainable), you could also gather concrete information about the complexity of the working class and its organisation within the Party and the CGT, and I emphasise that 'organisation' within the Party. Thus it was possible to discover, with some stupefaction, that the hard core of unquestioning militants in the vanguard in the Party remained unquestioningly loyal in their fierce defence of the Soviet Union and its interventions in Hungary, Czechoslovakia, and later Afghanistan, long after the XX Soviet Congress and the XXII French Congress. You discovered that these militants and the Party itself were completely cut off from sections of the working class which belonged to Force Ouvrière and the CFDT, from non-unionised workers, from the mass of immigrants (remember the bulldozer at Vitry), from all kinds of employees, managers, intellectuals, and petit bourgeois people whose support the Party tried to enlist for various *ad hoc* organisations, following the official line on the 'Union of the Left'. The same thing was true of the Catholics who made a great fuss of those theologians, priests, and monks who agreed to sign all the petitions and appeals to vote communist (I have always curtly refused to sign anything canvassing electoral support and almost every other kind of petition). The same thing was also true of those Catholics whose underlying motives were basically despised by important figures in the Party (Garaudy and later Mury and then Casanova) who did not comprehend their reactions even when they were publicly favourable to the Party, and so on. You also gained considerable experience not only of Party practices in its alliance with its political 'allies' but of those allied political groups as well. What is more, you were in the advantageous position of making critical comparisons between the stridently projected official image which the Party sought to convey from behind the walls of its fortress in the rue Fabien and from within the federations which were kept under close supervision by members of the Central Committee and the Politburo, and the actual ideology, attitudes, and behaviour of those political groups. And I am not talking about the peasants, whom the Party never tried to understand in spite of having MODEF [the Movement for the Defence of Farming Families] at its disposal. (Hélène had direct experience and was uncompromising on this issue. She had carried out surveys on the ground in connection with proposed motorways and other projects which brought her fame within the organisation for which she worked, Sedes, but was frowned on in the Agricultural Committee of the Party.)

Can you think of any other organisation, whether the PSU, the Communist League, or any of the tiny left groups, which would have enabled a militant to gain equivalent social, political, and ideological experience of the class struggle to that which could be gained by those who belonged for a while to the Party? No one can contradict this. But obviously, if the Party wanted to analyse and take control of social relations, it could have nothing more to do with any movement, especially if it was linked to the salaried class, which was concerned solely with wage rises, etc., in order to tackle the *whole process of production*; but that has only ever been done outside the Party and via the inept concept of self-management. And even if isolated individuals – such as Souvarine and Castoriadis who provided interesting information and good ideas on a good number of points but who were left alone, deprived of all *organic* contact (Gramsci's word is crucial in this connection) with the active and organised section of the population and outside any organisation involved in struggle – could express criticism and sometimes even (though this was much rarer) outline perspectives, organisations, practices, and struggles connected with 'popular movements' (so close to the heart of my friend Alain

Touraine, who had valuable things to say of a political and theoretical nature on this subject), what impact could these isolated
individuals have on the workers and the masses? It is necessary to
draw a sharp distinction between those who became disillusioned
or embittered and who *left* the Party because they were disgusted
with what they had seen and those who, affected by certain widespread ideological rumours, have always been disillusioned, embittered, and hostile without ever having passed through the Party.
An embittered person who has had direct and concrete experience
of Party practices and of the untenable contradiction between its
official principles and its actual practices is someone who is capable
if he so wishes, on the basis of what he knows, of *reflecting on
the causes of his disillusionment*, since he knows what he is talking
about. I am, I believe, one such person, like all those others who
have been rejected by the Party or left it as a consequence of
experiences which, if not personally distressing, were often appalling (happily, these have been rare in France, yet one only has to
think of Marty and Tillon!). One can reflect and therefore work
out one's own personal attitude and 'line' fully aware of the facts,
relatively speaking. Someone who is embittered either before joining the Party or without ever having joined it is embittered and
disillusioned *temperamentally* and not from experience. With his
own sense of rightness reinforced by horror stories of the Gulag
unbelievably put around by the likes of Glucksmann, B.-H. Lévy,
and others, all he does is to reflect upon some vague ideology of
which he is merely the bearer, having picked it up from somewhere
else, from that small band of Soviet dissidents who are totally cut
off from their own people. He accepts this ideology as a given
without the slightest critical evaluation, and is thereby rendered
incapable of true reflection on the politics of the Party or of
any other organisation or spontaneous mass movement, though it
might be valid and fully justified.

I cannot help thinking that this is the underlying reason for the
resounding failure of the leftism which grew out of May '68 in
France and Italy, and especially in Germany and Italy where leftists
became involved in the horrors of political assassination which
may have owed something to Blanqui, but much more to the
secret and, at the time unsuspected, manoeuvrings (it is only now
that we are beginning to be aware of these things) of international

secret services in which American, Soviet, Palestinian, and Israeli agents had common interests and engaged in similar practices. What they were involved in was an apparently insane form of subversion, the political results of which were quite considerable (above all, 'destabilisation' and demobilisation of the oppressed classes whose organisation was entirely legal and above board). They did not show up where one might have expected them to, not that serious research has been done on the subject: in the destabilisation of a certain part of the world opening the way either for Marxist-Leninist and even Maoist-style revolutions doomed to failure (Cambodia and the Shining Path movement in Peru) or for out-and-out dictatorships engaging in torture and under the influence of US imperialism. By cutting themselves off from the Party which detested them – and in no way do I wish to justify the Party – leftists deprived themselves of the only existing means *at the time* of acting *politically*, in other words having some effect on the course of history, which again *at the time* meant being involved in struggle within the Party. Things are different today, of course.

Those are the main points I wish to make about the 'effects' of my longstanding presence within the Party and the apparent paradoxes to which it gave rise. When I examine all this carefully, the arguments put forward by Rancière and his friends, which at first seemed respectable, now seem to me very lightweight. Whether people like it or not, I believe I served and served well, in very difficult conditions, not the Party apparatus, which I could not stand any more than Hélène could, but the cause of communism, not modelled on the loathsome example of 'actually existing socialism' and its debased Soviet example, but on the idea and aspiration of those in France and in the wider world (this is a fact, not at all a hypomanic illusion) who wanted, and still want, to think about the day, as yet unknown, when society will be rid of relationships based on the market. In the end, that is the down-to-earth definition of communism I come back to: a human community purged of all market relationships.

Things have now changed a great deal. For a long time Hélène had been right when she claimed that the Party, if not directly then indirectly, had 'betrayed the working class' which it claimed to serve. I have not renewed my membership since Hélène's murder in 1980. During that whole painful period the Party and *L'Humanité* treated me very decently. In law I was not allowed to take any initiative and I did not want to burden the Party with a dangerous 'murderer', which some would certainly have criticised it for.

I could also offer an explanation of the subjective basis of what was, for me, an exceptional 'encounter' with Machiavelli, Hobbes, Spinoza, and Rousseau. But I would rather save this for another little book.*

All I wish to say here is that the most valuable thing I learnt from Spinoza was the nature of the 'third level of knowledge', that of a singular and at the same time universal case, of which Spinoza offers us a brilliant and often misunderstood example in the singular history of a singular people, the Jewish people (in the *Tractatus Theologico-politicus*). Given that my own 'case' is of this kind, like any 'medical', 'historical', or 'analytical case', this means that it has to be recognised and treated as singular. The universality of this singular case emerges not from a Popperian verifiable–falsifiable law, but from the fact that certain constants are repeated, appear in every case, and allow one to infer from them the theoretical and practical treatment appropriate in other unique cases. Machiavelli and Marx work in exactly the same way, with a logic that has gone almost unnoticed and which should be developed.

Something else for which I am also personally and directly indebted to Spinoza is his remarkable conception of the body, which possesses 'powers unknown to us', and of the *mens* (spirit) which becomes ever more liberated as the body develops the activity of its *conatus*, its *virtus* or *fortitudo*. Spinoza thus offered me a bodily concept of thought, or rather of thinking with the body, or better still the body's own thought. This intuition made a direct link between the experience I had of appropriating and of 'reconstituting' my body, and to the development of my thinking and my intellectual interests.

The truly astonishing thing I got from Machiavelli was his extreme idea that chance is essentially no more than a void, and *par excellence* the inner void of the Prince, which brings to the

* The author is alluding to the book he planned to write and which was never completed, *La véritable tradition matérialiste*. Reference is made to this work in the Introduction (Editors' note).

fore in the balance and interplay of his passions his role as fox, allowing him to introduce a certain distance between those passions and the Prince-as-subject where being can appear as non-being and non-being as being. This astonishing conception, once it has been made explicit, coincides with the most profound analytic experience, that of distancing oneself from one's own passions, or to be more exact from one's own counter-transference. What I read in Spinoza and Machiavelli, I had experienced directly in my own life, and that is doubtless why I was so interested to 'encounter' it in them. Basically, what Machiavelli was enunciating was the problem and the question: what is to be done? And he did it long before Chernyshevsky and Lenin. Moreover, what Machiavelli revealed to us, through the figure of the Prince, was the key fact that political parties, including the Communist Party, form an integral part of the ideological apparatus of the State, the political, ideological, constitutional, and parliamentary apparatus, with all that that implies for the ideological moulding of the popular masses who vote and 'believe', with the Party's help, in universal suffrage. Machiavelli, of course, was not familiar with universal suffrage, but the ideological apparatus of the State did exist in his time and was formed by the popular-public image of the figure of the Prince. It is only a minor difference, but it warrants careful study from which parties today, and especially the Communist Party, would learn a great deal, since, as Gramsci understood so well, their aim is to achieve ideological hegemony as a way of taking over the apparatus of the State. This they seek to achieve not through its encirclement by so-called 'civil society', but through political organisations of the workers engaging in direct political struggle against the State apparatus itself.

XX

At the turn of the year, 1979–80, things looked promising. From October to December I successfully resisted the early stages of depression, on my own and without going into hospital. Despite our perpetual rows, separated always by long periods of calm and deep understanding between us, things were getting appreciably better. That was certainly true in Hélène's case. Her sessions with my analyst had produced results which were plain for everyone to see. She was infinitely more patient, less brusque, and was better able to control her reactions when she was at work. As a direct result, she had acquired new friends who admired and genuinely liked her. They described her to me as an exceptional person who, on account of her experience and understanding of social, political, and ideological mechanisms, had transformed the sociological methods of inquiry which were a speciality of Sedes, the organisation she worked for. She had perfected an original method of conducting research in the field which had been taken up by a number of her colleagues. It was no longer a question of me 'letting her see' my friends, she now took me to meet hers. When she retired (so that someone younger could take over), she very courageously organised a voluntary job for herself, doing some grass-roots research at Fos-sur-Mer, which she visited once a fort-night. It was an astonishing transformation. She ended up liking friends of mine, such as Franca, and she even went to see her in Italy when she became seriously ill, travelling alone and on her own initiative. When Franca's sister-in-law Giovanna became seriously depressed, Hélène organised a trip to Venice which she knew well. Giovanna still talks to me with feeling about that generous gesture of hers. She was very fond of Hélène, as were all those who had made an effort to get to know her, but she never imagined her capable of such thoughtfulness. I could give countless other examples.

Things were also getting better so far as I was concerned. I admit I was finding it more and more difficult to give my lectures – without really understanding why – and I slaved away at them without much success. I confined my activities to correcting essays and presentations done by my students, which I went over with them in private, making a few limited interventions on points relating to the history of philosophy. My relationships with my women friends had, however, undergone a dramatic change.

I am thinking in particular of one person I had known since 1969. Suspecting from the outset that she was passionately in love with me, I began by making advances and then backtracked sharply, which was my usual way of protecting myself. As she had a strong personality but was also extremely sensitive, highly strung, and given to emotional reactions, our exchanges were for a long time somewhat stormy, which was largely my fault as I readily admit. Then, either because I had sufficiently changed, as a consequence of my analysis, or because I realised she did not want 'to get her hands on me' and had 'no views about me', she soon became a real friend, and our relationship jogged along and gradually improved, not without certain ups and downs though they were much less violent than previously. She did a great deal for me during the long period I was in hospital (1980–83), which not all my friends appreciated to the same extent (according to them, and most of the nurses, she should have been much tougher with me), and it was largely thanks to her that I survived. Our friendship was mutual.

But I had also become extremely conscious of the way I approached women. I was able to prove this to myself towards the end of a book fair around 1975 when, with almost all the stalls deserted and the vast hall practically empty, I happened to notice a young woman with dark hair and the famous profile. Small, slim, and rather shy, she walked across the vast hall towards the stand where I was still on duty and bought a book from me. We talked, and I assured her that if I could help her with her studies I would do so willingly. That was all that passed between us, and I would have been extremely cross with myself had I behaved differently, believing quite firmly that, rather than lapse back into my old ways, I should treat her with the utmost respect, respecting her feelings. Of particular significance was the fact that my attitude had changed so much – a sign that something important, decisive even, had 'happened' within me. She telephoned me and I saw her, but nothing happened immediately. This revealed a wholly new attitude on my part, and what followed was a long process of two people slowly but surely feeling their way and discovering each other, without my forcing her in any way. I had the impression I was finally beginning to understand what loving meant.

Hélène and I were truly happy when one of her friends from work (a son of the economist, René Diatkine) invited us to Grasse for Christmas, to stay in the house of a friend of his, Jean-Pierre Gayman (the son of the man who in 1939 was the famous secretary of a cell!). We were happy again at Easter, when we made our second and final trip to Greece. In Athens, where the incident I have already described took place, I hired a car and we set off the way we liked to, without any definite plans, and discovered on the north-east coast a marvellous beach of coloured pebbles beneath tall eucalyptus trees and pines weathered by the wind and sun. How happy we were!

We returned to Paris and things began to go wrong for us, some of which were totally unforeseen and unforeseeable.

None of them were related to my intellectual initiatives. I was, I have to admit, enjoying a very creative phase, in which nothing seemed to stand in my way. Reflecting on the narrowly defined limits of our work on Marx and Marxism, and wanting to draw the practical conclusions from my antitheoretical self-criticism, I proposed setting up a research group, not to go on studying a specific social or political theory, but to draw together largely comparative elements on the theme of the uncertain material relationship between 'popular movements' and the ideologies they have acquired or accepted, and finally the theoretical doctrines they have come to believe in. It is clear that what I proposed was an investigation into the concrete links between the *practical* side of popular movements and their relationship (direct, indirect, perverse?) with the ideologies and theoretical doctrines, both past and present, which have been associated with them throughout history. Naturally, the issue as to how these movements became *organisations* was bound to be raised in connection with the formation and transformation of ideologies and theoretical doctrines. It was an integral part of a study which had enormous implications, and which I considered to be of immediate interest as a research topic and also in relation to theoretical and political life. So it was set up under the title of Centre for the Study of Popular Movements, their Ideologies and Theoretical Doctrines (CEMPIT). Those in charge of the École gave me their support, together with some funds; the ministry promised me some too, and I also secured the cooperation of over a hundred historians, sociologists, political scientists, economists, epistemologists, and philosophers, all with different interests and sympathies. In March 1980 I held an inaugural meeting at the École and several groups started work. It was our intention to work on 'cases' as different from each other as the Western workers' movement, Islam, China, Christianity, and peasant societies to achieve, if possible, comparative results. We held a number of meetings, and I managed to bring in specialists from the provinces and even from abroad. I had personal contacts with three quite remarkable Soviet scholars: a historian, a sociologist, and a philosopher. One worked on popular movements in prerevolutionary Russia, another on African religions, and the third on both official and unofficial ideologies in the USSR. The project had got off to a good start – though one or two close friends, sensing I was in a somewhat hypomanic state, feared the worst – and the groups we had established were hard at work when I had to deal with a minor and totally unexpected personal difficulty which was to have serious consequences.

At the end of 1979 in fact, I began to suffer severe pains in my oesophagus and more often than not brought up what I had swallowed. Dr Étienne, who was of course a general practitioner but a gastro-enterologist by training, made me have an endoscopy and as the results were rather disturbing he then had me X-rayed. This revealed a hiatus hernia. I had to have an operation, otherwise I would in time suffer ulcers in the oesophagus, the prognosis of which is often extremely serious. On two occasions a date was fixed for the operation, before Easter 1980, and each time I had a profound sense of foreboding (I told everyone that the 'anaesthetic would upset everything'), and so I had it postponed. Because the doctors were so insistent, however, I finally gave in. The operation took place, after our very happy holiday in Greece, at the Maison des gardiens de la paix, on the boulevard Saint-Marcel. Right up to the last moment I was working feverishly on papers which I had brought to my little hospital bed from CEMPIT.

Technically speaking, the operation was a success. I was given a strong anaesthetic and I woke up in an uncontrollable state of anguish (whereas some years earlier I had had two anaesthetics for an inguinal hernia and for appendicitis and had suffered no ill effects). This anaesthetic and my initial state of anguish gradually caused me to sink into a new 'depression', which, for the first time, did not seem neurotic and 'doubtful', unreal, but was a classic and acute case of *melancholia*. My analyst realised how serious it was and told me later: 'For the first time, to my knowledge, you presented all the symptoms of classic and acute melancholia, and what is more it appeared serious and alarming.'

I put up with things as best I could, through a succession of days which dragged endlessly and, as usual, did everything in my power, with the support of Hélène and my analyst, to overcome my state of anguish and my desire to be placed in a clinic so that I would feel secure. This time, however, I was clearly aware that it was not like previous occasions.

I continued to get worse and on June 1st, 1980, I again went into a clinic, but this time to the Parc-Souris clinic (rue Daviel) and not as previously to the Vésinet. M. and Mme Leullier, who were both psychiatrists and old friends of my analyst and who ran the Vésinet, had now retired, and my analyst did not know their successor. But that was not the main reason. He wanted to spare Hélène the interminable Métro journey (it took a good hour and a half, three hours there and back) between the École and the Vésinet.

You have to try to understand the sort of state Hélène was in. For years on end, she had borne the full burden and anguish of my states of depression, and hypomania, and not just my depressions but, what was far worse, the endless months (or weeks) when I was in a state of growing anxiety as I struggled along, constantly seeking her support, before deciding I had to go into hospital. Once I was in hospital, she was alone and the only thing she had to look forward to was visiting me practically every day and then returning home alone to an empty house in a state of anxiety. But what she found most difficult, and in the end unbearable, was the succession of telephone calls from my numerous friends and countless acquaintances who were constantly wanting to know how I was and asking for detailed reports on the state I was in. Hélène found herself endlessly repeating the same phrases and suffered greatly because no one ever asked how she was, about her own unhappy mental state. As far as all these friends were concerned, with a few rare exceptions, she no longer really existed. All these phone calls were made to find out how I was, never how she was. I know of no one who would have been able to put up with this over a long period – and it had been going on for nearly thirty years, intermittently, of course, but always following the same pattern. It was a torture for her, and she saw in it a lack of understanding and an injustice towards her which was intolerable. As she knew I was likely to have relapses, she was waiting for it to happen even during the periods when things were going better, and especially during one of my hypomanic states when I was truly unbearable. My constantly aggressive and pro-vocative behaviour wounded her deeply. She had no one to share her suffering, and whether from indifference, thoughtlessness, or for some other reason, none of my friends, with a few rare excep-tions, were either seemingly or genuinely aware of it. René Diat-kine did at least think of sparing her that tiring, three-hour journey every day on the Métro.

I remained in the Montsouris clinic from June to September in very trying conditions, as there was a greatly reduced staff, an unknown and not very approachable doctor, who seemed like a stranger, and a squalid little garden six metres square at the foot of the building with no view. It represented a brutal and traumatic change from the 'luxury' and comfort of the Vésinet where I had a large park, felt 'at home', if I can put it that way, and where I was obviously liked by the doctors and nurses or had won them round as I had got to know them.

I was prescribed Niamide (an MOAI), a drug that was rarely administered because of the dangers associated with it (especially the well-known cheese effect) and the spectacular side-effects. Previously, it had always worked wonders for me and, most unusually, had done so very quickly without any side-effects. To the complete surprise of my doctors, the reverse was true this time. Not only did the rapid effect fail to materialise, but I also swiftly lapsed into a seriously confused mental state, suffering hallucinosis and 'suicidal' persecution.

I will not go into the technical details, as those curious to know what they are can find out about them in any treatise on psychiatry or pharmacology. Antidepressants can actually have these sorts of effects, which are frequently seen in cases of acute melancholia. This time I was not 'putting on' an atypical or doubtful depression, a 'feigned' or 'neurotic' depression, and being admitted to hospital did not have the immediate calming effect I had experienced previously *on every occasion*. All the doctors who observed me at the Montsouris were agreed on this, not only the resident psychiatrists but Dr Angelergues as well, whom I knew and who often came to see me, and also my own analyst who, for a long time and more than anyone else, had been familiar with my usual reactions.

After Hélène's death, my analyst disclosed to me a hypothesis, not one that he himself had formulated, but which he had got from Dr Bertrand Weil, whom I had consulted in the past in connection with what seemed like organic problems and who had a vast knowledge both as a doctor and as a biologist. This man thought that my operation, or rather the strong anaesthetic I was given, had produced a 'biological shock' to my system, the precise nature of which was later explained to me, but I will spare the reader the details (essentially, it activated the metabolism of the drugs via the liver). The 'biological balance' of my body was seriously disturbed as a result of the shock of the operation and especially of the anaesthetic, and this had reverse and paradoxical effects.

Anyway, I lapsed into semi-consciousness and was at times wholly unconscious and in a confused mental state. I was no longer able to control the movements of my body, was constantly falling down, and vomiting all the time. I could no longer see clearly and lost control of my bladder. My speech was confused, to the extent that I often used one word when I meant another, as were my perceptions which I could no longer follow or connect. I was, *a fortiori*, unable to write and the things I said were nothing but ravings. In addition, I suffered terrible nightmares which went on for a long time when I was awake. Indeed, I 'lived' my dreams in my waking state, that is to say I acted in accordance with the themes and the logic of my dreams, taking the illusion of my dreams for reality. When I was awake, I was unable to distinguish between my oneiric hallucinations and simple reality. While I was in that state I endlessly elaborated themes reflecting my suicidal persecution to everyone who visited me. I was absolutely convinced that certain men wanted me dead and were preparing to kill me; in particular, a man with a beard who must have been a member of the staff I caught sight of when he was on duty at the hospital. I even thought a tribunal was taking place in the room next to mine which was going to condemn me to death. More than that, I believed men armed with rifles with telescopic sights were taking aim from the windows of the buildings opposite and would shoot me. Finally, I thought the Red Brigades had condemned me to death and would burst into my room either during the day or at night. I myself do not remember all the details of these hallucinations, which, except for a few flashes, have been completely blotted out by amnesia. I have got them from the numerous friends who came to visit me, from the doctors who looked after me, and by carefully cross-checking and matching the information I gathered from the accounts they gave me and the remarks they made.

This whole 'pathological' pattern was accompanied by extreme suicidal tendencies. Condemned to death and threatened with execution, there was only one course open to me: to anticipate the death that was inflicted on me by killing myself in advance. I imagined all sorts of possible ways of dying and, in addition, wanted not only to destroy myself physically but also to destroy all traces of my existence: in particular by destroying every one of my books, all my notes, by burning down the École as well, and 'if possible', while I was at it, by getting rid of Hélène herself. That at least is what I confided on one occasion to a friend, who reported it to me as I have described. (I have his unique testimony in relation to the last point.)

The doctors were, I know, extremely concerned about me. They were not afraid I would kill myself – I was protected against that, it seems, by the protective measures and surveillance operated by the clinic – though one can never be sure in such cases. What they feared most was that my serious disorder would lead to an *irreversible* deterioration in my condition which would condemn me to spend the rest of my life in hospital.

After a long period of this treatment, they decided to take me off the drugs which they believed responsible for the disturbing side-effects, and after the statutory delay (of a fortnight), they prescribed Anafranil which they gave me in a drip. The new treatment seemed to prove successful, and after a little while they thought I was well enough to leave the clinic, which I did and returned to the École. However, all my friends agree that I was in a very bad state when I left the clinic.

Hélène and I were together again and, as usual, we went off to the Midi for peace and quiet and sea air. We only stayed eight to ten days and then returned home, as my condition had worsened.

What followed was the worst period Hélène and I ever suffered in our life. Things had begun to go wrong the previous spring, but only intermittently, and the intervening periods of respite gave us hope. Now they took a definite turn for the worse and continued without a break until the end. I do not know what exactly I put Hélène through (I do know, however, that I was truly capable of the most terrible things), but she told me with a determination that terrified me that she could no longer live with me, that in her eyes I was a 'monster' and that she wanted to leave me for good. She began quite openly to look for a flat, but did not find one immediately. She then made practical arrangements which I found unbearable; totally ignoring me, though I was still there, in our own flat. She got up before me and disappeared for the whole day. If she happened to stay at home, she refused to talk to me and even to come face to face with me. She took refuge either in her bedroom or in the kitchen, slammed the doors, and forbade me to enter. She refused to eat in my company. It was an extraordinary experience, as if we were in Hell, with the two of us closeted together in a state of deliberately contrived solitude.

I was consumed with anguish. As you know, I always experienced intense anguish at being abandoned and especially by her, but being totally ignored, though I was still there, in our own home, was the most unbearable thing of all.

Deep down I knew she could not actually leave me, and I tried, in vain, to ease my anguish with this thought, though I was not entirely convinced of it. Then Hélène began to develop another theme, which had been there in the background for several months, but which now assumed a terrifying form. She told me there was no way out, given the 'monster' I was and the inhuman suffering I inflicted upon her, other than to kill herself. She quite openly collected the drugs she needed to commit suicide and left them on display, but she also talked of other, more violent ways. Had not our friend, Nikos Poulantzas, committed suicide recently by throwing himself from the twenty-second floor of the Montparnasse tower, in an acute state of persecution mania? She also talked of the possibility of throwing oneself under a lorry or a train, as if she were leaving the choice to me. And she assured me, in a tone suggesting she really meant it, which I knew too well to doubt her intentions, that these were not vain threats but an irreversible decision. She would simply choose the method and the time, obviously without warning me.

Again deep down I believed she was incapable of killing herself. I told myself there had been too many past occasions and that basically she was too fond of me, too deeply attached to me to be capable of carrying it out. But there again, I was not entirely sure. Then one day, to cap it all, she simply asked me to kill her myself, and the very idea, which was both unthinkable and unbearably awful, made me tremble convulsively for a long time. It still makes me shudder. Was she trying to suggest in some way that she was incapable, not only of abandoning me but also of taking her own life? All in all, there was only one option open to me. I would have to allow sufficient time to elapse for her to calm down, as had happened after so many acute crises in the past, to come to her senses and accept what she really wanted deep down: not to abandon me, not to kill herself, but to continue living with me and loving me as she always had.

As I have already indicated, this whole period of Hell was lived out behind closed doors. Apart from my analyst, whom she saw and I saw, we saw practically no one else (the École had not really started up again). The two of us were shut up together in our own private Hell. We no longer answered either the telephone or the doorbell. It seems I even put up some sort of handwritten notice outside my office for all to see saying: 'Temporarily absent; don't keep knocking.' Friends who tried to call on us and read this notice on the wall told me much later that they reproached themselves for never having tried to 'force my door'. Even if they had tried, they could only have done it by breaking it down since I was no longer opening it to anyone.

Time went by with us shut up together in this terrible isolation, in what our friends later referred to as an 'impasse', a 'Hell for two', or, to be more accurate, 'a Hell for three', if one includes my analyst as well as the two of us. They considered him fundamentally responsible for not having intervened.

Yet my analyst had intervened. I must have seen him for the last time on November 15th [*sic*, Translator] and he told me that things could not continue as they were and that I had to agree to go into hospital. He had made inquiries about the new director of the Vésinet, whom he did not know personally, and had obtained excellent reports. Disregarding the inconvenience of the Vésinet for Hélène, he considered that they would be happy to have me (I knew the Vésinet very well, I recall. I had been comfortable there and the drug treatment had worked rapidly and most successfully) and that I would be well cared for (he had unhappy memories of my stay at the Montsouris, where he felt the conditions had not been right for me). He telephoned the Vésinet, and they were able to admit me in two or three days. I obviously did not refuse, and in fact I do not remember exactly what my reply was.

Two or three days went by and nothing happened. I later discovered that Hélène saw my analyst on either Thursday, November 13th, or Friday 14th, and begged him to delay my admission to hospital for three days. My analyst doubtless gave way to her entreaties, and it was agreed that, unless something else happened, I would go into the Vésinet on Monday, November 17th. At a much later date, I discovered in my mail at the École an express letter from Diatkine, dated and postmarked the afternoon of Friday 14th, asking Hélène to telephone him back 'extremely urgently'. The letter reached the École on the 17th, though I do not know why (a delay in the post perhaps, or the porter had not been able to get hold of me as I was neither answering the phone nor the doorbell). At any rate, it arrived after the tragic event. I recall my analyst was unable to call either me or Hélène on the phone: *we were not answering it any more.*

At nine o'clock on Sunday, November 16th, I surfaced after an unfathomable night which I have never been able to fathom, and found myself standing at the foot of my bed, in a dressing-gown, with Hélène stretched out before me, and with me continuing to massage her neck and feeling intense pain in my forearms, obviously due to the massage. Then I realised, without knowing why, other than from her motionless eyes and the pitiful tip of her tongue showing between her teeth and lips, that she was dead. I rushed, screaming, from our flat towards the sick-bay where I knew I would find Dr Étienne. My fate was sealed.

XXI

Once he had given me an injection and made a few phone calls, Dr Étienne quickly drove me to Sainte-Anne's Hospital, where I was admitted as an urgent case. I entered another realm of darkness, and what I am about to recount I learnt from him, from my analyst, and from my friends, but only at a much later date.

It is 'standard practice' for someone suffering 'psychological disturbance' to be taken first to the police station (an annexe of Sainte-Anne's) for the usual formalities. The defendant is usually kept there for twenty-four hours, naked and in a padded cell with just a mattress on the ground, before being questioned for the first time and examined by a police psychiatrist, who decides whether he should be admitted to Sainte-Anne's next door. This is a standard procedure and exceptions can only be made in cases of extreme urgency and seriousness. I found out later that, when he discovered I had been taken straight to Sainte-Anne's without going via the police station, the Minister of Justice, Alain Peyrefitte, a former student at the École, was extremely angry and telephoned the Director of the École, Jean Bousquet, and gave him a rocket. Bousquet, whose behaviour was beyond reproach during this whole affair, replied that I was under his jurisdiction, that I was very sick, and that he entirely supported the initiative taken by Dr Étienne, who also learnt via a third party of Peyrefitte's anger.

It was doubtless an editor with the French Press Agency who informed my friends of Hélène's death, and they then passed the news around and quickly informed my analyst. All of them were deeply distressed and, until they received the results of the autopsy (which concluded her death had been caused by 'strangulation'), none of them, and especially my analyst, could believe I had killed Hélène, but imagined that, because I was suffering from hallucinations, I accused myself wrongly of causing a death that was accidental.

The news, which was quite a 'scoop', made the headlines in both French and foreign newspapers and rapidly gave rise in certain quarters to all sorts of 'analyses' and commentaries, as you can imagine.

I was very well known as an ex-student of the École, a philosopher, a Marxist, and a communist, married to a woman who was less well known but apparently remarkable. On the whole, the French (and the international) press behaved quite properly, but certain papers really had a field day. I will neither name them nor those sometimes famous individuals who put their signature to articles that were both wild and malicious. The authors elaborated five themes with obvious relish and self-satisfaction: they delighted in their political revenge, since the 'crime' at last gave them the chance to settle old scores once and for all, not only with me personally but also with Marxism, communism, and philosophy, not to mention the École normale. I will not be so cruel as to quote these extraordinary pieces of writing or to give the names of their sometimes famous authors. Let us simply draw a veil over their extravagant phantasies and the release of their pent-up feelings. Moreover, if they are in the least bit honest, they will recognise themselves in what I am about to say. It is for them to decide whether they can live with a clear conscience. In France and abroad, articles appeared on the following themes: 1) Marxism = crime; 2) communism = crime; 3) philosophy = madness; 4) it was a scandal that a madman, who had been mad for a long time, could have spent over thirty years teaching generations of philosophers at the École normale, who were now in *lycées* everywhere, guiding 'our children'; 5) it was a scandal that a criminal individual should have been openly protected by the 'establishment': think what would have happened to an ordinary Algerian in the same situation, was the line taken by one 'centrist' paper. Althusser was let off thanks to the 'protection in high places' that he enjoyed. The university establishment and intellectuals of all persuasions automatically closed ranks to keep things quiet and to protect one of their own from the rigours of the 'rules', and perhaps even of the law. In short, I was protected by the educational Ideological State Apparatus of which I was a member.

When you realise how long these press comments went on, first because it took some time for the results of the autopsy to come through and then because of the declaration that I was unfit to plead, you can imagine how distraught my friends were, given the atmosphere of the 'witch hunt' they were caught up in. It was made all the more alarming by the fact that it spread like the rumours which accompanied a dirty-tricks campaign from a certain section of the press. I speak of my friends since I no longer had any family. My father died in 1975 and my mother, although very lucid, was very old and totally indifferent. Bousquet, who was very dignified, had to intervene personally to correct totally inaccurate and defamatory statements in the press. He was courageous enough to do so publicly and prepared to take the risk. He affirmed that I had always fulfilled my obligations and teaching commitments in a totally honourable and irreproachable manner, that I had been an admirable colleague at the École, getting to know my students better than anyone else, and that as a sick person I deserved to be defended by my director. This gentle archaeologist, who lived only, and still does, for the excavations he did at Delphi, revealed himself to be a man of courage, of action, and of generosity. I was also 'defended', of course, by all the tutors at the École and by all the philosophers who, according to one journalist, 'were united behind Althusser'.

Naturally, I knew nothing of all this at the time, nor for a good while afterwards. The doctor who looked after me at Sainte-Anne's, whose attention and kindness so touched me, took care that no news got through to me. He rightly feared I would be traumatised by it and that my condition would get worse. That explains why he 'blocked' the huge amount of correspondence addressed to me, mostly by people I did not know who showered me with insults (as a communist criminal!), and most of which carried strong sexual overtones or even threats. It also explains why he took the decision to stop me having any visitors, not knowing who might turn up and what they might say to me. Above all (and the same fear must have inspired all the doctors not just at Sainte-Anne's but long afterwards at Soisy as well, where I was transferred in June 1981), he feared a journalist might manage to slip into the hospital, take some photos, pick up vague bits of information, and publish a scandalous article in the press.

This was not an imaginary fear. I have since discovered that a journalist from one of the major French weeklies managed to get hold of a photograph of me (doubtless by bribing a local nurse) in which I was seen sitting on my bed in front of the three people who shared the room. The weekly intended publishing this document under the title: 'The mad philosopher Louis Althusser continues to give his lectures on Marxism-Leninism to his co-detainees.' Fortunately, the lawyer my friends consulted (to find out what form the legal proceedings would take), doubtless having been informed by a journalist who found the whole business distasteful, intervened and the photo with its caption never appeared. But the fear of scandal-seeking journalists must have preoccupied all my doctors right to the end, even after my stay in hospital. And they were right, because long after I left hospital imaginary details about my life appeared in the papers, which were rarely very kind to me. As there are no personal scores I wish to settle, since I have neither the taste nor the desire for it, perhaps you will allow me to close this particular chapter which did however affect quite profoundly the conditions of my stay in hospital, my anguished state of mind, and especially my friends and my doctors.

So I was not allowed any visits, as they were considered too dangerous for all sorts of reasons. On the other hand, I remember being able to talk, almost every day around noon, with a great friend of Hélène's and mine who worked at Sainte-Anne's and who managed to come to see me, since she was free to go where she liked. What relief I felt at finally being able to talk to someone who knew Hélène very well and who also knew me! She told me later she first found me almost totally prostrate, incapable of following a conversation, but pleased to see her. On the other hand, I have very precise memories of my discussions with the experts who were appointed to examine me. Three elderly men in dark suits came in turn to fetch me from my room in order to take me to a sort of office up in the attic (a minute room in which, if you did not take care when you stood up, you banged your head against the roof joists). They each religiously sat down in front of me, took a sheaf of papers and a pen from their briefcase, asked me questions, and wrote things down at interminable length. I have no recollection either of their questions or of my replies.

My analyst also came to see me very frequently, and always in the same office in the attic. I remember asking him the same question over and over again: how could I have killed Hélène?

I later discovered that, two days after I was admitted, the examining magistrate came to question me, as is the practice, at Sainte-Anne's, but it seems I was in such a state that he was unable to obtain any statement from me.

I do not know if I was given antidepressants at Sainte-Anne's (other than the MOAI). The only memory I have is of swallowing each evening enormous doses of chloral, an old and very effective drug, which, to my great satisfaction, made me sleep so well (despite the very long, curtainless windows) that I had the greatest difficulty in waking up each morning. This prolonged sleep was pleasant, as is anything which enables you to escape the brutal return of your feelings of anguish. On the other hand, I was aware of receiving a dozen shock treatments, which suggests I must have been very depressed. The shocks were, of course, administered after I had been given a narcotic or curare, as had been done at the Vallée-aux-Loups and formerly at the Vésinet itself. Before the discovery of MOAI drugs I can still picture the young, rosy-faced doctor who came to my room with the electric-shock 'machine' and who, before setting to work, gave me long and, I might even say, cheerful lectures about shock treatment and the advantages of it. As a result, I faced my 'little death' without too much apprehension, yet I still had my old horror of the whole business.

The physical conditions in which we lived at Sainte-Anne's were truly unimaginable, especially the huge refectory where you had to pick up a plate and your knife and fork (these had to be washed after the meal in a revolting sink of water, though not the plates, for some reason I never understood). We sat with whomever we liked and the staff brought huge communal dishes of basic food to the table. It was there, however, that I made a real friend, a former primary-school teacher no longer able to teach, a 'chronic' case to use the awful jargon of the place, who was allowed out and later on brought me newspapers. Dominique, too, was sick. He was a teacher like me and let me talk and understood me. I could confide in him utterly as a true friend, sure of his discretion. I have not forgotten his kindness and generosity but though I tried to find him again, I did not succeed. If he should read this little book one day, I would like him to get in touch. I compromised him later on, as a result of a harmless initiative of mine which caused a stir in the hospital.

I have since found out that, during this whole period, my closest friends felt quite helpless because they did not know exactly what might happen to me and were waiting for the results from the experts and then for the decision as to whether I was fit to plead (which came through only at the beginning of February). They did all that was possible or what they could to help me from the outside. It was at this time that the most faithful and devoted of them revealed themselves. Strangely, in most but not all cases it was those who were closest; while some of the closest definitely distanced themselves. This division gave me something to think about later on. Some men and women can be frightened by madness, psychiatric hospitals, and confinement and cannot confront or think about them without inwardly feeling considerable anguish, which can prevent them from visiting their friend or even intervening in any way. In this connection, I cannot fail to mention the heroic behaviour of our dear friend Nikos Poulantzas, who had an absolute horror of all psychiatric hospitals. Yet he had regularly visited me when I was admitted to hospital and was always cheerful, though he must have been screwed up inside; something I only discovered very late on. I remember he was almost the only person I agreed to see in the year preceding Hélène's death. I did not know at the time that he had already tried to kill himself once. He described it as a pure accident, saying he had been struck by a lorry in the dark on a great wide avenue. In fact, I learnt from his companion that he had thrown himself under the wheels. I did not see Nikos at home, but in the street near the École, and I later learnt he was already suffering from the acute persecution mania which he ended with his spectacular suicide. Yet Nikos was cheerful with me, never said a word about his own suffering, nor about his first attempted suicide which he disguised as an accident, talked to me about his work and research projects, and asked me about mine. He embraced me warmly when he left, as if he expected to see me again the next day. When I later discovered what he had in mind, I could not contain my admiration for what had been not only an exceptional gesture of friendship on his part but also a truly heroic act. Not everyone reacted as he did, however. I have since discovered, for example, that one female friend disappeared completely after a journalist referred to my relationship with 'an ideologist'. As she was a specialist in the history of ideas (but in no way an ideologist!), her friends who only knew me by name took fright (she did not) and pointed out the danger to which she was exposing herself: endless questioning, a public trial at which she would certainly have to testify, etc. They also wanted to protect her. She dropped out of the small band of my active friends. Some disappeared for unknown reasons. Others, having been of great practical help to me, disappeared from one day to the next, without warning, brutally, and my letters and calls have remained unanswered to this day. I can think of one person who came to see me every other day and who was my most devoted and my closest friend for years while I was at the École. If he happens to read this, I want him to know my door is open and that, if he does not come, I shall one day knock on his door. After what I have lived through, I think I am capable of understanding anything, even the behaviour of those who seemed to withdraw at a certain point without giving any reasons. But, apart from my astounding encounter with Nikos, the visit of this nature which touched me the most was the one I received one day at Soisy. An 'old student' who had become a very dear friend, and who was an extraordinary man, came to see me. He asked me not to say anything but to listen to him. For two hours he talked only of himself, of his terrible childhood, of his father who had been in and out of psychiatric hospitals, and he finished by telling me: I came to explain why I can't come to see you. I can't cope with it. A year later, when he was undergoing analysis, he planned his suicide over a long period and never confided in anyone, not even the courageous young woman with whom he lived and worked. He threw himself into the Marne, having cut his wrists and weighted himself down with heavy stones.

My reason for recounting these facts is not just because they distressed me deeply after they happened, but because they also gave me unusual insights into the behaviour of very close friends when confronted with the drama in my own life. It was not just the drama itself, however, but their own anguish and perhaps even the perverse and insistent public 'rumours' about me which certain media people kept alive, unaware or disdainful of people's suffering and tragedies, and who found some personal satisfaction (I do not want to know what it was) in keeping these perversely ambiguous rumours alive.

These circumstances also have to be borne in mind if certain aspects of the behaviour of my doctors are to be understood.

At last, after the shock treatment and its beneficial effect on me, my doctor agreed, little by little and with a great deal of caution, that I should be allowed to have visitors; initially two, then three, then five but no more, and having completely satisfied himself that these friends could be trusted. Thus I saw again certain close male friends and two female friends, one of whom had incredible difficulty being accepted and was only successful as a result of interventions and her own forcefulness. I did not always find these visits restful. They stirred up past memories and reminded me of the outside world and the terrible fear it inspired in me (I believed myself finished for good, and the outside world, which I thought I would never see again, caused me enormous anguish). In one respect my doctor was right: visits can reawaken feelings of anguish or make them worse. But I could not bear being alone, an old obsessive fear of mine which later had such a devastating effect on me, and I begged them to allow my friends to come. My doctor was wise enough to accept a compromise which I was able to live with throughout my stay at Sainte-Anne's.

One day, however, I thought I would play a clever trick on him. I gave my friend Dominique, who was allowed out, a list of telephone numbers and insisted he contact other friends to fix dates and times when I hoped to see them. He carried out this commission. I do not know how my doctor found out about it, but he appeared in my room, absolutely furious (the only time I saw him like this), told me I had no right to invite friends without his authorisation, asked for their phone numbers, and informed them they were not to come. It was the only time there was any 'coolness' between us, but it soon passed.

Time went by, and I began to feel better. I was however distressed to learn that, urged by the authorities and without consulting or even notifying me, those in charge at the École had moved all my things out of my large flat in the rue d'Ulm, a flat which had meant so much to me in my life! (Moreover, from an administrative point of view, I was simply on sick leave and could therefore return if my health improved.) This measure seemed to condemn me to permanent confinement, since 'they' on the outside had literally blotted me out, in spite of my rights. So far as my flat was concerned, my physical surroundings, it was as if I no longer existed. This business of being moved out of my flat haunted me for a very long time, for years – only now am I coming to terms with it.

I was also distressed by something else I learnt. Having been confined officially by a decision of the prefect and deprived of all my rights, which were entrusted to a representative of the law, I remained at the mercy of the prefect who, as always in the case of those in hospital for a considerable time, could transfer me, that is have me moved to another establishment. Those, it seems, were the rules. Now, for a long time in my case, there was some question of my being transferred to Carcassonne! You can imagine how confused I and my friends felt. How could I have expected them to visit me or relied on them being near? It would have been a disaster.

The truth, however, was infinitely worse as I have only just discovered in the last few months. I initially found out about it from my doctor at Soisy who said he heard it from my doctor at Sainte-Anne's, and he confirmed it quite openly. The doctors at Sainte-Anne's had come under 'very sustained' pressure on the part of certain *administrative authorities at the highest level* to have me locked up in a 'secure hospital' in the provinces, 'to settle the Althusser affair once and for all'. Now everyone knows how rare it is for someone to get out of one of these secure hospitals which are much worse than prisons. You usually rot your whole life away there. Thank goodness my doctors at Sainte-Anne's had the courage (that is the right word, as medical law was on their side, but they needed simple courage to invoke it) to defend me, saying I was neither dangerous nor violent (which was perfectly obvious). That is how, unknown to me, I escaped the most terrible fate which I would not have survived; at any rate I would never have got out, I am sure. But my friends would certainly have publicised it and things would not have gone as those 'at the highest level' might have wished. At that point, the 1981 election took place and the Minister of Justice, my 'friend' from the École normale, was replaced by Robert Badinter. My friends breathed again, and I was sent to Soisy-sur-Seine.

However, my doctors' problems were not yet over. I did not want to leave Sainte-Anne's and fiercely resisted the arguments of my analyst who had to keep on wearing me down! I was rather comfortable at this hospital where, as on so many occasions in the past, I had made a 'niche' for myself and also had a friend whom I did not want to lose. In addition, I found this huge historic building quite a lively place because the people were constantly changing. Furthermore, I had made friends with one of the nurses, a stocky West Indian from the Antilles who was full of tact and understanding and always frank and good-humoured. I had a great fear of change and naturally was not short of arguments for staying: I knew Soisy, of course, but it was forty kilometres from Paris, and how would I have been able to have visitors? However much my analyst told me – and I knew from experience – that I would receive better treatment and be more comfortable; that being away from Paris and its dangers I would have much more freedom of movement, if only within the large grounds; that it would be easier for him to follow my progress and that he would visit me regularly, I remained unconvinced. I stuck to my decision: I did not want to leave Sainte-Anne's. But in the end, believing it was a choice between Carcassonne and Soisy, I gave in, though with a heavy heart.

So, in June 1981, I left Sainte-Anne's in an ambulance. As a precautionary measure, my doctor had announced I would be going at five in the afternoon, but the ambulance left at two o'clock. The journalists and photographers who might have turned up had been caught napping.

XXII

Thus I arrived at Soisy in June 1981. The huge green park was dotted with white wards between tall trees. It was springtime and the grass had been mown. I was admitted to ward seven, which was to be my home until July 1983.

I felt lost. My change of surroundings and the fact that I had new doctors and nurses and above all no friends there came as a severe shock. It took me some time, a long time in fact, to agree to accept and come to terms with the 'transfer', and to realise the doctors were right. The patients comprised for the most part 'chronic cases', unfortunate individuals who were shut away often for life in the same room with the same thoughts and without any visitors. There were the schizophrenics, the permanently insane, in particular two wretched young women, one of whom was seeking the Virgin Mary and the other constantly muttering the same incomprehensible remarks, as well as former alcoholics. Yet there were very few acute cases, whereas at Sainte-Anne's they had been more numerous, and as most of them got better and left, there was a constant turnover of inmates. Then there was the ward containing the pitifully senile men and women, who were dragged out into the sunshine and who remained there, enclosed in their own silence.

I got to know the impressive young doctor who was assigned to me. He looked after me right to the end and still keeps in touch. Having been analysed himself, he had a 'way of listening' to his patients which made that obvious. But it took me some time to get used to him and also to the nurses who worked as a group, according to the principles of 'team care', and who discussed things with the doctor on the basis of their observations, though I know they did not always agree with his methods. Some of them criticised him for paying me too much attention and granting me privileges not accorded to other patients. Psychiatrist colleagues of his also criticised him for this on one occasion. He agreed: 'It is true, I don't treat him like the others. But I do treat him on the same basis as I treat of all my patients; that is to say I grant them things according to who they are, their status, their demands, and their anxieties. If I ignored the fact that Althusser is well known, has preoccupations relating to his position, which includes having enemies, it would, in my view, be totally artificial.' Not that he ever granted me everything I asked for, far from it; nor did he accede in the least to the sometimes extravagant requests of my friends, far from it. In my case he always stuck to principles he had adopted and never deviated (and the same was true for all the others too – to judge from what I saw); I considered his position both fair and unassailable.

First they tried giving me Anafranil, but to no effect. They then immediately switched to Niamide (an MOAI), which had the same effect as previously. I got into a severely confused mental state, had hallucinations and feelings of persecution and became suicidal, exactly as at the Montsouris. I will not go over these symptoms again. But they became dramatically worse when, for want of anything better, it was decided to double the dose of this MOAI. The consequences were catastrophic. I could no longer eat or even drink without vomiting straight away, I kept falling down, and even broke my arm. My nightmares continued when I awoke and for a good part of the day, and I desperately looked for a branch in the nearby wood from which to hang myself. But how could I get hold of a rope? As a precaution, my dressing-gown cord had been removed as had my shoelaces. As always in these circumstances I longed for a little respite and oblivion at night, but my nights were appalling. I felt I could not sleep and in addition I had a great deal of trouble with the night nurses who were supposed to give me medication (chloral again and worse) at eight o'clock in the evening. But, like most of the patients, they watched television until ten o'clock, which meant there was an appalling two-hour delay in the official timetable for my medication. It was then that I realised the doctor did not have total control over the nurses, that he had to compromise, and even turn a blind eye (I was never given my evening medication at the right time, except for one occasion when a very pleasant young medical student was on night duty, but it did not last long). I even began to think, somewhat exaggeratedly, that in this very liberal and well-organised set-up, and doubtless *a fortiori* in less 'advanced' set-ups with less well-informed nurses, the doctor must submit to 'the dictatorship of the nurses'. And even if this impression of mine needs qualifying, it is, I think, crucial for a proper understanding of the relationships and the atmosphere which prevail in all enclosed psychiatric establishments; and the consequences are very damaging!

When the doctor finally reached my room in the morning, I had long been anticipating his arrival and was eager to hold his attention once he was there. I made an enormous effort to emerge from my nightmares, which lingered on even after I had woken up, and, still in a dreamlike state, I recounted to him the terrible dreams I had had. He listened and said a few words, but this 'listening' on his part was what mattered most to me. Sometimes he ventured an interpretation, always cautiously. I gave the appearance of hanging on his every word. But I would often then go and find a nurse and ask the question: 'Does the doctor really know what he's doing? Does he know what he's saying?' Again doubts and feelings of anxiety invaded me: anxiety at being alone again, at being abandoned, as always.

My analyst came to visit me once a week, on Sunday morning, in the almost totally deserted ward (with only one emergency duty-nurse). I endlessly went over with him the deep-seated reasons for the murder I had committed, yet without ever feeling guilty. I remember putting forward the following hypothesis (I had already suggested it to him at Sainte-Anne's): Hélène's murder was 'a suicide via a third party'. He listened to me, neither agreeing nor disagreeing with what I said. I discovered later from my doctor that my analyst saw him from time to time and gave him his support. Already on one occasion, when I had been admitted to Sainte-Anne's for resuscitation, my analyst had managed, after incredible negotiations, to visit me in the intensive-care unit and to talk to the specialist looking after me. He believed it was the end and that I would not recover physically from what I had gone through. It was the only time he had doubts about my survival. But so long as I survived, he never doubted that I would be psychologically 'cured'. When my doctor was very worried about what might happen (as he sometimes was), my analyst supported him in the belief that I would recover – he never faltered. Without him, the doctor might perhaps (?) have resigned himself to the idea of my becoming another 'chronic case', like those whose lifelong wretchedness I observed all around me.

The MOAI reduced me to such a state (obviously, I remember nothing of what happened at the time) that I again had to be admitted for resuscitation at Évry. Once again, too, I recovered. The lethal MOAI were suppressed and I slowly recovered. I even experienced a period of exhilaration at Soisy, spent two months in my flat, and, almost without sleep as in my earlier hypomanic states, I typed (between November 1982 and February 1983) a two-hundred-page philosophical manuscript which I have kept. Though very disjointed, it does not in the least suggest delirium. Actually, I expressed for the first time in writing a certain number of ideas I had carefully stored away in my mind for over twenty years, ideas I told no one else about as they seemed so important to me (!). I had kept them for future publication, when they were fully developed. But rest assured that they are not ready yet.

Contrary to what I feared, I received countless visits from my friends: one a day. Indeed, they had arranged things so that I should not be left alone for a single day. I owe them so much! Yet I have to tell the truth and admit that I absolutely and tyrannically *demanded* these visits both of them and the doctor. My doctor understood their importance and since the conditions at Soisy were different from those at Sainte-Anne's, he gave me ample latitude. I thus spent long afternoons in the company of my men and women friends. The important thing was their presence. So, one of my women friends would knit in silence at my bedside while another would arrive with a book. I found it very easy to accept their silence, since I was no longer alone. But why was I so demanding, so tyrannical (truly) over visits? Doubtless because of the 'overwhelming nature of the depression', and also because I was able to use the power it gave me over others to escape, if only temporarily, the fear of being alone and abandoned which gripped me so intensely. When someone failed to turn up, or when a male or female friend somehow gave me the feeling I was abandoned, I sank back into a worse depression.

This happened at the beginning of 1983, when I succeeded in spending a few weeks in my flat. Not alone, of course; as, on the strict orders of my doctor who insisted on this precaution (since I talked to him of throwing myself from the sixth floor), my friends were with me day and night. But the impression of being abandoned cast me back into an extreme state of depression which meant that my doctor had to readmit me to hospital. He sent me to the Vivalan, which slowly produced some sort of a recovery and then, in the end, my extremely precarious departure from hospital in July 1983 to spend a holiday in the country in the east of France.

But so much happened in the intervening period! My doctor felt (he later confided to me) that I was so seriously ill and had been for so long that I would never recover and that I was so defenceless I would never be able to leave the security and protection of the hospital. That was what he feared the most. But he 'held on', which was the one basic line he quickly adopted; he 'held on', and though he followed the ups and downs of my illness, he stuck to his position. Yet things were not easy for him; on the contrary, I did everything I could to make them complicated.

I had a terrible fear of the outside world; not so much of the malicious interpretations and interventions which obsessed the doctors and nurses (though the issue did not arise at Soisy) and which my own doctor continued to fear on my account even though I was no longer sensitive to them, but of the very reality of the outside world, which I considered for ever beyond my reach. For a long time this anxiety assumed a specific form. All my things had been moved (my friends spent whole days on it) from the École to a flat in the Twentieth District which I had bought with Hélène in preparation for retirement. My friends described the state of the place to me: there was such a clutter of boxes full of books that it was practically impossible to get into the flat. What was to be done? Not only did I think I would never be able to leave hospital and return to the outside world; even if I did, I had the feeling I would be unable to get inside my flat. So it was decided I should go to have a look. A nurse I greatly liked went with me one day in the hospital van. I was dismayed to see piles of boxes right up to the ceiling and refused to enter. I came away with a sense of dread which continued to haunt me, not an empty fear of something which might happen, but of something terribly concrete. Without doubt, I was done for.

It was then my doctor came up with what he was later to refer to as one of his 'far-fetched solutions', an absolutely absurd 'medico-bureaucratic' idea, namely: the hospital van would go to fetch my boxes of books, which would be unloaded in an empty hall in the hospital where I would sort them. They would then be taken back to my flat to be arranged on the shelves. But where was I to obtain the shelves? Three of my friends then offered to put up some basic bookshelves which could be bought at the Bazar de l'Hôtel de Ville and which they transported in pieces on the Métro! However, I was not much further forward. Only I could sort out the books, but I felt totally incapable of doing it. The whole plan was going round and round in my head. Without saying a word to me, my friends put up the shelves, piled all my books on to them as best they could, and then came one day and announced that I could at last get into my flat whenever I liked. In fact, I was able to get in, as I have already said, during my first stay outside the hospital in November and December 1982, which had such an unhappy ending. The problem was I could not find a single one of my books, so I had to begin to sort them, but how was I going to tackle this mammoth task? I had thousands of books though I had read only a few hundred of them, having put off reading the others (as I imagined) until the right moment. Again, I was filled with dread. But I have proved that it is possible to live with one's books in a state of disorder as I have still not managed to arrange them sufficiently to find what I want, apart from the odd one or two, and yet, all things considered, I feel quite at home in this disorder. Yet another proof that everything 'is in the mind'.

But that wasn't the worst thing. For what I now want to come to was both horribly specific and most unusual. Certainly, I looked on being in hospital as I had always done on previous occasions: as an almost complete refuge from the anxieties of the outside world. It was as if I were in a fortress, confined to solitude by the walls of my own impenetrable anguish. How would I ever get out? My doctor was fully aware of this and, since he understood, he played along with me, with my anguish, and thus became affected by it, anguished in turn, as were all the nurses to whom I constantly conveyed my feelings of anguish. I even remember one day putting the terrible question to my doctor, thinking of one specific occasion when I had looked in terror at the base of a woman friend's neck and asked myself in a state of anguish: what if I were to do it all over again (strangle a woman)? My doctor reassured me, saying of course I would not! – but without giving me any further explanation. I later found out that the women nurses were frightened of coming into my room alone, in the evening, frightened I would jump on them and strangle them – as if they had 'sensed' my horrifying desire, cloaked in feelings of anguish. Confinement unavoidably gives rise to this contagion, which is why I have mentioned it. The anxiety of the patient, the doctor, the nurses, and visiting friends is communicated, and it communicated itself totally in my case, thereby intensifying its effects, to the extent that on several occasions my doctor's position became critical, if not in relation to the nurses (he never spoke about them to me), at least with regard to my friends, who certainly noticed it. How can the doctor escape this interplay of multiple anxieties, in which he is both actively and passively caught up? It is an extraordinarily difficult situation, which can only be resolved by making compromises, which my doctor did. There were, however, certain secondary effects.

I believe I can locate the principal source of these secondary effects precisely, connected as it is with the 'nature', both objective and phantasised, of the 'fortress' which afforded me protection and provided a refuge against the anxiety of some impossible contact with the outside world. Now the outside world was not solely a product of my own phantasies, but was brought to me each day by my friends who came from that outside world and returned to it again each day. I will give one example. Foucault himself came to see me twice, and I remember on both occasions we discussed everything that was happening in the intellectual world, as I did with virtually *all* my friends; the characters who were part of it, their projects, their books, their conflicts, as well as the political situation. I was quite 'normal', wholly in touch with everything; my ideas started to come back to me, and I would sometimes even get in a dig at Foucault, who went away convinced I was getting a lot better. When he came on another occasion, Father Breton was with me. There then took place between them, under my aegis as umpire, an extraordinary exchange of ideas and experiences which I shall never forget as long as I live. Foucault spoke of his research into Christian 'values' in the fourth century, and made the very important observation that, while the Church had always valued love highly, it had always profoundly mistrusted friendship, which classical philosophers and especially Epicurus placed at the heart of their ethical practices. Naturally, as a homosexual, he could not avoid drawing a parallel between the Church's repulsion against friendship and the repulsion against homosexuality, that is to say (ambivalence again) the predilection for homosexuality, of the whole apparatus of the Church and of the monastic life. At this point Father Breton intervened quite astoundingly, not to make various theological points but to share his personal experience. As a baby, without knowing who his parents were, he was taken in by the local priest; this man realised he had a lively mind and sent him to the seminary at Agen, where he completed part of his secondary education. At fifteen he became a novice and led the extremely austere life of a young monk – an impersonal, selfless existence (since Christ was not a person but an impersonal being subsumed in the Word), involving strict observances. In his obedience, the self was ignored in favour of something higher: 'Your thinking was done for you in accordance with the rule, and because someone else thought for you, your own personal thoughts were considered a sin of pride.' It was only later, when practices had evolved, that the uniqueness of the individual began to be respected a little more, but not much, as a consequence of what was referred to as Christian personalism! In this sense, and picking up a comment made by Foucault, Breton suggested that 'man was a very recent discovery' in monasteries. Breton did not have a single friend in his life, since friendship was always considered suspect because it degenerated into special friendship, a latent form of homosexuality. A repressed attraction towards homosexuality certainly existed in the Church, which made itself apparent in the exclusion of women. There would never have been such insistence on the danger of special friendships had homosexuality not been a constant danger and temptation. The superiors were obsessed with special friendships, which they feared as a widespread evil. Then there were so many priests, saintly priests at that, who detested women, which explained their instinctive purity and, since woman is a dirty creature, many priests believed they were turning their backs on impurity by having nothing to do with women and 'enjoying boys' instead. There was, for example, the case of the saintly priest who faithfully said mass and carried out all the observances and who one day took his charming little server into the sacristy after mass, opened his flies, and cut off a few pubic hairs to place in a sort of reliquary (the box containing the host). Friendship in such cases was always suspect, and what Foucault said was quite understandable. Love was a way of freeing oneself from friendship, in the broadest sense of the term, when expressed both to one's neighbour and to others at large.

There I was between the two of them, listening to Foucault and Father Breton, taking part in a conversation which had nothing to do with the stronghold I was in, namely the hospital. I had got right away from my anxiety about being shut in and protected. The same thing happened *with all my friends*, thus enabling me to escape the famous prison 'security' in both mind and conversation and to experience the outside world.

Obviously, my doctor knew relatively little about this aspect of my life, and I did not tell him about it. I only told him of my anxieties. It was on this basis that he built up his picture of my confinement in the fortress hospital. I would venture to say he was much more fixated and anguished than I was by my obsession with being confined and my fear of the outside world. I recently had a long talk with him about these past issues and I realised that, having detected signs of the anguish I felt, he projected his own anguish in a much more radical form on to me. It is true I thought I was completely done for, but not so much on account of my fear of the outside world as for deeper reasons which I will explain.

But before doing so, I would like to emphasise the damage done by the very existence of psychiatric institutions. It is a well-known fact that a number of sick people, suffering from an acute and, therefore, transitory crisis, who are automatically and routinely confined in a psychiatric hospital, can, because of drugs and their confinement, become 'chronic cases', truly mentally ill and incapable of ever leaving the hospital grounds. This effect is well known to all those who have tried to put a stop to automatic hospitalisation, preferring more limited interventions, such as day visits and hospital or community clinics, etc. That is the essential thrust of the reforms achieved (or rather called for) in Italy by

Basaglia. What Basaglia wanted to do was to prevent the acute cases and those which had 'become chronic' from suffering the ill-effects of confinement by closing psychiatric hospitals and sending the patients either to clinics or to families prepared to take them in. Naturally, such a reform could only be conceived of during a period of great popular upheaval, with the help of the unions and workers' parties. It is scarcely conceivable in France, given the ever-present repressive mentality. In Italy itself, as you know, the Basaglia reforms totally failed. What can now be done to free the mentally ill from the Hell created for them by the combined operations of all the Ideological State Apparatuses?

But what is less known about is the effect of psychiatric confinement on the doctors themselves, on the way they see their patients and their anxieties. In my own case, it is striking that the most well-intentioned doctor in the world and the one best equipped to 'listen' to his patients projected on to me his own anxiety about the absolute 'fortress' and, as a consequence of this projection and confusion, was partly mistaken about what was really happening inside my head. It was not so much the external world which caused my anxiety as the intense fear of finding myself *alone* there and abandoned, of being incapable of solving any difficulty whatsoever; an inability quite simply to be or to exist. While my doctor's attention was fixed on a specific anxiety which he passed to me rather than observed in me, thus shifting it from its 'object', or rather from the absence or loss of any 'object', to the representation of his own anxiety projected on to me, a wholly different 'dialectic' was developing within me: that of 'mourning'.

Several friends have reported the same experience, which was always equally disconcerting. For a long time – it seemed interminable – I 'lost' everything: my dressing-gown, my shoes, my socks, my glasses, my pencil, my pullovers, the key to my cupboard, my address book, and goodness knows what else. I see now the unconscious significance of this strange behaviour, which related to *objective*-objects. It was the 'coinage' of a wholly different, unconscious loss, the loss of a subjective-object, in other words an inner thing, the loss of the person I loved, Hélène, which reawakened another, earlier loss, that of my mother. The initial loss of the inner, subjective-object was transformed unconsciously into an indefinitely repeated mechanical act: the loss of specific *objective-*

objects. It was as if, in losing the subjective-object which determined everything to which I attached emotional importance, in losing the unconscious source of all this, I lost simultaneously and indefinitely any capacity to attribute value to specific objective-objects. I lost everything because I had lost the Everything which mattered to me, and I was mourning that loss. This business of indefinitely losing everything was a psychological working-out of my grief, the working-out of that loss and of the loss of that earlier subjective-object.

At the same time, I suffered in every part of my body: in my eyes, my ears, my heart, my oesophagus, my intestines, my legs, my feet, everywhere. I was actually losing my body to the effects of some sort of universal illness which was depriving me of the capacity to use it. I thus lapsed back into a state in which my body was 'fragmented'.

Another aspect of my behaviour was, however, equally strange and significant. All the friends who saw me then have confirmed it in a most striking way. I talked endlessly to them about suicide. With one, I spent a whole afternoon going over the different ways of killing myself, starting with the oldest, classic forms derived from antiquity and ending in fact with an earnest request to bring me a revolver. I asked him equally insistently: '*What about you, do you exist?*' Above all and at the same time, I was constantly *destroying* – the word itself is important – any prospect of getting out of the wretched state in which I found myself. I was never short of arguments, on the contrary, it seems my reasoning was implacable, and I spent my time *proving* to my friends the absolute futility of any help, whether physiological, neurological, chemical, or psychiatric and psychoanalytic, and especially psychoanalytic. Resorting to philosophical arguments, I demonstrated the fundamental limitations of all forms of intervention, its arbitrary and, in the end totally futile, nature, at least in my 'case'. My friends were unable to say anything and finally fell silent, even those who were experienced in the 'dialectics' of philosophical debate (and I was often confronted by extremely talented philosophers), and they went away completely bewildered and in despair. They would then telephone each other, but only to admit among themselves there was nothing to be done; that was it, I was doomed. What was the 'purpose' of these arguments of mine, which resembled a succession of trials of strength from which I unfailingly emerged victorious? In the destruction of another's existence, and in my implacable rejection of all forms of help, support, and reason which people tried to offer me, I was quite clearly seeking *proof*, the counter-proof, of *my own objective destruction, the proof of my non-existence*, proof that I was well and truly dead so far as any hope of being saved was concerned, of coming back to life. Indeed, in this proof and counter-proof, I sought to demonstrate to myself the radical impossibility for me of being saved, *that I was therefore already dead*, which, in another guise, was connected to my desire to kill myself, to destroy myself. But that self-destruction was symbolically achieved through the destruction of others, above all my closest and dearest friends, including the woman I loved the most.

It was truly 'the working-out of the process of mourning', the process of self-destruction in which I was engaged, at the time of Hélène's destruction which I caused; but it was not just Hélène's destruction. One day I had a visit from an analyst friend of long-standing. I told him of my anxieties and of the question I turned over and over in my mind: what exactly was the explanation for Hélène's murder? To my great surprise, he told me that through Hélène I had unconsciously wanted to kill my own analyst; a slightly 'wild' interpretation, at least in a formal sense. I had not thought of it in those terms and was most astonished and incredulous. But in fact my attempt to effect the radical destruction of any reality attached to psychoanalysis fitted in with this. I could have confirmed it, moreover, had I had the least suspicion of it, when I made a determined effort to get rid of my analyst, abandoning him for another one, a woman in fact of Polish-Russian origin (like Hélène) whom someone had mentioned to me. It was all done on the phone through friends who were my accomplices. I even mentioned it to my analyst on one occasion who told me I was perfectly entitled to make my own free choice and made no objection to what I proposed. I continued to give it some thought! But things dragged on, and it was practically impossible for me to leave hospital for an appointment such a long way away, so in the end I did not carry out the plan which I had very seriously considered.

I have good reason now for thinking that everything hung

closely together: the loss of the subjective-object was translated into the loss of countless real objective-objects, just as my generalised hypochondria revealed itself simultaneously as a desire to lose and destroy everything: Hélène, my books, my reasons for living, the École, my analyst, and myself. What recently alerted me to this and practically inspired me to write this little book, was the remark made by a woman friend I was so fond of. She had never reproached me in the slightest nor had she ever said what she really thought of me, but then quite recently she revealed almost instinctively: 'What I don't like about you is your will to *self-destruction*.' Her remark opened my eyes and revived the whole memory of those difficult times. In fact, I did want to destroy everything: my books, Hélène whom I had killed, my analyst, but all because I wanted to be sure of destroying myself, about which I phantasised in my suicide plans. Why was I so bent on destroying myself? Deep down, unconsciously (and my unconscious desires endlessly found expression in reasoned arguments), I wanted at all costs to destroy *myself* because I had never existed. And what better *proof of my non-existence* could there be than to draw from it the conclusion I should *destroy myself*, having destroyed those closest to me, all those on whom I could rely for help and support?

It was then I began to think that my life consisted of nothing but endless artifice and deceit, that it was totally inauthentic, with nothing true or real about it, since that old original compulsion of mine, which had recurred so often and in so many guises (cf. the episode with the rifle), had begun to resurface as a consequence of the terrible, primitive anxiety brought on by depression. In the meantime, however, I had found a way of living as a teacher, a philosopher, and a political animal. I also thought that death had been part of my very existence from the beginning, via Louis's death which held my mother's attention, beyond me. She thus condemned me to the same death that had befallen him in the skies over Verdun and which she compulsively relived in her heart and in her repulsion at the desire I constantly embodied.

It was then I understood (and I did so on the basis of my friend's most perceptive remark) that my mourning for Hélène did not date from her death (from when she was killed). I had been living it, working it out *from the beginning*. In fact I had always been in mourning for myself, for my own death, brought about by my mother and with other women assuming the same role. As tangible proof that I did not exist, I had desperately sought to destroy any evidence of my existence, not just Hélène, the supreme evidence, but secondary evidence such as my work, my analyst, and finally myself. I had not, however, noticed that there was one exception to this generalised slaughter: the woman who had recently opened my eyes by saying that what she did not like about me was my will to self-destruction. This was not a chance occurrence, given that I had tried to love her in a quite different way from the other women I had known before. She was thus the one exception in my life.

Indeed, I had never stopped mourning for myself, and it is doubtless the same grief I have experienced in those strange, regressive depressions of mine which were not genuine attacks of melancholia, but a contradictory way of being dead to the world by behaving in the same all-powerful way that I did in my hypomanic phases. A total incapacity to be equals total omnipotence. We are constantly faced with the same terrible ambivalence, the equivalent of which is found in medieval Christian mysticism: *totum = nihil*.

May I skip the rest, which is of no interest to anyone? I do, however, now see where the changes I was undergoing were leading me: they were all part of a process of my (re)taking in hand my own existence. It began with an initiative of mine to have my 'lawyer' come and free a trade unionist from what I considered to be political imprisonment (the CP). My doctor never knew *anything* about this intervention. The next occasion was when I asked my doctor to prescribe me a new drug, Upsène, which in fact did me some good. I left Soisy in July 1983 and spent an uncomfortable period holidaying in the country house of some close friends of mine in eastern France, but I was still feeling under the weather. I succeeded in not being readmitted to hospital on my return in September 1983, and my doctor took a (considerable) risk in this respect. My friends organised the equivalent of day-and-night supervision for me in my flat. Thanks to them I got used to my new abode in the end and was no longer frightened by it. Since then, I have deliberately treated my analyst as just an analyst and refrained from asking him to be a psychiatrist or a doctor. Since then I have also gradually reassumed responsibility for my affairs, my friendships, and my attachments. I have also, I think, learnt what it is to love: being capable, not of 'exaggerated' initiatives, of always going one better, but of being thoughtful in relation to others, respecting their desires, their rhythms, never demanding things but learning to receive and to accept every gift as a surprise, and being capable, in a wholly unassuming way, of giving and of surprising the other person, without the least coercion. To sum up, it is a question simply of freedom. Why did Cézanne paint the montagne Saint-Victoire at every available moment? Because the light of each moment is a gift.

So, despite its dramas, life can still be beautiful. I am sixty-seven, and though it will soon all be over, I feel younger now than I have ever done, never having had any youth since no one loved me for myself.

Yes, the future lasts a long time.

XXIII*

I showed this text to an old doctor friend of mine who had known Hélène and me for a very long time and naturally I put to him the following question:

'What did take place between Hélène and me on that Sunday, November 16th, which resulted in such an appalling murder?'

This, word for word, was his reply:

'I would argue that an extraordinary set of events came together, some of which were purely accidental, others not, yet the whole configuration could in no way have been foreseen but might very easily have been avoided at little cost if . . .

'In my view, three things stand out:

'1. *On the one hand*, as three expert doctors have already pointed out, you were in a "state of dementia", and therefore not accountable for your actions. You were suffering from mental confusion and hallucinations and were totally unaware of what you were doing both before and during the act. At a deeper level you were in an acute state of melancholia and could therefore not be held responsible for what you did. This explains why you were declared unfit to plead, which is statutory in such cases.

'2. *On the other hand*, one thing struck those conducting the police investigation: there was no trace of disorder in either of your two bedrooms, or on your own bed, nor was Hélène's clothing in any disarray.

'The story of the "blanket" which had protected Hélène's neck from any marks of strangulation was the hypothesis of a journalist seeking to explain the absence of external marks of strangulation. But this hypothesis, which in any case was only found in one article and rejected by a number of others, was formally rejected

* This chapter, numbered to follow on from the others, was also entitled 'No ground' (Editors' note).

by the investigation. The skin on Hélène's neck bore no external marks of strangulation.

'3. *Finally*, the two of you had been alone in the flat, not only for the previous ten days, but also that morning.

'There was obviously no one there to intervene. Furthermore, for some reason, Hélène made no effort to defend herself. Someone, quite rightly, made the following observation: given your state of confusion and insensibility (and perhaps also suffering the harmful effects of the MOAI drugs, following the "biological shock" which produced those adverse effects), had Hélène given you a good slap or made some serious effort it would have been enough to stir you from your state of insensibility, or at least to halt your own unconscious actions. Then the whole course of events might have been different. But she did nothing.

'Does that mean she was aware of her impending death and wanted to die at your hands, and thus passively let herself be killed? It cannot be ruled out.

'Or does it mean, on the contrary, that she feared nothing when, out of kindness, you began to massage her, which was something she had long grown used to? If I am to believe you, however, I have to point out that you had never massaged the front of her neck only the nape. This, too, cannot be ruled out. You are aware that the neck is *extremely delicate* (all anatomists, anyone who engages in armed combat, and also killers are fully aware of this). Only the slightest of blows is needed to fracture the cartilage and small bones, causing death.

'Fundamentally, did Hélène wish to end her life (she had talked incessantly of killing herself during the previous month but you knew she was incapable of doing so)? Did she passively accept death at your hands, having begged you to kill her? That again cannot be ruled out.

'Or did you so want to help her, as you had done throughout your life, help fulfil her most fervent and helpless desire, that you unconsciously satisfied her desire to end her life? It is what is known as "suicide via an intermediary" or "altruistic suicide", something one comes across quite frequently in cases of acute melancholia such as yours. This again cannot be ruled out.

'But how can we choose between these different hypotheses?

'Almost anything is conceivable in these circumstances. But

basically one can never be *absolutely certain* since so many elements combine to trigger the dramatic event and they are both subjectively complex and indeterminable and objectively uncertain for the most part.

'What in fact would have happened, for example – and this is perfectly objective! – had Hélène not begged your analyst to give her three days to "think" about it, whereas he wanted to admit you to hospital straightaway? What deep-seated reason did she have for begging your analyst to grant her this delay? And above all, above all, what would have happened if the *express letter* from your analyst, posted on Friday 14th at four o'clock in the after-noon and asking Hélène to telephone him *most urgently,* to set in motion your *immediate* admission to hospital despite her pleas for a delay, had reached the École, not on Monday 17th, after the tragedy had occurred, but either on Friday 14th in the evening or on Saturday 15th at nine o'clock in the morning? It is most unlikely the postal service was at fault. But the caretaker at the École, who receives all the ordinary mail as well as express letters, was evidently unable to reach you on the internal telephone, nor could he get you to open the door when he rang the bell, since for at least ten days you had no longer answered either the tele-phone or the doorbell – all your friends have testified to this (including those who wished they had been able to "force the door open"). If by some miracle or exceptional circumstance you had answered the phone or opened the door, Hélène would have received the *express letter* from your analyst and, had she wanted to, could have called him. It is clearly beyond dispute that every-thing would then have been different.

'From the beginning to the very last moment, this tragic event in your life remained unfathomable, this is an objective fact not a phantasy.

'All that can be said is, if the numerous imponderable factors are discounted – but how can they be disregarded? – Hélène accepted death without doing anything to prevent it and to protect herself, as if she wanted to die and indeed to die at your hands.

'What can also be said is that you did undoubtedly kill her, and thus sought to fulfil your own death wish, while at the same time doing her the immense service of killing her (which she was quite incapable of doing herself), though you only wanted perhaps to massage her carefully, and it must be remembered no external marks of strangulation were found. Thus you sought unconsciously your own self-destruction via the death of the person who believed in you most so as to make sure you remained that same artificial and deceitful character you were always obsessed with. The best way of proving you do not exist is to destroy yourself by destroying the person who loves you and above all believes in your *existence*.

'I know there will always be people, friends even, who will say: Hélène was his illness and he destroyed that illness. He killed her because she made his life impossible. He killed her because he hated her, etc. A more elaborate version might be that he killed her because he lived with the phantasy of his own self-destruction, and this self-destruction "logically" involved the destruction of his work, his fame, his analyst, and finally Hélène who summed up his whole life.

'The most unfortunate aspect of this line of argument (very widespread because very comforting – it offers, after all, an indisputable "cause"), is the *"because"* which creates an unchallengeable explanatory link, without in any way taking into account objectively uncertain elements.

'Now all of us have unconscious, aggressive phantasies, indeed homicidal, murderous ones. If all those who had such phantasies were to carry them out, we would all inevitably, you understand, become murderers, all of us. As it happens, the vast majority of people can live quite contentedly with even their homicidal phantasies, without ever realising them in acts.

'Those who say: he killed her *because* he could no longer bear her, *because*, even if only unconsciously, he wanted to be rid of her, understand nothing, or are unaware of what they are saying. If they applied this logic to themselves, which is ultimately that of *unconscious premeditation*, and given that they are subject to the same logic of aggressive and murderous phantasies (and who is not?), they would all have been put away long since not in psychiatric hospitals but in prison.

'In the life of an individual as in the life of a people there is no definitive truth except that of hindsight after they are dead, once things have come to an irremediable end, as Sophocles so rightly said. No one, above all the dead, can then alter anything. It is the finality of death which provides the perspective from which it is possible to decide (in the case of Sophocles) whether the dead person was happy or not, and in Hélène's case the "cause" of her death.

'But things don't happen like that in real life. A person can die as a result of a simple accident without "fulfilling any desire". But when a "desire" exists or is suspected, there are countless people who, with *hindsight* reinforced by a *fait accompli* which they find irresistible, invent an explanation based on the idea of a murderous phantasy which they then turn into the "cause" of the murder, even unconscious *premeditation*. The word itself is charged with meaning, signifying as it does *anticipation and unconscious planning of the murder* with the unconscious intention of carrying it out. Such people find it necessary to do this not only because they need to understand what happened but also to defend their own interpretation of it in order to protect themselves, to protect their friend or accuse someone else, in this case some doctor or other who did not do what seemed essential from a "supposedly objective" and "obviously" external point of view.

'Friends such as this, who are too well-intentioned towards their friend and – or – themselves, confuse the irreversible and *factual perspective* afforded by life itself with *that afforded by psychological insight* which gives *meaning*. In the first place, everyone, including a person's friends, needs to form with hindsight his personal point of view which suits him (though I in no way use the word pejoratively), enables him to come to terms with the shock of what actually happened and to face up to it in public. But each one of them, or almost, has his own interpretation; this is bound to make things worse as far as their relationship with their friend, the murderer, is concerned and even their relationships among themselves. They cling rigidly to their *personal point of view*, around which they construct an image of the murderer, and live with the private apprehension that the person concerned will one day challenge or correct their interpretation in terms of his own. In this sense your doctor was right to tell you that your explanations, quite as much as your lack of explanations, risked alienating very close friends. I hope with all my heart it will not be the case, but there again one can predict nothing with certainty.

'The patient's own private interpretation, arrived at after the event, is quite a different matter, first because it is part of his own experience, but above all because phantasies are always *ambivalent* rather than having a single meaning. The desire to kill, for example, or to destroy oneself and everything connected with oneself, is always matched by an immense desire to love and be loved in spite of everything, an immense desire to become one with the other person and thus to save them. In reading what you have to say, it seems to me that this is extremely clear in your own case. How can one possibly invoke the *"causally"* determining factor of a particular phantasy without at the same time invoking the other *"causally"* determining factor, the ambivalence, which expresses itself in the same phantasy as the radically opposing desire to that of killing, namely the desire for life, love, and salvation? In fact, it ought not to be described as *causal* determination at all, but as a welling-up of *ambivalent meaning* within the fractured unity of desire, which is only realised, in its wholly ambivalent ambiguity, because of some external "chance occurrence" which enables it to gel, as you say of Machiavelli. But the realisation itself, which is terribly dependent on contingent factors (your analyst's letter which Hélène did not receive, Hélène's total failure to defend herself, the isolation in which you both lived – if someone else had been at hand, what would have happened? who knows?), can in reality only take place in circumstances which are themselves highly fortuitous. Those who claim to be in possession of some *causal* explanation understand nothing of the ambivalence of phantasies and of inner meaning, *in life rather than with the definitive perspective afforded by death*, nor do they understand anything of the role of those fortuitous, external circumstances which enable the fatal event to occur or (as happens in the vast majority of cases) to be averted.

'So really, in order to understand the incomprehensible, you have to take into account uncertain and imponderable factors (of which there were so many in your case) but also the ambivalent nature of phantasies, which introduces a whole host of opposing possibilities.

'I have, I believe, put all the cards on the table, only some of which, the most obvious to any observer, are needed for one to argue that you were not responsible for your actions when you committed the murder.

'Having said that, you cannot prevent anyone from thinking differently. The essential thing is that you have explained yourself clearly and publicly for your own satisfaction. If there is anyone better informed, let them, if they wish, make something more of it.

'Anyway, I interpret this public account of your behaviour as a way of taking responsibility again for yourself, your grief, and your life. As they said in ancient times, it is an *actus essendi*: an act of being.'

One final word: I hope those who think they know more or have more to say will not be afraid to do so. They can only help me live.

L. A.

THE FACTS

1976

As I am the one who has organised everything, I should introduce myself straightaway.

My name is Pierre Berger. Actually, that is not true. It was my maternal grandfather's name and he died of exhaustion in 1938, having ruined his health working on his own as a forest ranger for the National Forestry Commission in the mountains of Algeria. He lived out in the wilds with his wife and two daughters.

I was born at the age of four in their forestry house in the Bois de Boulogne overlooking Algiers. As well as dogs and horses they had a large pond with fish. There were pine trees, and in winter I used to pick up great strips of bark which had fallen from the giant eucalyptuses. There were also lemon, almond, orange, and mandarin trees; and best of all medlars. I particularly enjoyed feasting on the medlars, and my aunt, who was a young girl at the time, would clamber up the trees like a goat and pick me the choicest fruit. I was a little bit in love with her. One day there was a great scare as we also had bees which were looked after by an old man who used to go to talk to them without wearing a veil. For some unknown reason, perhaps because he was muttering to himself, my grandfather was attacked by them. He therefore ran and leapt into the pond, greatly alarming the fish. But life was peaceful up in the hills. You could see the sea in the far distance, and I used to watch the boats arriving from France. One was called the *Charles-Roux*. For a long time I was puzzled by the fact that I could not see its wheels.

My grandfather was the son of poor peasants who lived in the Morvan. He sang at mass on Sundays and sat with a group of boys who were good singers in the stalls at the back of the church. From there he could see the whole congregation, including my grandmother praying with the others. She was a frail young girl and went to the school run by nuns. When the time came for her to get married, the nuns decided that Pierre Berger was suitably poor and upright to be her husband. The matter was agreed between the two families, despite my great-grandmother's complaints. She could not be persuaded to leave her cow and she had as little to say as it did. Before the marriage took place, however, there was a bit of a fuss. My grandfather, who did not have a penny to his name and owned no land, took it into his head to become a forester in the colonies, and lured either by Ranavalo or the Catholic press, decided he would go to Madagascar. It was the period of French imperialism which was strongly supported by Jules Ferry. But my grandmother soon put a stop to these plans, imposing certain conditions: Madagascar was out of the question, though she was, at a pinch, prepared to go to Algeria. If he did not agree, she would not marry him. But Pierre Berger did agree, because Madeleine was irresistible.

This is how my grandfather came to take up his exhausting job in the most remote forests of Algeria. I came across the names of these regions again in communiqués put out during the war of liberation. Living in houses deep in the forest which were totally cut off and a long way from any village, my grandfather looked after absurdly large areas completely on his own, protecting them against fires and the minor depredations of Arabs and Berbers. He constructed roads and firebreaks, which also served as communication routes. Yet for all this work, which required numerous different skills and carried enormous responsibility, he received less than a primary-school teacher's salary. Tense as he was, he never spared himself, but worked hard night and day and rode his horse until it was ready to drop. He was always on the look-out for the slightest thing and slept only a few hours. He also had a racking cough caused by smoking too many cigarettes which he rolled himself. He ruined his health there. From time to time, directors or inspectors would 'descend' on him. They had a room in the forestry house and spare horses. My grandfather kept his distance, but respected them for coming out to visit him, reserving his disdain for those who stayed behind in their office. He particularly respected a man called Peyrimoff who came out into the mountains and was prepared to discuss the things that mattered. He still talked about him late in life when he had retired and returned to the Morvan. He was someone who did his job properly.

My grandfather and grandmother had the same blue eyes and were equally stubborn. For the rest. . . . My grandfather was small and stocky and spent his time coughing and cursing everything. But no one attached too much importance to it. My grandmother was tall and slim (at a distance I always thought she looked like a young girl), did not say much, thought about things, and showed compassion (I remember her comment when I read her a piece from Malraux's *L'Espoir* one day, in which he describes the suffering of the Spanish Republicans: 'the poor things!'). But if it was necessary, she showed determination. When the popular, armed uprising, known as the Margueritte, occurred in Algeria at the beginning of the century, the events took place in the mountains not far from the forestry house. My grandfather was absent that night, out on his rounds as usual. My grandmother was alone in the house with her two daughters, who were about three and five years old. Though she was loved by the local Arabs, she was under no illusions, recognising that an uprising was an uprising and that the worst might happen. She stayed up all night with a rifle and three cartridges, which were not intended for the Arabs. The night passed and dawn finally came. My grandfather returned shortly afterwards, grumbling about the rebels he had met: the poor devils will get themselves killed.

I was born in the forestry house which he lived in at the end of his career. It was in the hills above Algiers and life there was a bit quieter. About five o'clock one morning in October 1918, my grandfather set off on horseback to the town and returned with a Russian woman doctor whose name I have forgotten. She, it seems, suggested I would know a lot one day, at least a lot of silly nonsense, 'given the size of my head'. At the time my father was a lieutenant in the heavy artillery at the front in Verdun and had gone back after a period of leave. During this leave he visited my mother, then engaged to his brother Louis who had just been killed in a plane over Verdun in which he was serving as an observer. My father considered it his duty to take his brother's place and my mother felt obliged to accept. You have to realise that marriages were in any case arranged between families, and the views of the children counted for little. My father's mother, herself married to a man who worked for the National Forestry Commission, but only in their offices, arranged the whole thing. She saw my mother, a pure, modest, and hard-working young girl, as just the person for her favourite first-born son, who had already been accepted at the École normale de Saint-Cloud. Louis was the favourite for the simple reason they did not have enough money to educate two sons and therefore had to choose. He had been chosen for reasons connected with my paternal grandmother's views on Écoles normales. My father, on the other hand, was obliged to go to work at the age of thirteen, initially as a messenger in a bank. Being intelligent, he had then climbed the ladder even though he lacked formal education. He often talked to me about the Fashoda incident as an example of his mother's tough and calculating approach to life. She counted every penny and made provision for the future. Immediately there was a threat of war she sent him straight out to buy kilos of dried beans, the best thing to have at a time of food shortages. In doing this, perhaps without realising it, she was following the age-old tradition of poor people in Latin America, Spain, and Sicily. Provided you protect them against insects, dried beans keep indefinitely, even in time of war. I have never forgotten this same grandmother shelling out for a tennis racket for me one July 14th as we watched from her balcony the troops parading on the quayside in Algiers.

My father often took me to the football stadium where there were epic encounters between French teams or French and Arab teams. Things got very heated. It was there I heard a shot fired for the first time in my life. People panicked, but the game continued as the referee had not been wounded. My father also took me to the races, this time with my mother. He could get in easily as he knew someone, through the bank, who worked on the gate and let him in without any fuss. He gambled, not very large sums of course, and though he always lost he enjoyed it, as we did too. My father also eyed the beautiful women a little too keenly, judging from my mother's silences which I also noticed on other occasions. He took me just once on my own to a huge military firing-range, which echoed with the noise of shots hitting the distant targets. It was quite different from the fairground shooting-gallery, which I was good at, having worked out how to hit the egg bobbing around on the water and win the bar of chocolate. It was much more difficult and frightening at the range. When I held the rifle to my shoulder and pulled the trigger, I felt a violent kick, as if I had fired behind me. The bullet had, however, gone straight ahead, to judge from the flags being waved above a trench indicating I had completely missed the target. My father told me I had done all right as a beginner and began to give me quite a lecture about artillery fire: how you adjusted your aim if a shell went too high or how you hit a target you could not see; my first introduction to the principles of Machiavelli, which I only got to know later. We also went as a family to play tennis and to the beach. My father had an excellent serve, a bit like Tilden's, and my mother had a formidable lifted backhand. I tried as hard as I could. I was taught to swim by my mother who did the breast-stroke and was less idiosyncratic than my father – he liked to swim on his back, taking care to keep his toes out of the water so that he could look at them without getting them wet. Much later, I started to do the crawl, having taught myself, and it still shows.

I was of course a good pupil at school, following the example set by my mother. She became a good schoolteacher, and the friend of other good teachers who used to ask me before class what the fruit of the beech tree was. When I replied: the beechnut, they told me I was a good boy. I attended a mixed primary school (by which I mean little Arab and French boys of the same age, rather than boys and girls). I was ceremoniously taken to school by our cleaning lady, which made me ashamed, as, apart from being accompanied, I was allowed into the school yard before everyone else, which was where I used to meet the nice master who asked me about the fruit of the beech tree.

My first period of schooling was marked by two dramatic events. One day in class, the pupil behind me decided to let out a fart. The master looked at me reproachfully for a long while: 'You, Louis. . . . ' I did not have the courage to say to him: 'It wasn't me,' as he would not have believed me. The second occurred in the school yard when we were playing marbles, which I was very good at. We were also swapping plain and coloured marbles. I do not know why, but I began quarrelling with another child whom I suddenly slapped. As a result, I got into an absolute panic and ran after him, offering him everything I had on me if he would keep quiet about it. He did. I have to confess, this episode still makes me shudder.

Compared with this incident, what happened in the Bois was insignificant, though it surprised me as much as the slap. My mother, my sister, and I were out enjoying the fresh air, sitting on the grass with a friend of my mother's who had brought her two children, a boy and a little girl. Again, for some trifling reason, I suddenly heard myself calling her a 'Nincompoop', a word I had read in a book and thought was offensive and which I applied to her for no apparent reason. My mother apologised and the incident was forgotten. I remained astonished that you could have ideas which you were unaware of.

On the other hand, an incident which occurred later in Marseille made a lifelong impression on me. I was walking with my mother along a fairly wide though slummy street near the place Garibaldi, when we saw one woman being violently insulted by another and dragged along the ground by her hair. A man who was standing motionless and enjoying the scene kept repeating: be careful, she has a revolver. My mother and I pretended we had seen and heard nothing. It was quite enough that we each carried away an image of the scene we had witnessed and tried to come to terms with it. I never did cope with it very well.

After primary school, I entered the first form of the *lycée* in Algiers of which I have only one memory: of a magnificent, white, open-topped Voisin car with a chauffeur who wore a cap and waited for another boy at the school who never spoke to me. I also remember visiting an Arab landowner, whom my father knew, and being given candied gourd before tea, which I have never seen since. We also used to be taken to the mountains by one of my father's friends in his old Citroën. We visited the place where, many years earlier, my grandfather had saved the lives of a team of Swedes, I believe, who had gone out in a blizzard which caused them to lose all sense of direction. My grandfather, who detested decorations (as did my father), was given the Military Cross with a special decoration and citation for this exploit. I kept all these things after my grandmother's death.

The forestry house in the Bois de Boulogne remained in my memory because of its exceptional situation, overlooking the whole of Algiers, the bay, and the sea, which stretched away to the horizon. I used to spend a long time on my own, under the carob trees, looking out to sea and rubbing the scented leaves of this tree between my fingers. When we came for two days at the weekend with my parents, we used to look in spring at the anemones which grew in the part of the garden bordering a medical laboratory and another bourgeois residence belonging to a former army man, who was married with two children. There were often dramas in this family. I was interested in the little girl. She had long hair and said nothing, but I never dared speak to her. Their almost grown-up son rebelled against his father who got into violent tempers and locked him in his bedroom on the first floor. One day we heard loud banging on the door which suddenly gave way, and the young man fled into the woods. The father took down his gun and went after him, while the mother wept. But it was just histrionics and order was soon restored.

As we were about to leave, my father regularly picked a large bunch of gladioli which he gave to a mysterious lady who lived on the square de Galland. My mother pretended not to notice, but I saw this lady one day. She had languorous eyes, was wearing scent which smelt of wisteria, at least that is what I thought, and was waiting for him to speak to her. As always, my father said something amusing, which did not fool anyone.

My father had had an affair before he married with an impecunious young girl called Louise and broke with her the moment he married my mother (he never saw Louise again, because he was a man of principle, even when she became ill and died). He did not seem to have many friends. There was one who worked with him at the bank, a gentle, unenterprising character, who always needed propping up. He was married to a woman called Suzanne who had many attributes and was bursting with energy. My father saw them often and flirted with Suzanne in his own way, always joking and making fun of her figure, which she greatly enjoyed. I remember on one occasion when my sister had scarlet fever and we had to be kept apart, I was sent to stay with these friends and spent over a week with them. Early one morning, I got up and went to the kitchen where I suspected I would find Suzy (you have certain intuitions at that age). I half opened the door and saw her standing there naked, making the coffee. She said: oh, Louis ... so I closed the door again, wondering what all the fuss was about. She had a way of embracing me, hugging me to her bosom, something she did quite readily, which made me think seeing her naked was less significant than being hugged like that. It was in her house that I had a strange dream, which I still remember. I dreamt that an enormous shapeless creature, like some gigantic, endless worm, was emerging from the top of the cupboard at the end of the room which had slowly opened. It terrified me. Much later in my life, I came to understand what might be the meaning of this incomplete dream I had had while staying with a woman who clearly wanted to sleep with me but decided not to out of respect for convention; I also wanted to sleep with her though the idea scared me. Meanwhile, her husband suspected nothing. He smoked a long-stemmed pipe filled with mild tobacco and had a little dog which he took for a walk on Saturday afternoons in the parc Galland. Someone once took a photo there of me. I had a thin body crowned by a heavy-looking head and a high forehead, which was out of proportion with my slender, frail-looking shoulders. I resembled a pale stem of asparagus which had been forced in a cellar. The sun was high in the sky, and I cast a thin shadow, though shorter than I actually was. I was completely alone, holding the dog on the end of its lead. Alone.

The relationship between my mother and father was a strange one. My father had divided his life into two rigidly separate compartments: on the one hand, there was the world of work which absorbed him completely, on the other, the family which he left entirely to my mother. I do not remember him taking any part in the upbringing of his children. He handed the whole task over to my mother. This meant that my sister and I were at the mercy of all my mother's fantasies and fears. She made my sister learn the piano and me the violin, so that we could play together, which she saw as part of a good, cultured upbringing. She became infatuated with a progressive doctor and decided one day to put the whole family on a vegetarian diet. Thus, for six or seven years, we ate natural products, without any meat or animal fats and without butter or eggs. Only honey was acceptable in her eyes. My father refused to go along with it. A steak was ostentatiously cooked and solemnly served to him as a sort of protest; meanwhile we ate grated carrot and almonds and chestnuts stewed with cabbage. It was a splendid sight: my father ate in silence, sure in the strength of his position, while we commented on the relative and unequal merits of meat-eating and vegetarian diets so that all might hear and take heed. But my father took no notice and continued to cut his rare steak with a firm hand.

My father was given to violent outbursts which frightened me. One evening, when our neighbours on the same landing were singing, he took a saucepan and ladle, went out on to the balcony and set up a terrible din which frightened all of us, but put a stop to the singing. My father also suffered nightmares which ended in long and terrifying wails. He was quite unaware of this and when he woke up claimed he remembered nothing. My mother used to shake him to make him stop. They never said anything to each other which suggested they loved each other. But I remember one night hearing my father, who must have been holding my mother in his arms as they lay in bed, murmuring to her: 'You're mine . . .', which gave me quite a shock. I remember two other episodes which surprised me. One day, just as we had got back to our flat in Algiers, having come off the boat from France, my father had a turn on the balcony. He collapsed while sitting on a chair. My mother was frightened and spoke to him, something she never normally did. I also remember being in a train one night on our way to the Morvan when my mother had a turn. My father made us get out in the middle of the night at Châlons, where we tried to find a hotel to open up and agree to take us in. My mother was very ill, and my father, who was very worried, spoke to her, something which he never normally did. These two memories carry with them a whiff of death. Doubtless they did love each other though they never spoke to each other. In the same way, people remain silent when they are by the sea or when death is at hand. They did, however, venture the odd word just to make sure the other was still there. It was their own business. But my sister and I paid dearly. I only became aware of this much later.

Talking of my sister, I also recall an incident which took place in the hills above Algiers where we found the tiny cyclamens by searching beneath the bushes. We were walking calmly along a dirt road when a young man suddenly appeared on a bicycle. I do not know what he was doing, but he knocked my sister down. My father pounced on him, and I thought he was going to strangle him. My mother intervened. As my sister was hurt, we hurried home with me still holding a few cyclamen flowers in my fingers though I was no longer interested in them. My father's violent behaviour seemed strange to me. My mother, however, was completely indifferent to it, or so it seemed, though she spent her time complaining about her great suffering and the sacrifice she had been forced to make by my father in giving up her career as a teacher, which was something she enjoyed. Though he seemed so self-assured, he would suddenly get carried away, unable to control his violent impulses. Yet I have to admit he did actually control them in a way, as he usually got what he wanted when he resorted to such behaviour. He was always lucky, with things turning out to his advantage. Yet he also held back from doing things when it was necessary. He was, for example, the only manager in the bank not to join Pétain's Legion when he was in Lyon between 1940 and 1942. Nor did he support General Juin when he undertook to 'make the Moroccans eat straw', and, even though he had mixed feelings as a *pied-noir*, he was not against De Gaulle when the turning-point came and agreed to Algerian independence. He grumbled a great deal, but that was all.

After my father's death, I learnt from members of his staff that he ran the bank in a very idiosyncratic way when he became manager. If not a principle of his, it was at least his custom not to say anything or to make absolutely unintelligible remarks. His subordinates dared not admit they had understood nothing, but went off and usually managed very well on their own, though they still wondered if they might not be mistaken and this kept them on their toes. I never knew whether my father did this deliberately or not, as he adopted almost the same practice with us. When he was with his customers or his friends, however, he never stopped talking and was perfectly comprehensible. He was always joking, which disconcerted those he was talking to, putting them under his spell and in an inferior position. I perhaps inherited something of his delight in provocation. My father's banking methods were rather peculiar. He often lent large sums of money in the bank's name and without interest, especially when he was in Morocco. This disconcerted his rivals and placed them in a difficult position. But almost always the customers paid the interest themselves, though it had not been asked for, thus proving as my father said that Moroccans had a sense of honour and that you could trust them. However, my father would never accept the smallest gift, other than flowers for my mother, or an invitation to visit a farm where he was offered mint tea and the local sweets. He was very critical of his superiors who, to all intents and purposes, allowed themselves to be bribed. He did not hide his feelings, treating them with a disdainful silence, which spoke much louder than words. I remember one of them in Marseille, who had a beautiful house near Allauch with a tennis court. He had a young wife, whom I found most attractive, and who used to say as she was about to serve: 'You'll see, it'll be like the Folies-Bergère'. And when she pivoted on her right leg, her short skirt blew up revealing a nice pair of buttocks and the pink knickers she was wearing, which set me day-dreaming. I wish she had talked less and come with me into the laurels, whose flowers were pink as well. In the end, however, this manager came unstuck since his weakness had been to accept too many things in front of too many witnesses, including my father who never said a thing. My father was later to pay for his silence when the senior management of the bank pensioned him off at very short notice, whereas tradition-ally a person of his calibre would have gone to the head office. No, he was pushed aside, in favour of someone less good than himself who had been to the École Polytechnique and married a daughter of the Protestant family which owned the bank; this was standard practice both for the bank and for a student from the Polytechnique. My father retired and told me it was perfectly normal, since it was a family affair and the only thing he had done wrong was to marry a woman who was not their daughter. You cannot control what you feel in your heart. But in fact he was not distressed at this outcome, which to him was like an unintentional honour. There are those who are not decorated, he said fiercely. Actually, he had refused all decorations.

I continued my secondary education in Marseille, in the fine, tall buildings of the Lycée Saint-Charles, presided over by a head-master who was an amateur painter and run in a friendly manner by distinguished teachers, including one old man who openly wept in English lessons because his daughter had died. We were all very sad. We took our revenge on the PE teacher and the caretaker. The one made us play nothing but football, which was much appreciated. The other kept guard rather aggressively at the exit and chased away any girls who ventured anywhere near it. It was there, in opposition to the views of my father, who was thinking of the Polytechnique, that a distinguished teacher of literature began to turn my thoughts towards sitting the entrance exam for the École normale. To start with, he entered me for the open exam for secondary-school pupils. I took this exam in all subjects but did not get a single certificate of merit. I have to admit I did invent quotations and translations, which was not the done thing.

My father was then transferred by the bank to Lyon. There he continued to play tennis and to go to the opera, where there are some very beautiful women to be seen. I went too and entered *hypokhâgne* at the Lycée du Parc. That is where I got to know Jean Guitton, who was constantly preoccupied with proving the immortality of the soul, and Jean Lacroix ('The man taking over my position and who isn't very well known,' Guitton told us, 'is someone called M. Labannière'). Unlike Jean Guitton, who taught with his back to us, bent over, clasping his forehead with his right hand, a small piece of chalk casually held between the fingers of his other hand, Jean Lacroix talked to us face to face, emphasising what he said with blows to his unfortunate right ear and with phonetic explosions, which we identified with some difficulty as the equivalent of *beuhl*, the name we immediately gave him, though not with his consent. There was also Henri Guillemin, who gave us an hysterical performance on Chateaubriand, before returning to his post in Cairo, from where he sent us a superb photo of himself wearing a red fez. We sent him a telegram in reply: 'The work is different, but the hat remains the same.' Above all there was 'Père Hours', a stocky individual and a native of Lyon who was the spitting image of Pierre Laval. He was a Gallican, fiercely Jacobinic in his sympathies, who spent his time speaking ill of the Pope and Georges Bidault. He also kept his eye on the career of French politicians with the help of index cards he had on each of them. He drew some surprising political conclusions (in 1936–37), claiming that the French bourgeoisie would betray France, fearing the Popular Front more than Hitler, that it would give in to the Nazis after a phoney war, and that France in return would owe any future it might have to its people, roused to resist by the left, led by the communists. The relationship between 'Père

Hours' on the one hand, and Jean Guitton and Jean Lacroix on the other, were rather unusual. Hours could not stand Guitton, whom he accused of being a mother's boy. He was in political agreement with Lacroix, but found his philosophical and religious emotionalism hard to take. It was, however, greatly to Lacroix's credit that he defended his views and contributed, alongside Mounier, to the review *Esprit*. Born into an average middle-class family in Lyon, he had married a young woman who belonged to one of the most exclusive upper middle-class families in the district. Lacroix was ostracised and denounced as the devil. When he attended a family gathering which brought together hundreds of people who were related to each other, it took a certain amount of calm courage to face the insults which were heaped upon him. Jean Lacroix always stuck to the same line, remaining faithful to Mounier, even though his successors steered the review *Esprit* into easier, murkier waters. Hours's career after the war, on the other hand, was wholly unexpected. Convinced by one of his children who was a Jesuit and who had lived in Algeria for a number of years that Islamic people were inherently incapable of rising to the intellectual challenge of scientific knowledge, because of their religion and their writing (*sic*) (even though the Arabs were the heirs of Archimedes, invented a revolutionary form of medicine, and also translated and interpreted Aristotle), he got it into his head that the French should not leave Algeria and became a fervent supporter of French Algeria, at a time when De Gaulle was preparing to give in to the demands for independence on the part of our old colony. Hours died suddenly in a state of anger and consternation a few days after his wife.

There was another character in *khâgne*, apart from the students, who also stood out. He pretended to teach English language, his head held high, as he recalled his memories as an interpreter with the 'Anglo-Saxon' troops in the 1914–18 war. He spoke pure Oxford English and became enraged whenever I opened my mouth, proclaiming at the top of his voice that I had picked up a terrible American accent down at the docks. As he enjoyed being ragged, we did not deny him that pleasure. It was all part of a very British notion of fair play. A pupil, chosen in advance, stood behind the master's desk, while he sat a few feet away, and began to comment in English on some text or other, usually one in that language. Meanwhile, we had agreed among ourselves that, at a key point in his commentary, he would put in a line from Béranger: 'May God grant you a pleasant death, my children' or 'How at home one feels in an attic when one is twenty'. It never failed. Each time the person doing the commentary reached the crucial point and began to say: 'This passage irresistibly recalls to mind that line of Béranger . . .', the teacher stood up, as if propelled by a spring, and put on the greatest display of anger I have ever seen, which went on for ten minutes. He kicked the boy out of the class and continued the commentary himself without mentioning Béranger. You could see how happy he was from his thick hair and quivering hands.

One day someone played a trick on him. The boy in question, a splendid fair-haired lad who was himself a bit of a poet and permanently in love with a girl in our group whom I will say a word or two about in a moment, was commenting on three lines of John Donne. He began by giving his version of it in translation:

> *Je t'ai aimé trois jours durant*
> *Je t'aimerai trois jours encore*
> *S'il fait beau.*

It was pouring down that day, but that did not matter. He returned to the original version of these three lines to evoke certain 'associations'. He began: 'I have loved you irresistibly brings to mind the song by Tino Rossi . . .' and went on in the same banal fashion. He cited all the popular songs of the day, linking each one to a specific word in the poem. The teacher said nothing until the name of Béranger cropped up. At that point, as always, he got into a rage.

On another occasion another boy, who subsequently became a celebrated Oratorian and who was known to everyone as Fanfouet, because he came from Savoy, and whose father was in charge of a station which had been closed (you can imagine the jokes we made about the name of the station), did a commentary on another text, in English as always, but using an original analytical method. He put forward exactly forty-three different approaches, beginning with the classic ones such as the historical and geographical approach and ending up with somewhat uncommon ones such as the ornithological (highly successful with the master who liked sea birds), the culinary, and other such inanities. Béranger featured, inevitably, under the poetic approach, provoking the customary rage.

When it was my turn to perform, I adopted another tack. I consulted a friend of mine doing Spanish and also looked in some of his books for a quotation from a sixteenth-century monk and seasoned inquisitor, Dom Gueranger, which I introduced, lowering my voice at the right moment. Thinking he had heard the name Béranger, the master was on the verge of his customary rage, and I had immense difficulty getting him to see his error and convincing him Dom Gueranger had nothing whatsoever to do with Béranger, having been born two or three centuries earlier and never having written any poetry. He bought us all a drink at the end of the year at the kiosk under the trees in the park. There were girls out on the lake in boats, and we wondered what they were doing there since it was so hot.

We also challenged the authority of 'Père Hours'. Whenever he had to pronounce a word in English, such as Wellington, he usually stopped talking, went up to the blackboard, wrote up then underlined the word in question so that everyone would understand, while apologising for the fact that he 'couldn't pronounce English'. He extemporised, leaning with one hand on his desk and flicking through with the other, for appearance's sake, a few sheets of paper which were apparently devoid of notes. There was no stopping him. He would say: 'Did I tell you England was an island?' and wait for the answer which did not come. He drew all sorts of conclusions. One day, after the war, he told me, in front of Hélène who had fought in the Resistance, that it would have been truly impossible in England, not because it was an island but because the English lived in cottages and the Resistance fighters would not have had any secret bolt-holes as they did in Lyon. I played my own trick on him one day when I had to give a talk to the class on the First Consul and his foreign policy. I so organised it that the final word of my talk was the name of a famous battle. As I was on the point of saying it, I got up slowly, picked up a piece of chalk in my right hand, and approached the blackboard, saying: 'Forgive me, but my Italian pronunciation is very bad.' Then I simply wrote the word: Rivoli. 'Père Hours' took it very well, as a professional. So he tended to go on at great length, but there was a huge boy in our class who would have made a world-class rugby or tennis player, but who was too idle to do anything. As if to challenge everyone's expectations, he later became one of the best-known journalists working for the French press. Scarcely had Hours begun talking than he would slump on to his desk and go to sleep, to our great delight, as he snored loudly. All that we were interested in was: for how long? because 'Père Hours' always noticed him in the end. He would then creep up on the sleeping boy, shake him vigorously, and shout out: 'Hey, Charpy! We've arrived. Everybody out!' Charpy opened just one eye, keeping the other one closed, and went back to sleep. 'Père Hours', taking the view he had more than done his duty, would begin again to tell us that England was an island.

Most of us were royalists at that time (except for the poet and another boy who, without telling anyone, set off for Spain one day to join the International Brigade, where he was killed like all the others). It was the fault of Chambrillon and Parain, the one a brilliant aesthete, the other, whose father manufactured ribbon for hats at Saint-Étienne, an excellent pianist, in love with a woman he had yet to meet. But you could picture her from the attitudes and feelings he expressed. Our royalism, in support of the Comte de Paris, was a thing of the moment that could doubtless be explained by the fact that Boutang had briefly and flamboyantly made his mark in *khâgne* a few years previously; for us at least it was not very serious. We made a few well-chosen and pointed remarks, addressed to imaginary enemies such as the Popular Front which had delivered France up to the Jews and the common people.

I saw something of the Popular Front when a huge procession of workers marched down the rue de la République one day. Seething with rage, I watched them from a small window of the flat in which my parents were then living in the rue Arbre-Sec, a name to conjure with. But I reconsidered all this in the light of what 'Père Hours' told us about the French bourgeoisie and ordinary people, and it was enough to draw me away from my royalist friends.

Our poet's mind was on other things. He spent his time making advances to one of the two girls who went around with us, a young woman with jet-black hair called Mlle Molino. She was a fiery individual beneath her calm exterior and would explode if one as much as touched her. There were stormy and dramatic scenes in public during the three years I was at the *lycée*. The poet declared his love for her in front of everyone, even in English, but she did not want to know. One day the two of them disappeared, and we believed they were dead, but they reappeared a few days later, seemingly in good health. Within a matter of hours, however, they were at each other again, breaking off their relationship. It was a more enjoyable sport than watching the abysmal local football team which never scored any goals but let in dozens. I ought to mention that Édouard Herriot was mayor of Lyon and spent his time running the Radical Party, refining his thoughts on culture (it seems he spent ten years at it) and preparing to die having made his peace with the Church.

I learnt a little of his preparation for the after-life from a tall, thin Jesuit who had the finest nasal appendage I have ever seen, which did not however prevent him from enjoying life. I went to find him one day at the seminary where he lived up in Fourvières as I needed his help in founding a student Christian movement in *khâgne*. He greeted me warmly, though he was a little surprised that I had sought him out, going over the heads of the municipal, university, and church authorities; but in the end he agreed. That is how, with his agreement, I formed my first political cell. I never needed to form another. We recruited members and held irregular meeting, and thus I came to discover that the Church was concerned in its own way with the 'social question'. Coming as it did from the Vatican, this concern made 'Père Hours' cross. One day we set off, including the royalists, for a retreat in a monastery in the Dombes where there were numerous lakes. The monks were unctuous, relaxed, and bound by their vow of silence. They worked on the land by day and at night they got up five times to say their prayers out loud. The building had an incredible smell of wax, soap, oil, and filthy sandals. It was a wonderful way to learn something about detachment from the world and how to concentrate spiritually. Furthermore, on each floor there was a huge clock which chimed the quarters and kept everyone awake, especially at night. I tried to absorb the atmosphere and prayed on my knees, convinced that Pascal would overcome my spontaneous

materialism with his materialist arguments. I even gave a sort
of homily one evening on meditation which earned me Parain's
unqualified esteem. But I told him I did not deserve it, since my
text had been written in advance. I remember this period as a time
when perhaps I had a religious vocation which fizzled out and a
certain predisposition to ecclesiastical eloquence.

Though it would have altered nothing, there was not a single
girl staying in the Dombes. One did come across girls everywhere
else however; not only Mlle Molino whom I had no intention of
attempting to take away from Bernard (our poet), but those seen
in parks and gardens, in the street as well as in the famous café
where, like all the members of our group, I was expected to buy
a beer and tell all. A few of my friends remembered what I said.
They were there just to terrify the rest of us, which they did, and
we shuddered at the thought of how much enjoyment we might
give them. Finally the moment came, and I remember beginning:
'Lav, lav, lav, lav', said the little boy. 'Why didn't you do a wee-
wee before coming in?' replied his mother. After this decisive
opening, what followed was of little significance. It was, I think,
a pastiche of Valéry in which, among other things, I said: 'It is
not for nothing that I have hung up my sword', without explaining
why or what the sword or the nothing referred to. The meaning
was, however, not lost on everyone, as I was soon made to realise
when I was aggressively questioned on my love life, which was
something one had to expect. I handled it as best I could by telling
the truth: that there was one young blonde girl I had seen at a
distance coming home alone through the woods when I was in
the Morvan. I said how I would have liked to go with her and
take her in my arms. There was another girl I had got to know
much better on a beach in the Midi where we used to spend
the summer months in a house belonging to one of my father's
colleagues, when he was in Marseille. But things did not go very
far, except for one marvellous afternoon spent in the dunes when
I trickled sand between her breasts and caught it as it came out at
the top of her thighs. I could not see her again because my mother
was opposed to my relationship with a girl she considered too
young for me, since she was a year older and scowled. One day,
when I wanted to cycle to meet her at a beach where she would
have been dangerously alone, my mother said no, so I set off in

tears at breakneck speed in the opposite direction, to La Ciotat. There I bought a stiff drink and thought how I might have been holding her in the sea, as I liked doing, with one hand under her breasts and the other in her crutch. This was something she did not mind at all and furthermore it would not have made her pregnant. They listened to all this without mocking me in the slightest and, when I finished, there was a long silence which they covered by drinking their beer.

Without realising it, despite the horrors being committed in Spain, war was gradually drawing nearer. When it finally broke, I was taking a thermal cure at Saint-Honoré where I enjoyed doing running dives into the pool and walking in the shade under the tall trees in the park. It was September 1939 and I still had not received my call-up papers which I had been expecting. I had very painful rheumatism in my left shoulder which disappeared as soon as I received them. It is a well-known fact that most men's aches and pains are cured by war. My father was sent to the Italian border, where they waited for the Italians to fire a few shells as a way of demonstrating they were really taking part in the war. My mother went back to the Morvan and there enjoyed the happiest period of her life, without her husband and children. She took on the job of town-clerk in the local town where lots of refugees fled after May 1940, in the wake of the defeat. As for me, I was sent with other students to the Training Centre for Reserve Cadet Officers in Issoire. There was a great concentration of men and women of all ages in this rather provincial town as well as horses and ancient cannons, because of the horse-drawn artillery. We were instructed in the art of war by an amateur warrant-officer, Courbon de Castelbouillon, who was completely round and, like Napoleon III, short in the leg, but a fine-looking man when mounted on his white horse. He swore like a trooper as the horses went round and round resignedly in the sand. They would go forward and of course remain still without anyone having to lead them and from time to time they dropped a sizeable dollop of dung or let out a stream of piss which surprised everyone. We greatly enjoyed the processions on the parade ground, the keys to which the warrant-officer claimed had been lost at the time of Louis XIV, and especially the general chaos caused by the fact that not one of us was able to make his horse go forwards, backwards, jump, or lie down. We laughed a great deal, in spite of Courbon's rages. Though he did not mind at all having to deal with such distressing recruits, he told us that, given the circumstances, we would lose the war which would teach us and the Popular Front a thing or two. What really delighted us was our walks along the high ridges bordering the valley of the Allier which were covered in blackthorns. We loved the fruit that rotted in winter, especially when we picked it high up or close to an abandoned chapel. We returned exhausted but happy. There was a group of friends who were as thick as thieves and who always had some quotation or other to add humour to the conversation. Among them was Poumarat, whom I have met up with again and who now has a beard, a wife who suits him, and several children who get on well together. He goes gliding and is always craning his neck by looking at the sky to see if there are any good air currents. He writes good novels but deals with topics that are too outmoded for a publisher to accept them. Béchard, a friend from *khâgne*, was also there. He was a great bean-pole who cast an enormous shadow and had a huge head of hair. He spoke with a Morvan accent, played the violin, and expressed himself in English when he was in a good mood. He died around 1942 in Morocco, at the same time as his wife, as a result of tuberculosis from which they both suffered. I do not know what he was doing there; getting away from Pétain, I presume. There was another stocky character who was only interested in women. He came across one who slept with the horses and made love to her in the straw, claiming it was absolutely marvellous, because she was not at all affected and always wanted more. He even rented a hotel room for her which cost him a lot but was more practical, except that when he came back he told us she was a bitch because she had given him the clap. It was not easy to get treatment for it at the time. This reinforced my view that one definitely had to beware of women, especially if they slept in the straw with the horses.

As time went by and the war was continuing without any progress being made, we were asked if we would like to volunteer for the air force. Béchard and the others said yes. I took fright and fell ill, long enough to escape having to make a decision. My temperature was just high enough, and I think I also deliberately rubbed the thermometer to achieve the desired result. The doctor came to see me, looked at my chart, and did not press me. In the meantime, the others had gone. I remained alone with Courbon, who preferred horses to aeroplanes. But there was no longer any fun.

The remainder of us were sent to Vannes in Brittany to complete our training. I joined a new, less homogeneous, and less amusing company. We now had more serious business, however, including night exercises, looking for spies (one day, we found torn-up papers belonging to Spaniards who were on the run), mock firing over marked-out terrain, forced marches, written exams, etc.

During this period floods of refugees kept arriving in a sorry state. And before long the Germans got nearer as we were preparing to defend the Breton stronghold of Paul Reynaud. He himself took off for Bordeaux with the rest of the government, which had fled in disarray. Vannes was declared an 'open town', and we resolutely awaited the Germans, mounting guard in our quarter to prevent refugee soldiers returning home as deserters. This was done on the orders of General Lebleu, who was implementing a carefully devised plan, the intention of which was to deliver us up to the German army, on the principle that it was politically safer for the men to be taken to Germany as prisoners rather than to go south, where Heaven knows what they might do, even follow de Gaulle. It was an effective and faultless piece of logic.

The Germans arrived in side-cars and respectfully accepted our defeat. They were courteous, promised to liberate us within two days, and kindly informed us that if we escaped we would suffer reprisals as they would catch up with us. Some turned a deaf ear and took off without any qualms. All you needed were some civvies and a few francs. In fact it was what my uncle, who had been a prisoner in 1914, did. He knew the score and was not easily taken in. He somehow got hold of a civilian suit, stole a bicycle, and set off, even managing to cross the Loire, on the pretext that he was going to pee on the other bank ('I'm a left-banker, sir'). He turned up one day to the total astonishment of his wife: 'You'll get us all into trouble.' My uncle was sufficiently bad-tempered to be left in peace. He later died, having raised his family and thoroughly aggravated his wife, but that is a separate issue.

Before we left, the Germans carefully transported us from one place to another in Brittany, visiting several camps, as they called them, but none were very secure. I remember one where all you had to do was climb in the ambulance in order to escape. In another, you got out of the truck, wandered off into the village behind the little station, and you were free. But that would have been desertion and there was the promise that everything would be done according to the rules. Besides, the Germans had taken my little Kodak camera given me by my father, which they naturally said they would keep safe before giving it back to me. We could write. Things looked fine. It was just a matter of waiting.

During this period we had taken the statutory written exams for Reserve Cadet Officers. Father Dubarle came out top. As with the Concours général, I failed them all and do not know if I was even graded, since they did not have time to publish the results because of the Germans. (In the entrance exam for the École normale, on the other hand, I came sixth, I believe, in July 1939. I got no less than 19 out of 20 for Latin, and 3 for Greek, for which I ask Flacelière to forgive me. I produced a philosophical essay on efficient causality which I knew damn all about; that simpleton Schuhl liked it but not Lachièze-Rey, who told me with good reason that he 'hadn't understood a word'.) The Germans considered us second-class soldiers and therefore sent us to a camp for ordinary troops. First, however, we were sent to a general transit camp near Nantes where we fought over water and where Dubarle, who was far-sighted, organised the surveillance of military convoys on the nearby railway so that the information could be passed on to those outside. This was in June 1940, I recall, before De Gaulle made his appeal.

Things began to get serious when we were put in a train with a truck full of soldiers armed with machine-guns at the rear. There were sixty of us to a truck, we had to pee into a bottle, and there was nothing to drink but our own urine. We were extremely restive. The journey lasted for four interminable days and nights. In the daytime we stopped at various stations, where people offered us something to eat. We also stopped out in the countryside where peasants were cutting their hay not more than a dozen yards away. Some of the lads managed to rip up the floor-boards and crawl out on to the bogeys, while others complained, 'You'll get us all shot'. But they continued to do it and ended up jumping off at night into the brambles. We heard a few shots and a dog barking, but the dog was a good sign. We all dreamed of escaping the same way, but we were afraid and there was not time, and supposing the Germans had found the trucks empty! We gave addresses and messages to those who escaped as well as all sorts of advice and entrusted them to God's hands.

We knew when we had crossed the German border because it was raining. Germany is a country where it always rains. As Goethe said to his king: it is preferable to have bad weather than no weather at all. He was right. But the rain drenches you. The pallid Germans we saw standing on stations were soaked. They did not give us anything to eat. They seemed bemused by their victory. It had surprised them when they got up in the morning, before they had had their black coffee, and they had not yet recovered from the shock. They obviously knew nothing about the concentration camps, and neither did we, but they were better placed than us.

We finally arrived at a nameless station in the middle of an area of heathland which was swept by wind and rain. We were made to get out and then had to march forty kilometres, threatened all the while with guns and whips. A number of prisoners fell by the wayside, but for the most part the Germans did not finish them off. Horses were sent to drag them along. I recall I had pinched a sort of British raincoat made out of rubberised material just in case, having kept in mind what Goethe had said, and wore it under my shirt so that the Germans would not confiscate it. I marched the forty kilometres with this thing next to my skin, and you can imagine how much I sweated. Once we were in the tents, I was afraid I would catch a cold at the very least. But I didn't, and anyway, the next day the Germans confiscated my pseudo-shirt, claiming they would find it useful. I am sure it was. From then on I got used to the rain and discovered that you could get wet without catching a cold.

The night we spent under canvas was incredible. We were hungry and thirsty, but above all we were totally exhausted and fell into a deep sleep, so much so that they had to shake us by our feet the following morning to get us up for the various prison-camp checks. But I had discovered that men keep warm, especially when they are tired and unhappy, and that by and large things work out all right.

They did not work out for everyone. Our camp was right next to another one in which we saw half-starved people wandering around – they must have come from eastern Poland as they spoke Russian. They did not dare approach the electrified barbed wire, and so we threw them a little bread and some clothes and said a few words, though we knew very well that they would not be understood. This didn't matter as it bought them a little comfort, and us as well, feeling that we were not so alone in our wretchedness.

Then we were divided up into different units. Together with a few students and three hundred other prisoners of peasant stock or lower middle-class origin, I was allowed to go to a special camp, where we had to dig underground tanks for the *Luftwaffe*. First, we had to destroy the old houses on the site, clear woods, fill in ponds, and enclose the whole thing with barbed wire. My lack of skills meant that I was allocated to these latter tasks: digging holes, putting in posts, and fixing the barbed wire. We imprisoned ourselves. Watching over us was a guard who had fought in the 1914–18 war and who had had enough of killing, which he never ceased telling us. From time to time, he gave us a little bit of his lunch, as ours was somewhat meagre. I remember that one day, when I had some *Lagergeld* (money valid only in the camp with which one could buy a tooth brush or a cigar), I got it into my head that I would visit the baker's shop about three hundred yards away. There was good German white bread, also black bread, and even a plum tart. It was to no avail; my money was worthless as the woman wanted proper money for her bread. As our guard said: 'That's war!', and spat on the ground as if to underline his feelings.

Most of the people I got to know there were peasants who were full of memories: of their land, their animals, the work they did, their wives and children. They had a special sense of their own superiority: the 'Boches' did not know what work was as they would soon discover. And they set to work just to show them. But two or three of the students disagreed with them and made their feelings plain. They said we should do as little work as possible, even if we starved, and that we should sabotage things if we could! They were troublemakers, in the minority. There was also an agricultural labourer from Normandy called Colombin who had a huge moustache, a wide flat beret, and silent convictions. He did not give a damn. Every now and then, he spat into his hands, leaned on his shovel, and said: I need to have a good crap. And he would go and shit somewhere close by, in full view of the astonished Germans. He told me lots of stories.

Not as many, it is true, as other prisoners. I am thinking in particular of a young man from Normandy who had managed to keep his gold watch, a present from his wife, and who showed it to everyone, swearing he would not swap it for a crust of bread. One day, to his great surprise, he could not find it under his mattress. He accused the Germans, who told him they did not need his watch, that they had confiscated all the others – and one more or one less was of no interest to them! It had simply vanished. But when the chap returned home, he dicovered his wife had it and that she had been given it by an American officer. Funny things happen. But there was another cultured individual, a journalist on a daily paper in eastern France, who was Russian in origin and therefore had a number of things to say about the Nazi–Soviet pact and its consequences. He also had quite a lot of stories about women which, given the lack of them, he told with great facility and success. In particular, he said that possessing them was as easy as falling off a log, and to prove it described how he had stroked one under the table at an official banquet, in front of everyone. He had then gone back home with her in the evening and pressed her against her front door until he managed to get her legs apart and reach the crucial parts. This he had done with the consent of his adversary who was, he made a point of telling us, completely naked under her dress. That set us all daydreaming, including Colombin who spat on the ground.

The same journalist embarked on the sexual education of our guards. Actually, this is a bit of a lie. What he told them was that a black woman's thing went 'crossways', which created quite a stir among them. They sent for a medical officer who listened attentively to what they said, bought an encyclopedia in which he found nothing conclusive, passed the problem on to someone higher up who told him that it was true of all races who ate garlic, but as the blacks did not eat it, unlike the Jews and the French, it could not be true in their case. The whole business finished there, but our friend was granted an extra ration of bread, which he shared out.

I was then given the job of sweeping up as I had got a bad hernia from lifting tree trunks out of the pond. While my friends were absent, I therefore remained in the camp all day wielding my broom. A broom is made up of the handle and the head. The important part is the handle and the way you manipulate it. The dust is secondary; like the Supply Corps, it follows. I got the hang of it and did in two hours a job which should have taken twelve. I therefore had time to myself. I began writing a tragedy about the young Greek girl whose father, the general, wanted to sacrifice her to produce a wind. I wanted her to live and so arranged things that it became possible, with her agreement. The two of us would sail away in a boat at nightfall and make love at sea, providing there was no wind but just a slight breeze for our enjoyment and to keep us cool. I did not have time to finish this masterpiece, in which I, the Giraudoux of the sweepers-up, had a role, because I became seriously ill. It seems I had kidney problems, according to the French doctor in the camp, a proud, competent northerner, who told the Germans that I had to be sent without delay to the main camp hospital as it was urgent. A white ambulance came, and for the first time I was driven slowly through mile after mile of desolate countryside to the camp at Schleswig. I went into hospital, where I was well cared for by a weary German doctor who said I was cured and sent me back to the camp after a fortnight. But this time it was to the main camp. It was very crowded. The Polish prisoners, who had been the first to arrive, occupied all the key positions, and there were minor battles between the French, the Belgians, the Serbs on the one hand, and the Poles, who agreed in the end to give up one or two jobs. I was fit to do outdoor work, such as unloading coal, digging trenches, gardening, before I managed to get a job inside the camp: in the sick-bay which was run by the doctor who had got me into hospital and a lewd dentist who spent his time sending bars of chocolate to the Ukrainian women prisoners in the camp opposite so that they would show him their fannies from a distance. So I became a 'nurse', without ever having been one before, and looked after all sorts of sick people. I saw an unfortunate Parisian cabaret singer die from gas gangrene brought on by an operation done in a field hospital by a young Nazi doctor who wanted to get some practice. Most of them were pretending to be ill. They grew thin by fasting in order that they would be diagnosed as having a stomach ulcer which would show up on an X-ray falsified by swallowing a piece of string of the right length with a small ball of aluminium foil on it. It did not always work. I tried but to no avail. I attempted to get myself declared unfit to be a nurse by having papers sent to me which I then pretended to find in a parcel, as if by chance, under the very nose of a guard. That did not work either, because I had forgotten to tear from my military pass various certificates proving I had been a Reserve Cadet Officer.

The experience of doing forced manual labour taught me a number of things. First, that you have to learn what you are doing. Secondly, you have to discover how to pace yourself, quite deliberately, which involves knowing your own rhythms of breathing, physical effort, and tiredness. You have to go slowly if you are to sustain the exertion involved. Finally, I learnt that continuous work of this kind, tiring though it is, is in the end less difficult than intellectual work, as 'Père Hours' had told us over and over again during lessons; at least it puts less strain on one's nerves. I also learnt that men engaged in physical work throughout their lives acquired a genuine culture which, though non-verbal, was extremely rich. It was not just technical but commercial, financial, moral, and political as well (remember, I was in the company of peasants throughout this period, the Germans having sent the workers among the prisoners into factories where they provided skilled labour). I discovered that a peasant is a true *polytechnicien*, though he does not know it, as he has to understand an incredible variety of things, from the weather and the seasons to the uncertainties of the market, not forgetting technical and technological matters, chemistry, agro-biology, the law, and union and political struggle – whether as an active participant or passively. I learnt about this later from Hélène. Not to mention agricultural forecasts relating to the medium term, debts incurred in the purchase of machinery, investments which could not be counted on due to the vagaries of the market, etc. In addition, I discovered there were poor peasants in France, where one might have thought such conditions did not exist, living off one cow in a small meadow, a few chestnuts, and some rye or, as in the Morvan, by rearing a pig or two and fostering a child in care. Gradually, I began to get some notion of the existence of a genuine popular, or at least peasant, culture, which I had barely suspected, which had nothing to do with folklore, was rarely visible, yet which was crucial for an understanding of the behaviour and reactions of peasants, especially their uprisings, which date from the Middle Ages, and which even the Communist Party found disconcerting. I remember what Marx said in *The 18th Brumaire of Louis Bonaparte*: Napoleon III was elected overwhelmingly by the French peasants, who were not so much a social class as a sack of potatoes. I began to get the measure of their isolation: each one for himself on his land, separated from the others, but dominated by the big farmers, even in their cooperatives and agricultural unions. Nothing has changed since the war, even though Catholic organisations have gained influence among the young farmers: the rich farmers are still in control and dictate what the average, the small-scale, and the poor should do. The peasants have not learned from industrial capitalism, unlike the factory workers who come together at work, are subjected to the disciplines of the division and organisation of labour, are savagely exploited, and obliged to organise themselves quite openly for their own protection. The peasants remain isolated, each one working for himself, and do not come to recognise their common interests. They are a ready prey for the bourgeois State, which treats them prudently (taking almost no taxes, giving them loans, etc.) and is thus able to exploit them as a docile electorate. They are one of the persistent 'obstacles' referred to one day by the secretary of a Party federation around 1973, after the Party's vote had reached its peak in the elections. Though I had not met any workers, I did know a number of lower middle-class people, who were either career officers, civil servants, white-collar workers, shopkeepers, or university teachers. They belonged to another world, and were talkative, anxious to get on with things, longing to get back to their wives, their children and their jobs, ready to swallow any bits of news they heard, especially the women, afraid of the Russians, more afraid of them than of the Germans, wily, and prepared to do anything to get themselves repatriated. They cursed De Gaulle, even if they had nothing good to say about Pétain, because De

Gaulle was prolonging the war. They had splendid parcels sent from France which they freely shared with everyone, were most concerned about their appearance, and talked about women all day long. I remember a Corsican who was forced to lie down on his wooden slatted bed, had his trousers removed, and was masturbated against his will. This took place in a hut where every evening a teacher from Clermont called Ferrier put on a 'radio programme'. All the huts sent their representatives, and Ferrier gave the military and political news of the day which he heard on a German radio in the office where he worked and where he had gained the confidence of his guard, a German communist. Ferrier kept up the morale of everyone in the camp. All that is needed sometimes is for one individual to take the initiative and the whole atmosphere changes.

I resigned myself to remaining in the camp where I had numerous friends: de Mailly, who had not yet received the Prix de Rome; Hameau, a young, penniless architect; Clerc, the former captain of Cannes football team which had won the French Cup in a memorable match (this tiny little man, who was a phenomenal player, had escaped four times in incredible circumstances and been caught again on the Swiss border, having already crossed it and inadvertently crossed back into Germany); a priest called Poirier; and above all Robert Daël.

By virtue of the Geneva Convention there was in all the camps a trusted prisoner for each nationality. The first one we had was a young car-salesman called Cerrutti. The Germans liked him and he took up his position without being elected. When, by way of reward, the Germans repatriated him, there was a great deal of unrest in the camp. The Germans had chosen his replacement, but we would not accept him as he was a Pétainist. We agreed we should elect Daël, and he won hands down with everyone supporting him including the dentists, to the astonishment of the Germans. Daël's first act, which no one understood, was to take on the Pétainist candidate the Germans had wanted as his deputy. This pleased them. A month later, Daël got the Germans to repatriate the man and chose me to replace him. I have never forgotten this simple yet brilliant political lesson. Daël was very strong and had his own way with the German staff running the camp, getting two officers transferred whom he found bothersome and taking control of everything sent from France: food, parcels, and mail. He reorganised the whole network of links between the central camp and the different outposts, which were often left to their own devices. He was not to be argued with. He spoke his own form of German, and the difficulty he had pronouncing it meant his listeners had to pay attention. He never made any mistakes and everyone appreciated him despite the fact he was not very talkative. I remember an incident which occurred in the camp theatre, where people always fought to get the best seats, a great number of which were reserved for the Germans and for important people in the camp. Daël one day pinned up the following notice: 'From today, there will be no more reserved seats in the theatre, with one exception: mine.' No one objected and the Germans queued like everybody else to watch light comedies in which men dressed up as women.

On one occasion, however, a woman came to the camp: a very beautiful French singer, and everyone was overwhelmed. She sang in the theatre, and then Daël invited her to his private quarters for an intimate chat which must have turned out well. He, too, liked women and was always ready to talk about them. He talked about the parties he went to in his youth, the games of 'strip poker' he played with young women, including the daughter of the Chinese Ambassador, and about how he always made sure he lost which enabled him to get what he wanted. He managed to win over the officer delegated to accompany him on his visits to the various units, to which they were driven in a lorry by a young Parisian worker with a very marked accent called Toto. He one day persuaded this officer to take him to Hamburg, where a very beautiful Polish lady was waiting in a room for him. She looked after him very well, but the whole incident was not without risk to those involved. To my knowledge, Daël never went further than that. On his return from captivity, he convinced a young woman whom he had not met before that they could get on and build a life together, and have children. He wrote to me: you cannot imagine what it is like to hear the sound of high heels on the pavement beside me. . . . He did exactly as he said he would and kept his word, though he was reduced to selling films for other people. What a come-down for such a remarkable man. He did at least raise fine children. His wife survived him and lived somewhere on the Channel coast. There are, I am sure, a number of men in France (he never attempted to get in touch with anyone) who still think of him, and will do for a long time to come, as a marvellous, semi-mythical character.

I must also recount another episode in which Daël and I found ourselves in a difficult situation. When Daël, who was worn out, had given up his position as the trusty and we had reflected at length on the impasse in which we found ourselves, we thought we should perhaps try to escape. The difficulty lay in the fact that during the three weeks following every escape all the resources of the German army, gendarmerie, and police were mobilised to look for those who had escaped and so they had practically no chance of getting away. This was the difficulty we had to overcome, and the solution we came up with was as follows: what we had to do was to allow the three weeks to pass and not escape during that period in order to avoid triggering the control measures. This was only possible on one condition: we had to remain in the camp for those three weeks while officially letting it be thought we had escaped. Thus all we had to do was hide somewhere and wait, provided that our hiding place was secure.

As it happened, nothing could have been easier than finding a secure hiding place in the main camp. We hid ourselves away with the help of a few trusted friends, who brought us food and cheering news of the commotion caused among the Germans, and allowed three weeks to go by. We then escaped quite easily, and Daël even saluted the astonished sentry, as was his custom. Things went smoothly, the way we had planned, except for an unexpected encounter with a minor post-office official in a village who asked us the precise address of someone we did not know. This made him suspicious and earned him the expected reward.

If I am to be wholly truthful, I should add that I have described things exactly as we planned them, but that we never left the camp, believing our effort in dreaming up the plan and thus in principle solving the probem was itself sufficient reward. I did not forget it once I got back to philosophy, since it is the nub of all philosophical (as well as political and military) problems: how to escape the circle while remaining within it.

When the English forces were within a hundred and fifty kilometres of the camp, and the collapse of the German army was accelerating, Daël resorted to other strategic measures. He went to the Germans and offered them a deal: if you agree to leave and we take your place, I will give you certificates stating you behaved properly. They accepted his offer and departed one night, leaving everything in good order. All we had to do was take over. Our life changed quite dramatically. First of all, Toto took advantage of the situation and was able to sleep with the German woman working in an office whom he had detected at a distance on account of her perfume. Couples were formed and given a blessing, more or less, by Poirier. Fresh supplies were organised on a grand scale, with groups going off and bringing back bucks and hinds, as well as hares and other animals, vegetables, and lastly alcohol. We re-routed a river for water. Finally, we produced French bread. We gathered everyone together to inform them and shape their thinking from a political point of view. We taught young German boys and girls English and Russian and also how to handle guns. They were terrified at first but then reassured. We played football and put on plays with real women. Every day was a holiday; in a word it was communism.

But the blessed English had still not arrived. So Daël and I had the idea we should set off to meet them to tell them of the situation. We commandeered a car and a (slightly dubious) driver and went all the way to Hamburg where the English received us so coolly that we preferred to slip away (with the help of the driver) back to the camp. There we were given a very bad reception because our friends, including Poirier, thought we had abandoned them. He had high moral standards (believing there were things one did not do). We consoled ourselves with a fine venison stew and waited to see what would happen next.

The English finally arrived and allowed us to leave on condition we left behind all our personal valuables. We went by plane, first to Brussels and then on to Paris. I then travelled to Morocco, where my parents were living and where my father was still playing tennis and zooming around the country at over one hundred miles an hour, except when his road was blocked by camels, which never got out of the way. He had a Spanish driver who said: 'Madame he is afraid of camels, but Monsieur she is not.'

I found our reunion very difficult. I was feeling old and that I had missed the boat, that I had no guts and did not have a thought in my head. I felt I would never be able to return to the École, though my place was still open and they had sent me some books. That was when I had my first depression. I have had so many over the past thirty years, some of which were so serious and dramatic (in all I must have spent fifteen years in hospitals and psychiatric clinics and would still be there were it not for analysis), that I will be forgiven for not talking about them. Indeed, how does one talk about such a truly unbearable state of anxiety, which is almost like being in Hell, and about the unfathomable and terrifying emptiness one feels?

I feared I was sexually impotent. I consulted a military doctor who poked and prodded me and assured me I was fine. I travelled around Morocco with my father, played tennis too, and swam. I knew no girls (obviously), heard lots of stories about Sidna and his court, his friends and doctors, about the Governor-General and his rages; in other words, I got some inkling of the class struggle in Morocco and was struck by the arrest, in dubious circumstances, of Mehdi Ben Seddik.

But I had to return to Paris. My father entrusted me with several bottles of bourbon he had found, which had been in the sea several years as part of a shipwrecked cargo, and he also entrusted me with my sister. The whole lot was loaded on to another cargo boat, which was rather peculiar in that it only went in a curve that the captain had constantly to correct; and this was how we progressed. The conditions on board were appalling: the heat, the promiscuity, the rats, everything you could imagine. We finally arrived at Port-Vendres and I returned to dry land. Paris was not far away.

At the École normale I was greeted by people I did not know. As it happened, I was the only man in my year to have been a prisoner, all the others having pursued their studies in the normal way, though not without certain difficulties which lived on in their memories. Everyone else was young, but some of them had heard the 'legendary tales' of my Lyon days, kept alive by Lacroix, and had themselves been active in the Resistance. It was through one of them, the communist Georges Lesèvre, that I met Hélène.

Talking of communists, I would like to mention that the first one I ever met was in captivity. It occurred towards the end, after the Germans had gone and Daël was no longer the trusty and when a certain 'disorder' prevailed in our little communist society. Courrèges arrived, thin and unhappy, having come from a punishment camp. He quickly recognised what was wrong and took things in hand. It was quite spectacular. Within a few days, he showed himself to be a sound and sensible man of the people, capable of driving reason into the few recalcitrant individuals who wanted to take advantage of the situation and thwart the course of justice. Everyone followed him. I have never forgotten his example, which I came across again in Hélène and others. Communists do exist.

I met Hélène in special circumstances. Lesèvre had invited me to visit his mother who lived in the rue Lepic where she was recuperating from a serious illness she had contracted as a deportee. He said to me: I am going to introduce you to Hélène. She is slightly crazy but worth getting to know. That is how I met her, outside a Métro station with the streets of Paris under snow. To stop her from slipping I took her arm, then her hand, and together we walked up the rue Lepic.

I know I was wearing the shabby pullover and suit given by the Red Cross to all home-coming soldiers. We talked about the Spanish Civil War with Elizabeth Lesèvre. All of us had things to say, but during our silences something began to develop between Hélène and me. I saw her again and I remember one day in a hotel on the place Saint-Sulpice she made a gesture which frightened me: she kissed my hair. She came to see me at the École and we made love in a tiny room in the sick-bay. I immediately fell ill (not for the last time), suffering such intense depression that the best psychiatrist in the whole of Paris whom I consulted diagnosed 'dementia praecox'. I was admitted to that hellhole the Esquirol, where I discovered what a modern psychiatric hospital can be like. Hélène, thank goodness, who had seen worse, arranged for Ajuria* to visit the hospital and examine me. He diagnosed severe depression which he treated with twenty electric shocks, given at that time directly on the bare skin without either a narcotic or curare. We were all together in a large, bright room, our beds almost touching, and the person designated to treat us, a stocky individual with a large moustache whom the patients nicknamed

* The pet name of the psychiatrist Julian de Ajuriaguerra (Editors'note).

Stalin, went from one to the other with his electric box and headband which he placed on each of us in turn. We watched the patient next to us writhe as always in a kind of epileptic fit and had time to prepare ourselves, gripping the well-chewed towel between our teeth which ended up tasting of the electric current. It was for all concerned a most edifying spectacle.

As one always emerges from depression, I emerged from mine, to discover Hélène was living in a wretched hotel, having sold her first editions of Malraux and Aragon in order to live, and having herself been in hospital for an abortion, knowing that I would not have coped with the idea of having our child. We left Paris for les Alpilles, in the Midi, where we camped in a wooden cabin near Saint-Rémy, as we had no money. Young people lit fires and one day I cooked the best bouillabaisse I have ever made in my life, Algerian style (first frying the fish with the onions). As I had to get over my illness, I went straight on to a place in the Alps which took in students who were convalescing. There I got to know Assathiany and his wife, and also Simone, whom I treated very badly, as she did me. But I had to write my thesis on Hegel's concept of content. Since returning from captivity, I had got to know Jacques Martin, to whom I dedicated my first book in 1965. He had the sharpest mind of anyone I have ever met, was meticulous, as rigorous as a lawyer, and had a macabre sense of humour which was the bane of the clergy. Anyway, he not only taught me to think but above all made me aware there were other ways of thinking than those we were taught. Without him, I would never have put two thoughts together, or at least of the kind we agreed on. I wrote this thesis at my grandmother's house in the Morvan while she did the cooking. At my request she invited Hélène, who typed out my text in the evening. Hélène was obliged to spend several months in the house as there was nowhere else in the village where she could stay. Her only friend was the old woman who lived opposite, La Francine, who gave her eggs and talked to her. My grandmother died a few years later from a heart attack one freezing cold morning as she was sitting in her pew at mass. She was buried next to grandfather Berger, at the top of the windswept cemetery where my aunt planted a few flowers from time to time. I have the most vivid memories of this village in the Morvan where my grandfather spent his last years after his retirement and where we used to spend our summer holidays as a family, except for my father, who stayed behind to work in Algiers and then in Marseille. There was a garden which ran down from the house, a well which I had watched being dug through the granite, fruit trees planted or grafted by my grandfather which we had watched grow, wonderful strawberries, flowers, rabbits, hens and therefore eggs, cats which came when you called their name, which is unusual, but no dogs. There were two large cellars, one for fire wood, the other for wine. In the summer, my grandfather used to sit there in the cool on a little wooden bench reading *La Tribune du fonctionnaire*. There was also a deep water tank from which on two occasions I rescued one of our cats which had fallen in. It was a horrible sight watching the animal splutter. One day the same cat got its head stuck in an empty jam tin and I had to pull it out, which I did by some miracle. The cat let out a terrified yowl and disappeared for several days. On the other hand, I was spared the job of killing the hens and rabbits. I was very fond of these stupid animals which were quite unable to defend themselves. To show how much I liked them, I even made a syringe from an elder branch by hollowing out the pith and squirted them from a distance, which always made them jump. The stately hens clucked with surprise as they viewed this assault on their dignity with their heads held high and eyes wide open, while the rabbits dashed round and round in their cages. But when it came to the moment of truth, I was asked to leave. I know my grandfather knocked the rabbits on the back of the head and that my grandmother cut the hens' throats with a rusty pair of scissors. If they wanted to kill a duck, they simply chopped its head off with a billhook and the duck continued to run around for a few seconds.

Potatoes and sorrel were our staple foods, together with chestnuts in winter (at that time people made a living rearing three things in the Morvan: pigs, cattle, and children in care). I went to the village school. Its high walls were close to the well behind a very tall pear tree which produced small, hard fruit with which my grandmother made a red jam I have not come across since. About twenty local children, eight or nine of them in care, studied under a socialist teacher called M. Boucher, who was a kind, good-looking man. I was subjected to the usual ragging for at least a month. The other children particularly enjoyed chasing one of their number, bringing him down, and removing his trousers to look at his privates. They then ran away screaming and yelling. I discovered later that this practice closely resembled what was done in certain primitive societies. I had to go through it and then I was left in peace. I used to play on the bars in the playground and was quite good at it, which earned me a certain amount of respect. As the teacher considered me to be a good pupil, everything went well. On one occasion he made me sit the scholarship exam in Nevers. That day my grandfather put on his Sunday suit and a new cap and we set off on the train. He took trouble choosing a hotel, and I was able to visit the splendid church of Saint-Étienne which has the most marvellous effects of light and shade in the world. I came sixth in the exam and, at my request, my father gave me a rifle as a reward. I had a very strange experience with this rifle. My father had acquired twelve acres of land with an old farmhouse some six kilometres from our village. It was on a hill beyond the railway line and almost inaccessible because it was completely overgrown with bracken and chestnut trees. When he was free, my grandfather almost always set off for Les Fougères around five o'clock in the morning, on foot naturally (there were no cars in the district at the time). Being a hardened forester he cut a path up to the house. There were beehives there. My parents had wanted to keep bees ever since they had observed them at the forestry house in Algiers where M. Quéruet looked after them. There were hives, too, at Bois-de-Velle where my grandfather owned a field which he showed me how to cultivate. He grew all sorts of things but especially wheat, which he also taught me how to cut and bind, and potatoes which I learnt to dig up without damaging them. We visited Les Fougères as a family and I used to wander round the paths in the wood on the look-out with my loaded rifle. One day, when I was not lying down firing at a target as I had done in Algiers with an army rifle, I spotted a turtledove. I aimed at it and missed then reloaded my rifle and continued on my way. All of a sudden I had the crazy idea of turning it towards my own stomach to see what would happen. I was convinced there was no bullet in the barrel but at the last moment I hesitated and opened it up. It did contain a bullet. I broke into a sweat but did not brag about what I had done.

We often went to Les Fougères in a cart pulled by a plump mare which jogged along quietly and was driven by a placid young peasant who became the local mayor during the Popular Front. I sat next to the driver and watched the mare's fat rump as it laboured to pull the cart. In the middle was a lovely moist slit which fascinated me, though I did not know why at the time. My mother's imagination ran ahead of mine, however, which is why she made me sit on the bench at the back where I could not see the mare, but watched cockerels instead jumping on the hens at the side of the road. They looked comical and I laughed as I pointed them out to my mother, but she did not find it funny and scolded me, telling me not to laugh in front of M. Faucheux and that he would think me ignorant. But of what? I never knew.

The specialities of the region were the goats' cheeses and the cows' milk, and also the snow in winter which covered the landscape, bringing silence with it. I drew a picture of this landscape on one occasion, and the teacher congratulated me. The snow, like the rain which I liked listening to as it fell steadily on the slate roof, gave me a profound sense of security. No one heard my footsteps when I walked in the countryside, where I stumbled on the tracks of animals. The silence was more peaceful than that of the sea or of sleep, safer too, as there were no dangers now that the snow had fallen. It was like being in my mother's womb.

There was also a priest and a château in the village. We saw the priest at the church where he took the catechism class before school, very early in the morning while it was still dark. We sat round a little stove which glowed red, and he taught us very simple things. Having been at Verdun, he had shed most of life's complications. He went around in a soldier's beret with a pipe in his mouth. He was a good man. I consulted him at a later date, when a Jesuit I knew in Lyon had left me in some doubt concerning an Alexandrian bas-relief showing a naked girl playing a flute which interested me rather too much. He told me it was very simple to explain; that the Doctors of the Church had confused things, that he, as a matter of fact, had a housekeeper who was also a good friend, that it was not for nothing that God was made man, and that had he not done so he would not have understood man's needs. So the whole business was sorted out once and for all, and much better than my mother had done with her mares and cocks. The priest had a harmonium which I learnt to play after a fashion. When there were ceremonies which involved music I would play a few tunes in my own way which he seemed to enjoy. He maintained I ought to learn music. I replied that I already played the violin. My mother had in fact sent my sister and me to learn the piano and the violin respectively in Algiers at a school run by a brother and sister who were friends of hers. They taught us the basic principles and how to play together. But it was not a great success and the fact that my father drove us to Sunday concerts in Marseille while he went off somewhere else did not help matters either. It bored us stiff watching the conductor's back as he attempted to bring some order to the noises emanating from the platform until, for an unknown though comprehensible reason, everyone suddenly stopped, having reached the end of the last page, and we all applauded.

So life went on and I became a student at the École normale, and finally my grandmother died in 1961. At the École, I had the viva on my thesis with Bachelard, who asked me very cautiously: 'But why did you use two epigraphs, first René Clair's remark: "The concept is obligatory since the concept is freedom", and then Béranger's quip: "The content you have is worth two you can only think of".' I replied: 'It sums up the nature of content.' He remained silent for a moment and then said forcefully: 'But why do you talk about the circle in Hegel, would it not be better to talk about the circulation of the concept?' I replied: 'Circulation is one of Malebranche's concepts, along with reproduction. The proof is that Malebranche was the philosopher of the Physiocrats, and Marx said they were the first theoreticians of circulation in the field of reproduction.' He smiled and gave me a mark of eighteen out of twenty. This was in October 1947. After my terrible depression in the spring, I had spent the summer hurriedly writing up my thesis which I quickly delivered up to the 'gnawing criticism of the mice'. Martin had done a very good thesis on the individual in Hegel, also with Bachelard, and had used obscene drawings as an epigraph. He discussed things I only half understood, despite his explanations. Everything was subordinated to the concept of the problematic, which set me thinking. It was a materialist philosophy which sought to give a proper account of the dialectic. He discussed Freud, offered a balanced critique of Lacan (that long ago!), and he ended up by talking about communism; I remember this phrase of his: 'in which there are no longer human beings, but individuals.'

At the École I got to know Tran Duc Thao, who achieved fame very early on when he published his thesis on phenomenology and dialectical materialism which was strongly influenced by Husserl. He remained a Husserlian, to judge from the articles he sent to *La Pensée* from Hanoi, where he has lived since 1956. Thao gave us private lessons and explained: 'You are all transcendental egos, and as egos you are all equal.' He was preoccupied at the time with a theory of knowledge which remained quite close to Husserl, and which I later heard Jean-Toussaint Desanti put forward. He was similarly concerned to marry Husserl and Marx, which was contrary to Martin's position. At the time Thao knew Domarchi very well; a brilliant theorist of political economy who was appointed to the École. He gave a dazzling and incomprehensible course on Wicksell and then disappeared as he had fallen passionately in love with a woman whom he relentlessly pursued but was unable to marry. Thao and Desanti carried the hopes of our generation, as did Desanti later. Husserl was to blame for the fact that they did not fulfil them. I should perhaps say a word about Gusdorf, who struck terror into the hearts of those preparing the *agrégation** in philosophy at the École during this period. He had produced his thesis while he was a prisoner, collating all the private diaries he was familiar with, and he gave it the title *La Découverte de soi*. One day he received a letter from the Director of the Palais de la Découverte, the gist of which was: everything to do with the discovery of the self is of interest to the Palais de la Découverte, and I would therefore be grateful. . . . Gusdorf went to the palais and returned with their congratulations, their brochure, and the feeling he had been taken for a ride. Subsequently, however, they did have his book on the shelves in their library. Gusdorf had a habit of responding to any slightly embarrassing question by saying: 'Get lost!', and when you left his office, in which he had a reproduction Louis XV writing-desk,

---

* Highest competitive exam for teachers in France (Translator's note).

he would say: 'Forgive me if I don't come with you', a phrase he also used on the telephone, as well as 'keep your hat on'. He had very few expressions but he always used them most effectively. He did not get on well with Pauphilet, who was appointed Director of the École because of what he had done in the Resistance, in place of Carcopino, who, it seems, had more or less collaborated. Pauphilet was well known for his confirmed laziness, the affected vulgarity of his speech, his ignorance of his own specialisation (the literature of the Middle Ages), and his predilection for cheap dance-halls, where he regularly sought out rather special pupils to whom he recited poems by François Villon which he knew by heart. He was buried behind the caretaker's lobby at the École, so that he would be on home ground. No one knows this, or everyone has forgotten it, but some very fine roses do happen to be growing there which the caretaker waters regularly until they wilt. I always imagined that Pauphilet, who liked women and flowers, enjoyed this attention.

Gusdorf had his own very personal method of preparing us for the *agrégation*, which proved excellent. He gave us no lectures and he did not get us to do any written work. He simply read us without comment extracts from his thesis on private diaries. I learnt one useful lesson from this; that the best way of preparing for the *agrégation* is by not attending lectures, and so also by not giving them, but by reading extracts from anything. It was most important that I got the *agrégation*, but it cost me another bout of depression. By the end of the year, however, I was totally prepared. I came first in the written exam (Alquié told me my first essay on the subject 'Is a science of human action possible?', in which I drew on Leibniz and Marx, was worth nineteen out of twenty for the first part, sixteen for the second, but with all the stuff about Hegel and Marx in the third part, he was sorry, but it was only worth fourteen). I came second in the oral, having misinterpreted a passage from Spinoza where I read 'solitude' for *soleil* (sun), which was a little too Aristotelian. Hélène was waiting for me at the end of the rue Victor-Cousin and embraced me. She was greatly afraid I had not got over my depression. Poor Hélène, I was for ever frightening her with my depressions.

Philosophical life at the École was not particularly intense. It was fashionable to pretend to despise Sartre, who was in fashion and who seemed to dominate all possible modes of thought, in France at least. This little 'philosophical group' in Royan seemed to have freed itself from our traditional spiritualism and was absorbed by neo-positivism. Sartre was recognised as having certain qualities as a publicist and a bad novelist, political goodwill, and, it goes without saying, great honesty and independence. We looked on him as 'our Rousseau', or at least as a Rousseau of a stature for our times. We had greater respect for Merleau-Ponty as a philosopher, even though he had the lay-person's religious obsession with transcendental idealism. He was exceedingly academic in his approach, to the extent that one would gain his approval if one wrote an *agrégation* essay in the style and with the solemnity of *La Phénoménologie de la perception*. Merleau visited the École and gave a splendid course on Malebranche (he demonstrated quite brilliantly that one only had to look at his theory of natural judgement to see that his conception of the *cogito* was obscure and of the body opaque). He taught us that the secret of success in the *agrégation* lay in communication (put yourselves in the position of the examiners; it is summertime and very hot; they have not got much time; you have to make yourself understood, do their thinking for them while giving them the impression they are thinking for themselves). He made a few comments about painting, space, and silence, said a few words about Machiavelli and Maine de Biran, and then left, as discreet as ever. At the Sorbonne, Bachelard gave lectures which were like free-wheeling conversations, enlivened with remarks about violets and camembert. You never knew in advance what he was going to say, and neither did he, which meant you could join one of his lectures at any point and leave if you had an assignation or a medical appointment. No one took him seriously, and nor did he, but everyone was content. He was always prepared to see people, concerning exams or theses, at any hour of the day or night, which had its advantages; when he was not dealing with his daughter, who caused him a lot of anxiety, or his tramps, who gave him a lot of pleasure. Alquié was the authority on Descartes and all Cartesians, including Kant, whom he considered a slightly heretical Cartesian because he was German. When addressing his audience, he exploited in a masterly way, and almost as well as Jouvet, the unchanging characteristics of his different stammers. He was a great professor who knew a lot. With him, at least, as an examiner for the *agrégation*, you knew for certain and in advance what mark he would give a particular piece of work, which was invaluable. Schuhl, a sweet-natured man, who wore thin-rimmed spectacles and intermittently had a small moustache, cautiously explained Plato to us, but in such a fragmented way it was impossible to follow what he was saying. He quickly sought refuge in a research seminar on Greek antiquity where he achieved a very high level of scholarship. Jean Wahl, peeping like a pale, timid, and frightened Pavlovian mouse over the top of his lectern, went through *Parmenides* word by word imperturbably repeating for the umpteenth time what he had written in his own book and forgotten about. At the end of each commentary, which he kept brief, he would say 'you could equally well take the opposing point of view', which left his audience somewhat confused. They came seeking one interpretation or the other but went away with both. He had married one of his students, who bore him several children and quickly took him in hand, as he was totally distracted about everything, including women and children. Later, when I talked about Lenin at the French Society for Philosophy, which he chaired, and quoted Diezgen's harsh comment on professors of philosophy as 'almost all certified lackeys of the bourgeoisie', he quickly picked up what I said and protested on behalf of his fellow professionals, who were clearly less offended than he was. As chairman he felt it was his duty. We were scarcely aware of Lévi-Strauss at this time, and even less well acquainted with Canguilhem, who was to play a crucial role in shaping the way I and my friends thought. He was not yet at the Sorbonne, but was filling everyone with terror in the secondary sector, where he had accepted the post of School Inspector in the mistaken belief that he could reform the way philosophy teachers thought by shouting at them. He soon gave up his painful experiment, quickly finished his thesis on the reflex, and was appointed at the Sorbonne where he turned his anger on his colleagues rather than on his students, who detected beneath his gruff exterior a fund of understanding and generosity. At a later date he gave a lecture at the École on fetishism in Auguste Comte, which people talked about for a long time. He also observed our initial skirmishes with ironic detachment but with a sympathetic air too. He told me one day that it was as a result of reading Nietzsche that he began his researches into the history of biology and medicine.

Lacan was beginning to make a name for himself, giving his seminar tucked away in the Institute at Sainte-Anne's. I went to hear him on one occasion, when he talked about cybernetics and analysis. I did not understand a word because of his tortuous, baroque way of speaking, a phoney imitation of Breton's splendid language. He clearly did it so that his listeners would be awestruck. They were, and their reactions were contradictory: some were filled with fascination, others with hatred. Martin helped me understand him, and I was won over by some of the things he had to say. I referred to them in a short article I published in *La Revue de L'Enseignement philosophique*, in which what I said more or less was that: just as Marx criticised homo economicus, Lacan deserved praise for his critique of homo psychologicus. Within a week, I received a message from Lacan saying he wanted to see me. He invited me to dine with him in an expensive little restaurant. He was wearing a frilled shirt which came from London, a casual jacket, and a pink bow-tie, and his eyes behind his rimless glasses were veiled and unresponsive apart from occasional flashes of attentiveness. He spoke intelligibly and spent most of the time gossiping about former disciples of his, their wives and large properties, and about the connection between these social circumstances and interminable analysis. We readily agreed on these topics which touched on historical materialism. I left thinking it would be a good idea to invite him to transfer his seminar from Sainte-Anne's to the École, as he was under threat of having to leave there. Hyppolite agreed straight away. After all, this was the man who 'took the child of a night in Idumaea' to a session devoted to the translation of Freud's text on denial-negation. Thus for several years Lacan held his seminar at the École. Every Wednesday at midday, the pavements of the rue d'Ulm were blocked with the most fashionable luxury cars, and people squashed tight into the smoky salle Dussane. It was the smoke which put a stop to the seminars because it drifted up to the library immediately above – Lacan was unable to prevent his audience from smoking. For months and months there had been complaints, and then one day Flacelière asked the 'Doctor' to go somewhere else. He made a frightful scene, claimed he was the victim of veiled censorship (Flacelière was not very keen on stuff about the phallus, and Lacan had been unwise enough to invite him to a session concerned only with that topic), petitions were signed; in short there was quite a to-do. I was in a clinic at the time, and Lacan phoned Hélène, whom he may or may not have recognised, I do not know, but got nothing from her despite a great performance of trying to seduce her. She simply told him that unfortunately I was not there and could therefore do nothing. Lacan resigned himself to what had happened and found somewhere to go in the Faculty of Law. Some students at the École had been quite impressed by him, among them Jacques-Alain Miller, whose famous concept had been plagiarised and who was wooing Judith Lacan, and Milner, who never went anywhere without his umbrella and subsequently became a linguist. Once Lacan had gone, his popularity diminished at the École, and as he no longer needed me, I did not see him again. I discovered through an intermediary, however, that he had become interested in mathematical logic, after his Möbius strip, and in mathematics, which seemed to me not a good sign. He had an undeniable influence on me, as on many other philosophers and psychoanalysts of his day. I was going back to Marx and he to Freud, which meant that we understood one another. He fought against psychologism, as I fought against historicism, which was another reason for us to understand each other. I was less attracted than he was to structuralism, and I found his attempt to offer a scientific theory of Freud premature. In the end, however, he was essentially a philosopher, and there were not too many philosophers in France one could follow, even if the philosophy of psychoanalysis he developed, claiming it was a scientific theory of the unconscious, perhaps seemed risky. But one can no more choose one's influences than the age in which one lives. As well as Marx, who was not much of a philosopher, there was someone else who influenced me: Spinoza. Unfortunately, he was not teaching anywhere.

I have a curious memory from the École of Georges Snyders, whose Jewishness was recognisable at a hundred yards. By some miracle he had returned from Dachau, though very weak, and survived. He was an extraordinary pianist, and roped me in one day with Lesèvre, a talented cellist, to play some Bach. Snyders played with passion and gave the impression he was not listening to anyone else. At the end of the piece, he simply said: there were no wrong notes, but your playing had no soul. I never picked up the violin again. Snyders adored good food and used to go to the Grand Véfour, but instead of beginning with the classic hors d'oeuvres, he would order a sugared cream, and would end up with saveloy and crushed pear, without redcurrants, which went against the traditions of the establishment concerning the order in which dishes should be served. He could not care less about such things and only ever drank a glass of white wine or sour milk. It always cost him a lot, but even though he now has a chair, has been decorated, has a wife who is a mathematician, is the father of a student at the École ('he was a bright lad'), he still goes quite happily to that terrible area around Les Halles where he has discovered the kind of restaurant he likes, where they serve him pig's trotters with blackcurrant jelly. Snyders had a grand scheme which unfortunately he had to abandon: he wanted to create a National Centre of Culinary Research. He claimed one might have achieved interesting results with fried blotting-paper and straw jam. That remains to be seen.

Before he died, Pauphilet appointed Prigent, who came from Brittany, and got rid of Gusdorf from the École. I was appointed in his place, thanks to the friendship of 'Old Mother Porée', who had been running the École for almost forty years despite a succession of different directors. Initially, she was in charge of linen and then became secretary to the Director. She had character, as well as views about correspondence and teaching, and she knew how to deal with the Germans who turned up one morning to arrest Bruhat. I owe her a great deal, and I am not the only one. She was on her own when she died in a dreadful old people's home, where almost no one visited her. It was a hundred kilometres from Paris in the middle of a forest. Things like this will be forbidden when we have changed society.

Once I had passed the *agrégation* and was appointed tutor, I had to look after my young friends who were preparing for the same exam. They included Gréco, Lucien Sève, and more than a dozen others. Despite Gusdorf's warnings, I felt obliged to give them a course, which I did, on Plato. I told them a whole lot of stuff about the theory of Ideas and about reminiscence as a screen-memory theory masking problems relating to the class struggle. I

produced some splendid flourishes concerning Socrates as forgetfulness, the body as forgetfulness, and therefore Socrate's body as
forgetfulness, and about Menon's body as remembrance. I extri-
cated myself as best I could from that impossible work of Plato's,
the *Cratylus*, in which he claims and refutes the idea that one can
call a spade a spade. What fascinated me about Plato was that he
could be so intelligent and so conservative, reactionary even, that
he cultivated kings and also young boys, spoke equally well about
desire and love, about all the different occupations people had,
and even talked about mud, which also has its Idea somewhere in
Heaven, along with shoes and the Good. He was also a man who
enjoyed doing different things; he knew how to make jam, which
I mentioned to Snyders one day, and he thought I was mad. I was
indeed still mad, suffering my almost annual bout of depression,
which solved the problem of my courses. The students at the
École were in the habit of passing the *agrégation*, except when
they went off to India on their travels or had some great love
affair, for which Mme Porée was on the look-out (wait until you
have your *agrégation*, young man, then you will be able to do
what you like); so in the end my absence did not matter much. In
any case, old Étard, the librarian at the École, took over where
Lucien Herr left off and gave them all the useful bibliographical
information they needed. He was a nice enough chap, but the only
trouble was, you needed to have cancelled all your appointments
for a good week in advance when you bumped into him. He
talked endlessly about the history of religions, referring to some
project he had in mind for a doctoral thesis but which he did not
have time to get down on paper. He talked besides about everyone,
from Herriot to Soustelle, who had not yet made a name for
himself in Algiers. Étard said of him that he was incapable of
doing anything on his own and would always play second fiddle.
He was right. Before the war, he had run a research centre under
Bouglé, housed in the École, which Aron and several Germans
who had fled Nazism were involved with. I believe Horkheimer,
Borkenau, and one or two others were there. Borkenau unfortunately went astray and ended up working for the Pentagon, I
believe, but many things can be put down to the war. When Bouglé
died, the centre disappeared. It was not until Jean Hyppolite came
along that it was set up again, but on a different basis, more in

tune with the contemporary concerns of political economy and computer science.

Dupont, a chemist who was a specialist on pine resin, succeeded Pauphilet. His comment was: 'I'm terribly sorry, but I was given the job because the better candidates died in the war.' Unfortunately, it was true. As a director he was indecisive and sometimes gave way to brief and harmless fits of temper. Raymond Weil, a Greek tutor at the time, wittily summed him up when he said: 'It's absolutely essential . . . that someone shoulders my responsibilities.' On the arts side, Dupont was represented by the good-natured Chapouthier, who naïvely expressed astonishment that 'such young and handsome lads get married so quickly', which offended him. When he remained at the École during the summer with the students, waiting for the results of the *agrégation*, he ate with them, and got them to pay for him most of the time, as his wife did not give him a penny. He was surprised one day to discover Michel Foucault was ill, but I told him it was not serious. Even so, he was surprised that Foucault had not spoken to him in the corridor, when he came across him looking drawn. Foucault got the *agrégation* that same year. He ended up, as everyone knows, at the Collège de France, where he had friends.

When Chapouthier died, Hyppolite arrived as Deputy-Director, before taking over the running of the École. He was a thick-set, sturdy individual with an enormous head full of ideas. He had a fertile mind, smoked incessantly, slept only three hours a night, and constantly sought the friendship of the scientists who were headed by a brilliant organiser, Yves Rocard. Hyppolite laid his cards on the table when he gave his inaugural address: 'I always knew I would one day be Director of the École. . . . I expect the École to be an open institution; I hope I make myself clear.' He began to set up seminars which he was always talking about. This became known, and one day he received a long letter written in a shaky hand, signed by a retired colonel in the cavalry, who was living in Cahors. He told him he was interested in what he was doing, referred to his own teaching experience in the army, adding that he, too, had organised seminars over a long period, and proposed an exchange of ideas. There was another letter attached, signed by his daughter, saying that daddy was really interested in the whole thing and asking him to reply. Hyppolite did reply, and a correspondence began which was to last many years. Despite his war wounds, the colonel visited Hyppolite in Paris and gave a lecture at the École which went down well, even though his vocabulary was a little too militaristic. The colonel's name was C. Minner.

Hyppolite ran the École in a highly personal manner: the bursar's office followed his lead. In fact, it took the initiative under the leadership of Letellier, who had a lordly manner and did not worry about what he spent. The new buildings at 46, rue d'Ulm date from this period. There was room for the old laboratories and the new ones, as well as the new Centre for Human Sciences after Hyppolite's death, and study bedrooms for students. A violent argument ensued over the division of the vast area occupied by the biologists, but the laboratory director had his way, much to the annoyance of the physicists, who only wanted a few dozen square metres of space.

When Hyppolite left the École to go back to the Collège de France, he gave another rather melancholy speech in which he said: 'I believed I would have an intellectual influence on the place, but in reality I shall simply be remembered as the Director who instituted a system of tickets and got the new buildings at number 46.' (The tickets controlled access to the refectory and put an end to irritating squabbles, in which Prigent sometimes tried, unsuccessfully because he had too many friends, to exert his authority. At the same time, he grumbled quite openly about the Director – something he was always doing – whom he described as a 'mouselike creature', incapable of doing a damned thing.)

In his own discreet way, however, he achieved something else of importance. He brought about a reconciliation between Sartre and Merleau-Ponty, who had had nothing to do with each other for seven years as a result of a political quarrel. Hyppolite invited Sartre to give a lecture to the students in the salle de Actes. But looking around, there were some well-known faces in the audience, such as Canguilhem and Merleau. Sartre spoke for an hour and a half on the notion of the 'possible': a model *agrégation* lecture, which surprised everyone as they had not expected it. He ended by reminding us of the great slave revolts in South America in the sixteenth century, and talked about the value of human revolt. No one asked any questions. We all went off to Piron's (a local café run by a former member of the Resistance), and people began to talk more freely. Sartre's only response was to express approval of each question he was asked. Merleau was also there, but he did not say a word. We left the café very late and bade each other good night. I left with Merleau, who began to comment on the questions I had asked Sartre about the war in Algeria which was going on at the time. Then we spoke about Husserl and Heidegger and about Merleau's own work. I criticised him for his transcendental philosophy and for his theory of the body. He answered by posing a question I have never forgotten: but you yourself have a body don't you? A week later Merleau's own body suddenly failed him: he had a heart attack.

When Hyppolite died, we organised a commemoration for him in the theatre. It was attended by some of the most senior figures in the university, including Wolf, the Director of the Collège de France. We listened to eulogies of the deceased. As I had been asked to say something, I prepared a short speech, which I showed to Canguilhem in advance for his opinion and which he approved. I include in an appendix the text of this speech,* which caused a great scandal for reasons which were quite ridiculous since I was only repeating the judgement which Merleau himself had made in front of me on Hyppolite's philosophical work.

Flacelière succeeded Hyppolite and took charge of the École during what was perhaps the most difficult period in its history. Kirmmann, another chemist, looked after the science side. Flacelière was a man of character with a ruddy complexion, brought up on Plutarch. He was given to violent outbursts (he even struck a student in 1969 and then immediately apologised). He was traditional in his outlook and did not himself have anything to do with innovations at the École. For these he relied on his younger colleagues who trusted him. It was at this time that the events of May '68 erupted. There were barricades right up to the École. The students did not get involved, however, and contented themselves with taking in those who had been injured and sustaining those doing the fighting with cups of tea as ammunition. Flacelière stood impassively in front of the lodge, as he had done elsewhere in the 1914–18 war. Several times he stopped the CRS from pursuing

* This text was not found among Althusser's papers (Editors' note).

students who had taken refuge in the École. He had an air of confidence which he inspired in others. He subsequently lost his composure when, in the aftermath of May '68, the École was used for meetings which went on uninterruptedly day and night. Its walls were covered with graffiti insulting to Flacelière himself and to his wife. Then, with the inevitable delay, it experienced its own famous 'night' in 1970. This was the occasion when extreme left-wingers organised a 'celebration of the Commune', adopting as their only slogan 'as much wine as you like'. Six thousand young people invaded the old building, followed by a number of trouble-makers who smashed their way into the cellars with pickaxes and took everything. They even broke down the doors of the library which was courageously defended by Petitmengin. They burnt some books, spread petrol on the floor and the ceiling (it was a miracle the École did not burn down), and besides doing other damage they went in for wild antics (like making love in the open air to guitar music). The next day a deathly silence pervaded the École. Flacelière offered his resignation, which was accepted (the ministry considering him responsible for what had happened). Flacelière stepped down and then published a little book about the affair, in which he heralded (wrongly) the demise of the École. The walls were repainted, the damage repaired, with ministry help, and order was gradually restored.

Both Mandouze and Bousquet contested Flacelière's post, which the latter obtained for apparently political reasons, as it was gener-ally acknowledged that he was friendly with Pompidou. He was in fact a calm man who had been in the Resistance in Bordeaux, a Catholic with left-wing sympathies who preached a sort of British philosophy full of humour and patience. He was just the Director the École needed, alongside a precise, headstrong, and determined mathematician, Michel Hervé, and a new bursar who was discreet and efficient.

During this whole period we were naturally involved in politics. All those I had been at school with in Lyon and whom I met up with again at the École were for the most part members of the Party. Hélène had been a member until the war, but I will explain in a moment why she ceased being one in 1939. Communism was in the air in 1945, after the German defeat, the victory at Stalingrad, and the hopes and lessons of the Resistance. I remained hesitant for a while, however, and was content to play an active role in the (Catholic) 'Tala Circle' at the École, where I managed to get the chaplain, a certain Abbé Charles, thrown out, as I could not stand the vulgarity of either his language or his arguments. He is now in Montmartre, having had an enormous influence on Catholic students at the Sorbonne for many years. I was also active in the 'Students' Union', which was illegal but fighting to gain official recognition. If I may say so, it was there that I had my first political success involving a large group of people. With the help of Maurice Caveing, I got the committee, made up entirely of socialists, to resign.

I also remember an angry incident which brought me into conflict on one occasion with Astre, who belonged to the teachers' union. The ancillary staff at the École were on strike and wanted to go to demonstrate outside the ministry. Astre opposed it, but I managed to arrange things so that we all went, ancillary staff and academics together. Astre told me I was a 'commie'.

Politics became more serious for me when I joined the Party in October 1948. The cell at the École was led by a young biologist torn by the issues raised by Lysenko. He threw himself off the roof of the École, and his shattered body was removed on a stretcher with no chance of him being revived. It was a terrible object lesson. I later discovered that his suicide was also precipitated by an unhappy love affair.

Jean-Toussaint Desanti was lecturing at the École at this time, where he gave courses on the history of mathematics or of logic. They were unusual in that he would begin, linger over the introduction, and never manage to get any further. 'Touki' was something of a Husserlian, having been trained in this school of philosophy, and though he claimed he was a Marxist he never entirely disowned Husserl. But he was a member of the Party and had achieved a certain renown at the École before the war for having fired a revolver at the ceiling, for never revealing his thoughts, and for having fought alongside Victor Leduc against the fascists in the Latin Quarter. He also had a stormy and well-publicised relationship with Annia, who was known as Dominique. Most importantly, however, he was a Corsican, the son of a shepherd, he said. This explained everything, including his relationship with Laurent Casanova, then the Grand Ideological

Inquisitor of the Party. It was hard to explain Touki's particular affection for Casa, other than in terms of clannishness or their shared liking for goat's cheese and rosé wine. Anyway, he followed him everywhere like a little dog, and his pet phrase was: let us go forward in a fighting spirit. I got some idea of what this fighting spirit was when Touki took me to see Casa in December 1948. We waited for over an hour in a corridor of the Party headquarters, and through the door of his office I listened to him subjecting someone to a form of torture as he gave him a terrible moral lecture. Casa was concerned with the political and scientific conscience of Marcel Prenant, an eminent biologist and a member of the Central Committee at the time, who gave no credence to Lysenko's discoveries. Casa called him all the names under the sun and told him from time to time that he should realise that $2 + 2 = 4$ was true only in terms of a bourgeois ideology. Prenant came out looking deathly pale. Casa then greeted us in a very relaxed manner; it seemed it was an everyday occurrence for him. He listened to me as I outlined the plan formulated by our cell to create a Politzer Circle at the École, to which we intended to invite leading political and union figures who would tell the students something about the history of the workers' movement. That is how Racamond and Frachon came to talk to us, as well as Marty (who came twice and spoke with great professorial authority).

This was the time of the Cold War and of the Stockholm Appeal. I went canvassing in the area around the gare d'Austerlitz, and got almost no signatures at all, apart from a refuse collector, whom we persuaded to join the Local Committee, and a young woman who signed because she felt sorry for me. We put up a noticeboard in the rue Poliveau, and each morning I would come and put up the latest information about the threat of war and the progress being made by the popular opposition. No one tried to stop me, but few people read what we put up.

This all came to an end in a most unpleasant manner. I have already mentioned the Local Committee in the Fifth District. It was not exactly the same as the local section of the Party, though certain militants belonged to both bodies. One day, when Hélène went to collect some posters from the rue des Pyramides, a former official of the Young Communists in Lyon recognised her and immediately denounced her as a well-known agitator who went

under the name of Sabine. The repressive machinery of the Local
Committee was set in motion, despite an appeal to Yves Farge,
who could have intervened but said nothing.

In order to understand this whole business, we have to go back
in time. Hélène was one of the very few not to question the
Nazi–Soviet pact and had been a militant in the Thirties in
the fifteenth district [in Lyon] alongside Michels, Timbaud, and
others to whom she was very attached, but like many others she
was cut off from the Party in 1939. None the less, at the same
time as being active in a non-communist organisation in the Resistance she constantly tried to establish links with the Party, but in
vain. She had known Aragon and Elsa very well, and also Éluard
and a number of other communists involved in the Resistance,
who had also been unable to establish links with the Party. All
these friends, and many more besides, used to meet at Jean and
Marcou Ballard's, the headquarters of the *Cahiers du Sud*. Aragon
quarrelled with Hélène over a stupid incident, referred to as the
affair of 'Elsa's stockings'. He had wanted a certain colour, and
Hélène had been unable to obtain them. In an almost identical
fashion, Lacan, whom Hélène had got to know in Nice, broke
with her because she had not been able to find the safe accommodation needed by his wife, who was Jewish. At the time of the
liberation of Lyon when the legal fate of Nazi prisoners and
French collaborators was at stake, Hélène was given certain
important responsibilities. It was then that her break with the
Aragons became much more serious, as she became the subject of
a fierce attack orchestrated by Cardinal Gerlier and the whole
band of local collaborators, led by Berliet. She was accused of
imaginary crimes and of having protected war criminals, whose
execution she had in fact tried to prevent in order to extract
precious information from them or to exchange them for Resistance prisoners held at Montluc (such as Father Larue, who was
executed by the Germans the day before the town was liberated).
She did indeed use the pseudonym Sabine and the name Legotien
as well. Thus she had three names, which was considered suspect
and held against her. It was only a short step from accusing her
of being an agent of the Gestapo, which is what those leading the
prosecution on the Local Committee soon did. While she was in

Lyon, Aragon had already accused her of being a member of the intelligence service.

It was in these circumstances that I attended the meetings of the Local Committee. Hélène's attempts to invoke the testimony of members of the Resistance who knew her well and were aware of what she had done in Lyon were ineffective and to no avail. She was accused of all sorts of crimes and of having concealed them. Certain members of the committee maintained a dignified silence, uncertain as to the verdict they should pronounce, but they did not have sufficient weight in the face of the others who condemned her from their position of strength.

Hélène was thus excluded from the Local Committee on the basis of these infamous accusations. The members of the Party went along with it. I remember the primary concern of the members of my cell, as well as of the Desantis, was to 'rescue Althusser'. They put pressure on me though their aim was not altogether clear. But I took no notice of them.

Hélène and I left for Cassis to put this dreadful business behind us. It was a truly hallucinatory experience watching the sea relentlessly and impassively breaking on the shore, beneath a burning sun. We recovered, though I am not sure how, and returned to Paris a fortnight later.

The Party then took the issue up. Gaston Auguet interviewed Hélène at length, bringing out all the old accusations. He told her murky stories put about by a certain Gayman, who had been expelled from the Party and could not therefore be heard. He, it seems, knew whether or not Hélène belonged to the Party in 1939, at the time of the pact. Thus it was impossible to establish if Hélène was still a member of the Party. This was how Auguet left things, telling her she could appeal. At the same time, he told me I should leave Hélène immediately, which I did not do.

This whole frightful business made me ill (I almost committed suicide), and coming as it did on top of the suicide of the first person to have been secretary of our cell, opened my eyes to the sad realities of the Stalinist tactics within the French Party. I did not have the serenity of Hélène, who hardly let it get to her because she was sure of her facts and in any case considered that it only concerned her, whereas for me it was an appalling personal ordeal. At all events, it ended a certain number of our friendships.

As happens to everyone who is expelled, we lived in almost total isolation, since the Party did not believe in doing things by halves. As a loyal friend of Casanova, Desanti became more distant, though he was still reasonably friendly towards me. The comrades in my cell, led by Le Roy Ladurie, would have nothing more to do with me. But most of the candidates taking the *agrégation* were on my side, as was my dear friend Lucien Sève, who always stood by me, and Michel Verret who understood. But they were very few in number, and it was like a journey through the wilderness.

I went on working, however, and gradually managed to produce several articles. I was active in the Association of Teachers of Philosophy, and one day, at the instigation of Maurice Caveing who was the author with Besse of a *Manuel de philosophie*, which sadly had a rather negative impact in those terrible times, we decided to take over the committee of the National Association. It was simply a question of organising the vote which most of the members did not take part in. We won easily, but then found that most of the members were against us, and they then had the vote declared void. Another one was arranged which we lost. Those were the wholly undemocratic tactics adopted at the time.

During this period I was working on a commission attached to the Central Committee which was preparing a critique of philosophy. We met each week and in the end produced an article in which we declared that 'the whole question of Hegel was settled a long time ago' (Zhdanov), except where it has resurfaced among people like Hyppolite and has taken on an overtly hostile tone. That was the way people thought at the time.

I have described elsewhere how I came to write some of my new articles, which though unorthodox were published in *La Nouvelle Critique* (thanks to Jacques Arnault) and in *La Pensée* (thanks to Marcel Cornu). It was not without difficulty. I was banned from publishing anything with the Éditions sociales, though I do not know whether Krasucki, Garaudy, or Aragon was responsible for this, or even if anyone was. In any case, all that is now in the past. What I do recall relates to the Central Committee at Argenteuil. The day after the meeting, I was surprised to receive a telegram from Garaudy saying: 'You were defeated yesterday, come to see me.' But I did not go. Three months later, I had a friendly message from Waldeck, who was then General Secretary of the Party, inviting me to come for a chat. I spent three hours with him one beautiful spring morning. He talked slowly, and was a warm and honest man. He said to me: 'You were criticised at Argenteuil, but that's not what matters. We had to criticise you in order to criticise Garaudy too, as the things he says make us feel uneasy. Some of the things you have written, however, we find interesting.' I asked him some questions, such as: 'You, who are in touch with the workers, do you think they are interested in humanism?' 'Not in the slightest,' he replied, 'they couldn't care less.' 'What about the peasants?' 'It's exactly the same,' he said. 'Then why do you put so much emphasis on humanism?' This, word for word, was Waldeck's reply: 'Well you see we have to speak the same language as all those university people and socialists. . . . ' And when I questioned him about the political position of the Party, this was his exact reply: 'We have to do something for them, otherwise they'll all leave.' I never discovered what he meant by 'all'; whether it was the members of the Party (which was probably the case), or the intellectuals, or the workers. I left feeling rather puzzled.

Both before this meeting and since, I have had the opportunity of meeting leading figures in the Party, though they did not have the stature of Waldeck. I did however find it interesting listening to them. I am not referring to Guy Besse, who was modesty itself ('I've got no illusions, I was made a member of the Politburo to counterbalance Garaudy', though he may have acquired some illusions since). I am thinking of Roland Leroy whom I met four or five times between 1967 and 1972. A shrewd individual, concerned with his appearance and favouring a slightly decadent, Florentine sort of elegance, yet at the same time very sharp and lively, but whose fine 'intellect was held in check by his will', Roland Leroy also talked to me of his difficulties (how to defend his philosophical position), of the things he was sure about (the Common Programme with the Socialists: the knives will be out I promise you. The only advantage the Soviets have over us is their social mobility. Jacques Chambaz was there too, and he agreed). I also met René Andrieu, one of the most popular leading Party officials because of his aggressive attitude on television. He was worried about the future of *L'Humanité* and told me that he was anxious to introduce a readers' column where people could express their views quite openly, as happened in *France-Nouvelle*. This was premature, however. I had a brief encounter at a congress with Georges Séguy, whose populist but non-demagogic language I have always admired. He talked to me about the postal strike and said it would soon come to an end because a lot of people were out of work and one strike on its own could not be sustained for long. I met several others as well. The higher they were in the hierarchy, the more free they were with their comments. The ordinary journalists on *L'Humanité* and *France-Nouvelle* had nothing at all to say, no comments to make.

Since this is my chance to say everything I want to, I should also point out that other famous people I have met include Pope John XXIII and De Gaulle.

Through my friend Jean Guitton, I had contacts in Rome. I met John XXIII in some gardens as he did not like the Vatican except for his palace. It was springtime, and this pure-hearted man was enchanted by the flowers and the children. He had the appearance of a Burgundian who enjoyed red wine, but beneath that exterior he was a totally artless and profoundly generous man with a slightly Utopian vision, as you will discover. He took an interest in me as a member of the French Communist Party and explained at length that it was his desire to effect a reconciliation between the Catholic and the Orthodox Churches. He needed intermediaries to obtain the basis for an agreement on unity from Brezhnev. He was quite open about it. I pointed out to him the ideological and political difficulties of such a venture, the position of Mindszenty, for whom he expressed total disdain (he is fine where he is, let him stay there), and quite simply the state of international tension which existed and the prevailing anticommunism within the Church. He said he would take care of the Church if the communists were prepared to make a gesture. I suggested it would be very difficult to get them to make such a gesture, that even the Italian Party would not do so and that the French Party was even less well placed. He was almost sharp with me at this point, saying that since the French Church was Gallican it should be of some help and that there was a longstanding alliance between France and Russia, etc. I left with a feeling of distress at my own impotence, having failed to convince him that I was not in fact the only person concerned. I saw him on two other occasions, and he remained as resolute and as bothered by this issue which meant so much to him.

I met De Gaulle, whom I did not know personally, in surprising circumstances in a street in the Seventh District. A tall man with a cigarette dangling from his mouth asked me for a light, which I gave him. He then immediately asked me who I was and what I did. I replied: I teach at the École normale. He remarked: the salt of the earth. I said: of the sea, the earth isn't salty. Or do you mean it is salacious? No: it is dirty. He then said: you have quite a way with words. I said: it's my job. He replied: military men don't have it to the same extent. I then asked him what he did, and he said: I am General de Gaulle. This is true. A week later, in a panic the telephone operator at the École put a call through to me from the Presidential Office inviting me to dinner. De Gaulle asked me endless questions, about myself, my life, being a prisoner-of-war, politics, the Communist Party, without saying a word about himself. It went on for three hours and then I left. I saw him again during my period in the wilderness, and on this occasion he did the talking. He said all the things one would have expected him to say: he was very rude about the army, spoke highly of Stalin and Thorez (as statesmen), was very critical of the French bourgeoisie (it could not be bothered to produce statesmen, the proof being that it had to call on military men who had other things to do). He too was preoccupied with the Communist Party: 'Do you think they are capable of understanding that I'm the only person who can keep the Americans at bay and who can introduce something resembling the socialism they want into France? You can have as much nationalisation as you want and I'm prepared to have communist ministers. I'm not like the socialists who kicked them out on the orders of the Americans. I have made Russia a particular concern of mine. The great issue is the Third World. I have given all the countries their freedom apart from Algeria. You'll see the goddam French bourgeoisie call on me when things start going badly for them. Guy Mollet is their man but he's incompetent, and Lacoste is even worse. Am I alone? Yes, I am, as I've always been. According to Machiavelli, you always have to stand alone when you start something big. But the French people are Gaullists, and I have a few trusted friends like Debré and Buis. I have fulfilled some of their dreams.' Malraux made a tidy sum recording some of the great man's comments, which he dressed up in his own literary style, but when I read them I remember De Gaulle's simple remarks, their abruptness and grandeur. He walked the political tightrope with consummate skill. But he was very hard on the peasants; he claimed they were only concerned with taxes even though they were dealt with leniently in this respect. He was equally hard on the Church which he said spent its time bleating in the hope that it would tame the wolf. What they did not realise was that they had to be more wolflike than the wolf itself. None the less, he did have some respect for certain Catholics like Mandouze; they knew what it was like to be isolated. It made me realise that a certain degree of solitude is sometimes necessary if one is to be listened to.

I experienced solitude in the psychiatric clinics where I regularly went. I also experienced it during those very rare moments when I resurfaced, as I was getting over bouts of depression, and seemed to be lifted out of myself by some unknown force into a sort of elation where everything became easy. Without fail, I would become involved with some new woman who became the love of my life. I would take her the first hot croissants of the day at five in the morning and red currants in the early summer (curiously, it was always May or June when I was recovering. My analyst mischievously told me that all months were not the same, that holiday months were rather special, and most of all those immediately preceding them). During these periods I did all sorts of crazy things which alarmed Hélène, who witnessed my manic behaviour at close quarters, and which also worried those around me, even though they were used to my uncontrollable whims.

I had a thing about the sort of kitchen knives which rust, and stole several from a shop which I returned the next day on the pretext that they were not what I wanted, selling them back to the same astonished employee. I decided also to steal an atomic submarine, an affair which, quite naturally, was hushed up by the press. I telephoned the commander of one of our atomic submarines in Brest, pretending to be the Minister for the Navy and telling him he had been given an important promotion. I also told him his successor would be arriving almost at once to take over. Indeed, someone wearing an officer's uniform did turn up, exchanged the appropriate documents with the former commander, and took over the ship. The other officer then left. The new captain called the crew together and told them they were to have a week's special leave to celebrate the promotion of their former captain. This was greeted with cheers. Everyone left the ship except the cook who nearly foiled the whole plan by claiming he was simmering a ratatouille. In the end, he too left the ship. I took off my borrowed cap and telephoned a gangster who wanted to get hold of a nuclear submarine in order to do a deal for international hostages or with Brezhnev, telling him he could take delivery of it. During this same period I staged a first-rate non-violent hold-up in the Bank of Paris and The Netherlands to win a bet with a friend and former fellow-student, Pierre Moussa, who was the manager. I hired a strong-box at the bank, was escorted to it, opened it, and ostensibly deposited a considerable number of forged banknotes (in fact I had bundles which were the shape of five hundred franc notes) in front of the bank official. I then went up to Moussa's office and told him I wished to make a sworn statement of the value of my deposit, namely a billion new francs. Moussa, who knew my links with Moscow, did not show surprise. The next day I went back and had my strong-box opened, only to find to my astonishment that it was completely empty. Some very clever gangsters had been there during the night, having got through all the doors. The most extraordinary thing of all was that they must have known how much was in my box, because they had not broken into the other boxes (in fact they had the keys to my box). The bank official, who had seen the box full the previous day, was summoned and he agreed it was now empty, as did Moussa, who had Lloyds pay up within a week. But Moussa was no fool. He asked me to make a small contribution to the benevolent fund for retired bank managers and also to the alumni association of the École. A record of these contributions can be found in the association's accounts. The Prefect of Police at the time, I have to admit, behaved most properly, which goes to show that top public officials knew how to conduct themselves. I told my father about it and he had a quiet laugh as he knew Moussa well. In fact Moussa had visited him in Morocco to explain the local situation. My father had listened to him without saying a word and then said goodbye, giving him the addresses of several beautiful Finnish women (Moussa was keen on girls of this type at the time) and some bourbon which had been in a shipwreck. I stole many other things as well, including a grandmother and a retired cavalry officer, but this is not the place to discuss such things as it might cause difficulties with the Vatican, since the officer belonged to the Swiss Guard. I had good relations with the Vatican having been received by Pope Pius XII (along with one hundred and ninety-two other Parisian students who were taken to Rome in 1946 by Abbé Charles). The Pope appeared to have a liver complaint but spoke very good French distorted by Italian phonemes, like a piano accompanied by a doubtful cellist. He asked me if I was a student at the École and if I was doing arts or science, or if I was a philosopher, to which I said yes. He then said he hoped I would read St Thomas and St Augustine in that order, and that I would be 'a good Christian, a good father and a good citizen'. I have done my best to live up to his expectations, which he expressed with true feeling. I knew neither that marvellous man Pope John XXIII, who was like Canon Kir but saintly, nor Pope Paul VI, that gentle, worried old woman, who was always gallivanting about, and whose one desire in life was to meet Brezhnev. But I knew them through Jean Guitton, whose books were their bedside reading, and who corresponded with them. That is how I knew of all the goings-on in Rome and how I was able to pull off the stunt with the cavalry officer, who wanted to rejoin the woman he loved in the Grisons, once he was back in civvies.

Of course this mad phase of mine, in which, on top of everything else, I fell in love with an Armenian living in Paris, did not last. Her skin was the colour of a beautiful piece of cloth, her hair different again, and her eyes moved gently to and fro at night. I went back to one of the clinics I had been in, but I had progressed since leaving Esquirol. I went to Soisy, where they did not do shock treatment, but artificial sleep treatment instead, which gave me the impression I was getting better. I remember a rather amazing experiment taking place at Soisy which should provide ammunition for the anti-psychiatry lobby. Everyone, except the doctors and the caretaker, was brought together in a large room filled with chairs: the patients, the male and female nurses, etc. We all talked about ourselves and then became silent. This went on for hours. First one patient would get up to go and have a pee, then another would light a cigarette. Sometimes one of the female nurses would burst into tears, and then when we had all finished talking, we would go to eat or lie down ready for the sleep cure. I always had a great deal of admiration for the doctors. They always managed not to come, and you could not even see them in private. They claimed their absence was part of the treatment, which did not prevent them spending a lot of time outside the hospital looking after private patients who needed their services; or else they were busy running after the nurses, whom they either married or got pregnant. I realised how dangerous sleep therapy could be, contrary to established opinion which took no account of sleep-walking, as a result of an incident which occurred in the middle of winter when there were eight inches of frozen snow on the ground all around us. I was found at about three in the morning, out in the snow and more than two hundred yards from my ward, completely naked. I had also injured my foot on a stone. The nurses, who were very alarmed, put a small dressing on my wound, gave me a hot bath, and put me back to bed. I did not see a doctor on this occasion either. They had no specialist knowledge of sleep-walking. I was profoundly thankful that Béquart was there, who was interested in philosophy and whom I saw in the company of his charming wife. There was also Paumelle, who had set the whole thing up, not without certain misgivings, and who worried about it over his whisky and talked on occasions to Domenach, a former fellow-student of mine in Lyon. Derrida, Poulantzas, and Macherey also came to see me. We ate chocolate éclairs in a local cake shop and then went for a walk and a chat in the fields. Derrida talked with extreme tact of his own depression which occurred after his marriage, Nikos told me all about his girlfriends (he was a one!) and spoke of the disputes between the internal and external parts of the Party, and Macherey discussed philosophy and referred to his accommodation problems. I did my best to pass the time, which is in fact the most difficult thing in the world to do when you have a deep-seated, physical sense of anxiety. But the depression always came to an end, and I returned to the École where those taking the *agrégation* were preparing for the exam on their own, and where there were the usual political intrigues. Hyppolite and his wife welcomed me back in a friendly manner. The only one who really suffered was Hélène, because everyone thought that if I became ill it was her fault as she was such a nasty piece of work. And when I disappeared, everyone ignored her, which meant that she was bearing not only the burden of my illness but also a sense of guilt that she was to blame. None of our friends even contacted her to ask her out for a drink or to go to the cinema. The nearest and dearest of someone who is ill are always treated as lepers, because people in general, and especially those who are close, fear that they will fall ill in their turn. To cite another example; not once in thirty years did either my mother or my father visit me in a clinic, though they certainly knew the address. A sort of curse seems permanently to have hung over Hélène, and she is terrified of being hard-hearted, which she is not in the slightest. On the contrary, she is extremely kind to people. She can, however, be a little brusque on occasions, but not maliciously so, if they speak to her too early in the morning when she is having breakfast or if they make a rude comment in front of her about Stendhal, Proust, or Tintoretto, or even about Camus (whom she knew well during the Resistance), etc. They are niggling things; but just as one can start a large fire with a few twigs, so a great deal of harm can come from a few niggles.

So I was still involved in politics. It had all begun in the spring of 1964 when I received a visit in my office from Balibar, Macherey, and Establet, who were then students at the École. They came to ask me to help them work on Marx. I said yes, took in their commentaries, and realised I knew more than I thought. Still at their request, we organised a seminar on *Das Kapital* during the academic year 1964–65. Rancière set it going and got us over all our initial difficulties, for which he deserved our thanks, as no one else was prepared to start the ball rolling. In fact he talked three times for two hours each time. It was a masterly exposition, which was published by Maspero, slightly formalist and Lacanian perhaps (the 'absent cause' kept coming up) but it showed real ability. I spoke after Establet, Balibar, and Macherey, who was teaching at the time at La Flèche. I deserved no credit for it as they had done all the work. Duroux, who was the cleverest of us all, unfortunately kept quiet as always, though he was full of ideas and not afraid to share them. Jacques-Alain Miller, who was already going out with Judith Lacan, displayed great initiative in October 1964, which brought him to prominence, and then disappeared completely (he had gone off with a girl to the forest of Fontainebleau and was teaching her how to produce theoretical concepts). He reappeared again without warning in June 1965 to reveal, much to everyone's astonishment, that someone had 'stolen one of his concepts'. I was no longer manic at that time, and it cannot therefore be attributed to me. Miller claimed it was Rancière's fault and said he had stolen the concept of 'metonymic causality' he had dreamt up in an idle moment but which he firmly believed in. Rancière stoutly defended himself and in October 1965 declared it was my fault. Miller then had a frightful row with me, which was subsequently to have quite an effect on Régis Debray when he was freed from Camiri (he refers to it in his most recent book as a symptom of the mental disorder prevailing at the École both in general and in particular cases). In actual fact, it was quite exceptional. Concepts circulate freely as they are being developed without any controls being placed on them.

They circulated to such an extent that the Union of Communist Students soon included them in pamphlets for their famous schools of theory. These schools grew out of the extremely theoretical conviction which prevailed among us at the time that, faced with the impossibility of political action within the Party, it was necessary to adopt Lenin's point of view, as expressed in *What is to be done?*, and fight on the only front open to us, that of theoretical education. The project was very successful, relatively speaking, unexpectedly so. Schools of theory were set up in almost all the universities of Paris and were led by a small group of philosophers, the most active and able of whom was without doubt Robert Linhart. There were political consequences, as had been anticipated. The students who formed the original group in the rue d'Ulm virtually took control of the Union of Communist Students, because it was weak and being undermined by those with 'Italian' leanings and by the 'psycho-sociologists' in humanities at the Sorbonne. The Party, which was not very strong there, tolerated this until the group in the rue d'Ulm and their friends took the initiative of breaking with the Party which clearly gave them a great deal of pleasure. I gave them a real rocket and said they were behaving like children, not engaging in political action. But they had taken the step. They then founded the Union of Communist Youth (Marxist–Leninist), UCYM-L, which became well known for its activism and its carefully thought-out initiatives, above all the continuation of theoretical education, the creation of a review (*Les Cahiers marxistes-léninistes*, to which I contributed, as you will see, two bad articles which the Party pretended not to notice), and especially the formation of the extremely successful grass-roots Vietnam committees, which in the end gave the Party cause for concern. With their theoretical political awareness, their passion, and their imagination, these young people, in spite of everything, understood some basic principles of agitation and mass action and had begun to do something. After a difficult start, *Les Cahiers marxistes-léninistes* sold very well. For their first number, devoted to the recently initiated Cultural Revolution, I gave them an unsigned article (which I here acknowledge, after Rancière), in which I put forward a simple but false theory based on the premiss that there are three forms of class struggle: the economic, the political, and the ideological. Thus three distinct organisations are needed to promote it, whereas we have two: the union and the Party. The Chinese, on the other hand, have just invented a third: the Red Guards. QED. It was a bit simplistic but it went down well. I then produced another very long, signed article on 'dialectical and historical materialism', in which I defended the basically sound idea that Marxist philosophy was not to be confused with the Marxist science of history, but my arguments were, to say the least, schematic. Well over a year after the UCYM-L had been founded, I remember receiving an invitation from Paul Laurent to come to visit him. At that point I was about to go into a psychiatric hospital and was unable to take up his invitation. I always regretted it because, from a distance, Paul Laurent always seemed to me to be an interesting man, at any rate calm and lucid. This was on the eve of May '68. As I was leaving by car for hospital, I saw groups marching beneath the Red Flag. It had begun.

In May '68 the Party had completely lost touch with the student masses in revolt. Those belonging to the UCYM-L went, like good Leninists, to the factory gates, where the workers had just launched the biggest strike in the history of the labour movement. It was their downfall. The workers did not need the students' support, even those who were 'organised', and things were happening elsewhere: in the Latin Quarter where, for a month, battles raged with cobble-stones and tear-gas, but without a single shot being fired, the CRS obviously having been given orders, by a Prefect of Police whose daughter was among the demonstrators, to handle the students carefully, most of whom were the children of the upper middle class. They showed less clemency at the Peugeot factory, where three workers were shot.

Everyone knows how De Gaulle brought this spectacular revolt to an end by staging another show: his own unexpected disappearance. He did not go to the factory gates or to the occupied Sorbonne, however, but to Germany, to Massu's headquarters (at least this was the official version), only to return two days later to give his famous breathless speech, thus paving the way for the Grenelle talks, which brought Pompidou face to face with Frachon and Séguy, and the elections which gave him an exceptional majority, after the demonstration along the Champs-Élysées.

The events of May, where striking workers and students in revolt briefly and tentatively came together (the great procession which marched through Paris on the 13th), gradually fizzled out. Once most of the major claims of the workers were met at Grenelle, they gradually, if sometimes reluctantly, went back to work. The students took longer to accept the idea of defeat, but they gave up in the end and the Odéon and the Sorbonne were vacated. A great dream came to nothing. Yet it lived on in people's memories. People remembered and will go on remembering for a long time that month of May, when everyone was in the streets and there was a real atmosphere of fraternity, when everyone felt they could talk to each other as if they were lifelong friends, when everything suddenly became natural, when everyone believed that 'imagination ruled', and that beneath the pavements lay golden sands.

After May, the student movement broke up into sects or small groups. The UCYM-L split. Robert Linhart, Jacques Broyelle, and others left, while those that remained followed Benny Lévy who founded the Proletarian Left with Alain Geismar of the Movement of March 22nd. This organisation founded both a daily and a weekly paper but, despite the protection and financial support given them by Sartre, who believed he had seen in the events of May the embodiment of his theory of seriality (the CGT) and of the group (the student demonstrators), it stagnated and then disappeared. A number of its leaders and militants close to it, like

André Glucksmann, ended up by adopting an antiMarxist stance, something which is likely to happen to any ideological movement that is antiauthoritarian and anarchistic. It was a sad end, despite the huge demonstration of protest against the assassination of Overney, which I described as the funeral not so much of Overney but of the extreme student Left. Naturally, all the extreme left-wingers were present at the burial of the extreme left. And many more besides, which fostered a certain number of illusions for a month or two. But the reality of the situation soon became clear, though it prompted no analysis whatsoever as everyone was in a state of confusion. Lévy, however, continued imperturbably to give orders which no one followed, before publishing his conversations with Sartre, who had taken him on as a private secretary.

The genuine extreme left, that of the workers, which was anarcho-syndicalist and populist, took refuge elsewhere: in part of the PSU and in the CFDT. But this was something the French students were unwilling to admit: that there were two extreme lefts, the one associated with the workers, which had been in existence for a very long time, and the student movement which was of very recent origin. Nor would they admit that the older one, which was part of the workers' movement, had a future, whereas the second was in principle bound to grow away from the workers' movement. The situation in Italy and Spain is different for historical reasons, since to the left of the Communist Party there exist a number of political organisations which have a combined student and worker base, something quite unthinkable and impossible in France. The leadership of the French Party knows this full well and showed as much by the tactics it adopted both in May '68 and in the aftermath. All it had to do was to withdraw into its 'workers' fortress', the CGT and the Party, and despite its imprecations simply allow the extreme student left, whether Maoist or otherwise, to wither away on its own.

I must mention here an initiative some of us took in the spring of 1967 of founding a study group, which we named quite transparently after Spinoza. Most of my friends belonged, whether they were members of the Party or not. The experience was interesting, because it was prophetic. We were convinced that things were about to happen in the universities, and it gave rise to a book, published simply under the names of Baudelot and Establet because of political differences, on *L'École capitaliste en France*, and another great work by Bettelheim on the class struggle in the USSR.

We had also undertaken a study of the relations of the class struggle in France, but due to lack of time and funds it was not completed. In the end the group simply broke up (at the time of one of my depressions, economic recession, and the departure of Alain Badiou, one of our most brilliant members, who decided he had to reunite the Maoist groups in France in order to renew the Party). Badiou is currently bringing out some interesting volumes with Maspero, in which, curiously, one finds the Sartrian philosophy of revolt, which he has never disowned, used as the basis for his analysis of certain texts of Mao, against a background of voluntarism, of pragmatism, and of idealism which is typical of the great Chinese communist leader's thought.

In order not to cover up any of my ignominious theoretical writings, I ought to add at this point that in the spring of 1966, at the same time as the bad article I had written on 'theoretical work' appeared in *La Pensée*, I published a major work on theoretical education, which was translated by the Cubans and sought after by people everywhere. I wrote another, more ambitious, book on ideological (*sic*) and scientific socialism, which, fortunately, was not published. One can judge, when reading these essays, to what extent I succumbed to the temptation I later criticised as 'theoreticism' which was in the air at the time, due to the real success of the schools of theory set up by the UCYM-L. This temptation or deviation was not merely verbal, as it affected what they did in political terms, though it had to take account of the need for effective action. Experience showed that theory was not entirely unwelcome, since it at least gave those who adopted it a sense of the importance of theory. But what it could not give them was a sense of the impact of practice on that theory, in other words it could not teach them to 'put theory into practice', keeping praxis in mind, that is to say the balance of forces within the class struggle, the range of meaning which words carry, and an evaluation of the effects of both theory and practice. It was an interesting experience for these young people, and among those who did not lose their way by joining the antiMarxists there were a number who derived benefits from it some of which already look most promising, to judge for example from Linhart's book *Lénine, Taylor et les paysans*.

With reference to the celebrated 'epistemological break' which I borrowed from Bachelard, I stumbled on certain strange formations such as classical political economy, which are at one and the same time prescientific and theoretical, and theoretical without being truly philosophical, and in addition bourgeois. This last determination was far and away the most important. I had therefore to accept and think in terms of the ideological class nature of the substratum of the bourgeois theory of the political economy. At the same time I had to recognise that this bourgeois ideological formation presented itself in the shape of an abstract, rigorous, and, to a certain extent, scientific theory. This was how Marx dealt with the ideas of Ricardo and even Smith, deluding himself into thinking that these theories were perhaps scientific, because the class struggle in England had been temporarily interrupted (*sic*), a theory which Marx's work as a whole contradicts. It now seems to me of crucial importance to discover, via this delusion of Marx, not just in his early writings but in *Das Kapital* too, the origin of numerous misunderstandings which have led to a misinterpretation, and even a willful falsification, of Marxism. If Marx truly founded a science then this science, like all sciences, has to be at least re-evaluated if not revised, its principles more firmly established, and its conclusions more precisely drawn. This simple idea should prove fruitful. It will lead to a considerable simplification of a body of work which Marx, labouring under the same delusion, believed was necessarily 'difficult at the beginning', as was the case with all science. This, however, is false. A revision is needed of the first section of Book 1 of *Capital*, which I drew attention to several years ago, and especially a careful distinction between what Marx wrote in *Capital* and in the various notes on his reading, such as the 'Theory of surplus-value', in which he was often content simply to copy out what Smith wrote on the productive worker, for example; a theory, which is not the same as that of productive labour, and which disappeared from *Das Kapital*. Much remains to be said about all these misunderstandings which are carefully kept alive by people who have a special interest in falsifying Marx's work. This I shall try to do.

For the present, I will content myself with saying a word or

two about Marxist philosophy. Having thought for a long time
that it did indeed exist, but that Marx had neither the time nor
the means to formulate it, and having also thought for a long
time that, all things considered, and despite the publication of
Materialism and Empirio-Criticism, Lenin, too, had neither the
time nor the means to formulate it, I arrived with difficulty at
two conclusions. First, that, contrary to what I had believed and
asserted, Marx did not discover a new philosophy, in the way that
he discovered the laws of the class struggle – but adopted a new
philosophical standpoint, in a field (that of philosophy) which
both pre-existed him and continued after his death. Secondly, this
new standpoint of his stemmed in the final analysis from his class
position as a theorist. But if this last proposition was true, it
implied that any philosophy (at least any major philosophy and
perhaps even some minor ones too) was ultimately determined
by the class position of the person who formulated it, and thus
philosophy as a whole was in the end nothing more than 'the class
struggle in the realm of theory', or the continuation of the
class struggle by means of theory, as Engels clearly realised. This
thesis, of course, raised enormous problems, not only in relation
to when philosophy began but also to the different forms the class
struggle took and to the obvious relationship between philosophy
and the sciences. One had to acknowledge, therefore, that philosophy was not the property of professional philosophers, their
private property, but of all men ('every man is a philosopher',
Gramsci). Yet one also had to recognise that philosophers' philosophy took a specific form, which was that of systematic and
rigorous abstraction, as opposed to ideologies (religious, moral,
etc.), and that when *philosophers practise philosophy* something
is being worked out which is not wholly insignificant but has
repercussions in the sphere of ideologies which represent something like the stakes in a philosophical class struggle. But what
was this thing which was being worked out when philosophers
practised philosophy? For a long time I believed it to be a sort of
compromise, a way of repairing the damage done to the fabric
of philosophy by the irruption of the sciences into the hitherto
unified world of philosophy (epistemological breaks causing philosophical ones). But I came to realise that things were less mechanistic and that philosophy, as borne out by its history, had a certain

relationship with the State, with the power of the apparatus of the State, and specifically with the constitution, that is to say with the unification and systemisation of the dominant ideology, which is the keystone of the ideological hegemony of the class in power. It then struck me that philosophers' philosophy was responsible for bringing together the contradictory elements of ideology which every dominant class is confronted with when it comes to power to help form a dominant ideology for both the dominant and the dominated class.

From this perspective, things became relatively clear or at any rate intelligible. It became clear that everyone was a philosopher, as he lived within an ideological framework impregnated with the fall-out from philosophy, which occurred as a result of its attempt to forge a unified dominant ideology. It became clear, too, that the dominant class needed professional philosophers to create that unified ideology. It became clear finally that philosophical categories were used in science, since no science in the world, including mathematics, is developed outside prevailing ideologies and the philosophical struggle to turn the dominant ideology into a unified one. Things noticed earlier began to fall into place, and the unusual silence of Marx and Lenin began to make sense, as did the failures of philosophers (such as Lukács) who had tried in vain to create a Marxist philosophy, and even more so the failures of those (such as Stalin and his imitators) who reduced philosophy to a simple ideological tool of pragmatic justification. Marx and Lenin were able to remain silent on the question of philosophy, since it was sufficient for their purposes for them to adopt a proletarian class position in order to deal subsequently with the philosophical categories they needed, whether in relation to the science of class struggle (historical materialism) or practical politics. Naturally, this does not mean that it became unnecessary to elaborate more fully the philosophical consequences of adopting a proletarian class position, but the task became quite different. It was no longer a question of creating a new philosophy in the classic mould, but of reworking the categories which had always existed in the history of philosophy and still did on this new basis. Marx's remark in *The German Ideology*, to the effect that philosophy had no history, took on a new and unexpected meaning, because the same struggle has been repeated throughout the history of philosophy; what I referred to a little while ago as the same demarcation line, the same 'immeasurable distance taken'. Thus we were now able to embark on a quest for the best examples of this in the whole history of philosophy; and the best were not necessarily the most recent. And we could give a materialist meaning to the old spiritualist intuition of *philosophia perennis*, with the difference that for us this 'eternity' was nothing more than the repetition of the class struggle. No, philosophy is not, as the young Marx would have it, revealing himself in this respect the true disciple of Hegel, 'the self-awareness of a given historical period', but the battleground of the continuing class struggle which only achieves its most approximate forms at certain historical moments and in certain thinkers: for us, above all, Epicurus, Machiavelli, Spinoza, Rousseau, and Hegel, the true precursors of Marx. I had long since recognised the philosophical virtues of Spinoza, and it was not fortuitous that, in trying to understand the 'philosophy' of Marx, I made a detour via Spinoza. But it was while working on Machiavelli that I became aware, quite unexpectedly, of the unusual and illuminating link which existed between them. I shall explain it one day.

In the meantime, Jacques Martin had committed suicide. His body was discovered during the hottest period of August 1963 in the room he occupied in the Sixteenth District, a long way from everyone else. On his body he had placed a long red rose. Like us, he was familiar with Thorez's remark about communism as bread and roses. He could not be resuscitated.

For more than fifteen years, Martin had been receiving treatment from a man who called himself an analyst, but who practised narcosis. He was in a state of confusion after the war and had been given this doctor's address by some young students who were seeking help for their neuroses. I, too, was treated for twelve years by the same doctor and, thanks to him, gradually became more acquainted with analysis and its problems. S. made me lie down, gave me an injection of pentothal, just enough to make me intoxicated, and I began to talk. He was interested above all in my dreams, which he meticulously interpreted, underlining both their positive and negative meaning. When I began to get depressed again, S. was very attentive in trying to help me, but he had definite views about life. I remember, in the summer of 1963, the answer he gave when an Italian woman friend I had got to know during the previous holidays asked him what he thought about my condition and my feelings: it's only a holiday romance, was his reply. He seemed to have no sense of time, was always very late, and never seemed to mind how long the sessions went on.

The analyst I saw next took a completely different view of things. He thought about it for some time before taking me on, and I fitted in with the normal rhythm of his sessions. It was quite different. This man was not in the least bit interested in my dreams, did not resort to narcosis, never commented on the positive or negative aspects of any symptoms, and was always ready when I arrived. My sessions with him went on over a period of fifteen years and have almost come to an end now so I can say a little about them. I discovered for myself what Freud described in his books, namely the existence of unconscious phantasies, their fundamental lack of substance, and the extreme difficulty one has in gradually getting rid of them. We talked face to face, and to complicate things still further he also saw Hélène at a much later date just once a week for half an hour. There were dramatic incidents, fifteen bouts of depression, and also short-lived moments of manic exhilaration when I did all sorts of extraordinary things. For example, I started to steal, not because I wanted things but simply to show I could do it.

I ought to say something at this point about my analyst. I belong to a generation, at any rate to a social class, which did not know that analysis existed and that it could cure neuroses and even psychoses. Since 1945 things have changed a great deal in France in this respect. I have already said how I came to be treated by a doctor who used narcosis, and how a dear friend of mine persuaded me one day to go to see D. 'whose shoulders are broad enough to take you on'. In fact, he needed broad shoulders to help sort me out, because my depressions, in other words my resistance, went on for fifteen years. Nothing could be more simple than the unconscious elements which analysis deals with, yet the combinations they assume in individual cases could not be more complex. As a friend once said to me, the unconscious is like knitting; all you need is wool, but the stitches can be infinitely varied. What soon happened with me, as always, was that screen-phantasies began to occur, and above all the twin themes of artifice and of the father's father. I had the impression that everything I had achieved in life I had done fraudulently: especially my academic success since I had copied things out and invented quotations in order to succeed. And as I only followed my teachers' example to demonstrate that I was better than them, deception and my achievement were one and the same thing. I kept going over and over these same themes for a long time, before others manifested themselves. Above all, there was my fear of the female sex organ, a black hole in which one might be swallowed up for ever, my fear of women and of my mother, who never ceased moaning about her life and who was always preoccupied with the notion of the pure male whom she could trust – her fiancé who had died in the war and whom she thought of all the time unconsciously. She found him, for instance, in the naturist doctor with whom she could exchange ideas without there being any sexual contact. My mother was afraid of the male sexual organ, afraid of sexuality. I then became aware that this was how my mother loved me, as a sexless male who was pure minded. And even when, to my great anger and disgust, she poked about in my sheets and found what she believed were the signs of my first wet dream (you are a man now, my son), and thus literally interfered with me, it was to steal and to deny me my sexuality. The same thing happened with my father. As she passively submitted to his sexual advances, her mind was elsewhere, in the skies above Verdun. My father loved her quite differently, in a wholly virile manner, and I still recalled that double endearment of his 'my mine' which he used to utter as a way of assuring himself that my mother was truly his, and not someone else's, his brother's for example. This cast light on my need to resort to deception and to play the role of 'father's father'. As I was loved in an ethereal way, as a non-sexual being which I was not, I had to take charge of myself and fabricate a false persona. This would enable me, given that I was no ordinary man, to demonstrate my superiority over my father and any other father-figure and to prove to myself, at the expense of other men, that I really was a virile man and not the a-sexual being my mother wanted me to be. The fact that it took fifteen years of analysis in its present form for me to come to terms with these products of my unconscious is partly explicable in terms of the depressions I suffered, but the depressions themselves were undoubtedly a way of resisting the progress of the analysis. It took all this work, all this *Durcharbeit* to overcome these simple phantasies.

All this was happening at the same time as I was working on Marx, and I was constantly struck by the extraordinary affinity between the thought and practice of the two authors. Both of them give primacy not so much to practice itself but to a certain relationship with it. In both cases there is a profound sense of the dialectic linked to *Wiederholungszwang*, an 'instinct of repetition', which I discovered in the theory of class struggle. Both of them suggest, in almost identical terms, that observable effects are no more than the result of extremely complex combinations of very basic elements (in Marx, for example, the elements which contribute to the processes of labour and production). But these combinations have nothing in common with the formalist and structuralist combinatory that one finds in Lévi-Strauss or even Lacan. I came to the conclusion that historical materialism should in some way reveal itself in analytic theory and even felt that it was possible to put forward the proposition that 'the unconscious works like ideology', which cannot really be sustained in these terms, though in itself it is not wrong. Since then, interesting work (by Godelier) has produced important insights into these issues, though a long way, obviously, from the preoccupations of Reich who had little knowledge of Marx . . .

WORKS BY ALTHUSSER IN ENGLISH TRANSLATION

L. Althusser, *For Marx*, trans. Ben Brewster, Allen Lane, 1969 (reprinted by Verso, London, 1979).

L. Althusser, and E. Balibar, *Reading Capital*, trans. Ben Brewster, New Left Books, London, 1970.

L. Althusser, *Lenin and Philosophy and other essays*, trans. Ben Brewster, New Left Books, London, 1971.

L. Althusser, *Politics and History. Montesquieu, Rousseau, Hegel and Marx*, trans. Ben Brewster, New Left Books, London, 1972 (reprinted as *Montesquieu, Rousseau, Marx: Politics and History*, Verso, 1982).

L. Althusser, *Essays in Self-criticism*, trans. Grahame Lock, New Left Books and Humanities Press, London and Atlantic Highlands NJ, 1976.

L. Althusser, *Essays on ideology*, Verso, London, 1984.

L. Althusser, *Philosophy and the Spontaneous Philosophy of the Scientists and other essays*, ed. G. Elliott, Verso, London, 1990.

NOTE: Except in the case of *For Marx*, the essays collected in these books do not correspond to those in the French works with similar titles.

Essays on Ideology contains no new material; it reprints a selection of essays from the earlier volumes. *Philosophy and the Spontaneous Philosophy of the Scientists* contains some previously untranslated material as well as some essays from earlier volumes.